GENTLEMAN
AND
SOLDIER

GENTLEMAN
AND
SOLDIER

A Biography of Wade Hampton III

★ ★ ★

Edward G. Longacre

Rutledge Hill Press™
Nashville, Tennessee

A Division of Thomas Nelson, Inc.
www.ThomasNelson.com

A postwar tribute to General Wade Hampton, C. S. A.:

"Seeing him often in many of those perilous straits
which reveal hard fibre or its absence,
I always regarded him as a noble type
of courage and manhood—
a gentleman and soldier 'to the finger nails'."

—JOHN ESTEN COOKE

Published by Rutledge Hill Press, a Division of Thomas Nelson, Inc., P.O. Box 141000,
Nashville, Tennessee, 37214.

Library of Congress Cataloging-in-Publication Data

Longacre, Edward G., 1946–
    Gentleman and soldier : a biography of Wade Hampton III / Edward G. Longacre.
      p. cm.
    Includes bibliographical references and index.
    ISBN 1-55853-964-6
    1. Hampton, Wade, 1818–1902. 2. Generals—Confederate States of America—
Biography. 3. Confederate States of America. Army—Biography. 4. Confederate States
of America. Army. Hampton Legion. 5. United States—History—Civil War,
1861–1865—Cavalry operations. 6. South Carolina—History—Civil War, 1861–1865.
7. Reconstruction—South Carolina. I. Title.
E467.1.H19L66 2003
973.7'3'092—dc21

                                                   2003006296

Printed in the United States of America

03 04 05 06 07—5 4 3 2 1

In memory of
my highest-ranking cousins:

Brevet Major General Hugh Boyle Ewing, U. S. A.

Brevet Major General Thomas Ewing, Jr., U. S. A.

Brigadier General Charles Ewing, U. S. A.

Brigadier General Francis Marion Cockrell, C. S. A.

CONTENTS

★ ★ ★

ACKNOWLEDGMENTS

★ ★ ★

M y sincere thanks goes to several individuals and institutions without whose assistance this book would not have been written or, if written, would have taken longer and have imposed heavier burdens than I was forced to bear. Rod Gragg of Conway, South Carolina, and Larry Stone of Rutledge Hill Press were instrumental in bringing the project to fruition. Geoff Stone oversaw the editorial process and helped shape the final manuscript. My research assistants, J. Frank Byrd of Aiken, South Carolina, and Anne Dodenhoff of Charleston, helped locate source materials essential to a well-rounded portrait of Hampton. Eric J. Wittenberg of Columbus, Ohio, made available a typescript copy of the 1864 diary of one of Hampton's most trusted subordinates, J. Frederick Waring. As on several past occasions, Paul Dangel of Berwyn, Pennsylvania, produced a series of maps that complements and enhances the narrative. Again, too, my wife, Ann, assisted in every stage of the research and writing.

Others to whom I am indebted include Patricia G. Bennett, Charleston (South Carolina) Library Society; Marianne Cawley, Charleston County Public Library; Margaret Cook, Earl Gregg Swem Library, College of William and Mary, Williamsburg, Virginia; Brian J. Cuthrell and Sam Fore, South Caroliniana Library, University of South Carolina, Columbia; Wade Hampton Dorsey and Robert McIntosh, South Carolina Department of Archives and History, Columbia; Andre Fleche, Charlottesville, Virginia; Emily Guthrie, The Academic Libraries, University of North Carolina,

Chapel Hill; Lisa Hazarian, William R. Perkins Library, Duke University, Durham, North Carolina; Bruce Kirby, The Manuscript Division, Library of Congress, Washington, D.C.; Nancy F. Lyon, Yale University Library, New Haven, Connecticut; Julie Mills, Seymour Library, Knox College, Galesburg, Illinois; and Paulette Schwarting, Virginia Historical Society, Richmond, Virginia.

PREFACE

★ ★ ★

W riting in June 1898, Confederate veteran and amateur historian Edward Laight Wells of Charleston, South Carolina, observed that "no life of Gen. Hampton, or account of his services has ever been published. Such a book would, I think, find readers, because of the inherent interest of the story and the popularity and widely known reputation of the man." At the time, Wells was completing *Hampton and His Cavalry in '64*, a tribute to his former commander, which would be published the following year. A decade later, he would write an unabashedly southern account of his subject's postwar political career, *Hampton and Reconstruction*. While both works contained a certain amount of biographical material, Wells, despite his belief that a life study of Hampton would find an audience, never undertook such a work. Perhaps he realized that a dramatic story and a popular subject were not enough to ensure literary success.

More than a century after Wells proposed a study of the man, Wade Hampton continues to be neglected by book writers. Manly Wade Wellman's *Giant in Gray*, published in 1949, remains the only book-length biography of this formidable soldier and influential politician. That study is marred, however, by factual errors and questionable interpretations; moreover, it is skewed toward its subject's pre– and post–Civil War career, which accounts for almost 60 percent of its text. Yet, in many ways the period 1861–1865 was the most significant and memorable in its subject's life.

As Wells observed, Hampton's life story is so inherently interesting as to be almost irresistible. Known in some circles as the wealthiest man in the prewar South, Wade Hampton III, the son and grandson of upcountry South Carolinians renowned for their economic, political, and military accomplishments, refused to succumb to the life of the idle rich. He worked long and hard to make his plantations in Mississippi and his native state models of scientific farming. The owner of several thousand slaves, by all indications he treated his chattels with a degree of civility unusual in one of his station and time.

Despite possessing no military experience beyond a few militia musters, when the Civil War began Hampton quickly proved himself, as one admirer described him, "every inch a soldier." In addition to his military talents, he placed his personal fortune at the disposal of the Southern nation, sending cotton to Europe in exchange for rifles and cannon. With these resources he armed a one-thousand-man force of infantry, cavalry, and artillery, which he raised, recruited, and then donated to the military forces of the Confederate States of America. Commanding this little army with the rank of colonel, Hampton helped win battles, while exposing himself so boldly to enemy fire that he acquired two wounds.

In mid-1862, after recuperating from his second wound, Hampton, now a forty-four-year-old brigadier, made a remarkable transition to cavalry service, that branch of the nineteenth-century army reserved for zealous youngsters. For the next two years he served as ranking subordinate to the "Beau Sabreur of the Confederacy," Maj. Gen. James Ewell Brown Stuart. While never a bosom friend of Stuart, whom he faulted for his gaudy lifestyle, cavalier mentality, and favoritism toward fellow Virginians, Hampton ably served his superior. Stuart admired his tactical acumen and frequently adopted his advice in preference to that of the professional soldiers who served under him.

After Stuart's mortal wounding at Yellow Tavern in May 1864, Hampton, by then a major general, became the de facto successor to the Beau Sabreur. For three months, however, Robert E. Lee declined to make his promotion official, fearing that the South Carolinian lacked the youth and energy demanded of the position. In August 1864, following inspired performances at Haw's Shop, Trevilian Station, and the opening battles of the Petersburg campaign, Hampton was officially installed as commander of the Cavalry Corps, Army of Northern Virginia. Through the remainder of his stint in Virginia, he proved to all who observed him that Lee had acted wisely, if belatedly, in elevating him. In fact, he became such an indispensable component of the army's hierarchy that when Hampton left Virginia in early 1865 to defend his native state against the hordes of William T. Sherman, Lee claimed his loss made inevitable the surrender of the Army of Northern Virginia at Appomattox Court House.

In the spring of 1865, following the defeat of Rebel forces in the Carolinas, Hampton returned to his plantations, which had been vandalized and burned. He spent the next decade trying in vain to restore his wealth and opposing the excesses of military and congressional Reconstruction. In 1876, he was persuaded to reenter politics (before the war he had served in the state legislature). Early the next year, following a race marred by fraud and violence on both sides, he was elected governor of South Carolina by a margin of thirteen hundred votes out of more than one hundred thousand cast. He took office, however, only after a five-month standoff against Republican officials who claimed victory and upon the removal of occupation troops from his state.

Although Hampton was hailed as a redeemer by white constituents desperate to throw off the yoke of Reconstruction, his single term as governor was notable for the moderate racial policies that prevailed throughout. Despite intense pressure to champion white supremacy, Hampton consistently acted on the belief that South Carolina's whites and African Americans could not only live and work side by side, but also prosper. His influence in state political circles, however, was challenged by radical factions inside his party and lessened by his election in 1879 to the U.S. Senate.

In Washington, as in Columbia, Hampton was a voice of moderation, conciliation, and unity, while also a strong proponent of the political, economic, and social interests of his state and region. Prevented by new opponents—followers of the agrarian racist Benjamin R. Tillman—from winning a third term, he relinquished his Senate seat in 1891. Following a stint as U.S. railroad commissioner, he retired again to his home state, this time for good. By his death in 1902, Hampton was hailed as a bridge between the Old South and the New. He was also remembered for a dramatic series of contradictions. The quintessential slave owner, he had questioned the ethical underpinnings of the Peculiar Institution and had argued against reopening the African slave trade. A prewar spokesman for sectional harmony, he had become one of the most avid Confederates. A model Christian who condemned violence and abhorred dueling, he personally dispatched more opponents in battle than any other general officer, with the possible exception of Nathan Bedford Forrest. The man who "redeemed" his state from black rule, he extended more political benefits to African Americans than any other Democratic governor in the postwar South.

Despite the best efforts of Wells and Wellman, the man behind these dichotomies remains elusive. Some of his more controversial actions have never been adequately explained, nor have the motivations behind them. This book, which concentrates on its subject's war career, attempts to reconcile the conflicting attitudes and contradictory behavior of one whose views, policies, and actions materially influenced the life of his state, his region, and his nation.

ONE

"I will sacrifice everything but principle and honor."

The past two days had been a frustrating mixture of delay, tedium, and slow, almost imperceptible movement toward the seat of war. Understandably, the 620 members of the Hampton Legion were in something less than an amiable mood when, at two-thirty on that summer Sunday morning, the aged, overburdened "camel-back" engine pulling their troop train lurched to a stop a mile south of the depot at Manassas Junction. To the accompaniment of squealing metal and hissing steam, the raw recruits clambered out of the boxcars that had carried them north from Gordonsville, Virginia, the final leg of an excruciating journey that had begun in Richmond twenty-six hours earlier.[1]

In common with the hundreds of other recruits who had come north in recent days from Richmond, site of the capital of the fledgling nation known as the Confederate States of America, the men of the Hampton Legion had reached their destination none too soon. They alighted from the cars to the distant but alarming thump of cannon fire. Though desultory, these exchanges between light artillery units positioned well to the north and west hinted that before many hours had passed, the new arrivals would find themselves in the thick of battle. Five days before, more than thirty-five thousand recruits under Brig. Gen. Irvin McDowell had left the drill fields around Washington, D.C., heading for Richmond. The roads they trod led to Manassas via Fairfax Court House, Centreville, and a meandering watercourse, Bull Run, that flowed about three miles north of the depot. Along that stream, miles of breastworks had been thrown up to block the Yankees' route. They were held by twenty-two thousand equally inexperienced Southerners under Brig. Gen. Pierre G. T. Beauregard, one of the early heroes of this young war. Well aware of his precarious position, on the eighteenth Beauregard had called for reinforcements—specifically, for the twelve thousand troops who had gathered in the Shenandoah Valley under Gen. Joseph E. Johnston. Beauregard hoped this force would reach him in time to even the odds in a confrontation that promised to decide the fate of the Southern nation and the duration of its experiment in rebellion.[2]

As uncomfortable as the train ride had been, the ordeal of the Hampton Legion had been immeasurably worsened by a lack of rations. Neither officers nor men had eaten anything since leaving Richmond shortly before midnight on July 19–20. Rumor had it that the legion's commander had wired ahead to have food and drink ready for the command at Gordonsville. Yet, as Pvt. Johnny Coxe recalled, upon arriving at that station, fifty-five miles south of Manassas, a little after 6:00 P.M. on the twentieth, "instead of a sumptuous supper . . . we found only a few negro women standing about with pies, cakes, and sandwiches for sale. The place was small and couldn't get together such a big supper." Because the legionnaires had yet to answer a pay call since joining the Provisional Army of the Confederacy, only those brazen enough to steal from the local vendors could quiet their protesting stomachs.[3]

The situation rankled the commander of the hungry men, who seethed inwardly and swore aloud. He focused his wrath on the local tavern keeper, who had received the order to prepare a legion-sized meal. The display of temper produced no result, but it relieved the colonel of at least some of his frustration. Forty-three-year-old Wade Hampton was a patriarchal figure to the troops of the military unit that bore his name, and he treated their current plight as a personal affront. Since the earliest days of the legion's recruitment and formation, the tall, bewhiskered planter had regarded the officers and enlisted men who had flocked to his standard as his personal charges—almost as his kinsmen.

Hampton's paternalistic attitude stemmed from his intimate involvement in the legion's formation. He had paid the cost of its armament, as well as a certain amount of its equipment and, conceivably, some of its clothing, out of his own pocket. Such generosity, while not unheard of among the wealthier citizens of the South, had produced a unique organization. Wealthy patriots in many quarters of the infant Confederacy had defrayed the cost of raising companies, battalions, and regiments of cavalry and infantry. Wade Hampton, however, had recruited an army all his own, consisting of six companies of foot soldiers, three (and later four) companies of cavalry, and a battery of light artillery.

While most of the troopers supplied their own uniforms and arms as well as horses, Hampton had purchased at least four hundred Enfield rifles, the finest infantry arm of the day, as well as four English-made rifled cannon, currently en route by steamer from Liverpool to Charleston. Such extraordinary largess was made possible by the benefactor's vast wealth. One of the largest landholders in the South, Hampton managed a half dozen plantations in two states, on which more than fifteen hundred slaves produced a variety of cash crops, principally cotton, tobacco, and rice.[4]

Even if affordable, his generosity bespoke a turnabout of personal philosophy. Until mid-April of 1861, when South Carolina cannon fired on a U.S. Army garrison in Charleston Harbor, initiating nationwide hostilities, Hampton had counseled fellow South Carolinians against precipitate action, either military or political. He had opposed with special vehemence his state's December 1860 announcement that it had seceded from the Union, an act he considered not only rash, impractical, and unconstitutional, but also ruinous to the interests of his state.[5]

Despite Hampton's best efforts, when his troops reboarded the cars of the Orange & Alexandria Railroad for the long run to Manassas, most of the legionnaires continued to endure hunger pangs. And when, in the wee hours of the twenty-first, their overburdened conveyance arrived at its destination, the men had to endure additional discomforts. It was bad enough that, due to a backup of troop trains, they were halted a mile or so from the depot. But when ordered off the cars in the stygian darkness, the men found they had to scale a steep embankment to reach level ground. Muttering at the inconvenience of it all, the legionnaires clambered blindly up the west wall of the cut, in the process dirtying their natty uniforms. Private Coxe recalled that "as we disembarked some one inquired the time, and Lieutenant Lester pulled out his watch and said: 'Half past two'."[6]

In response to their officers' orders, the men sullenly filed into marching formation. After several minutes of standing about, Colonel Hampton appeared at the head of the column. Astride the warhorse that had made the trip from Richmond in one of the few available freight cars, he guided the men along the right-of-way toward the junction, their movements bathed in

3

the glow of trackside bonfires. Upon reaching the depot, they joined hundreds of other new arrivals, some of whom were lolling about in open fields, boiling coffee and frying bacon and ham. Fortunately, rations were in abundance at the depot, and in a matter of minutes the legionnaires were themselves breaking ranks and wolfing down a hearty breakfast. "We greatly enjoyed our feast," Coxe recalled, "and by the time it was over day was breaking."[7]

As the men consumed the last fragments of bacon and biscuit, they became more attuned to the pulsing din of artillery fire. As the sound grew intense and insistent, the makeshift bivouac became a scene of much activity. Company officers alerted everyone to stand ready for marching orders. Then the legion's quartermaster and his assistants passed among the men, doling out the 577-caliber ammunition that fed the rifles Hampton's patronage had provided. When the men had loaded and shouldered their pieces and had filled their cartridge boxes with the remainder of their issuance, they began to march. On either side, other units began moving in the same direction.

Although it was now past 6:00 A.M., few men could see where they were heading. The wooded road to Bull Run lay thick with dust that, when kicked up by hundreds of moving feet, formed an almost impenetrable cloud that obscured vision and parched already-dry throats. Well before the end of their brisk two-mile jaunt, the men in the ranks were not only panting from exertion but also coughing and hawking to expel grit from mouths and throats.[8]

As per the orders he had received from one of General Beauregard's staff officers, Hampton directed his column toward Portici, the plantation home of a family named Lewis, which stood directly south of a stone bridge that spanned Bull Run. The strategically located manor house was now the field headquarters of one of Beauregard's brigade commanders, Col. Philip St. George Cocke, whose troops guarded two nearby fords. Hampton's original intent had been to support Cocke's command at and near the bridge. When almost to his objective, however, the colonel met a scout from Beauregard's headquarters with a piece of alarming news.[9]

The scout had come up from points west, where he had observed a massive column of blue-clad infantry and artillery crossing at Sudley Ford, beyond the Confederate left flank. The invaders were threatening to envelop and crush a force that had rushed into their path, a couple of regiments under Col. Nathan G. Evans. The defenders were spunky and full of fight, but they were too few to halt the enemy drive. Unless quickly supported, they would be crushed or swept aside, with dire consequences for the entire Confederate line.[10]

Unknown to the scout, but not to Hampton, Colonel Evans had already alerted his superiors to the threat at Sudley, and Beauregard had ordered some recently arrived reinforcements to the critical sector: Alabama, Mississippi, and Tennessee infantry, plus a Virginia battery, all under Brig. Gen. Barnard Bee, followed by two regiments of Georgia foot soldiers under Col. Francis S. Bartow. Hampton, however, suspected that, given the reported size of the blue column, even these troops would prove unequal to the crisis. Therefore, the colonel ordered his troops into motion once again. This time he led off, as he later reported, "at a right angle to the course I had been pursuing, and guided by the sound of a heavy fire which had just opened, marched toward their [the enemy's] advancing lines."[11]

At the end of a mile covered at the double-quick, Hampton's command neared the east-west–running Warrenton Turnpike and, beyond it, the Yankee position, fronted by a bank of artillery. On the crest of a ridge over-looking the pike a battery was exchanging shells with the attackers—the Staunton Artillery of Capt. John Imboden, part of Bee's brigade. Hampton positioned his men within supporting range of the battery. While the gun crews continued to work their pieces, oblivious to incoming rounds of shell and canister, the commander of the legion went forward, in company with some of his officers and a few curious enlisted men, to try to gain a closer view of the enemy position.

From the edge of the high ground, he enjoyed a deep and wide view of the field of battle beyond the turnpike. What he and the other onlookers saw did not bode well for the future of their army. Thousands of blue-clad troops were pressing forward from the direction of Sudley Ford, their bayonets flashing, as Johnny Coxe said, "like silver in the bright sunshine." Covered by the fire of their well-positioned cannon, the Yankees had begun to drive in Evans's and Bee's troops. To the rear, Bartow's Georgians were trying desperately to nail down a position capable of halting the onslaught. While a concerned Hampton looked on, a Yankee gun sent a shell in his direction. The round burst only a few feet from the colonel's mount, showering horse and rider with dirt and grass. Only the instincts of a born equestrian kept Hampton in the saddle.[12]

After several minutes spent in close proximity to the enemy without firing a shot in their direction, the Hampton Legion received new orders, directing them to Bartow's assistance. Turning to his second in command, Lt. Col. Benjamin J. Johnson, and his senior company commander, Capt. James Conner, Hampton leveled a volley of instructions. Within minutes, the legion was sweeping down the ridge in line of battle, exactly as it had rehearsed during weeks of drill in camp on their commander's plantation outside Columbia. Reaching the base of the rise, Hampton led his recruits through a woodlot south and east of a farmstead belonging to a free African American named Robinson. In this position the legionnaires for the first time came within rifle range of the Federals pressing Bee and Bartow. Here they suffered their initial casualties, a couple of officers and several men.[13]

Ignoring the leaden rain, Hampton led onward until he reached the foot of another stretch of high ground, a few hundred yards from the turnpike. There one of Bartow's regiments, which had gained a precarious lodgment, was in need of assistance. Again Hampton rode forward to observe the action at close range. Minutes later, he returned to the body of his command to announce: "Men of the Legion, I am happy to inform you that the enemy is in sight!"[14]

At his shouted order, the forward ranks of the legion started up the rise, their Enfields at the ready. By the time they reached the summit, as Johnny Coxe recalled, "bullets were singing all about us." One struck and killed his lieutenant, an old friend from his hometown of Greenville. Redoubling their pace, as though speed made them impervious to bullets, they eventually reached a line of fencing in the Georgians' rear. Behind this barrier, which provided minimal protection against rifle balls, the legion returned the enemy's fire so stoutly as to stun the nearest Federals, a few of whom turned and broke for the rear in what Hampton called "great confusion."[15]

The legionnaires' coolness under fire and good marksmanship exerted a calming effect on the comrades they had come to assist. When one of Bartow's subordinates rode up to Hampton and asked, rather nervously, whether the legion intended to hold so exposed a position, the planter-turned-soldier replied, with a burst of emotion: "Certainly!" His reply heartened the Georgian, who declared that he "wished to hold it too, but his men were extremely anxious to retreat to a wood in the rear." The officer rode back to his outfit and informed its men "that the South Carolina battalion would remain and that they should do so, too." Thus reassured, Bartow's brigade held its ground in front of Hampton's men even as wide-eyed members of Evans's and Bee's commands raced past them to the rear.[16]

Within minutes of his defiant declaration, Hampton had cause to second-guess himself. After being halted by the accurate fire of the legion, the Yankee infantry re-formed and, covered by their artillery, resumed the advance, apparently in greater strength than before. Hampton quickly found his position "entirely exposed" to musketry in front as well as to an enfilading fire from a battery in a concealed position opposite his left. The combined fire took a grievous toll; among its victims was Lieutenant Colonel Johnson, who fell dead with a bullet in his skull. Hampton himself was dashed to the ground when his mount was killed by an artillery shell. With the assistance of Captain Conner, the senior surviving line officer, the dazed but unhurt officer led the legion back to the high ground south of the Robinson place. Bartow's men, their position also untenable, followed suit.[17]

The withdrawal, which was conducted efficiently despite the trying conditions under which it was performed, failed to save Hampton's people from additional harm. No sooner had the command reassembled on Henry House Hill than yet another body of Union infantry materialized off the right flank. Even as this force opened on the legionnaires, the battery on their left galloped toward them up the turnpike, supported by another phalanx of foot soldiers. To complete Hampton's predicament, the main enemy force, several thousand strong, pressed forward on the road from Sudley Ford, aiming for the legion's center.

All too clearly, Hampton saw that "we were nearly surrounded," vulnerable to simultaneous, crushing blows from three sides. A sudden thought struck him with the force of a mule kick: This, his first battle, was also apt to be his last.[18]

The world into which Wade Hampton III was born on March 28, 1818, had been largely shaped by the father and the grandfather whose name he shared. He would live long enough, however, to see that world ended by the equally devastating effects of war and social change.

His ancestry, which lent him a powerful sense of self-identity even in early youth, was a lifelong source of pride. He was born in a historic Charleston house, the home of his mother's family—in fact, in the very room overlooking Hasel Street that she had occupied in girlhood. Edward Wells would observe that from his mother Hampton inherited "the mingled blood of Saxon and Celt, of Briton and Huguenot," while "on his paternal side he came of that sturdy stock, large and vigorous in frame, active in mind and body, brave men, and true women, the Virginians, who did such patient work and gallant deeds in winning empire from the wilderness." Combining as it did the social, cultural, and economic influences of the Upper and Lower South of the early nineteenth century, his was a heritage that should have impressed the most discriminating devotee of pedigree.[19]

The house in which Wade Hampton III was born

In fact, the family into which the third Wade Hampton was born was notable less for a long, illustrious heritage than for its vast wealth—wealth that it had amassed only since the end of the Revolutionary War. The first three generations of Hamptons in America had been small farmers who through hard work and determined thrift gradually merited the grandiose title of "planter." Historians and genealogists trace the family's roots to Staffordshire and Middlesex, England, where Hamptons had resided since the eleventh or twelfth century. From Middlesex came the first American émigré: Rev. Thomas Hampton, an Episcopalian minister who made the perilous voyage to the New World in 1729, followed a year or two later by his wife, Joan, and their three children.

The family lived briefly in Jamestown, then the capital of Virginia, from whence they relocated to Gloucester County, on the colony's Middle Peninsula. There the first American-born Hampton, Thomas, came into the world. Thomas, like his father, entered the church, but his eldest son, John, born in King William County, made his living from the soil. In the process, and thanks largely to the labor of the few slaves he had been able to purchase, John Hampton became moderately wealthy, if not socially prominent. John also made a name as a soldier—the first of his line to do so—by leading militia troops against hostile Indians who threatened the settlers of James City County. John's military abilities eventually gained him the rank of captain.[20]

Thomas's second son, Anthony, the great-grandfather of Wade III, was the first Hampton to settle in South Carolina. Abandoning a career as a flax-breaker, Anthony carved a farm out of the wilderness along the Tiger River, which borders present-day Spartanburg. There, about 1774, he built a modest cabin in which he resided with his wife and five sons, his married daughter, and her husband. The second son, Wade, received a limited education but one substantial enough to enable him to school the children of neighboring settlers. Enamored of hunting, an avocation that his son and grandson would enthusiastically adopt, Wade, accompanied by his three younger brothers, was in the woods tracking game on the tragic day in July 1776 when Cherokees in war paint attacked the family cabin, burned it to the ground, and killed every inhabitant, including Anthony Hampton's newborn grandson.

With a grim determination that would mark his lifelong quest for fortune and position, Wade, after burying his family, armed himself and his brothers, enlisted the help of neighbors and friends, and pursued the Cherokees. Deep in the forest they overtook the war party. With Indian-like stealth, they surrounded its camp, attacked with a war whoop all their own, and dispatched almost the entire band with muskets, knives, and gun-butts. Bloodied, exhausted, their thirst for vengeance slaked, the attackers elected not to pursue the few escapees.[21]

Hampton's grandfather, Wade Hampton I

The brothers Hampton, very much at loose ends, could not bear to return to a life of farming. Instead, they gave themselves over to the struggle against invading whites—British regulars and Hessian mercenaries who had invaded America to suppress a seething rebellion against the rule of King George III. The previous spring, a tense standoff in the upper colonies had turned into a shooting war in Massachusetts. Now the struggle had spread to the South, where it had taken on a particularly vicious tone, with few participants on either side observing the rules of civilized warfare. In such a war Wade Hampton, seeking an outlet for his rage and frustration, rose to prominence. Strong and intelligent, backwoods-savvy, he excelled as a member, and later as a leader, of partisan forces, before attaining the rank of captain in the Second South Carolina Regiment. Later he transferred to dragoon service. Manly Wellman observes that he "rode like a Bedouin, and showed talent with a broad, curved saber, not good for thrusting but capable of dealing a terrible slash when wielded by a strong arm."[22]

Although never vanquished, the captain was twice captured. On the first occasion, as a member of the garrison at Charleston that was surrendered to the British in May 1780, he was freed on parole. After a few months of inactivity he returned to duty, enraged and sickened by British atrocities against civilians and wounded soldiers. He was also incensed that the Indians who had butchered his family had been encouraged in their depredations by the Redcoats, with whom they had formed an alliance. The second time he fell into enemy hands, he found himself liable to execution as a parole violator. Before the sentence could be carried out, he wrested a musket from an inattentive sentinel, shot and bludgeoned his captors, escaped into the wilderness, and rejoined his unit. He went on to distinguish himself in combat at Hanging Rock, Rocky Mount, and Eutaw Springs.

After Cornwallis surrendered his army in Virginia, effectively ending the British intervention, Captain Hampton was willing to leave military life for the more settled existence of a farmer. He prospered in peace as he had in war. In the late 1780s he purchased an estate on the Congaree River outside Columbia, the new capital of South Carolina. Through the labor of a dozen slaves, he planted large quantities of corn, beets, and other vegetables, as well as various cash crops.[23]

Tobacco gained him his first touch of wealth, but by the end of the century he had put most of his capital into cotton. A pioneer in cultivating this crop, which had recently become a profitable enterprise thanks to the invention of the cotton gin, he assumed many risks in introducing it to a climate and a soil others considered unsuitable to its growth. Refusing to gamble small, he planted, as one admirer observed, "nearly one thousand acres of the seed, while his neighbors were afraid to venture upon more than would grow in their flower gardens. He was quite successful with his first crop, having gathered about five hundred bales, which were sold in Liverpool at a handsome profit." In quick time, the plant brought Wade Hampton a fortune, one that continued to expand almost magically. He had truly become a gentleman farmer, the first of his line to merit that designation.[24]

By the turn of the nineteenth century, the first Wade Hampton had outlived two wives, married a third, reared three sons and three daughters, and become one of the largest landowners in the Deep South. His possessions included a mansion on Blanding Street in Columbia as well as a manor house on his home plantation, Millwood, five miles east of the city. He had acquired more than one thousand slaves—so many, it was said, that "he did not know them when he met them, and that they were constantly introducing themselves to him." Increasingly, he was able to pursue outside interests including reading, private study, and other forms of self-improvement, as well as avocations including hunting, fishing, the importation of prized livestock—cattle, sheep, swine, and hounds—and the breeding and racing of thoroughbred horses. He bred and trained some of the finest racing stock in South Carolina, saw them win every major turf trial in his state, and helped found the South Carolina Jockey Club. Having amassed untold wealth, in later life he divested himself of large amounts, contributing generously to the faith of his forebears (although he considered himself a "loose" Episcopalian) as well as to educational institutions including Columbia's South Carolina College, later the state university, on whose board of trustees he served for many years.[25]

He never lost his interest in things military. He served faithfully in the state militia, and in his late fifties he returned to federal service as a colonel of horse, eventually with the rank of brigadier general. He retook the field when the War of 1812 broke out, although his second confrontation with the British was not as successful as his first. In 1814, after leading a failed attempt to capture Canadian garrisons, he resigned his commission, the result of quarrels with fellow officers and clashes with his superiors. By contrast, his eldest son and

An antebellum photo of the arbor at Millwood

namesake, who cut short his studies at South Carolina College to serve on the staff of Gen. Andrew Jackson, made a distinguished war record, notably as a courier bearing important dispatches. Reportedly, Wade Hampton II was the first messenger to inform official Washington of Jackson's pivotal victory at New Orleans.[26]

The second Wade Hampton parlayed his war record (he rose to, and in later life was universally addressed as, Colonel), as well as his family's resources and political prominence (the first Wade had served several terms in the state legislature and two in the U.S. House of Representatives), into even greater wealth and power than his father had amassed. By 1835, when the elder Wade died, his son owned a successful plantation near Columbia. His father bequeathed to him the remainder of the family's property, which by now encompassed not only Millwood—with its Greek Revival plantation house, five acres of flower gardens, and clusters of slave cabins—but several estates in South Carolina's Richland District. Other holdings included a three-thousand-acre plantation (Walnut Ridge) in Issaquena County, Mississippi, where cotton was the principal crop; Houmas, a twelve-thousand-acre plantation on the Mississippi River near Donaldsonville, Louisiana, which produced several hundred thousand hogsheads of sugar each year; and thousands of uncultivated acres in Texas. The family also owned hunting lodges in Virginia and Cashiers Valley, North Carolina.[27]

Even before coming into his inheritance, Wade II had extended his social influence, and improved his financial health, by marrying Ann Fitzsimmons, daughter of an Irish immigrant who had made a fortune in the shipping industry. His wife's dowry included a plantation near Augusta, Georgia, worked by seventy-five slaves. Her family was politically as well as socially prominent: Ann's older sister, Catherine, was married to James Henry Hammond, future governor of, and U.S. senator from, South Carolina. Each of Wade Hampton's sisters also married politicians, two of whom were elected governor.[28]

Although akin to his father in some respects, including his managerial ability and love of fine horseflesh, Colonel Hampton was more educated and refined, less rough-hewn and backwoods-tough. One historian describes him as "ideally the gracious, benevolent, cultured country gentleman of the traditional Old South . . . [who] lived in the grand manner of the storied Southern planter, accumulating a great library, entertaining lavishly, and sparing no expense in maintaining a racing establishment. . . ." Spared the necessity of making a fortune, he was less acquisitive than his father and more inclined, at an early age, to part with his possessions. When his family's vast holdings were deeded to him, he at once divested himself of half of them. Believing that the two surviving daughters of his father and his third wife were in greater need of financial security, Wade II did "what few men ever did before or since. He tore it [his father's will] in a hundred pieces and then made an exact and equal division of all his father's property between himself and half-sisters." As part of the arrangement, he relinquished title to the house on Blanding Street and the sugar-production estate on the Mississippi.[29]

When his eldest son was born in 1818, the second Wade imbued the boy with an interest in education, a love of fine things, and an appreciation of manners, mores, and social graces. During his first seventeen years, the boy was influenced just as heavily, if not more so, by his formidable grandfather. Wade I captivated the youngster with stories of his exploits against redskins and Redcoats and awed him with displays of sacred heirlooms—the spurs, knives, and pistols with which he had tamed the wilderness; the gilt-encrusted uniform he had worn in two wars; the saber he had wielded with enough power and precision to gain a reputation as a master swordsman.

Wade Hampton III spent most of his youth at Millwood, with frequent excursions to the family's outstate holdings. When not in the company of his doting parents and grandfather, he was cared for by a black nurse named Nelly, described as "a kind, intelligent and faithful house servant, who later was nurse and playmate to younger Hampton babies." Those infants included Wade's brothers, Christopher ("Kit") and Frank, and his five sisters: in order of their birth, Harriet, Catherine ("Kate"), Ann, Caroline Louisa, and Mary Fisher. While ever on good terms with his brothers and sisters, Wade III grew especially close to the youngest of each: the handsome, unfailingly cheerful Frank, and the petite, kind-hearted "Fisher."[30]

A prewar drawing of Frank Hampton

Like each of his siblings, Wade III inherited defining traits from his grandfather and both of his parents. The Hampton men bequeathed to him not only an aesthetic sensibility but also a sound physique and a love of outdoor recreation. He also inherited a native reserve that some observers would mistake for diffidence or even arrogance. This tendency was relieved, however, by an amiable disposition that appears to have been the early influence of the mother who died when Wade III was fifteen. As Manly Wellman notes, "among those who did enjoy his friendship and confidence he was unusual for geniality and generosity even among the open-handed plantation gentry of the antebellum South. He was able to gather around himself the most devoted of companions, from aristocrat to slave. All through his long life, with its triumphs and its tragedies, they clung to him."[31]

More than for his quiet demeanor or his determined sociability, Wade the Third, even as a boy, was notable for physical and mental toughness. Wellman tells the story, supposedly taken from family lore, of how, when barely past the toddler stage, he attacked and dispatched with his toy sword a large, angry drake, lord and master of the duck pond at Millwood. In later years, he wielded a heftier blade with uncommon power, as well as with exquisite mastery; a long line of human opponents, if pressed, would have testified to his prowess.

In his early teens, he began to display the physique of a body-builder or a pugilist. His strength was largely in his upper body, which featured muscular arms, broad shoulders, a barrel chest, and a bull neck. Yet he was not massively built, even by the norms of his era. In his early twenties, he reached his full height of six feet, and for years thereafter his weight hovered around 175, although by the time he was fifty he had put on another seventy pounds. Thus he was only four or five inches above the average male stature, but his well-developed torso and his habitually ramrod-straight posture made him look taller still. Many—especially those Yankees he engaged at close quarters—spoke of him as a giant, as he must have appeared in the heat of battle.[32]

In addition to his mastery of the sword, Hampton displayed an early proficiency with firearms. While a good shot with a rifle, he was especially adept with a pistol, which he wielded with instinctive accuracy. During the war, he declared to a subordinate that he "never took sight when shooting a pistol, that he looked at the object and pulled [the trigger] as soon as he raised the gun, not waiting a second." Nine times out of ten, he struck the target square. Hampton was such a student of the handgun that a suggestion he made, before the war, to Samuel Colt prompted the arms manufacturer to add a technical innovation to his celebrated "Peacemaker." Hampton received no royalty for his proposal, but a grateful Colt sent him an ornate presentation piece.[33]

Even in his youth, Hampton showed himself to be an accomplished horseman, as he was throughout his life. In later years, in common with other male members of his clan whose physique approximated his own, he favored large but fleet-footed steeds, the offspring of the prized animals his father had imported from England. Although hardly the embodiment of a jockey, Hampton loved to race his thoroughbreds in genteel but earnest competition with friends and relatives. He took great pleasure in breeding the family's horses and introducing them to the turf. He was careful, however, never to overwork them, and he never neglected or mistreated them. Usually he rode with single rein, a curb bit, and lightweight spurs, and it was said that his seat was light enough to make "a heavyweight in pounds a burden easily and pleasurably carried by the horse."[34]

He melded his interests in weaponry and horsemanship through hunting, which became his lifelong passion. The country in which he grew to maturity, teeming with deer, quail, and other game, fostered his interest in this sport. While small game provided much enjoyment, he hungered for bigger, more dangerous prey. By the time he reached his mid-twenties, bear had become his preferred quarry. Black bears inhabited the woods of his native region and also the hills of western North Carolina and Virginia where the family maintained lodges. Astride well-trained mounts, accompanied by similar-minded sportsmen and packs of hounds, he would track bears to their habitat deep in the woods and mountains. When he brought them to bay, he would dispatch them with the rifle and, on occasion, with the knife, another weapon he wielded with both force and precision. At times he would venture so close to his prey that he would return home with holes in his jacket and breeches and claw marks on his arms and legs. It was dangerous sport, to be sure, but he pursued it until a freak riding accident, in his sixties, resulted in the amputation of his leg and ended his hunting days for good.[35]

At an early age, the third Wade Hampton was tutored in the responsibilities incumbent upon an heir to southern aristocracy. By instruction and example, his father and other family elders impressed on him that he, like they, had certain obligations to his race, class, and region. In every situation, and especially in the face of adversity, he was expected to comport himself as a gentleman—sober, self-composed, and unfailingly polite. Above all else, he must uphold his family's honor, never allowing shame or disrepute to tarnish the Hampton name. For a southern gentleman, honor was a sacred trust, a code to live by, and a defining measure of a man's character and worth.

The young man learned his lessons well. Throughout his life he would carry easily the burdens—the intellectual and emotional baggage—of his status as a white southerner of breeding and means. Even so, he refused to succumb to the romantic myths that colored the self-perceptions of other mid-nineteenth-century southerners. As a boy, he fed on the chivalric tales of Sir Walter Scott and the lachrymose verses of Lord Byron. Even then, however, he seems to have regarded these works as escapist lore rather than as guides to right living.

Certain attitudes and concerns that found general acceptance among his class stirred doubts and raised questions in the young man. He avoided the dissolute behavior in which so many sons of the plantation aristocracy indulged. He did not use tobacco; he rarely imbibed alcoholic beverages (although he later developed a taste for fine wines, an affection that found expression in a two-story wine cellar); and his name was never linked to sexual indiscretions of any sort. As proficient as he was with the pistol, he came to abhor the practice of dueling, by which generations of southern gentleman made public display of their honor and courage while indulging in carefully controlled violence. So forcibly did he make known his distaste of the *code duello* that he was never forced to engage in it; and whenever possible, he dissuaded friends and relatives from resorting to the practice.[36]

Only once did he drop his opposition to dueling, this in response to an

egregious offense against his family. As a boy, he and his brothers and sisters enjoyed visiting at Silver Bluff, the Beach Island, South Carolina, plantation of their uncle James and aunt Catherine Hammond. There, in company with their cousins, Wade, Kit, and Frank fished, hunted, and engaged in outdoor sports. When Hammond, a former U.S. congressman, was elected governor of South Carolina in 1842, his nieces and nephews became regular visitors at his house in Columbia.

The Hampton girls became especial favorites of their uncle, who, apparently unknown to his widower brother-in-law, was possessed of a nigh-uncontrollable libido which had led him to take a succession of female slaves as his mistresses. First at Silver Bluff, then in the governor's home, the thirtyish Hammond was captivated by the beauty, naiveté, and budding sexuality of the four oldest girls: Harriet, then nineteen; Catherine, seventeen; Ann, fifteen; and Caroline, fourteen. Lacking a mother's supervision, the sisters showed little restraint in vying for the affection of their uncle. When in his company, they showered him with kisses and intimate embraces, while apparently encouraging him to reciprocate. Unable to resist so great a temptation, Hammond, when alone with the "four lovely creatures," began to molest them. This behavior, which he carried on for more than two years, involved, as he admitted, every form of physical intimacy "short of direct sexual intercourse."[37]

Hammond managed to keep his indiscretions a secret until April 1843, when Catherine abruptly and vocally rejected his advances. Stung by her reaction, Hammond apologized profusely and ended his intimacies with the girls. If he expected to escape exposure and scandal, he was mistaken, but the storm did not break for another eight months, when Catherine finally brought his conduct to her father's attention. Twenty-five-year-old Wade Hampton III immediately proposed to challenge the miscreant to the field of honor; later, he considered administering a public beating or flogging. His father reacted more calmly, if no less angrily, to the news.[38]

Hammond, having learned of Catherine's revelations, feared physical harm and even assassination; he began to arm himself when walking to and from his office. Weeks passed, however, and nothing untoward happened. At first he suspected that his position made him unassailable; later he realized that his powerful relative intended to exact a slower, more satisfying, revenge. Instead of threatening Hammond physically, Wade Hampton II and his family set out to ruin their relation by disclosing his conduct to influential friends. By this tactic they succeeded not only in blackballing Hammond from respectable

17

society but also in thwarting his professional designs. Whenever the ambitious politician sought office, the Hamptons engineered a whispering campaign that never failed to bring him low. To do so they had only to display a letter that Hammond had sent his brother-in-law in an effort to excuse his conduct but which served, instead, as an admission of guilt.[39]

Not until 1857, by which time the elder Hampton had left South Carolina for permanent residence on his Mississippi plantation, did Hammond gain high office, being elected to the U.S. Senate. By then, although his political reputation had been somewhat rehabilitated, his health and spirit had been broken, as had his marriage and numerous family attachments. But James Henry Hammond was not the only victim of the sordid affair that continued to exile him from high society. By publicizing his relative's indiscretions, Colonel Hampton ensured that his daughters suffered humiliation and ostracism. Their youth and gender failed to protect them from the punishment accorded to notorious violators of early-Victorian mores. As one political official observed to a colleague, "after all the fuss made no man who valued his standing could marry one of the Hampton girls." In fact, all four were condemned to lifelong spinsterhood.[40]

Another entrenched institution of mid-nineteenth-century southern society that Wade Hampton III apparently came to question, perhaps even to condemn, was the one most critical to the survival of his way of life—chattel slavery. As a member of the landed gentry, one who would inherit thousands and purchase hundreds more, his dubious attitude toward the practice may appear incomprehensibly ironic. But from youth he appears to have been bothered, and in later years appalled, by the indifference, callousness, and cruelty that too many masters, including some of his kinsmen, displayed toward their chattels. He also came to abhor the most inhuman elements of the slave trade, especially the willingness of many masters to break up slave families by selling off fathers, mothers, and children strictly in the interest of financial gain.

When he himself became a slaveholder, Hampton resolved to treat his chattels as considerately as possible. He provided them with snug habitations, warm clothing, abundant food, and other basic comforts, while on many occasions—not merely holidays—presenting them with small gifts and unexpected luxuries. Whenever disease struck—measles, diphtheria, typhoid fever,

smallpox, and other lowland maladies made regular visits to Hampton's plantations—he would ensure that his chattels received medical care on a par with that given his family. Supposedly, he hired his overseers with an eye to fair dealing and an even temper, and he enjoined them to manage the workforce as humanely as possible. This is not to say that none of his chattels was overworked or treated harshly, but the master neither condoned nor excused such treatment. Through his paternalistic behavior, he endeared himself to his bondsmen, many of whom praised him to the slaves of other planters and bragged to white folk that they worked for "Marse Wade."[41]

And yet too much can be made of Hampton's professed aversion to the Peculiar Institution. In all probability, his views on slavery did not differ markedly from those of many of his contemporaries. Dozens of planters, before and after Hampton became a slaveholder by inheritance, expressed misgivings, and even guilt feelings, toward slavery, but they perpetuated it nonetheless. Although Hampton may have questioned some of the assumptions on which the practice was founded, he never unambiguously publicized his doubts, even after gaining political office. In December 1859, as the shadow of civil war spread across the land, he rose in the South Carolina senate to speak against reopening the overseas slave trade. His oration elicited praise from northern abolitionists as well as from liberal-minded southerners. While sincerely committed to keeping the ban in effect, he may well have acted, at least in part, from self-interest. The trade with Africa had been closed in 1808 primarily to prevent a disastrous glut on the American market, one that would devalue slaveholders' property. Fifty years later, that consideration would still have carried weight with planters of Hampton's stature. Then, too, as he freely admitted, his primary goal was to avoid antagonizing the North and precipitating the breakup of the Union. The speech did include criticism of slavery as an institution. But implicit in Hampton's oration was the notion that slavery was a regrettable necessity, not a stain on America's soul.[42]

However strong was Hampton's antislavery impulse, it rested on ethical rather than moral or religious grounds. Like his father, the third Wade Hampton was rather loosely connected with organized religion. Nominally an Episcopalian, especially through the first half of his life he appears to have displayed little interest in his faith beyond its ability to polish his reputation as a Christian gentleman. He never argued against slavery as a sin, an offense against God as well as man. Nor did he see the practice as at odds with acceptable political philosophy. Conversely, in the manner of slavery's most avid apologists, he condemned the tactics of abolitionists and others who sought at every turn to interject the slavery controversy into the political process.

Nor did he make any attempt to translate his beliefs into action. So far as can be determined, he failed to emancipate any of his chattels, young or old. Along with many other seemingly enlightened planters, he may have felt constrained from doing so by the all-too-evident plight of freed slaves in the South. Their lack of education and job skills, their unfamiliarity with freedom, and the legal and political restrictions imposed on them by a society steeped in prejudice and discrimination combined to deny most freedmen a respectable existence. But to cite this undesirable condition as a defense of slaveholding was to argue that ex-slaves were inherently incapable of betterment.

At bottom, while he may have been committed to ameliorating the most objectionable features of an institution that troubled him, Wade Hampton III took no steps to end the practice—nor did he attempt to persuade others to do so. Viewed in this light, he was no different from the hundreds of other southerners who saw evil in slavery but not enough evil to demand its eradication.[43]

Colonel Hampton had attended, but had not been graduated from, South Carolina College. He was determined, however, that his son would complete the full course of study at the institution of which he, like his father before him, was a benefactor and trustee. In 1832, Wade III matriculated at his state's premier institution of higher learning, embarking upon the broad classical education that constituted the core of every college curriculum of the day. Rather than simply immerse himself in learning, he attended college with a view to studying law—principally, it would appear, as a steppingstone to political office. He was well prepared for higher education, having attended, with his brothers, the well-appointed academy that flourished at neighboring Rice Creek. Then, too, he had benefited from daily exposure to the ten thousand volumes in the library at Millwood, which embraced virtually the sum total of human knowledge of the period.[44]

The undergraduate did well in his studies, winning especially high grades in Latin, Greek, and modern literature. Yet he was neither a bookworm nor a professional student; he looked forward to time outside the lecture hall, much of which he spent hunting and fishing and on vacation with his family in the

Appalachians. There the Hamptons not only relaxed but helped civilize their less aristocratic neighbors. Edward Wells claimed that the family's extended stays at Cashiers Valley and their other remote hideaways were of "material and lasting benefit to their surroundings in the improvement of manners and morals." He elaborated, in his trademark purple prose: "Many of the inhabitants of this sparsely-settled region were descendants of those who, coming from other communities, had left . . . to seek a refuge where trackless forests and mountains barred the service of legal process. . . . To these people in that day was thus afforded by the Hamptons the civilizing, educating influence exerted by those of gentle birth and culture. Fair hands and kindly hearts dispensed charity by gracious words and deeds in many a rude log-cabin clinging to the mountain-side or nestled in the lonely 'cove.' No wonder that among them Hampton became a name to conjure by."[45]

The third Wade Hampton left South Carolina College, sheepskin in hand, in the spring of 1836, the year after his grandfather's death. While he captured no academic prizes during his four years there, his college career had given him the polish and self-confidence of an educated man as well as a host of fond memories, primarily of classmates with whom he forged friendships and those faculty members who had impressed and influenced him, including Francis Lieber, the eminent professor of political science. In later years, wishing to "manifest my gratitude to my Alma Mater," he funded two full scholarships, which he stipulated should go to those "who tho worthy of an education, are unable to procure one."[46]

Upon graduation, Wade III shared more fully than ever before in the operation of the several plantations the family had acquired. His growing involvement in financial affairs occasionally took him far from home—to Richmond, to New Orleans, to New York City. When at Millwood he paid increasing heed to the demands of polite society, being introduced to, and being received into the homes of, the best families of his region.

He found the time to reacquaint himself with kinfolk from whom he had been separated by years of schooling and business affairs. These included his half-cousin, Margaret Cantey Preston, a childhood companion whose mother, Harriet, was half-sister to Wade Hampton II. By 1837, Margaret had grown from a determined tomboy into "a girl of famous beauty and dignity." As she had in years past, but now for different reasons, she caught the gray blue eye of Colonel Hampton's firstborn, who over the same period had matured into a husky and attractive, if not classically handsome, young man of nineteen.[47]

Soon after he left college, the couple began courting. The romance blos-
somed, and in the fall of 1838 "Mag" and Wade were wed during a lavish ceremony at the bride's home in Alexandria, Virginia. Returning to South
Carolina, the couple set up housekeeping on a small estate known as Sand
Hills, a gift of Colonel Hampton, which sat squarely between Columbia and
Millwood. Wade's brothers continued to reside on the local plantation until
they married and inherited land of their own. The unmarried sisters (who
would become known, corporately and fondly, as "the Aunties") would
remain at Millwood for nearly thirty years, until their majestic home fell prey
to war's violence.[48]

During their brief life together, two sons and two daughters were born to
Wade and Margaret Hampton: Wade IV, in 1840; Thomas Preston, named for
one of Margaret's relations, in 1842; Sally, in 1846; and Harriet, in 1848. The
three oldest children had the good fortune, and good health, to reach maturity. Although the fates would later conspire against them, the boys grew into
strapping replicas of their father—impressively tall, muscular, and vigorous,
while Sally became the embodiment of her graceful mother. Little Harriet,
however, was frail and sickly almost from birth, causing her parents growing
concern, and later untold grief.[49]

With the exception of his daughter's health, Hampton appeared to have
few concerns beyond the normal vicisstitudes of business. He felt fulfilled in
both his personal and professional life, especially when he could combine
business and pleasure, as he did during a memorable journey to the British
Isles in the summer of 1846.

While primarily a business trip, aimed at making commercial contacts and
opening markets for southern cotton, the excursion proved to be a whirlwind
tour. Hampton's party visited London, where they dined as guests of the Duke
of Wellington, and Blenheim, seat of the Duke of Marlborough. Exposure to
British society was a heady experience for the young South Carolinian. As he
admitted to Margaret, instead of a brief visit, "I would like to spend two weeks
in such society, the entre [sic] to which we could now easily have."[50]

Before departing London, the travelers visited Parliament, where they
observed the verbal jousting of Henry Brougham and Lord John Russell, the
new prime minister. Moving on to Oxford, they toured the august university,
its equally famous Bodleian Library, and churchyards with graves dating to the
eighth century. Plunging into the English countryside, the party visited the
Bard's home at Stratford-on-Avon, before inspecting the factories of

Birmingham and the furnaces of Sheffield. A foray into Scotland, which included stops in Edinburgh and Glasgow, provided Wade with the opportunity to hunt grouse on the moors. He and his companions even made a pilgrimage to the Abbotsford grave of Walter Scott, patron saint of southern romanticism.

Uncertain transportation induced the travelers to cancel a side trip to the North of Ireland, but they returned home via the Continent, where they walked the boulevards of Paris and supped at its quaint cafés. The trip—which introduced Hampton to princes and poets, soldiers and statesmen, and worthy folk of all classes and walks of life—furnished him not only with business connections but also with a reservoir of fond memories to be tapped now and again during the dark and mournful days that lay ahead.[51]

For several years after his return from England, Wade Hampton III prospered and matured and knew true contentment. Then came a stunning series of personal tragedies. In June 1852 his wife, who had been unwell since giving birth to her fourth child, died at Millwood. Eighteen months later, five-year-old Harriet succumbed to the illnesses that had plagued her since infancy. The double tragedy, almost unbearable in its cumulative effect, left husband and father to mourn alone, to piece together what remained of his life, and perhaps also to question the beneficence of a God who bestowed on his children untold happiness, only to snatch it away so swiftly and completely.

Eventually, if only for the sake of the children Mag had left behind, he threw off his mantle of despair and bereavement. "My heart has been full," he wrote his youngest sister. "The past and present alike contributes to make me weak, but I shall hope to gather strength for the future. It is not a bright one but my duties are many & so are the blessing still left to me. I shall strive to discharge the one & be worthy of the other."[52]

He sought solace, or at least distraction, by throwing himself into the management of his ever-growing material possessions. During the two decades following his marriage, his land holdings had expanded to include four plantations in addition to Sand Hills, encompassing ten thousand acres and a workforce of more than a thousand slaves. Three of the estates, tilled by renters (Bayou Place, Otterbourne, and Bear Garden), were situated in South Carolina's Richland District. Despite its relatively compact size (835 acres), the fourth

23

plantation, Wild Woods, located in Washington County, Mississippi, produced the bulk of the cash crops, principally cotton, upon which the family fortune depended.[53]

The young master did his best to oversee affairs at each venue without meddling in the affairs of his tenants. The task entailed almost-constant travel, including weeks on the road to and from his Mississippi estate, which could only be reached by train to Montgomery, Alabama, then by steamboat down the Alabama River to Mobile, and up the Mississippi to his private landing. His custom was to spend several weeks each winter in Mississippi. He usually traveled there alone; in his absence, Margaret and the children had remained at Sand Hills, with frequent excursions to Millwood.

After his wife's death, the Hampton sisters cared for young Wade, Preston, and Sally whenever their father was away. The Aunties also looked after another niece, Annie, daughter of Kit Hampton. The second son had emulated his elder brother in ways both fortunate and sad: by acquiring a Mississippi plantation of his own (Linden, consisting of ten thousand acres, mostly in cotton), and by becoming a widower. Here was a cycle of prosperity and tragedy that would characterize the family for years to come.[54]

Despite his vast wealth, Hampton's father—Wade II—had a distressing habit of falling into debt. The value of his holdings in land, slaves, and the products of both might be unrivaled in the American South, but they never satisfied his craving for more. Undoubtedly from concern that large-scale cotton and tobacco production would exhaust the soil but also, it would seem, in response to a basic urge to acquire, the Squire of Richland District, beginning in the mid-1840s, began to mortgage his possessions, that he might buy more of them—more land, more farm machinery, more field hands.

This was a direct path to financial trouble, but Wade II went out of his way to worsen his problems. When relatives and friends attempted to expand their own fortunes via the same route, he invariably endorsed their notes, thereby increasing his own debt. Before long, the family's credit was under strain. Then, in the mid-1850s, the colonel took out a large mortgage on the plantation in Mississippi to which he had retired. When he died suddenly in 1858, he remained, in terms of material possessions, a Deep South Croesus, but he was more than half a million dollars in debt.

Unaccountably, he left no will, forcing his heirs to settle his complicated and muddled accounts. Wearing his responsibility like a badge of honor, his eldest assumed most of the family's debt—more than four hundred thousand dollars' worth. In return, Wade III received from his father's estate the 2,529 acres of bottomland that composed Walnut Ridge, along with a few dozen chattels. These were too few to work the plantation profitably; he would have to transfer slaves there from South Carolina. The remainder of the family's debt was shouldered by his brothers. Frank took on one hundred thousand dollars of it in exchange for title to two South Carolina plantations, plus live-stock, farm implements, and two hundred slaves. Christopher Hampton, who continued to live comfortably at Linden, endorsed the remaining notes, but renounced any claim to additional properties.[55]

As part of his financial responsibilities, Wade III provided generously for his sisters. He saw to it that the Aunties received the jewel of the family's land holdings. At Millwood—which comprised 1,079 acres and forty slaves—the spinsters-to-be could live out their lives in comfort amid splendid lawns, live oaks, and enough plant life to give the place "an appearance of eternal summer." Finally, miscellaneous properties in South Carolina, Texas, and other far-off climes were left undivided. Years later, when this land was sold to cover debts against the estate, the sisters, whom the war had dispossessed, were able to purchase a small tract on which to live out their remaining years.[56]

A few months after settling his father's accounts, Hampton tied up a loose end in his own life by remarrying. His second wife was Mary Singleton McDuffie, daughter of a close friend of Wade II, the late George McDuffie, former governor of South Carolina and U.S. senator. It is not known where or how the couple met; Wellman speculates that it occurred on a vacation trip—both frequented spas and resorts, including Virginia's White Sulphur Springs. However they came together, family connections and financial interests quickly drew them close. Mary, who had assumed management of her father's plantations upon his death in 1851, frequently sought financial advice from the son of his close friend.

On one such occasion, early in 1856, she wrote to Hampton in Mississippi, where he was wintering, soliciting his opinion on a number of matters. He replied warmly, assuring her that "the slightest aid I may be able to give you in the management of your business can put me neither to trouble [n]or inconvenience." He proved as much by appending three pages of instructions and suggestions. In recounting this "gentle beginning of courtship," Wellman portrays a handsome couple involved in romantic intimacy as well as business affairs. He neglects to add some details that cost the tableau some of its warmth and charm: Mary's inquiry and Hampton's advice concerned the most profitable disposition she could make of her excess slave population—specifically, whether to put her chattels on the block that year or the next. Hampton advised her to wait, predicting that some months hence the chattels would fetch prices as high as, and perhaps higher than, those then obtaining.[57]

A little more than two years after this episode, the couple were wed in South Carolina. From the start, the marriage brought Hampton pleasure and contentment, rescuing him from the melancholy into which he had slipped following Margaret's death. And yet the potential for tragedy hung over this union, as it had over his first marriage. Almost from the day they wed, Mary's health began to wane. His friends and relatives were struck by the fact that the robust outdoorsman had twice fallen in love with petite, frail women.

As if Mary bequeathed her constitution to their first child, George McDuffie Hampton, born in January 1859, was plagued by sickness throughout his early years, causing his father on more than one occasion to fear for his life. And yet this boy, known to his parents as "McDuffie," would survive well into the next century, as would Hampton's sixth child—his second by Mary—and third daughter. Born in January 1861 and given her mother's name, she was called "Daisy" to distinguish her from the many other Marys in the family.[58]

It has been observed that Wade Hampton III embarked on a political career more to please his father than to quench any personal ambition. In 1852, rather half-heartedly it would appear, he announced his candidacy for a seat in the lower house of the South Carolina legislature. His family's prominence in Richland District and its long affiliation with the Democratic Party assured him of victory, and in due course he entered upon a public life. He made an unremarkable record in the house, although he served creditably enough to win reelection in 1854. Two years later, when he moved up to the state senate, he took a more active and prominent role in the public debate on many issues. He was vocal not only on the perils of reopening the African slave trade but also on whether and how his state should seek redress of wrongs, real and imagined, by the federal government.[59]

His father and grandfather had been proponents of states' rights, but they had also manifested a healthy respect for federal authority. They had looked askance at earlier attempts by South Carolina to challenge the perceived usurpation of state prerogatives by the president and the Congress. In 1832, led by her native son, state sovereignty pioneer (and vice president of the United States) John C. Calhoun, South Carolina had attempted to nullify two acts that levied taxes on farm goods imported from Europe—the tariffs were so steep as to be considered ruinous to planter society. Calhoun's boss, the strong-willed nationalist Andrew Jackson, defied the Nullificators, declaring their effort to override Congress a "miserable mockery of legislation" one that posed "the threat of unhallowed disunion."[60]

Jackson's argument prevailed, but the president achieved an uneasy peace rather than a lasting victory. Calls for South Carolina to leave the Union were renewed several times over the next two decades. The clamor rose to high pitch following the passage of the Fugitive Slave Act of 1850, which many northern states not only failed to enforce but effectively obstructed. In 1852, a secession convention met in Charleston to air harshly worded grievances against the government. The delegates adopted an ordinance of secession, but agreed, for reasons of expediency (essentially, they realized that the rest of the South would not join their movement), to suspend its implementation. But antagonism toward the central government continued to percolate throughout the state, and the Secessionist impulse strengthened. More conservative observers such as Wade Hampton III understood that unless men of their persuasion failed to shape the public debate, civil war was a distinct possibility.[61]

In this context, Hampton's December 1859 speech against the renewed importation of slaves can be seen not as a humanitarian argument but as a desperate call to stanch a break in the dam of the Union, thus averting a national disaster. Hampton had long assured his constituents that he had no support for northern fanatics who viewed emancipation as a moral imperative—the true goal of such agitators was to break the political and economic power of the South. Yet if such people were not to be heeded, neither were those who, through an unreasoning fear of federal institutions, were willing to risk the death of the American experiment in self-government. By blindly pursuing a vendetta against Washington, these southerners sowed the seeds of their own destruction.

On that December morning—eight days after the execution of John Brown, the radical abolitionist whose failed attempt to foment a slave uprising had polarized sectional debate as no other single event—Hampton took the floor of the senate chamber in Columbia before an overflow audience. Surveying the packed galleries, he began to declaim in tones other than his normally soft, "watery" voice. He prefaced his comments with a legalistic summary of the legislation under consideration. Having set the boundaries of the question, he argued clearly and cogently against "a measure . . . fraught with a greater danger to the South than any other that has ever been proposed. . . . The South should studiously avoid making any new issue that might avert her from the only true one, which is *the union of the South for the preservation of the South*."[62]

He attacked the idea of repealing the slave trade ban—an idea already approved by the legislatures of Mississippi, Louisiana, and other cotton states—on a variety of grounds, including simple decency: It "would institute a practice which would necessarily involve cruel and inhuman practices; and would, by the introduction of barbarians from Africa, demoralize the slaves now owned in the United States and infect with evil influences the whole system of domestic slavery as now established. . . ."[63]

Still, the thrust of his argument was the preservation of the South's political power and her social and economic institutions, now threatened by the short-sighted policies of otherwise good and decent men. The only viable course was moderation, conciliation, compromise—not from fear of federal retaliation, but from a desire to preserve the best features of the southern way of life. In concluding his speech, he exclaimed: "Show me such a one" as would hew to the path he had set forth, "and I will sacrifice everything but principle and honor to place myself . . . by the side of the true patriots of the South."[64]

His appeal to political sanity brought only a smattering of applause, to the accompaniment of which he sadly retook his seat. The nature of the response told him that his argument had changed few, if any, minds, not only on the slave-trade question but also on the larger, more critical issues he had addressed. It may have been at this moment that Wade Hampton III began to despair for the future of his state, his region, and the fraying network of interests and institutions that was his nation.

TWO

"The legion is to serve wherever ordered."

The fears that underlay Hampton's opposition to reopening the slave trade were validated during the sixteen months following his senate speech. Thanks largely to the words and deeds of southern "fire-eaters" and radical abolitionists, sectional tensions increased exponentially while Hampton and other conservatives on both sides of the Mason-Dixon looked on helplessly. The tensions became especially acute after the spring of 1860. In April the Democratic National Convention, meeting in Charleston, deadlocked after almost sixty inconclusive ballots. Six weeks later the delegates reconvened in Baltimore, only to split again over the candidacies of the moderate senator Stephen Douglas of Illinois and the vice president, John C. Breckinridge of Kentucky, the pro-slavery proponent. Bellicose factions nominated both men, ensuring that neither would win the White House. On November 6, following a tense, often hysterical, and sometimes violent campaign conducted along the same divisive lines as the conventions, former congressman Abraham Lincoln of Illinois, reviled by southern extremists as the "abolitionist candidate," won enough electoral votes to be declared president. Lincoln, however, had polled almost two million popular votes fewer than his combined opposition, which included a compromise third-party candidate.[1]

Many southerners, including a clear majority of South Carolinians, refused to accept the results of the national canvass. Lincoln had risen to power upon a platform that opposed the extension of slavery into the western territories.

However, most southerners believed—or professed to believe—that the president-elect would interfere with the Peculiar Institution where it already existed. Slavery had become such an integral part not only of the southern economy but also of the social fabric of the region that the mere idea of a "black Republican" in the White House was cause for precipitate action.

Officials in Charleston and elsewhere in the state protested Lincoln's victory by hauling down the Stars and Stripes from the roofs of public buildings and the balconies of private homes and replacing it with a banner of defiance, the state's Palmetto Flag. Agitated crowds roamed the streets, poring over newspaper tabulations of the vote, haranguing anti-Secessionists, and applauding orators who vilified the president-elect. The state's leading newspaper, the *Charleston Mercury*, announced that "the tea has been thrown overboard, the revolution of 1860 has been initiated."[2]

In South Carolina, at least, the revolution got off to a quick start. Having flirted with secession as early as 1832, having approved the policy in principle two decades later, the state was more than willing to put it to another vote. Four days after Lincoln's triumph, the legislature reconvened in response to a call by Gov. Francis W. Pickens. Dubious about Pickens's political acumen and mistrustful of his motives, Senator Hampton refused to attend the special session. Without the benefit of advice from their colleague from Richland District, the august body called for a convention to meet at Columbia on December 17 to consider whether the state should formally announce her departure from the Union. As a direct result of this call, South Carolina's representatives in the U.S. Congress, including Hampton's lecherous uncle, Senator Hammond, resigned their seats and returned home to attend the convention. Hampton was heartsick but not astounded when, on December 20, the convention, which had reconvened in Charleston, adopted an ordinance of secession. The news spread to the corners of the country with the speed of a prairie fire.[3]

As if suddenly concerned that their actions would bring swift retaliation, hundreds of South Carolinians began to arm themselves and band together for mutual defense. Militia units, their ranks swelled by an influx of enthusiastic recruits, paraded through the streets of large cities and small towns throughout the state. In Charleston, the small U.S. Army garrison commanded by Maj. Robert Anderson attracted so many jeers, curses, and threats that on the day after Christmas the troops abandoned their old post at Fort Moultrie and, shrouded by early-morning darkness, rowed out to occupy the smaller but less accessible Fort Sumter, in the middle of the harbor.[4]

The garrison's covert transfer was considered provocative enough that land batteries went up all across the harbor. By the start of the new year, the muzzles of dozens of cannon and the mouths of numerous mortars—many of them purchased ten years before during the state's flirtation with secession— were trained on Anderson's new duty station. Looking on with a growing sense of dread, Hampton realized that the presence of Federal troops in the midst of a state that had proclaimed its sovereignty would soon prove intolerable to her citizenry. When South Carolina acted to remove the offending agent, open warfare would commence.

The thought forced the planter-statesman to confront the most fateful decision of his life. He had long cultivated a reputation as a political moderate, counseling others against precipitate action with a sectional bias. If such action triggered conflict, the result would be ruinous to his people. The material advantages of the North were too great to be overcome even by an army of fire-breathing zealots. From years of associating with Yankee businessmen and politicians, Hampton knew the North had the will to use every resource at its command to crush rebellion.

The coming confrontation was one that the South could not win except by a major intervention, foreign or divine. Hampton's familiarity with European industrialists—including those who had wined and dined him fifteen years before—told him that while the European powers might sympathize with the South's struggle for freedom, none was likely to provide it with direct military assistance. And he was enough of a deist to doubt that if and when civil war came to America, God would ally himself with either side.

If Hampton had doubts that his region could prevail in a shooting war, he did not doubt that he should take part in it. A southerner born and bred, a figure of prominence in his region's economic, social, and political life, he never considered abandoning South Carolina to her fate. Until December 20, he had done his utmost to prevent a clash of tempers and arms. Now that secession was the avowed policy of his state, he must adhere to it, regardless of its probable outcome or its potential impact on his family and his fortune. Henceforth, he would commit himself fully to a cause he had long distrusted.

Through the Christmas season, the Palmetto State remained a movement— or a nation—of one. Soon after the new year came in, however, she was joined in secession by the rest of the Deep South, as well as by the provinces of the southwest. On January 9, 1861, Mississippi became the second state to leave the union by the overwhelming vote of a secession convention. Over the next two days, Florida and Alabama adopted similar ordinances, although in the latter state a strong Unionist presence made for a relatively close vote. By the end of the month, Georgia and Louisiana had joined her sisters in rebellion, and by the first week in February representatives of all six states had met in Montgomery, Alabama, to organize a government and convene the first session of the Provisional Congress of the Confederate States of America.[5]

On February 9, the delegates ended days of discussion and debate by selecting as provisional president Jefferson Davis, a Mexican War hero, later the secretary of war, later still the senior U.S. senator from Mississippi. Hampton, who had become acquainted with the man during his part-time residency in Mississippi, applauded Davis's selection. His reputation as a sectional moderate and his long and distinguished record of public service gave the Confederacy instant credibility. Hampton was less knowledgeable about Davis's vice president, the diminutive but fiery Alexander H. Stephens of Georgia, and even less certain of Stephens's fitness for the position he would fill.[6]

In addition to a congress, the politicos who met in Montgomery created a provisional army and navy. These branches of service would become the major components of a permanent military establishment once the Confederacy secured her independence. Sons of the South who had served as officers in the armed forces of the United States promptly resigned their commissions and reported in person to the embryonic government in Montgomery or submitted applications for rank in the Confederate service—preferably

Confederate President Jefferson Davis

higher rank than they formerly held. In many cases, the applications were accompanied by endorsements from prominent politicians and other community pillars.

Worthy citizens like Hampton, who were committed to military service but lacked the requisite education and experience beyond a militia muster or two, could only look on as the defense forces of the South slowly took shape. In part, the slowness was the result of a general state of uncertainty. For a time, no one in authority knew how large a military establishment the South needed, or what shape it should adopt. Should it be composed primarily of ex-regulars, militiamen, or volunteers? If all three were needed, what was the proper ratio? Should officers be elected or appointed, and who should control their commissioning? How should regiments be raised and organized? These and other questions awaited a spark in the powder keg of war.

By all indications, the confrontation in Charleston Harbor would provide that spark. It nearly exploded on January 9 when a relief ship sent from the North by U.S. Commanding General Winfield Scott tried to reinforce and resupply Anderson's garrison. The *Star of the West* had crossed the bar into the main channel when she was struck by a single round from a masked battery on Morris Island, on the south side of the harbor. Though damage was slight, her captain elected to abort the mission, exit the harbor, and return to New York. That was the extent of hostilities thus far—Anderson's response to the hostile fire was limited to a written complaint to Francis Pickens. Though no admirer of the governor, Hampton concurred with the gist of his reply: As South Carolina was now an independent entity, any attempt to support a Federal installation on her soil amounted to a hostile act, one that demanded retaliation.[7]

For a time, many Charlestonians believed that war had already begun. Yet the status quo quickly resumed, and the next several weeks passed calmly enough. In early March, the pace of events accelerated with the arrival in the city of Pierre G. T. Beauregard of Louisiana, until recently a brevet major of United States engineers and now a brigadier general in the Provisional Confederate Army. The courtly Creole, a Mexican War veteran and former superintendent of West Point, became an immediate favorite among all classes of the citizenry, especially the female portion thereof. But Hampton knew the man had come to Charleston not to shake hands or flirt but to force the evacuation of the garrison whose presence had progressed from local irritant to intolerable affront to South Carolina's honor and dignity.[8]

33

The hero of Fort Sumter, P. G. T. Beauregard

For all his certainty that war was both inevitable and imminent, Hampton could not hold his life in abeyance while waiting for it to begin. For one thing, he had an annual excursion to make. In mid-March, he bade farewell to Mary, Sally, McDuffie, and the newborn Daisy (Wade Jr. and Preston were away at South Carolina College) and embarked by train and steamboat for the cotton fields of Mississippi. By the twenty-seventh, after a "very dull trip" down the river, he was in Mobile, the last major stopover before New Orleans, from whence he would proceed to his plantation by rail. The long, arduous journey seems to have depressed him. "Tomorrow is my birthday," he mused in a letter to his favorite sister, noting ruefully that he was quickly "growing old and no better. . . ." He had little news to impart and inquired after none, as if the war had become a distant abstraction. He asked Fisher to join Mary McDuffie Hampton in "Kiss[ing] the babies, and God bless you all."[9]

The remainder of the trip was as uneventful as the preceding, but momentous events were forthcoming. He had been at Wild Woods only a few days, seeing to his fields, his cotton gins, and his ledger books, when he learned that in the small hours of April 12 Beauregard had opened on Anderson's fort with every piece of ordnance at his command. The furious bombardment lasted for nearly thirty-six hours, almost without let-up. It blasted masonry from Sumter's walls, plowed up the earth on her terreplein and parade ground, and shot away the flagstaff from which the Stars and Stripes flew. For all the damage, no member of the garrison was killed or wounded. Anderson returned fire as best he could, though his few guns made the contest an unequal one throughout. Not surprisingly, those cannon also failed to kill or inflict serious injury. This all-but-bloodless opening to a war destined to be sanguinary in the extreme ended on the afternoon of the thirteenth, when Anderson, now almost out of ammunition, ran up a white flag.[10]

The news of Sumter's assault and surrender told Wade Hampton that his planter's life—and perhaps his lifestyle—was at an end. As soon as he could tie up affairs, he left them in the hands of tenants and overseers. Then it was back to the train and the steamboat to retrace the path he had taken only days before. He arrived in Charleston, where he was met by Mary, the baby, and Daisy's nurse, less than a fortnight after Anderson and his troops had been paroled and sent by steamer to Washington.[11]

By now Sumter was held by the forces of South Carolina. The newly adopted Confederate national flag, featuring a circle of seven stars, designating the states that had declared themselves out of the Union, flew from a makeshift staff. Beginning on the day of the surrender, Beauregard, Pickens, and other military and political officials had toured the shot-torn works in ceremonial acceptance of Sumter as a prize of war. After Hampton reached the city, Pickens assembled another group of dignitaries, including the new arrival, and returned to the fort. This time, a photographer was on hand to record the visit. His camera caught the tour group as it inspected a captured Columbiad, Hampton looking awkward in top hat and cutaway coat—formal clothing did not hang gently on his muscular frame—and towering above the others in his party.[12]

Wade Hampton (third from the left) inside Fort Sumter

Upon his arrival, Hampton found Charleston—as he had found New Orleans, Mobile, and the other cities along his return route—a hotbed of military preparation. Its cobbled streets were scuffed by thousands of would-be soldiers at drill—members of militia companies and newly formed volunteer regiments, many garbed in outlandish uniforms. Despite their sometimes ludicrous appearance, wherever they went they prompted wild cheering and bursts of excited emotion. Hampton discovered that many of these units had been bankrolled by Charleston's commercial, industrial, and financial elite, others by planters like himself. The recruits and their benefactors vied with one another to be the first to carry state and local pride onto the field of battle.

Observing the fruits of his neighbors' generosity, Hampton felt a sense of obligation to recruit, equip, and perhaps also to lead a unit of his own. Although he was not ruled by military ambition—at forty-three, he was well past the age at which one saw romance and nobility in war—his family had a long military tradition, as well as a history of civic duty. Since early youth, he had been steeped in military-like discipline; since young manhood, he had ordered others about, sometimes in drill-field fashion. If he was not a born soldier, he knew how to lead, and he carried the burden of duty and responsibility without stooping. Moreover, some of the most prominent men in the state, including many who were older than he, had not only financed volunteer units but also—clad in gilt-smothered uniforms—had led them into state service. Why should he not follow their lead? For one thing, he cut a more imposing figure in uniform than he did in morning coat.

Already he had offered his services to the governor, while making known his willingness to serve in any capacity Pickens considered him qualified to fill. If he was not deemed officer material, he would enlist as a private soldier. As Hampton must have foreseen, Pickens scoffed at the notion of South Carolina's wealthiest planter marching to war in the ranks. Thus, he was immediately receptive to Hampton's subsequent offer to finance the recruitment and organization of a combat unit. As befit his station, Hampton proposed to raise a small, self-contained army whose origins dated to Roman antiquity—a "legion," embracing several companies of infantry and cavalry, as well as a battery of light artillery. Part of the cost of fielding this two thousand-man force Hampton would pay from his own pocket—if the state contributed as well. He would fund most of its uniforms, equipment, and weaponry, including the long-range, rifled cannon that he envisioned for the battery.[13]

His offer left the governor equally impressed by his constituent's vision and generosity. He approved the idea virtually on the spot, conditional only upon the sanction of the Confederate War Department. He not only pledged state funds to augment Hampton's largesse but also promised to grant Hampton the proper rank—a colonelcy, at least—to command the organization. Almost at once, he wired word of Hampton's generosity to Montgomery, where, on April 27, Secretary of War Leroy Pope Walker approved the idea of raising a "regiment with legionary formation." Three days later, Pickens publicly announced the secretary's action. He added that he himself would take "great pride" in the legion's formation and declared that "no one could with more propriety be selected as commander of such a force than Colonel Hampton. I will contribute everything in my power to aid in its formation by furnishing such arms as may be at my disposal, and also in allowing any privileges consistent with the public service."[14]

Even before Pickens's proclamation appeared in the newspapers, Hampton made the rounds of Charleston's editors, whom he paid to run recruiting notices. Later he placed similar announcements in the newspapers of Columbia and other upcountry cities and towns. A typical notice, which ran in the May 3 editions of the *Charleston Daily Courier*, summarized Hampton's plans for the legion. He intended to raise six companies of "voltigeurs" (riflemen) for infantry service, as well as four companies of cavalry and a one-hundred-man battery of light artillery. The field officers would be appointed by President Davis, while company-level positions (as originally envisioned, each company would field a captain and four lieutenants) would be filled by vote of the rank-and-file.

If the command was accepted into the Provisional Confederate Army, it would serve for one year, unless hostilities ended sooner, in which case officers and men would receive an early discharge. Hampton proclaimed that "the Legion is to serve wherever it may be ordered by the President. . . . As soon as the companies report themselves ready for duty they will be ordered into camp for the purpose of drilling together. It is very desirable to have this corps ready at an early day, as I have every reason to hope that it will at once be ordered into active service. . . ."[15]

Hampton remained in Charleston to seek candidates for field rank in his organization. He interviewed former members of the U.S. Army, including West Pointers and graduates of the South Carolina Military Academy, later known as the Citadel. He looked especially hard at veterans with experience in drilling and instructing troops. He also spoke to civilian-soldiers with an active militia background as well as those who, like himself, lacked military experience but not leadership skills.

With his recruiting program off to a promising start, he returned to Columbia with his wife and daughter. There he met a couple of likely recruits—his sons, both of whom, along with every other member of the student body, had quit their university studies in order to enlist in a state unit. Another willing recruit was Frank Hampton, whose eagerness to enter the ranks overrode his natural desire to remain comfortably at Richland with his wife, Sally Baxter Hampton, a northern-born beauty of great poise and charm. Preston and Frank Hampton would join the cavalry portion of the legion, Frank eventually rising to become its second in command. Later, Preston would join his father's staff, while Wade Jr. would secure a position on the staff of Gen. Joseph E. Johnston.[16]

At the outset, Hampton feared that, because so many recruiters had gotten a head start on him, he would have a difficult time filling the ranks of his organization. He was wrong—from the first day of training camp, young men clamored to answer his call to arms. Many were members of militia companies whose commanders offered their units, lock, stock, and fancy uniforms, to Hampton. Some of the state's most venerable defenders would be represented in the organization, including the Washington Light Infantry of Charleston, a well-led, well-disciplined unit that became Company A of the legion's foot contingent. The only drawback to adding these existing organizations was that many were below the minimum strength demanded of wartime service. They were quickly filled up, however, by the dozens of raw recruits who responded eagerly, even frantically, to Hampton's recruiting campaign.[17]

The youngsters signed up for a host of reasons. The patriotic impulse was a major motivator, although more than a few were lured by the magic in the Hampton name and the prospect of soldiering in genteel fashion. The scions of the state's best families were numbered among the earliest recruits. They rode in on sleek, thoroughbred stock, some accompanied by body servants, a few by their favorite hunting dogs. When, days later, they reported at the training camp Hampton had set up on the edge of his Columbia estate, they—or, more often, their slaves—lugged steamer trunks carrying not only silk shirts and riding breeches (to be donned in off-duty hours) but also vials of French cologne, toilet articles of handmade ivory, tins of exotic cheeses, and bottles of claret. Young men of lesser estate also signed the muster rolls—the sons of small farmers from Edgefield and Richland, store clerks from Columbia, stevedores from the Charleston wharves. At first, however, the common folk were overshadowed by their blue-blooded comrades, ensuring that well before it went to war, the legion acquired the reputation of an elite command.[18]

So many responded to Hampton's recruiting pitch that by May 7, five days after he issued his first call to arms, he could inform Secretary Walker that he had on hand "many more troops than I am authorized to accept." Until the cannon he had ordered arrived from Liverpool, those who had signed up for artillery service would train as infantry. This gave the organization no fewer than 750 foot soldiers—enough to fill eight companies instead of the contemplated six. Hampton reiterated that all should go into training camp as soon as possible: "My desire is to have the Legion ready at a very early day to respond to any call you may make on it."[19]

In this letter, Hampton indicated that his generosity toward the Confederacy, while remarkable, had its limits. He would fund most of the weaponry necessary to arm the infantry and artillery components of his command. In addition to the artillery, four hundred Enfield rifles, paid for in Hampton family cotton, were on order from England. He expected, however, that South Carolina's armories and arsenals (including those Federal facilities the state had seized after December 20) would furnish the rest of the shoulder-arms the infantry needed.

The cavalry had already agreed to provide its own weapons, mainly sabers and pistols, although Hampton appears to have picked up the tab for much of its equipment. Each trooper would also furnish his own mount; for shouldering this expense, the government would compensate him at a rate of forty cents per diem. Hampton's artillery contingent, however, could not fund the battery teams that were essential to its operation. Hampton did not wish to incur this cost; he hoped that Pickens would follow through on a pledge to provide enough animals to mount the battery. In the end, he did. Hampton's preference was to organize the unit as horse or "flying" artillery, in which every cannoneer rode a horse, enabling his unit to keep pace with and closely support its comrades in the cavalry. If, however, Pickens could not provide the requisite number of animals, the battery would take the field as mounted artillery, whose men, when in motion, walked or perched atop the limbers and caissons that transported the unit's ammunition and tools. In the end, Hampton had to settle for the latter alternative. In the summer of 1862, however, the battery would be converted to horse artillery thanks to the patronage of Walker's successor, George W. Randolph.

It has become accepted fact that Hampton purchased the uniforms worn by his officers and men. Wellman not only repeats this claim but notes that the entire legion was clothed in uniforms of "rich gray with gilded buttons and braid, snug jackets, jaunty kepis and shakos." He bases his description on a portrait of a member of the legion's battery, found in a postwar collection of veterans' memoirs. The uniform he describes, however, was probably worn only by the artillerymen of the legion. As Hampton himself explained to the secretary of war, each of the infantry and cavalry companies would supply its own uniforms. The militia units, of course, already wore attire of their own pattern and color.[20]

Given the preference of these prewar organizations for natty and colorful uniforms not always suitable to active campaigning, it can be surmised that the legion, at least in its earliest weeks, displayed a variety of clothing styles and a full palette of hues. As time wore on and the original uniforms wore out, Hampton appears to have paid for replacement garb, or at least seen to their manufacture. By September 1861, by which time the legion had been in the field for three months, he wrote Mary Fisher Hampton to request that she and some back-home friends turn out new uniforms, declaring, "I want them made as soon as possible." Apparently the seamstresses answered his call. "You have all been very kind in making them," he later told his sister, "and I hope the Legion will be grateful."[21]

One day after informing the secretary of war about his recruitment efforts, Hampton wrote to Jefferson Davis, alerting him to the unexpected influx of recruits and offering to double or even triple the authorized strength of his command. He noted that the president had recently called for three thousand troops from South Carolina over and above the state's initial quota. To help meet the new goal, Hampton offered to turn the infantry of the legion into a full-sized regiment, composed of ten or more companies. He advised Davis that he had yet to accept into his ranks any of the proffered militia companies; these he would inspect in a few days with a view to their worthiness to join such a celebrated organization as his had become. Whether or not Davis cared to expand the size of the legion (he would, but would not do so until early 1862), Hampton hoped "in a very short time, to be able to present to Your Excellency a corps of which my State will never be ashamed."[22]

This hope rested, in large measure, on the caliber of the legion's officers. Relying on his personal interviews and the recommendations of trusted advisors, before May was out he had filled his complement of field and staff officers, including Benjamin J. Johnson—former commander of the Washington Light Infantry—as lieutenant colonel, James B. Griffin as major, Theodore G. Barker as adjutant, Claudius L. Goodwin as quartermaster, and Thomas Biggs as chief commissary officer. For the most part, the military experience of these men had militia rather than regular army origins, but each was a man of ability and resourcefulness, and both Johnson and Griffin could be counted on to instruct the men thoroughly in the manual of arms.[23]

A number of the company and battery officers would prove to be just as talented; no fewer than five would go on to careers as generals of infantry or cavalry. The list included Matthew Calbraith Butler, a young lawyer from Edgefield County, son-in-law of Governor Pickens, who commanded the "Edgefield Hussars," later Company A of the legion's mounted contingent; James Conner of Charleston, who had succeeded Johnson as commander of the Washington Light Infantry; Conner's first lieutenant, Thomas Muldrup Logan, another Charlestonian, a veteran of the campaign to neutralize Fort Sumter; Martin W. Gary, an Edgefield lawyer with a bald head, a hawklike nose, and a fiery temper, who led Company B of the infantry battalion; and Stephen Dill Lee of Charleston, the only member of the group with professional army experience—West Point graduate, regular artillerist, and commander of the legion's light battery. Destined to become the youngest lieutenant general in Confederate service, by May 1861 Lee had already made a reputation as a soldier of ability and a leader of men.[24]

In the last days of May and the first two weeks of June, officers and enlisted men assembled at "Camp Hampton," the training facility their commander had laid out on his estate outside Columbia. Units reported by train, while individual recruits arrived on horseback and afoot. Those who took the railroad from outlying points got an early taste of military life when they were marched the three miles from the depot to the camp. Upon arriving, however, they found pleasant surroundings. Johnny Coxe of the Davis Guards, a Greenville-area unit that became Company F of the infantry battalion, recalled Camp Hampton as "a fine place," adorned by "beautiful oaks, a good spring," a spacious campground, and a well cleared drill-plain. At first the Davis Guards shared the camp only with the Washington Light Infantry, but

Hampton's favorite subordinate, M. C. Butler

41

within a few days they were joined by the nuclei of Companies B, C, and D. In the second week of June, the mounted units under Butler and John F. Lanneau (the Brooks Troop) reported, followed by Companies E and F of the infantry, the remaining mounted companies, and the artillery. Some units arrived minus their commanders; Captain Lee, for one, was so long detained by business in Charleston that he failed to join his battery until late July.[25]

Once enough men were on hand to approximate a military organization, Hampton and his subordinates acted to make appearance reality. According to Private Coxe, "severe company drills were inaugurated under the eyes of Lieutenant Colonel Johnson, Major Griffin, and Adjutant Barker." The youngster noticed that Colonel Hampton rarely oversaw the proceedings, although he took charge at the dress parades that were held every evening under the gaze of "fine ladies and gentlemen from the city." The would-be soldiers managed a good showing, conscious that "the legion was made up of as fine a body of men . . . as marched and fought under the Confederate flag." One wonders if Hampton was absent from drill due to the press of other duties, or whether, conscious of his own inexperience, he was unwilling to display it before the legion and its spectators. For two weeks in early June, he had a good excuse for not appearing on the field of instruction. A "severe stretch of illness," apparently of an intestinal nature, had confined him to bed in his manor house.[26]

Following drill came target practice, which for a time was taken only by those recruits who had toted arms to camp or had shared in the initial issuance of state-supplied rifles. Apparently, the Enfields ordered from England did not reach Camp Hampton for several weeks after it opened. It can be assumed that target shooting produced impressive results from an early date. Unlike their counterparts north of the Mason-Dixon Line, South Carolinians, like their brethren in Virginia, Georgia, and other parts of the South, had been conversant with the care and use of firearms, particularly shoulder arms, since early youth. Armed with a rifle that fired the hollow-based, expandable Minié ball, many recruits could hit a target squarely—especially one they could mentally transform into an invading Yankee—at a distance of several hundred yards.

When not on the drill ground or target range, the men lived in tents of canvas and muslin laid out in a pattern of company streets. Hampton and his subordinates made the rounds of these habitations on a regular basis, inspecting the conditions that prevailed within. The men did not mess in small squads as they would during the active campaigning of later months. Instead, they supped at long wooden tables shaded by canvas tops. Probably because both groups drew largely from the same social class, officers and men dined together on soft bread supplied by a Columbia bakery and fresh beef prepared by black cooks in large kettles over a slow fire. Many other edibles were also available, although certain condiments and cream for coffee was scarce. Everything considered, many legionnaires recalled the days at Camp Hampton, despite the hard work they performed there, as the most enjoyable period in their army careers.[27]

By June 10, the legion's training program had barely gotten under way, and none of its companies had been formally accepted into Confederate service— the muster-in process would not begin until the twelfth. Already, however, Hampton viewed his command as fully organized and deserving of army affiliation. That morning he wrote to General Beauregard, who nine days before had been transferred to Virginia to take over the Manassas Junction–Bull Run line, asking that the legion be assigned to his command, which would soon become known as the Army of the Potomac.[28]

In the weeks since their meeting in Charleston, Hampton and Beauregard had forged a close relationship, based in part on shared experiences. They were of the same age, came from backgrounds of wealth and privilege, and were looked to by others for leadership. Their friendship had been sealed when Beauregard tendered Hampton a coveted position on his staff. Given his high regard for the Creole's acumen, Hampton had been tempted to accept, but in the end his preference for field command prompted him to decline with regret.

Now he informed Beauregard of his belief that the legion would soon be ordered to Richmond, successor to Montgomery as seat of the Confederate government. From Richmond, Hampton's command might be sent to any of several fighting fronts, including not only Manassas but also the Shenandoah Valley and the wilds of western Virginia. Because Manassas, which sat astride the most direct route from the U.S. capital to Richmond, appeared the most likely candidate to see large-scale action, Hampton wished to be assigned to that sector. Therefore, as he wrote Beauregard, "I most earnestly ask to be attached to your command," adding that "there is no one under whom I would so willingly & proudly serve as yourself."[29]

In the short term, his appeal both failed and succeeded. While it did not produce a formal assignment of the Hampton Legion to the Army of the Potomac, it appears to have generated a transfer to the Manassas line. On June 28, nine days after the last of the legion's original complement of companies was mustered into Confederate service, word came to pack up, strike tents, and march to the rail depot in Columbia. That morning Colonel Hampton bade a hasty farewell to his wife, to sixteen-year-old Sally, to the two-year-old son he called McDuffie, and to five-month-old Daisy, as well as to his brother, Kit (who had come up from Mississippi to help the Aunties manage the family's estates). Then, accompanied by his two oldest sons and brother Frank, the colonel took his place proudly at the head of the legion, which had formed into marching columns on the camp's parade ground, surrounded by a crowd of civilians come to see it off to war.

Many of the cheers and well wishes showered on the recruits were directed at the colonel, who cut a majestic figure on his thoroughbred charger as he led the column out of camp to the music of the legion's well-appointed band. He looked resplendent in a spanking-new uniform of rich gray broadcloth that, despite the gold lace on its sleeve cuffs, was less than showy. Around his waist hung a brace of Colt pistols and a scabbard holding a long, straight-bladed sword that, at six pounds in weight, only a soldier of great strength could have wielded effectively. A simple slouch hat sat atop a high forehead, below which bloomed a thick mustache and elegant-looking side-whiskers, facial adornment that would soon give way to a full beard. By any standard, he looked the part of the warrior. Few who knew him would have doubted that he would prove himself a warrior in deed as well as in image.[30]

Upon reaching the Columbia depot, the legionnaires boarded passenger cars, which carried them as far as Charlotte, North Carolina. There they transferred to less elegant accommodations, being packed, much like cattle, into freight cars bound for Virginia via Raleigh. Their ordeal was lightened whenever the train halted at depots and water stops, where the passengers were allowed to alight, rest, and partake of food served up by patriotic-minded women of the neighborhood.

Two days out of Columbia, the slow-moving cars chugged into the Richmond & Petersburg Railroad depot in the heart of the Confederate capital. To the applause of enthusiastic welcomers, the legionnaires assembled on the platform, dressed ranks, then followed their colonel through the streets of the city to Rockett's, the thickly populated suburb on the city's southeastern side. At the foot of Main Street, not far from the terminus of the Richmond & York River Railroad, the men halted amid a spacious field. At a signal, they doffed their equipage, rolled up their sleeves (a novelty for gentlemen unused to physical toil), and worked in unison to create a new Camp Hampton. They laid out the company streets and then cleared ground for a drill plain, upon which they resumed the training program they had quit upon leaving Columbia.[31]

Here the legion drilled, for the first time, in battalion strength as opposed to individual companies, each unit and each arm of the line in proper relation to each other, as on a battlefield. While the infantry and cavalry drilled in full panoply, the men of the battery simulated the discharge of shot and shell. Their cannon would not make the long voyage from England for weeks to come.

For the first days of the legion's presence in Richmond, its commander was not on hand to help instruct it. Lieutenant Colonel Johnson and Major Griffin drilled the foot and horse units and Capt. Richard Ward of Edgefield County, a veteran artillerist, filled in for the still-estranged Captain Lee in tutoring the erstwhile cannoneers. Hampton remained in downtown Richmond, conferring with a succession of officials including President Davis and Maj. Gen. Robert E. Lee, commanding the military forces of Virginia. While seeking a satisfactory assignment for his command, he also strove to complete its organizational and logistical structure. He was likewise prevented from joining the legion by his health, which remained unusually fragile. In fact, he seems to have suffered a relapse of the malady that had laid him low back home. Not until the early part of July could he inform his family in Columbia that "I have been improving and now I am quite well."[32]

When on July 4 he finally reported at the camp named in his honor, Hampton saw to it that the drill regimen increased in duration and intensity. He knew that little time remained for his men to master the basics—and no time to learn the nuances—of soldiering. From his political and military contacts, he understood that the Union recruits training in Washington and on the Virginia side of the Potomac could be expected to take the field at any day. Powerful politicians were joining the region's most influential editors in demanding that the nearly forty thousand troops under McDowell march on Richmond. The goal was to seize and occupy the enemy capital before the

Confederate Congress could convene there. En route, the Federals would cut the railroad that joined the Manassas region to the Shenandoah Valley.

If left unbroken, that rail line could cause McDowell untold trouble. At Manassas, Beauregard commanded only two-thirds as many soldiers as McDowell had at his disposal. In the Valley, however, another twelve thousand Confederates under Joseph Johnston were maneuvering in the face of an enemy force half again as large under an aged general of Pennsylvania volunteers, Robert Patterson. According to a rather open-ended plan put together by the Confederate War Department, Johnston and Beauregard were to unite against McDowell before the latter could strike the lines at Manassas. The railroad would play a prominent role in that plan.[33]

After rejoining his command, Hampton remained with it, unwilling to leave its side until assured it would acquit itself effectively in battle. As he informed his youngest sister, newspaper speculation that he had avoided roughing it by living out of a Richmond hotel was groundless: "I have remained in camp all the time." By the thirteenth, he could report that, everything considered, the legion was "getting on quite well, and our men are contented and in good spirits."[34]

Morale was strengthened by visits from distinguished guests, including South Carolina's congressional delegation, as well as from less prominent but no less welcome visitors—the relatives and friends of legionnaires. Representatives of both groups presented the legion with a battle flag. One banner was said to have been fashioned from the silken dresses owned by the wife of the legion's chief surgeon, Dr. Darby. This was a special gift indeed, and to mark the occasion President Davis came out from Richmond on July 16 to officiate at the presentation ceremony.

As Johnny Coxe recalled the event, the infantry of the legion were drawn up in a hollow square, with their cavalry and artillery comrades on either flank. After a salute was fired from some borrowed artillery pieces, Hampton and his ranking subordinates escorted Davis into the center of the square. The president then delivered what Coxe considered "a fine speech. He had a ringing tenor voice and spoke without apparent effort. I recall him as rather tall, straight, and slender. . . ." Davis's words have been lost to history, but whatever he said drew excited cheers from the legionnaires as well as from a bevy of spectators. Presumably, Colonel Hampton made a speech of his own in acceptance of the flag. After the ceremony, the men were released and Hampton hosted the president and his entourage at dinner held in his headquarters tent.[35]

Davis chose a momentous day to address the Hampton Legion. That morning, approximately thirty-six thousand eager recruits marched out of Washington and across the Potomac via the Long Bridge. After massing on Virginia soil, the attenuated column began the long, dusty trek that would lead it to Manassas Junction and neighboring Bull Run by way of Fairfax Court House, Centreville, and other points on the doorstep of the capital.

Alerted to McDowell's advance by spies out of Washington, as well as by scouts and outpost troops, Beauregard immediately issued a call for reinforcements. Word of the Yankees' coming was soon circulating through Richmond, and then it radiated in all directions. In the Shenandoah, Joe Johnston began to maneuver in such a way that, with luck and the continued timidity of his enemy, he might break contact with Patterson and take the railroad to Manassas.[36]

From the afternoon of July 16, Camp Hampton was alive with rumors of an impending transfer to Beauregard's sector. For three days, however, its occupants went nowhere. Then, on the morning of the nineteenth, newspaper accounts of a "Big battle at Manassas" reached Richmond. The previous day, McDowell's advance, having evicted the Confederate occupiers of Fairfax Court House and Centreville, had conducted a reconnaissance-in-force across Bull Run in the vicinity of Beauregard's right flank. The result was spirited fighting at Blackburn's and Mitchell's Fords, which ended with eighty-three attackers and nearly seventy defenders killed or wounded.[37]

Hard upon receipt of this electrifying news came word that the Hampton Legion was to prepare to strike tents and move out. At first the men were told to be ready to break camp by 2:00 P.M., but the time-consuming process of packing equipage and procuring transportation delayed the movement until early evening. Around eight o'clock Hampton finally led the legion through the streets of Richmond, halting at the Virginia Central depot in the heart of the city. There the men learned that a train of passenger and box cars was being made up to carry them as far north as Hanover Junction, then westward to Gordonsville. Dozens of civilians were also at the station, not to bid the men farewell but to meet a train from Manassas carrying those of Beauregard's troops who had been wounded on the eighteenth.

The legionnaires were told they would not depart until the Manassas train arrived. Although many had already become inured to the hurry-up-and-wait routine of army life, others turned restive, and a few unruly, during the unexpected delay. For weeks, these men had been drilled within an inch of their lives—now they wanted to get about the business of fighting. Hampton and his subordinates kept everyone well in hand, however, until, some time after ten, the hospital train chugged into the station and unloaded dozens of bandaged and blood-spattered passengers, many of them on litters. Suddenly, the Hampton Legion got a close-up view of the unromantic side of war.[38]

When at last the men were permitted to board their train, they met with further delay. Through someone's error, not enough cars were available to ship the legion's baggage, equipment, and horses. After much deliberation, a perturbed Hampton announced that the equipage would be left in piles on the depot platform, to be transported to Manassas by a later train. Alluding to the lack of accommodations, he also reported that while the infantry would take the cars, the cavalry and artillery would travel overland to Beauregard's headquarters, eighty dusty miles to the north. His words produced a certain amount of muttering and grumbling from the troopers and cannoneers, especially the former. Missing a train ride was bad enough, but, even worse, the horsemen would have to conform their pace to that of their artillery comrades, with their ponderous limbers and caissons. This undesirable situation ensured that neither arm would reach Manassas in time to be of material assistance to Beauregard.[39]

It was close to midnight before the train carrying the foot soldiers of the Hampton Legion left Richmond to the cheers of the few civilians who remained on the depot platform. In the darkened passenger cars, the roofs of which conveyed the patter of a light rain, officers and men settled back to enjoy the journey, heartened to be under way at last. Delay ended, tension and anxiety released, they looked with eager anticipation toward the fields of strife and glory that awaited them on the other side of the night.

THREE

"In the face of the enemy"

By two o'clock on the afternoon of July 21, 1861, the Hampton Legion was verging on extinction. At about noon, having been driven by the enemy's onslaught from its initial position around the Robinson farm, it had found some little shelter atop Henry House Hill, just east of the Warrenton Turnpike. In that position, however, the South Carolinians soon found themselves pressed hard in front, on the right, and in the right rear by the Union divisions of Cols. David Hunter and Samuel P. Heintzelman. Having surged across Young's Branch, a Bull Run tributary, as the maneuver wing of McDowell's surprise assault, the attackers were numerous enough to sweep all before them. The only coherent bodies of Confederates they faced were the South Carolinians under Hampton and, on their left flank, the Virginia troops of Brig. Gen. Thomas Jonathan Jackson. The Virginians formed a part of the little army under Joe Johnston that had reached Manassas Junction after a forced march and a railroad journey from the Shenandoah Valley that, in terms of delays and other aggravations, rivaled the legion's trip to war.[1]

For two hours Hampton's and Jackson's men had held their respective positions, holding back the blue onslaught at the cost of dozens of casualties, including Hampton's executive officer, Lieutenant Colonel Johnson. Despite the uneven odds and although a few of its members, unable to stand another minute in the path of the oncoming tide, had rushed to the rear, the legion had given the first serious check to McDowell's surprise assault. One South Carolinian suspected that his command's continued survival owed much to the local geography: "The whole battle was fought not far from the base of the mountains, and the ground was very hilly; so that they [the Federals] were unable to perceive the immense disparity between their numbers and ours. Had they known how few were the forces between them and Camp Manassas [Beauregard's headquarters], they would doubtless have advanced more confidently, and every man of us would have fallen upon the field. As it was, their movements were irresolute; they advanced and retreated alternately. . . ." Yet how long they could be counted on to display such irresolution, no one could say.[2]

The Confederates' stand had been so conspicuously stubborn that Jackson's people had already won an enduring nickname. General Bee, senior commander on this part of the field, whose own brigade had been so roughly handled that most of its survivors had fled, had marveled at the composure displayed by the Virginians on Henry House Hill. "There stands Jackson like a stone wall!" he is supposed to have shouted to his demoralized troops. "Let us determine to die here, and we will conquer!"[3]

Hampton's tenacious South Carolinians can be said to have deserved the same praise. Yet even heroic fortitude has its limitations. By now, a little after two, enough Federals had crossed Young's Branch that even the legion's combative colonel—who, after being thrown from his horse, had picked up a discarded rifle with which he blasted away at the foe—realized that the time had come to fall back yet again. At the urging of several superiors including Bee (then only minutes from a mortal wound), Hampton reluctantly but firmly issued the order to retire. As he noted in his after-action report, at least he had the satisfaction of knowing that his men had held their ground with little immediate support "for at least two hours in the face of the enemy, greatly superior in numbers and well provided with artillery."[4]

Under his supervision and that of Captain Conner and Adjutant Barker, the legion gathered up its wounded, broke contact with the enemy, and began to shift eastward across Henry House Hill, then down its back slope. It regrouped at the base of a rise that provided some shelter from the advancing foe. There Hampton and his men poured a steady and destructive fire at the enemy atop the ridge. After a few minutes, they found they were no longer holding back the bulwark virtually by themselves; reinforcements were hustling up in their rear and on their flanks. Assuming the burden of fighting in that sector as soon as they arrived were elements of Brig. Gen. Milledge Bonham's and Col. Philip St. George Cocke's brigades of Beauregard's command, followed by miscellaneous units, including the last troops to arrive from the Valley, Brig. Gen. Edmund Kirby Smith's.[5]

Although enjoying advantages of numbers and position, Hunter's and Heintzelman's troops were not prepared to find so many screaming Rebels in their path. At the sight, the Yankees seemed to wilt. By maintaining the offensive against a stubborn foe for several hours without water or relief from a blazing sun, the Federals had accomplished as much as anyone could have expected of rookies. Now, almost as a body, they turned about and withdrew. Many tossed aside their rifles and walked on, their backs to the Confederates, as if they no longer considered themselves soldiers.

As soon as the enemy began to give way, Beauregard and Johnston urged the new arrivals—most of them until recently uncommitted and thus fresh and unbloodied—to pursue with vigor. As the newcomers pressed forward, the men of the Hampton Legion—as if they had not already borne their share of the fighting—joined in. Their colonel proudly noted "my men advanced as rapidly as their worn out condition would allow." Spying a Yankee battery unlimbered and unsupported, Hampton shifted the head of his line in its direction. At his order, the front rank halted and delivered "a well-directed fire" at the gun crews, inflicting several casualties, then rushed forward to claim the prize.[6]

The battery may have been vulnerable, but it was not defenseless. When the would-be captors were only a few yards off, the crew sprayed them with canister at point-blank range. An iron fragment struck Wade Hampton full in the face, lodging under his left eye. If he lost consciousness, it was only momentarily. In an instant, he was back on his feet, ready to continue the advance, the only problem being that he could no longer see clearly, if at all. When it became obvious that he had been at least temporarily disabled, he was prevailed on to hand over the legion to Captain Conner and go to the rear for medical attention. To Conner went the honor of leading the battalion, side-by-side with the Eighteenth Virginia of Cocke's brigade, in seizing the enemy battery and putting a finishing touch to the Federal defeat.[7]

Later, having interviewed Conner and other officers, Hampton would report that after taking the cannon the legion continued its inspired, and inspiring, pursuit, splashing across Bull Run and on the north side advancing for two miles, until recalled. By then, it was past 6:00 P.M. and McDowell's retreat had become a full-fledged rout in the direction of the Washington defenses.

Returning to the starting point of its most recent advance, the legion bivouacked on the littered battlefield. Well into the evening, its officers and

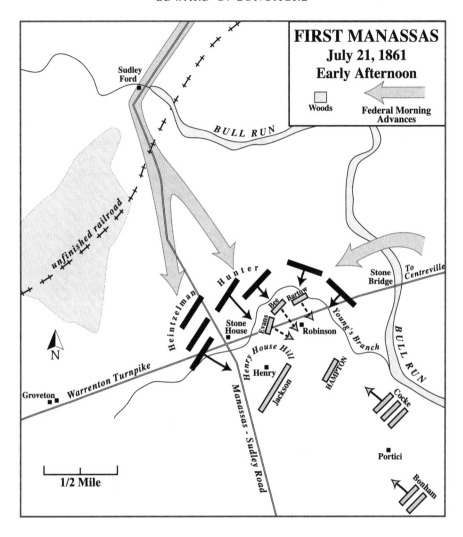

enlisted men continued to breathe in the intoxicating scent of victory. Many remained awake for hours after dark, so animated were they by the realization that they and their comrades had this day achieved the overwhelming victory that everyone in gray had been confidently predicting for the past three months.[8]

Eight days after the fight on July 21, when Hampton—still recovering from his wound—composed his report of the legion's operations on July 21, he was unstinting with praise for the command's conduct. The obvious pride with which he cited individual heroics was akin to that of a father glorying in the achievements of his progeny. The strong sense of paternalism that he, as oldest son, had long displayed toward his siblings and that he, as lord and master, had shown toward his slaves, had come to define his attitude toward the organization that bore his name.

He was especially laudatory toward those who had fallen in the thick of the fight. In the death of Lieutenant Colonel Johnson, "the service sustained a great loss, while the Legion has met with an irreparable misfortune. He fell with the utmost coolness and gallantry. . . ." Johnson's loss, coming so early in the action, had deprived Hampton of a critical conduit between commander and command. This being so, he commended Captain Barker and the rest of the staff for their "constant and efficient assistance," without which "my position would have been rendered as critical as it was embarrassing."[9]

Hampton reserved the majority of his praise for the rank-and-file, who, with few exceptions, had performed like the veterans they aspired to be. As he informed Beauregard, the recipient of his report, "the unflinching courage of the brave men who sustained their exposed and isolated position under the trying circumstances of that eventful day inspires in me a pride which it is due to them I should express in the most emphatic terms. . . . Compelled frequently during the day from the same cause to receive an increasing fire from different quarters while they withheld their own, the self-devotion of these faithful soldiers was only equaled by the gallantry of the officers whom they so trustingly obeyed. . . . Their conduct has my unqualified approbation, and I trust it has met the approval of their general commanding."[10]

If the legion was deserving of high praise, so was the man who had directed its movements. After the shooting stopped on that bloody Sabbath, President Davis, accompanied by the commander of Hampton's army, visited the colonel at his field headquarters near Portici. Beauregard, who was in an ebullient mood (he had been promoted on the field to full general), credited Hampton with much of the success that had been achieved on the left flank. Davis nodded emphatically and added warm praise of his own. He also inquired about Hampton's wound, proclaiming that the army could not afford to lose the services of such a skillful and tenacious soldier.

Such talk made Hampton uncomfortable. He later confided to Captain Conner, "they were so complimentary, that I have not ventured to write their remarks, even to my wife," lest he appear vain. Yet he was truly deserving of commendation, no matter how effusively worded. Forced to hold a nearly untenable position despite being wounded, he had shored up a sector of his army's line that had been verging on collapse, buying time for the arrival of reinforcements that turned the tide of battle. It was a performance that would have done credit to a twenty-year veteran of the regular service.[11]

That performance, however, had cost Hampton dearly. In tallying up the day's casualties, he found that the legion had suffered nineteen killed and almost one hundred wounded. The toll wore heavily on his mind, but all he could do was to ensure that the dead were buried with honors and the injured received the best of care. The primary burden fell on the legion's medical team, who performed creditably. One enlisted man who had received, like his colonel, a wound in the forehead, found that the surgeon who treated him "understood well the art of dressing wounds. He trimmed closely the hair around mine, washed out the clotted blood, bathed the wound, ascertained there was no split in the portion of skull exposed, and bound up my head nicely for me, strengthening me also with a glassful of excellent whiskey." The more seriously wounded were transferred from the legion's dressing-station to the army hospitals in the rear. Many ended up miles from their able-bodied comrades, at Culpeper Court House and Charlottesville, where some would remain for weeks or months of convalescence.[12]

Hampton himself was hors de combat for some days after the battle. When his loved ones at home learned of his injuries, they were gravely concerned but also relieved that he had been spared from death or maiming. From Millwood, Caroline Hamilton wrote her "dearest brother," expressing her thanks for "your great deliverance. . . . God grant your wound may be as slight as you telegraph it is. It is very hard to think of you so far from us and suffering alone." But he was not alone for long; within a week, his wife and youngest sister were at his side to monitor his recuperation. Mary Fisher Hampton wrote that upon arriving at Manassas Junction, they found her brother "well except [for] a very red eye. The doctors tell us it will be some time before it is quite well, but I feel anxious about it as it does not improve as I would like to see it do. The ball is still under the eye, and I do not think it will be well until it is taken out. But the doctors say it must be let alone, and of course they know best."[13]

In due course, the piece of canister was extracted, without damage to the eye. The two Marys rejoiced, but they remained at his side until they could confirm his recovery. They attended not only to the colonel but also to those wounded men who had been hospitalized locally. Their ministrations received favorable publicity throughout the army. In Richmond, Mary Boykin Chesnut, the charming, witty, and often acerbic diarist—wife of Hampton's political ally, Confederate congressman James Chesnut Jr.—observed that "Mary McDuffie Hampton & Mary Fisher have come to make a hospital of their own" on the edge of the recent battlefield. Referring to the well-known fragility of Mrs. Hampton, the self-appointed chronicler of the Confederate social scene wondered if the colonel's wife had the strength to complete her mission of mercy: "poor Mary Mc, can she do it[?]"[14]

She did. She and her sister-in-law remained with the legion for nearly three weeks, until persuaded that the colonel's health had been restored. They left for home on August 13, the day the battalion moved from Manassas to Bacon Race Church, nine miles to the east. There the legion established "Camp Johnson," named in honor of its fallen lieutenant colonel. The nurses may have left a few days too soon. Shortly after the move, Colonel Hampton, only recently returned to duty, experienced a relapse that left him feverish and weak for several days. Not until the first week of September, with the patient in bed at a private home a few miles from the battlefield, did he begin to regain his strength. "I do not know what there was in the attack," he wrote Mary Fisher, "to pull me down so suddenly and completely. But I was entirely prostrated and for some days suffered very much. I found I was obliged to move from the camp, for the noise there was distracting, and I came here, where I found some nice old people and a quiet place."[15]

By mid-September, 1861, having had his fill of peace and quiet, he was back with his boisterous command. More concerned with his men's health than with his own, he noted that in the weeks since the battle, with the legion mired in daily routine broken infrequently by picket skirmishing, the sick list had grown alarmingly long. Only as the summer neared its end did those on medical leave begin to return to duty in appreciable numbers.

It was well that the corporate health showed improvement, for it appeared that the legion would soon find itself on another field of battle. Rather than succumb to defeatism and demoralization, the army that fled from the sun-drenched field of July 21 had regrouped inside the Washington defenses, where, six days after the battle, Maj. Gen. George B. McClellan assumed command of it. This was hailed by the Northern press as the second coming of Napoleon. The West Pointer and ex-Regular had amassed a brilliant record as a military and civil engineer but a less grandiose one as a field commander. His claim to high station had been a series of victories over second-rate Confederate forces in western Virginia, victories actually won by less-conspicuous subordinates.

Whether or not deserving of army command, McClellan was determined to activate the potential he discerned in the vast horde of volunteers that had been placed at his disposal. Unwilling to take the field with the raw recruits who had failed his predecessor, McClellan would spend eight months instructing and drilling his newly christened Army of the Potomac before committing it to full-scale campaigning.[16]

The Hampton Legion would not enjoy so long a respite from active service. Although the Federals in Washington were unavailable for combat, their comrades who manned the outposts of northern Virginia were more bellicose. So, too, was the United States Navy, whose warships in the Potomac posed a continuing threat to the Confederate right flank. A threat of a less immediate nature was posed by the transport vessels that every day carried supplies to the troops in the capital. In hopes of interdicting the river commerce at least temporarily, on September 13 Beauregard's headquarters advised Hampton that the legion "may be required to make a diversion at a point on the Potomac."[17]

The site under consideration was Freestone Point, just north of the old port village of Dumfries. There, not far from river batteries already in place at Occoquan and Colchester, the artillery arm of the legion, supported by its infantry and cavalry battalions, could menace Yankee shipping, "without," as Beauregard's chief of staff suggested, "useless exposure or hazard of damage greater than any promised advantage would justify."[18]

Hampton had no doubt that his command would give a strong account of itself in riverine operations. In the six weeks since the fighting at Manassas, each of its service arms had been considerably strengthened. The organization now embraced almost a full regiment of infantry (eight companies strong, with two more to be added in the near future), as well as a four-company battalion of cavalry and not one, but two, batteries of light artillery.[19]

In expanding, Hampton's command had acquired a full complement of field officers. James Griffin had moved up to lieutenant colonel, while James Conner had been promoted to major in command of the infantry battalion. The highly competent Calbraith Butler had taken over the mounted arm, also with the rank of major. Captain Lee had finally assumed command of the legion's original battery, six guns strong. These included the Blakely rifles that Hampton had purchased, recently received from Charleston, whence they had arrived via blockade-runner from Europe. The legion's second artillery unit, currently stationed in the Richmond suburbs, was commanded by Capt. Willis Bachman. Manned almost exclusively by recruits from Charleston's sizable German-American community, it would become known throughout the army as the German Light Artillery.[20]

The personnel and matériel additions effectively made Hampton a brigade leader, and he was announced as such in General Order No. 15, issued on October 22 by the Adjutant and Inspector General's Office in Richmond. Over the next two months, however, he commanded only the legion. Not until late December or early January 1862 did his command expand to actual brigade size with the addition of three infantry regiments, the Fourteenth and Nineteenth Georgia and the Sixteenth North Carolina. For several months afterward, Hampton continued to lack the rank to match his increased responsibilities. Joe Johnston, who early in 1862 took sole command of the forces in Northern Virginia (Beauregard having been transferred to the western theater), recommended him for the wreathed stars of a brigadier, but without immediate effect.[21]

Hampton's superior and friend, Joseph E. Johnston

One week after alerted to a possible transfer, the legion was directed to leave Camp Johnson for Freestone Point. Early on September 20, Hampton led the command—minus the German Artillery, then en route to him from Richmond—down the historic Telegraph Road toward Dumfries. Left behind at Bacon Race were the sick of the legion, ministered to by one of surgeon Darby's assistants.

Reaching the river at the designated place, Captain Lee selected a suitable position for his guns, which now included a long-range 32-pounder cannon that had been wrested from the Yankees at Manassas. To protect the battery, fatigue parties set to work with spades and axes. Hampton noted with satisfaction that within an hour or so, "by the energy and willingness of my men the necessary field works and magazine were completed."[22]

He expected to unleash the battery as soon as the defenses were complete, but the necessary authority was withheld for some days. By the end of the month, however, Lee's guns were booming at intervals each day, threatening to sink any gunboat or transport that ventured near. Occasionally, the cannon dueled with water-borne artillery—the Yankees had outfitted several steam launches with howitzers and gun crews. The exchanges of shot and shell were sometimes damaging and always exciting. On one occasion, Hampton reported that "we had a warm little brush [with Union gunboats] and drove the whole concern off, luckily without any damage to us, though one big shell *scared* me very much."[23]

Whether Lee's guns inflicted material damage to the enemy is uncertain, but if they failed to do so it was not for lack of effort. By October 1, Hampton was informing his sister that he, his gunners, and their supports were "engaged nearly constantly." As a result, he frequently reported feeling "quite worn out," a hint that he had yet to recover fully from his post-Manassas illness. Tired or not, he was proud of the eagerness with which the legion took on a mission unfamiliar to them: "I am entirely satisfied with the conduct of my men."[24]

His superiors were just as pleased, and said so. Throughout October and into November, the legion and its colonel received plaudits from local commanders including Brig. Gens. William H. C. Whiting and Isaac Trimble, as well as from Johnston himself. In time, the army leader became Hampton's ardent admirer as well as a close personal friend.

Contemporary observers have suggested that the Johnston-Hampton relationship, rather than forged at this time, predated the war. Mary Chesnut is the source of a much-quoted story that Hampton, in antebellum years, invited then-Colonel Johnston to hunt with him on one of his South Carolina estates. This anecdote illustrates Johnston's excessive striving for perfection (although a better shot than his host, when the game was flushed he refused to fire because "the bird flew too high or too low, the dogs were too far or too near"). Yet the story fails to ring true in a number of particulars and cannot be accepted as proof of an early friendship.[25]

The Hampton-Johnston relationship was solidified in early December 1861, when the general presented his subordinate with an ornate, finely tempered broadsword of Spanish make measuring, from pommel to point, three feet, eight and a half inches. Engraved into the blade was a Spanish motto: "Do Not Draw Me Without Reason, Do Not Sheathe Me Without Honor." Hampton was touched by the unexpected gift. He wrote his commander a long note of thanks, calling the sword, "beautiful" as well as eminently practical and trusting that "it may do good service whilst in my hands."[26]

In the same letter, Hampton made bold to question his current assignment. By now the legion had been stationed at Freestone Point or at nearby Camp Wigfall (named for a friend of Hampton's, former U.S. senator Louis T. Wigfall of Texas) for more than two months. Its mission included guarding not only the west bank of the Potomac but also the west side of a meandering tributary, the Occoquan River. Early on, the assignment connoted importance, but in the weeks since then the legion's infantry and cavalry had experienced only desultory, long-range skirmishing with small bands of the enemy. "As there seems to be," the colonel wrote, "a great diversity of opinion as to the object of my being placed here and the course I should pursue, whilst there appears to be no general plan of action settled on, may I ask you to give me directions how to carry out best your wishes?"[27]

Ever since he had been on the river, Hampton's intent had been to make his position as strong as possible "and to hold it as long as I can." Although he rarely encountered a hostile force, it was always possible that the Yankees would launch a surprise attack in substantial numbers. Here he was being prescient: Only a few weeks later, a body of Union horsemen, estimated to number more than one hundred, came down from points north to attack his defenses. Having been alerted to the Yankees' approach, Hampton laid a trap for them. As they neared his position, twenty legionnaires hidden in roadside woods opened on them with a devastating flank fire, while Hampton led thirty of Butler's troopers in a frontal assault. As he later wrote, "I charged them[,] running them some distance and firing on them. We broke their squadron and emptied several saddles and if I had only taken more of my men with me, I would have cut the party to pieces."[28]

In his letter to Johnston, Hampton specifically asked what he should do if attacked by a force so heavy as to cut him off from other defensive positions along the river. Previously, he had suggested to army headquarters that roads be cut from Freestone Point all the way to Manassas to facilitate his reinforcing in a crisis. On another occasion he had recommended that a bridge be laid across the Occoquan to link Freestone Point with Colchester and Pohick Church. Those areas, which lay near the lowermost ring of Union outposts south of Washington, were even more tempting targets than Hampton's position, and he foresaw the necessity of supporting them if attacked. Apparently, none of these proposals had found favor with the high command, for they had gone unanswered.

Nor did Johnston, despite his high regard for Hampton, respond to his subordinate's request for specific instructions. In the end, all that was done for the legion was to send the German Artillery down from Bacon Race Church to bolster Captain Lee's battery. On Christmas Day, fatigue parties from the Sixteenth North Carolina helped the legionnaires build a line of heavy works near Wolf Run Shoals on the Occoquan River northwest of Freestone Point, to protect Captain Bachman's guns.[29]

Hampton continued to cover the Potomac and the Occoquan through the winter and into the spring of 1862. The changing seasons brought fluctuating weather that was sometimes severe enough to play hob with the health of Hampton's command. As early as mid-November, the colonel was reporting "one of the coldest and most windy days I ever saw and we had a little snow." The men, however, continued to sleep under canvas instead of in the well-chinked cabins that their comrades at Manassas had erected. Their commander preferred it this way, claiming that "it is healthier to live in tents, than in those miserable little huts."[30]

The results were predictable. Before November was out, he was reporting to his superiors that his command's sick list was lengthening. As he told sister Mary: "We are in want of men, and my numbers are cut down by great sickness in camp. Several good men have died and several more are very ill."[31]

Although he never admitted that his notions about winter habitations had anything to do with the poor health of his command, like a caring father he sympathized with the men's condition ("Poor fellows! It makes me feel very sorry to see them exposed to such hardships as they have to endure"). And yet he did not share those hardships. He spent the season indoors, having appropriated for his headquarters a private home, probably the property of one of the region's many Unionist residents. The place was so warm and snug that early in the new year, his wife and their youngest son arrived to live with him for an extended period.[32]

During their stay, Hampton was laid low by the third serious illness of his brief military career. This ailment, the origin of which remains unknown, so incapacitated him that by late February Johnston was seriously considering transferring command of Hampton's brigade to a healthier colleague, Brig.

Gen. John Bell Hood. Apparently, the patient recovered soon afterward, for there is no record of his being superseded. The illness demonstrated that a robust physique was no guarantee of protection against army-borne sickness. It also suggested there was something to Hampton's theory of the baleful effects of indoor confinement in winter.[33]

By the outset of March 1862, with Hampton's loved ones back in South Carolina, the Virginia weather began to moderate, and the roads that gave access to the enemy's positions began to dry. Stirrings in the camps in and below Washington indicated that McClellan was finally preparing to advance. From his Manassas headquarters, Joe Johnston fretted that his army, which numbered fewer than half the soldiers led by "Little Mac," made an inviting target. Afraid that he might soon be attacked and his route of retreat severed, Johnston had already asked Jefferson Davis for authority to withdraw to more defensible positions below the Rappahannock River, fifty miles from Manassas. Davis did not immediately reply, but by early March rumors of an impending movement were sweeping the Confederate camps along the Potomac. The rumors were swiftly followed by orders to pack up and stand ready to march.[34]

On the morning of March 8, at the direction of his immediate superior, General Whiting, Hampton assembled his regiments—his legion, the two batteries recently removed from their shoreline works, a third artillery unit temporarily assigned to the command, and the regiments from North Carolina and Georgia. Once under way, the southward march proceeded slowly but steadily. The deliberate pace was the result of many factors, most of which Whiting enumerated in his report of the movement: "An extended line, insufficient transportation, an active and superior enemy in his front [i.e., near Pohick Church], incessant skirmishing all along his outposts. . . ." Yet another factor was a recent thaw, which had transformed half-frozen roads into mires of mud and slush that stalled and sometimes immobilized guns, caissons, and supply wagons.[35]

Whiting had set a schedule for the withdrawal, and Hampton quickly began to fall behind it. To gain speed, he ordered his subordinates to jettison all impedimenta they considered expendable. Stephen Lee—now the major commanding both of the legion's batteries—lightened the artillery's load by destroying a dozen ancient battery wagons, some unserviceable horse equipment, several boxes of reserve ammunition, and a quantity of private baggage. Even before departing the Occoquan, the major had distributed excess commissary stores to "the poor people in the vicinity."[36]

The destroyed supplies and the lost baggage generated unfavorable commentary, mainly directed at Hampton himself. Two weeks after the army's withdrawal ended safely below the Rappahannock, Confederate Secretary of War Judah P. Benjamin, at the behest of President Davis, opened a formal inquiry into the matter. Hampton and Whiting were directed to submit a detailed report of the events attending their withdrawal. Hampton replied with a brief but forceful defense of his actions. He claimed the destruction of resources had been made necessary by inadequate transportation and a lack of advance marching notice, but that his brigade had carried off "all the public property that it possibly could." While he regretted having left behind so much private property ("it seems to be a hard case to make the soldier bear a loss which was caused by no fault of his own"), he stressed the necessity of it. For his part, Whiting praised the colonel as a "distinguished, active, and vigilant officer," declared that he had withdrawn from Freestone Point and Wolf Run Shoals "with consummate judgment, precision, and skill," and opined that the property lost en route "amounts to nothing."[37]

Apparently satisfied with these explanations, Davis and Benjamin pursued the matter no further. Even so, the controversy may have exerted short-term effects on Hampton's relationship with his president. Wellman suggests that at about this time a coolness developed between them; if so, it may have been caused by Hampton's belief that in opening an official investigation Davis had furthered a controversy that stung and embarrassed him. Any breach, however, was mended quickly enough. Neither man appears to have lost his confidence in the other as a result of the incident or its aftermath.[38]

On or about March 10, 1862, Hampton's command dug in along its army's new line of operations west of Fredericksburg. It may have lost some provisions en route south, but it had suffered no casualties, not even in the ranks of Butler's horsemen. The cavalry had held the post of greatest danger throughout the movement, covering the rear and flanks of the brigade against the enemy's pursuit, which, although conducted rather half-heatedly, could have endangered the entire command.

Newly promoted Brig. Gen. Wade Hampton

At the end of their journey, Hampton's men laid out "Camp Bartow," named for the fallen Georgian whose command they had supported the previous July. Surveying the woods, streams, and fields that surrounded him, their colonel pronounced the area "a much finer country than the one we left." Unlike their previous position, this one appeared free of the threat of imminent confrontation: "The country is as quiet as though no Yankees were about." The place did have some drawbacks. It was distant from any city or large town, and open ground was at a premium ("all Gen. Whiting's division are camped near us and we see nothing but soldiers . . . drilling all the time"). Overall, however, it was an improvement over life on the Potomac and Occoquan, and Hampton must have hoped he would linger here for a while.[39]

Thanks to the strategy of George B. McClellan, he was doomed to disappointment. Only days before Johnston evacuated his old line, the Union commander had been on the verge of transporting his 105,000 troops down Chesapeake Bay and the York River, up Virginia's Middle Peninsula, and into his enemy's rear. Caught off-guard by Johnston's withdrawal, McClellan decided to activate a contingency clause in his original plan. Now he would sail his army around the Middle Peninsula and into Hampton Roads, disembarking at Union-held Fort Monroe and marching overland against Richmond, eighty miles in the north. Until recently, this strategy would have been impossible to execute. The CSN *Virginia*, an ungainly but mighty warship, her hull plated in iron, had been menacing Union men-of-war in Hampton Roads, two of which she had sunk or run aground. On March 8, however, an equally unlikely looking ironclad flying the Stars and Stripes came down from the North to oppose the Confederate behemoth. For several hours the following day, the USS *Monitor* dueled her adversary to a standoff.

Suddenly neutralized, *Virginia* could no longer deny McClellan access to the waters that figured so prominently in his plans.[40]

By March 17, those plans were being implemented, and a few days later the advance element of the invasion force was debarking at Fort Monroe. After hauling ashore a vast quantity of matériel, the Federals poised to advance up the Virginia Peninsula by way of Yorktown. McClellan expected that Johnston would move south to reinforce the Yorktown garrison. But "Little Mac" knew he would get there first, and he had more than enough troops to overwhelm the local defenders.

As it marched up the Peninsula in the first days of April, however, the Army of the Potomac was slowed by fierce rainstorms; by roads that were few, narrow, and bottomless; and by the few but pesky Confederates inside Yorktown. Duped by the local commander, Maj. Gen. John Bankhead Magruder, into believing the place heavily occupied, McClellan decided he must besiege Yorktown into surrendering. He would entrap Magruder just as American and French forces had trapped Cornwallis's Redcoats eighty-one years earlier.[41]

Johnston was unexpectedly slow in reacting to the invasion, as were his military and civilian superiors. It was March 27 before he was ordered to reinforce Magruder, and not until April 6 did the vanguard of his Army of Northern Virginia draw within supporting distance of Yorktown. The movement south was slow to involve Whiting's so-called Reserve Division. On the eighth, the command, including Hampton's brigade, finally broke camp on the Rappahannock and moved south for the second time in a month.[42]

Grumbling at the new change of position, Hampton's men trudged down the line of the Richmond, Fredericksburg & Potomac Railroad. It is presumed that on the ninth, when they reached Milford Station, they joined other elements of their division in boarding boxcars and flatcars for the twenty-mile run to Ashland. At Ashland, Whiting's troops left the cars to make the balance of the trip to Yorktown afoot. By the middle of the month, if not sooner, Hampton was leading his leg-weary troops into bivouac along the defense line that ran west from Yorktown across the width of the Peninsula.[43]

Hampton's activities during the next three weeks are shrouded in obscurity. Presumably, he spent the time, as he had his stints on the Occoquan and the Rappahannock, building up his brigade's defenses, inspecting its camp and outposts, overseeing its continuing training, conferring with his superiors to keep abreast of the strategic picture, and, when not on duty, writing to the loved ones he missed as much as his Carolina upcountry. Throughout that period, he kept a close watch, via scouts and reconnaissance parties, on the Yankees on the other side of the Warwick River. McClellan's siege forces spent the time erecting a semicircular line south and east of Yorktown, studded with long-range cannon and mortars.

Joe Johnston did not like the looks of that line. By late April he was convinced, as he wrote Robert E. Lee—now posted to Richmond as Jefferson Davis's military advisor—that "the fight for Yorktown . . . must be one of artillery, in which we cannot win. The result is certain; the time only doubtful. Should the attack upon Yorktown be made earnestly, we cannot prevent its fall." Well before the close of April, Johnston, who never occupied a position he did not consider withdrawing from, was planning to transfer his army and Magruder's garrison to the approaches of Richmond. Official approval was slow to reach him, but by May 1 Davis gave his grudging permission, although complaining that the move would "involve enormous losses" of matériel if not of manpower. The president realized that by abandoning the line of the York River, Johnston would free the enemy to strike across Hampton Roads. One result would be the capture of Norfolk and the enforced scuttling of the mighty *Virginia*.[44]

Johnston's pullout began after dark on May 3. First to leave were Magruder's troops, their withdrawal covered by units farther west, including the corps of Maj. Gen. Gustavus W. Smith, of which Whiting's division had become a part. Magruder got off without incident and, to the relief of Hampton and his colleagues under Whiting, their men were also able to depart without molestation. In fact, the withdrawal took McClellan so much by surprise that it attracted only an occasional shot from the warships in the York that had pounded the port city throughout the siege.[45]

Early on the fifth, when the ever-cautious McClellan finally acknowledged his enemy's departure, he set in motion a pursuit spearheaded by his cavalry, under Brig. Gen. George Stoneman. While Whiting's men kept moving north in the direction of Barhamsville, Stoneman's troopers tangled with Johnston's rear guard, the horsemen of J. E. B. Stuart, on the outskirts of Williamsburg. The following day Virginia's colonial capital experienced heavier fighting between the Confederate infantry of James Longstreet and D. H. Hill, and those Federal foot soldiers who had come up behind Stoneman.[46]

Not content to smite the rear of Johnston's column, McClellan placed Brig. Gen. William B. Franklin's infantry division aboard troopships in the

York and sent it, escorted by two gunboats, twenty miles upriver. At an advan-
tageous point, Franklin was to debark, move inland, and attack the enemy's
right flank. If his men moved swiftly and struck aggressively, Franklin might
slice Johnston's column in two and halt its flight well short of Richmond.[47]

On the afternoon of the sixth, Franklin's little flotilla landed at Eltham's
Landing, a mile and a half below the confluence of the Mattapony and
Pamunkey Rivers and almost six miles northeast of Barhamsville. The sea voyage had been swift, but the disembarkation was a slow process, and it was not
followed by the aggressive advance McClellan had envisioned. It turned out
that Franklin was reluctant to take on a force of unknown size without prior
reconnaissance. Then, too, he had been promised reinforcements, but the three
divisions selected to support him were having trouble securing transportation.

The delay in attacking, which stretched into the seventh, gave Generals
Smith and Whiting, who were in the best position to block Franklin, time to
plot countermoves. These were urgently needed; for, while much of Johnston's
army had passed Barhamsville en route north, its supply train and rear guard
were still struggling up the muddy roads farther south; they would need
twenty-four hours to make good their escape.[48]

On the morning of the seventh, by which time most of Franklin's eleven
thousand troops were finally on dry ground, Whiting prepared to advance against
them. He would strike with Hood's brigade of Texas and Georgia infantry in
front, supported on the right by Hampton with his Carolinians and Georgians.
The rear of both forces would be covered by the Mississippi, Alabama, and North
Carolina brigade of Col. Evander M. Law. The overall intent was to pin the
unassertive Yankees to the cover of their gunboats and keep them there until
Johnston's column was beyond danger of being overtaken.

The operation began about seven o'clock. Hood moved out the road to
Eltham's Landing, aiming for the center and right flank of the Union line,
part of which was also in motion. Then Hampton's brigade advanced east of
the landing road, the Hampton Legion and the Nineteenth Georgia in
advance of the rest of the command. The brigade passed through belts of timber and briar-infested thickets, obstacles that not only slowed its progress but,
especially after the enemy unleashed a steady fire in their direction, threatened to disarrange its ranks. The opposition included not only musketry and
artillery fire but also salvos from the gunboats in the York.[49]

For a time, Hampton's column appeared to buckle under the onslaught.
The first rank shifted westward, nearly colliding with Hood's column, forcing

Hampton to ride forward and personally straighten out the line. Conspicuous in the saddle—twirling his outsized saber above his head, shouting instructions and advice in a voice audible above the noise of musketry and artillery—he guided the front line through the foliage to the open ground beyond. Then he led the way toward an even more formidable barrier, the infantry brigade of Brig. Gen. Napoleon J. T. Dana.

Responding to their colonel's urging, the Hampton Legion and their comrades broke into the double-quick, firing as they ran and keening a blood-curdling war cry—one of the first renditions of what would come to be known as the Rebel Yell. Startled as much by the sound as by the sight of their opponents, many of Dana's men threw down their weapons, turned, and ran. More tenacious comrades loosed a single volley before taking to their heels in the direction of the river.

Already hard-pressed by Hood's troops on the right, Franklin's division was staggered by the force of this assault on its other flank. As General Whiting later reported, "the enemy, though several times re-enforced, were steadily driven back. . . ." He noted that on at least one occasion, reinforcements massed opposite Hampton's right and tried to work their way around to his rear. Hampton's men coolly faced about and lashed the Yankees with repeated volleys. Soon afterward, Law's brigade made a belated appearance on Hampton's right, ending the flank threat. Soon afterward, Franklin's men began to quit the fight in droves, rushing back to the river and the protection of their gunboats.[50]

With his enemy on the run, Hampton recalled his forward rank, realigned the brigade, and held his position rather than pursue the beaten enemy. Whiting's intent had been not to destroy Franklin but to contain him; clearly, this had been accomplished. Five hours of long-distance skirmishing and close-up fighting had closed with Franklin's men hugging the banks of the York. There they would remain for the balance of the day, far from the road to Richmond that they had been assigned to block. They had suffered almost 150 casualties compared to the forty they had inflicted on Whiting's division. It would be many months before Virginia saw another such lopsided battle.[51]

In his after-action report, Hampton took pleasure "in saying that the conduct of the officers and men met my entire approval." Similar expressions of praise came from his superiors and colleagues, including Johnston, Smith, Whiting, and Hood. "Conspicuous gallantry" was the phrase most often used to describe the performance of Hampton and his men. The words were repeated by newspaper reporters not only from South Carolina but from many other points on the Confederate compass.[52]

More than favorable commentary appeared likely to come Hampton's way. In his report of the campaign, Johnston again called for the colonel's quick promotion. This time he sounded as if he meant to secure it come Hades or high water.

FOUR

"Remarkable for coolness, promptness, and . . . ability"

As if cowed by the check his army had received at Williamsburg and Eltham's Landing, McClellan followed Johnston up the Peninsula at a pace too slow to be called a pursuit. By the fifteenth, the rear of the Army of Northern Virginia had crossed the Chickahominy River to within three miles of the Confederate capital. Not for another week did the vanguard of the Army of the Potomac appear south of the stream. From across the water, the twenty-two hundred members of Hampton's brigade glowered at the enemy, exchanged volleys with them, and maneuvered for better positions in which to strike them. All the while, they hungered for an opportunity to land a blow severe enough to chase McClellan back to Fort Monroe, just as they had chased Franklin's men to the banks of the York.[1]

Colonel Hampton suspected that his troops would have their wish granted sooner rather than later. Even the defensive-minded Johnston would not permit an enemy to linger indefinitely on the doorstep of the South's most important city. Political pressure, if not military necessity, would compel Hampton's friend and superior to strike before time ran out on his command, his country, and his cause.

In the interim, Hampton tried to make the best of the waiting game. Through frequent inspections and consultations with the engineers of the army, he strengthened the defenses his brigade had recently erected, while keeping their occupants alert and vigilant. At night in his headquarters tent, he wrote by candlelight to Mary and the children, assuring them that "I am getting on well," and that, contrary to the fears expressed by politicians and editors, the army had not conceded the initiative to its opponent. Yet he was circumspect, as he had to be, about what he knew of coming events.[2]

After the twenty-fifth, he could send his family the happy news that his promotion to brigadier general had come through. The long overdue appointment, which was dated May 23, had hung fire to the last minute. Somehow, Johnston had gotten the impression that Hampton would decline the promotion, a misunderstanding that almost proved fatal to the colonel's ambitions. But the error had been cleared up, and Hampton could look forward to entering his next battle with wreathed stars on his collar and four loops of gold braid on his sleeves.[3]

As he had predicted, that battle proved to be imminent. By the last week in May, Johnston had concluded that the hard knocks his army stood to receive in assaulting a powerful foe were preferable to the slow wasting away that a siege would impose on it. He even thought he saw an opening for an offensive. Reconnaissance teams revealed that McClellan had positioned two of his five corps south of the Chickahominy. Their only connection with the troops on the north side was a rickety bridge over a stream swollen by recent rains. The army's posture appeared to leave it irresistibly vulnerable.

At first Johnston planned to strike the more numerous forces on the north bank. His scouts told him that heavy reinforcements were approaching McClellan on that side; a link-up was impermissible. By the twenty-eighth, however, Johnston learned that the reinforcements had been shunted westward to counter movements against Shenandoah Valley outposts by the general with the nickname "Stonewall." Thus relieved of the necessity of taking an even greater gamble, Johnston firmed up a plan to strike the south side of the Chickahominy.

On the morning of May 31, the men of Whiting's recently enlarged division, in common with most of their comrades outside Richmond, moved against the enemy via the Nine Mile Road. This thoroughfare led southwestward from Whiting's lines toward Fair Oaks Station on the Richmond & York River Railroad and, beyond, a road junction known as Seven Pines. The junction, Whiting's main objective, sat athwart the isolated right flank of Maj. Gen. E. D. Keyes's Fourth Corps, Army of the Potomac.

Whiting was well versed in the overall plan, and he would execute his part in it with precision and efficiency. Other commanders would perform less capably. Longstreet, for instance, mistakenly advanced toward Seven Pines via roads that had been assigned to other division leaders. The error created a mammoth traffic snarl, delayed the attack for several hours, and ensured that it would be conducted piecemeal. By early afternoon, D. H. Hill, who was to move south of Longstreet on the Williamsburg Road, grew tired of waiting for his colleague to attack, the signal for his own command to go forward. Tense from hours of fruitless waiting, Hill decided to attack Keyes's men at Seven Pines on his own. At his order, his troops swept relentlessly across swampy, wooded terrain, thrusting the Federals backward in chaos and panic. Soon the Union right flank was verging on collapse. Desperately, Keyes cobbled together a new line farther to the rear, and by early evening Hill's unsupported attack had spent itself, leaving the final result in doubt.[4]

Meanwhile, fighting belatedly surged along the Nine Mile Road. In midafternoon, Whiting's division finally cleared the road jam caused by Longstreet's blunder and attacked toward Fair Oaks. Under Johnston's personal direction, the troops advanced in two lines, overflowing the road on both sides. Hood's brigade was on the far right, with Law's brigade to its left and the brigade of Brig. Gen. J. J. Pettigrew farther north. The troops of Hampton and Brig. Gen. Robert Hatton formed Whiting's second rank, but as the division neared the railroad, Hampton, in response to orders from Johnston himself, moved up to extend the front line farther north.

Although the elongated line made Whiting's movement look formidable, both of his flanks were in danger. South of the Nine Mile Road, Hood's men were floundering through woods and swamps in a vain attempt to locate and link with the left of Hill's command. To the north, Hampton and Hatton were unknowingly approaching a sizable body of Union reinforcements. A large segment of Maj. Gen. Edwin V. Sumner's Second Army Corps had crossed the Chickahominy, undetected, via Grapevine Bridge. Arriving safely on the south bank, it had thrown up breastworks north of, and parallel to, the Nine Mile Road. When Whiting's line collided with its unforeseen opponents some time after 4:00 P.M., the result was carnage and chaos. Regiment upon regiment of Union infantry, covered by light artillery, blasted the advancing troops from many angles and brought them to a halt.[5]

Of all the commands thus ambushed, Hampton's suffered the most. Following his orders, the new brigadier advanced along a woods trail identified as a direct route to Keyes's right flank. Even before clearing the timber, his command came under fire from a pair of Sumner's batteries, which sent blasted tree limbs cascading down on everyone's head and shoulders. Hampton responded by ordering his lead regiment, the Sixteenth North Carolina, to attack and silence the guns. Leaning down from the saddle, he cautioned the officers of the Sixteenth to withhold fire "until you can feel the enemy on your bayonets!"[6]

At his word, the North Carolinians charged out of the trees and into a fusillade from foot soldiers and the cannon in their rear. Hand-to-hand fighting broke out almost immediately, men on both sides toppling from bayonet thrusts and rifle blasts at point-blank range. The contest swirled across clearings and through belts of timber, neither side gaining the advantage, until Hampton sent in reinforcements including his beloved legion. The additions tipped the balance of combat; minutes after they were committed, Sumner's artillery limbered up and wheeled to the rear, followed by its infantry supports.

The fighting appeared to be at an end, but it was not. Although driven "some distance through the woods," the Federals formed a new and longer line to which they continuously added troops until they threatened to lap around Hampton's left flank. Despite the odds, the brigade held its position and suffered accordingly. Here it lost the majority of the 329 casualties it absorbed this day, almost half of them in the ranks of the Hampton Legion. Hampton himself became a statistic when a Minié ball slammed into his foot, knocking it from its stirrup. Blood quickly overflowed his boot, prompting staff officers to call for a doctor. After a few minutes, the chief surgeon of Smith's corps reached the victim, inspected the wound, and, at Hampton's insistence, and while he remained in the saddle, carved out the slug.

By all accounts, Hampton not so much as flinched during the impromptu surgery. The wound was serious enough, however, that when he finally dismounted he could not put his weight on his injured foot. Perhaps because he refused to seek further medical care until the fighting tapered off after dark, the wound became infected, requiring an extended recuperation. It left him with a slight limp that would trouble him the remainder of his life. In fact, the wound would never heal completely—in later years it would suppurate occasionally, passing bone fragments to the surface of the skin and causing acute pain.[7]

At the time of his wounding, Hampton's command remained in imminent peril. Sensing as much, Smith rushed Hatton's brigade, augmented by an uncommitted regiment of Pettigrew's, to the rescue. The newcomers shored up Hampton's embattled flank, but the thickness of the woods and the approaching darkness prevented Smith from coordinating a general advance that might have swept the Yankees from Hampton's front. Lacking, as he lamented, "that concert of action almost absolutely necessary to success," Smith held his forward position until "it was too dark to distinguish friend from foe." Then, gingerly, he broke contact and pulled his corps back to a less exposed position.[8]

Having ended indecisively, the fighting at Fair Oaks and Seven Pines would resume early the next day. It would continue, however, without Hampton, who, within hours of Smith's withdrawal, was invalided to Richmond. As he would inform his family, for the first forty-eight hours after being struck, "I suffered greatly. . . . The ball [that hit him] . . . is mashed up and the bones feel pretty much in the same condition."[9]

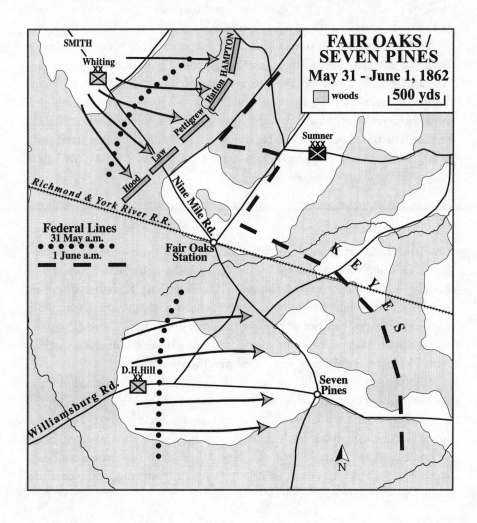

By June 3, he could finally report that "I am doing well," the pain having subsided. One reason for his improved condition may have been psychological—the knowledge that, although the second day of fighting between Johnston and McClellan had ended as inconclusively as the first, the latter's plan to besiege Richmond had been checked. Little Mac, cautious by nature, could be counted on to be more cautious still in the future. Then, too, Hampton was buoyed by the knowledge that, as at Manassas and Eltham's Landing, he had handled his command skillfully throughout the fighting, while displaying a commendable disinterest in his own safety. In fact, General Smith, in his report of the battle, described the South Carolinian as "remarkable for coolness, promptness, and decided practical ability . . . in difficult and dangerous circumstances." Such praise made even a disabling injury bearable.[10]

Yet Hampton cared less about his medical condition, or his reputation as a leader of men, than about the conspicuous service both of his sons had rendered in the fight—Wade IV as a member of Johnston's staff, and young Preston as temporary flag-bearer of the Hampton Legion's cavalry. From personal observation, their father testified that both had behaved "nobly, and I may well be proud of them. . . . Two braver and nobler boys never lived and I pray God to spare them to me." He could not know that, in time, only half of his prayer would be answered.[11]

Improved or not, Hampton's condition was such that he merited convalescent leave. Desiring to be cared for by his own family, on or about June 12 he hobbled to the depot of the Richmond & Petersburg Railroad, where he stowed his crutches aboard a passenger coach and entrained for South Carolina. He reached home late on the fifteenth, where he had a joyous reunion with Mary, herself just recovered from a troubling illness, as well as with McDuffie, Sally, Daisy, and his adoring sisters.

Although he spent at least a part of this period in bed, he decided he was well enough—physically, at least—to attend some social functions. The day after his arrival, he was received at the Columbia salon of Mary Chesnut, who found her guest in an unusually dark mood, a byproduct, she suspected, of his wounding: "A wet blanket he is, just now; Johnston is badly wounded. Lee is called King of Spades, because he has them all once more digging for dear life. Unless we can reinforce Stonewall, the game is up."[12]

As a summary of the fortunes of the Confederate armies, some of the views Mrs. Chesnut attributes to Hampton were accurate; others were neither true nor generous. General Johnston had indeed been wounded, twice, on the second day of the battle—he, too, had been sent to the rear to recuperate. Jefferson Davis had replaced him with Lee, who promptly withdrew the army to the Richmond defenses. Hampton was aware that Lee's experience in field command had not been uniformly successful. Indeed, as commander of the Department of South Carolina and Georgia in the fall of 1861, the Virginian had been better known for digging entrenchments than for engaging the enemy, hence the derisive nickname. There is reason to believe that Hampton, who had become quite close to Johnston, did not at first think highly of his successor. In time, however, he would come to consider Lee's rise to command of the army—a position he would never relinquish—as a stroke of great good fortune. As for Stonewall Jackson, his command in the Valley recently had been augmented to seventeen thousand troops, more than enough to outmaneuver or outfight every Yankee outpost in the region. Soon, in fact, Jackson would do the reinforcing, being called east to augment Lee for a better planned and better executed offensive than Johnston's at Seven Pines.[13]

After spending time with his family and their influential friends, Hampton paid a courtesy call at the governor's mansion. Pickens and his staff lavished praise on the wounded hero, waxed sympathetic over his injury, and listened intently to his accounts of the bloodletting around Richmond. Later he was guest of honor at a state dinner. There he bent uncomfortably under the flattery piled on him by political officials and other VIPs.[14]

He spent the remainder of his leave at home, resting his bandaged foot, struggling with the family's ledgers—flowing now with red ink, crop prices having become a casualty of war—and adding to his brood. By June 24, when Mary escorted him to the train for his return to the army, she was carrying the third child she would bear her husband, a son they would name Alfred.[15]

Three days later, he reached Virginia in better physical shape than when he had left it. His psyche, however, soon took an unexpected blow. Upon reporting at the headquarters of Whiting's division in the capital defenses, he was shocked to learn that he no longer had a command. In his absence, the army had been reorganized. During the reshuffling, his brigade had been broken up and its components distributed among Hood and three other generals.[16]

Why Hampton's regiments were summarily taken from him is difficult to determine. After all, he was not low man on the totem pole—Law, as junior brigade commander in Whiting's division, should have been the one displaced as a result of a redistribution of resources—yet the Alabamian retained a brigade under Whiting. Nor does Hampton's untimely absence from the field serve as an explanation. On May 31, General Pettigrew had been wounded and captured; but rumor had it that his brigade, although temporarily placed under Brig. Gen. William D. Pender, would be returned to him as soon as he was released from prison.[17]

Whatever the reason for his loss of position, Hampton accepted the situation with remarkable composure. One reason was that when he reported, the army was in the midst of a new offensive aimed at driving McClellan from the gates of Richmond. Thus it was no time to complain about usurped prerogatives. Then, too, Hampton was mollified when Lee, although deeply involved in supervising the operation, took the time to find him a new command.

On June 26 Jackson had arrived from the Valley to assist the Army of Northern Virginia in directing blows at an enemy that, with the exception of a single corps, was now positioned south of the Chickahominy. That same day, Lee's initial offensive, which struck the single Union corps north of the river near Mechanicsville, unhinged McClellan's right flank as well as his state of mind. Although his troops contained and then repulsed the attack, as soon as the fighting ended Little Mac commenced a retreat that would eventually carry him twenty-some miles from his original objective. The day Hampton returned to Virginia, Lee struck a second time, battering Maj. Gen. Fitz John Porter's Fifth Corps near Gaines's Mill, ten miles northeast of the capital. By evening, the Yankees were in full flight toward Harrison's Landing, their rear supply base on the James River.[18]

Late on the twenty-seventh, Hampton was assigned temporary command of one of Jackson's brigades—three infantry regiments and a light battery from Virginia—whose leader, Col. S. V. Fulkerson, had been mortally wounded earlier that day. Accompanied by Wade IV, who upon Johnston's incapacitation had joined his father's staff, Hampton reported to his new command on the edge of the Gaines's Mill battlefield. With no time to familiarize himself with his inherited subordinates, he assembled the brigade, which had occupied a reserve position during the day's fighting, and led it toward the Chickahominy River in company with other elements of Jackson's wing.[19]

Those elements saw no direct involvement in the next day's fighting, which closed with McClellan's men streaming across the Chickahominy on bridges they afterward destroyed. Stonewall held his people north of the river throughout the twenty-ninth as well, while, farther south, a division under General Magruder confronted Sumner's corps at Savage's Station. Undoubtedly, Magruder would have benefited from Jackson's assistance, and in fact Stonewall had been ordered to support closely the Confederate left. Not until evening, however, did he lead his men to the south side of the river under a downpour that had helped end the day's fighting. Hampton was nonplused by his superior's inactivity and apparent lack of interest in following given orders. Still, it was common knowledge that Jackson was an eccentric genius, and so his newest subordinate kept his misgivings to himself.

Through no fault of Jackson's, McClellan continued his retreat on the thirtieth. That morning his rear guard dug in behind treacherous White Oak Swamp while the rest of the army, accompanied by its supply train and cattle herd, continued its retreat to Harrison's Landing. Facing west, Sumner's troops confronted the pursuing forces of Longstreet and Maj. Gen. Ambrose P. Hill on the Long Bridge Road near Frayser's Farm. Farther east, meanwhile, two other divisions, plus miscellaneous supports, the whole under William B. Franklin, faced Jackson's men and the attached division of D. H. Hill across ruined White Oak Bridge.[20]

When his new brigade approached the swamp and surveyed the enemy positions on the far side, Hampton anticipated a swift and successful crossing. He was no seer: fatigue details twice attempted, but failed under fire, to repair White Oak Bridge. There seemed no cause for alarm, since several fords within a mile or so of the bridge offered a means of crossing and threatening Franklin's flanks and rear. Jackson accompanied his mounted commander, Col. Thomas T. Munford, across one of these fords, only to withdraw under a hail of sharpshooter and artillery fire. Leaving his superior behind, Munford then spurred his Second Virginia Cavalry a quarter-mile downstream. There he located a cow path that led to and across the swamp and gave access to dry ground beyond the Union right. But when he relayed the news to Jackson, Stonewall failed to act on it.[21]

While Munford ran his errand, Hampton made a reconnaissance of his own east of the bridge but west of Munford's passage. Accompanied by Wade IV and another aide, Capt. Rawlins Lowndes, he located a site where the swamp was no more than fifteen feet wide. The trio waded across through mud and mire and, like Munford, came out at a point beyond Franklin's right flank. Looking off to the right, Hampton discovered a body of Federals positioned in a ravine that blocked their view of the crossing site. An assault launched from the position Hampton and his aides occupied would come as a rude shock, one the enemy would be hard pressed to withstand.[22]

Recrossing the marsh unobserved, Hampton rode to Jackson's field head-quarters and calmly reported his findings to the commanding general. Jackson's response was so passive that it constituted no response at all. The dour Virginian listened silently to Hampton's news and when he had finished asked whether a bridge could be built across the site to accommodate a body of infantry. The brigadier replied that it could, whereupon Jackson ordered him to see to it.

Realizing—even if his superior did not seem to—that a golden opportunity might soon slip away, Hampton hastily assembled a fifty-man detail and set it to felling pine trees for construction material. In "a few minutes," pioneers and engineers fashioned a rough-hewn but serviceable bridge across the place where Hampton had waded the swamp. But when the brigadier reported back to Jackson, whom he found sitting on a pine log with his eyes closed and his face shielded by the lowered visor of his kepi, he received the same reply that Jackson had given Munford—total silence. In fact, for several minutes, Jackson, his mind befogged by days of overwork and nights without sleep, offered neither word nor gesture of response. Then, abruptly, he rose and lurched off as if in a trance.[23]

Knowing nothing else to do, Hampton returned to his troops, who had been drawn up in preparation for crossing the bridge, and returned them to their breastworks. There they and their comrades under Jackson remained for the balance of the day, softening up Franklin's position for an attack that was never launched. Meanwhile, to the west, Longstreet and A. P. Hill attacked vigorously and eventually broke through the center of Sumner's line near Frayser's Farm. Hastily summoned reinforcements—which a more aggressive Jackson might have pinned down—came up to stanch the gray wave. The fighting ended inconclusively about nine o'clock.[24]

As Hampton suspected at the time and understood more clearly in later days, the fighting of the thirtieth need not have ended this way. Had Jackson crossed near White Oak Bridge, he might have done more than prevent a detaching of troops to Frayser's Farm—he might have cut off McClellan's rear guard from the rest of its army. By any standard, Jackson's sleep-induced iner-tia had been costly. One of the army's most astute strategists, Col. E. Porter Alexander of the artillery, later wrote that, of the handful of occasions during the war when the Confederate forces stood on the brink of decisive military victory, "this chance of June 30th '62 impresses me as the best of all." Instead, it became one of the many might-have-beens of a conflict that seemed destined to drag on indefinitely.[25]

What followed the lost opportunities of White Oak Swamp and Frayser's Farm smacked of anticlimax. Permitted to disengage after nightfall, the Union rear guard made its way to the James via Malvern Hill. Along the northern slopes of that strong natural position, McClellan had organized a new and stronger rear guard—seemingly endless lines of infantry, anchored by no fewer than 250 cannon, 100 of them placed hub-to-hub on the summit. Almost inexplicably, Lee planned a full-scale assault. Late in the afternoon, following preparations made difficult by the devastating fire of McClellan's artillery and Union gunboats in the James, elements of three divisions attacked the position from the north and west, only to be blown apart well short of their objective. Hampton, whose brigade was not thrown into the cauldron, looked on in horror as the casualties mounted. When evening put an end to the fiasco, more than fifty-three hundred attackers lay dead or wounded as against thirty-two hundred defenders.[26]

It was a terrible note on which to end a successful campaign, but at least the threat to Richmond had been neutralized. Following the one-sided fighting of July 1, McClellan completed his withdrawal to the James, from which he displayed no inclination to bestir himself.

In later days, elements of the Army of Northern Virginia pushed nearly to the bank of the James. Reconnoitering the approaches to Harrison's Landing, Lee saw the inherent strength of the position, and forbade to attack it. Instead, in consideration of his troops, "who had been marching and fighting almost incessantly for seven days under the most trying circumstances," he pulled back to a point from which he could observe the length and breadth of McClellan's base, but beyond rifle-range of it.[27]

Given the sudden, dramatic decrease in the pace of operations below Richmond, Lee began to map a new campaign far to the west. At about the time McClellan withdrew from the doorstep of Richmond, the so-called Army of Virginia had been formed with the intent of operating between the Rapidan and Rappahannock Rivers. Assigned to Maj. Gen. John Pope, a transferee from the western theater with a reputation as a winner but also as a braggart and blowhard, this command was charged with several missions, including long-distance cooperation with McClellan. Little Mac's retreat to the James had precluded that possibility, but Pope retained authority to strike toward the railhead at Gordonsville, where he could cut the main line of communications between Richmond and the Shenandoah. Although Pope lacked McClellan's reputation as a latter-day Napoleon, Lee would have to keep a close eye on him and the threat he posed.[28]

In the meantime, the Confederate leader took the opportunity to reorganize his army, a chore he completed in the latter half of July. One result was the full integration of Jackson's command into the Army of Northern Virginia. Another was the expansion of the army's cavalry wing, under J. E. B. Stuart, from a large brigade to a two-brigade division. Both occurrences had repercussions for Wade Hampton's military career.

Maj. Gen. J. E. B. Stuart, Lee's cavalry commander

Following Malvern Hill, several high-ranking officers who had been on detached duty returned to the army. One was Brig. Gen. William B. Taliaferro, who during Jackson's Valley campaign had led the brigade that later passed to Colonel Fulkerson and then to Hampton. During this latest reorganization, two Alabama regiments were added to the three Virginia outfits that Hampton had commanded at White Oak Swamp and Malvern Hill. As seniority dictated, the enlarged force was assigned to Taliaferro.[29]

Hampton, who had realized that his most recent assignment was a provisional one, neither lodged a protest nor voiced a complaint over his displacement. Nevertheless, he was chagrined to find himself, for the second time in a month, without an assignment. On the other hand, having recently observed Stonewall Jackson at his worst, he may not have regretted relinquishing a position under the man. He hoped that another infantry brigade—preferably, one assigned to Longstreet, Lee's senior subordinate—would be tendered him before the army embarked on another campaign.

But no such opportunity came along. Instead, in the third week of July the Adjutant and Inspector General's Office in Richmond inquired if Hampton would be willing to accept transfer to the cavalry. The expansion of Stuart's command, which had secured its leader's promotion to major general, had created two vacancies at the brigade level. Although Stuart would not have the final say over the assignments, he had made known a single preference—that his favorite subordinate, Col. Fitzhugh Lee, Stuart's successor as leader of the vaunted First Virginia, be given one of the brigades. Robert E. Lee, Fitz's uncle, would approve Stuart's recommendation, but that left one billet to be filled. According to Jefferson Davis, the position was Hampton's if he wanted it.[30]

Gen. Robert E. Lee, commander of A. N. V.

Hampton appears to have had mixed feelings about accepting the offer. Stuart's prowess as an intelligence gatherer and a combat leader was well known throughout the army. From the earliest days of the conflict, he had launched well-planned, carefully executed, and often wildly successful strikes against Union outposts, supply depots, and communication lines. In the process he had taken on all comers, including infantry and artillery, in violation of textbooks that claimed cavalry could prevail in combat only against other cavalry.

Stuart's latest exploit had taken place in mid-June, when, ordered to reconnoiter Union positions north of the Chickahominy, he encircled McClellan's army. En route, at the head of a relatively small force of troopers, he outmaneuvered, outrode, and outsmarted hordes of pursuers. He returned to home base with minimal loss as well as with the timely intelligence Lee needed to plot the offensive that eventually drove McClellan from Richmond. The publicity the raid attracted assured Stuart's reputation, made him a household name in the North as well as the South, and rendered a posting to the cavalry a good career move for any officer.[31]

Thus, Hampton saw many advantages in accepting Davis's offer. In joining the cavalry he would serve in an elite combat arm under a capable and respected superior. As an accomplished horseman, a master swordsman, and a dead shot with a pistol, he seemed assured of a successful transition to mounted service. Then, too, under Stuart he would be reunited with Calbraith Butler and the cavalry of the legion he had organized and bankrolled. Along with the two batteries that had gone to war under his command, the mounted component of the legion had been permanently detached from its parent organization months ago. Although currently attached to a slightly larger unit with a similar organization, the Jeff Davis Legion, Butler and his troopers would soon expand into a full-size regiment under Stuart, the Second South Carolina Cavalry.[32]

As Hampton saw it, joining the cavalry also had its drawbacks. A talented soldier Stuart certainly was, but he was known to take risks with his own life and the lives of his men, sometimes during ill-conceived operations of debatable strategic value. The most recent example of this had occurred on July 3, when Stuart's battalions approached one of McClellan's encampments on the James, detached from its main army and thus seemingly vulnerable to attack. Instead of alerting the infantry, whose staying power would have ensured a successful assault, Stuart had amused himself by shelling the Yankees with his horse artillery, which he emplaced on a plateau overlooking the river. The guns created havoc and spread panic, and several Yankees were cut off and captured, but Union infantry and artillery eventually chased the assailants away. E. P. Alexander heard Hampton complain that Stuart had endangered his own command by flushing the game prematurely. Moreover, "had General Stuart waited for our infantry to come up before bringing on the fight," something of lasting significance might have been accomplished.[33]

Other facets of Stuart's reputation gave Hampton pause. The cavalry leader was known as a dandy, a preening cavalier, and, in some quarters, a buffoon. He favored polished jackboots, golden spurs, crimson-lined capes, and ostrich-plumed hats, and he rode to the accompaniment of his personal banjoist. He was susceptible to the flattery of men, especially the politically powerful, and, although supposedly happily married, he was always at the service of pretty women, especially those—and they were legion—who swooned at his displays of courtly charm.[34]

Such behavior was bad enough, but Stuart was known to surround himself with officers of similar tastes and tendencies—well-born Virginians in their twenties and early thirties, with a passion for hard riding and high living and to whom war was as much sport as struggle. Hampton was not certain he could flourish, or even survive, among such people, especially since his assignment, by making him Stuart's ranking lieutenant, might identify him as a devotee of the man.

At length, and after much inner debate, Hampton agreed to the transfer. He accepted the position as Stuart's senior brigadier, but with the stipulation that he could return to the infantry should a suitable command open up there. His new assignment was dated July 26. A day or so later, he bade his farewells to the men with whom he had been closely associated for fourteen months, including the officers of the legion that continued to bear his name. Then, accompanied by some of the staff officers who would make the transition with him, including Captains Barker and Lowndes and his two sons, he rode to Hanover Court House, fourteen miles north of Richmond, and reported at Stuart's headquarters.[35]

Hampton's introduction to the ways of the cavalry confirmed both the benign expectations he had formed and the dark suspicions he had harbored. He found his new superior to be polished and personable, without diffidence or hauteur, and quite capable of putting a newcomer at his ease. Stuart impressed him as frank, open, and aboveboard in his dealings with others. While something—a sly smile, a twinkle in his eye—hinted at a jovial personality, he was, Hampton quickly decided, a worthy specimen of the Virginia gentleman, refined in manners, correct in habits, courteous toward all, and considerate of the feelings of others. Above all, Hampton was impressed by the high regard with which Stuart's officers and troopers held him. It was obvious that he commanded not only their obedience but also their respect, their loyalty, and even their devotion. No wonder his people followed him so willingly on so many hazardous escapades.

If Hampton was agreeably impressed by Stuart's character and personality, he did not form the same opinion of the general's closest friend and most trusted subordinate. Although evidently an affable, even a jocular, sort, now-Brig. Gen. Fitzhugh Lee struck Hampton as representative of the most objectionable qualities of the Virginia aristocrat—vanity, ostentation, pomposity, and condescension. Upon their first meeting, Hampton also thought he detected in Lee's attitude a hint of disapproval, if not downright disdain—just what an outsider might expect from one entrenched in the society to which admission was being sought. The uncomfortable feeling that he was an interloper, a Johnny-come-lately, attached itself to Hampton. Months would pass before he could discard that sensation.[36]

Brig. Gen. Fitzhugh Lee

It did not help that he was fifteen to twenty years older than many of those who greeted him with curious glances as well as snappy salutes. An unusually high percentage of these youngsters wore stars on their collars and loops of lace on their cuffs. Upon being introduced, Hampton made an effort to hide his continuing limp. He may have been old, but he was determined not to appear infirm.

In his early days under Stuart, Hampton made the acquaintance of numerous colleagues, including the hulking, soft-spoken William Henry Fitzhugh "Rooney" Lee, Robert E. Lee's second son, Fitz Lee's cousin, and commander of the Ninth Virginia Cavalry; Thomas Lafayette Rosser, the self-absorbed, fiery-tempered leader of the Fifth Virginia; Pierce Manning Butler Young, the tall, handsome Georgian who led the Cobb Legion cavalry; the quietly competent William T. Martin, commander of the cavalry of the Jeff Davis Legion; and John Pelham, the boyish daredevil who commanded Stuart's horse artillery. Although Hampton would forge cordial relations with many, if not all, of these men, he was most comfortable in the presence of subordinates with whom he had prior acquaintance: not only M. C. Butler but also Tom Munford, whom he had gotten to know well during his stint under Jackson; and Hampton's old artillery subordinate, Col. Stephen Dill Lee, currently the provisional commander of the Fourth Virginia Cavalry.[37]

If his spirits were boosted by familiar faces, they sagged a bit when a couple of early gestures by Stuart called attention to Hampton's modest station in the local pecking order. In forming his division, Stuart had divvied up his units along geographical lines. As a native of the state, he had a decided preference for regiments raised in Virginia, almost all of which he had grouped into a brigade under Fitz Lee. There was no doubt that these troopers of the First, Third, Fourth, Fifth, and Ninth Virginia commanded the greater share of his patronage.

Lt. Col. (later Brig. Gen.) P. M. B. Young

The non-Virginians had been assembled into a second brigade, the one assigned to Hampton. They would serve alongside the Tenth Virginia, which appears to have gone to Hampton strictly to ensure numerical balance (each brigade consisted of five regiments or legions). Stuart's effort at geographical segregation might have seemed a trifle odd to some at first glance, but it was in harmony with the Confederacy's emphasis on regionalism. Moreover, Stuart probably supposed that Hampton preferred to lead Carolinians (Butler's regiment and Col. Laurence S. Baker's First North Carolina), Georgians (Young's outfit), and Alabamians and Mississippians (prominent members of the Jeff Davis Legion) rather than Virginians. Stuart would see to it that Col. J. Lucius Davis's Tenth Virginia transitioned out of Hampton's brigade as soon as another Deep South outfit was made available to take its place.[38]

In point of fact, Hampton did prefer to command regiments drawn from the lower South. But he did not appreciate the subtle (and not-so-subtle) hints by which Stuart, Lee, and other Virginians indicated they considered those outfits second-rate. Given this regional bias, what did the assignment of units say about Stuart's regard for his newest subordinate?

The thought was enough to disturb, but not to dismay, Hampton. He may have taken umbrage, however, at the numbering system Stuart devised for his brigades. In an apparent attempt to anoint Fitz Lee as his heir apparent, Stuart sent to army headquarters a suggested table of organization that referred to Lee's command as the First Brigade, Hampton's as the Second. Fitz's uncle approved the proposed structure but with the numerical order reversed: "The brigade commanded by General Hampton will . . . be the First Brigade, as he is the senior brigadier." Whether a protest by Hampton prompted this action is unknown, but as a stickler for seniority he would have been disturbed and probably also offended by Stuart's proposal.[39]

Regardless of whether Hampton gained the early approval of his new associates, from his first days in the cavalry he impressed numerous officers and troopers with his well-bred manner, his calm and kindly demeanor, and his air of self-assurance. In time even his lack of flair and flamboyance, at first regarded as a mark against him, won many admirers. One of these, who observed Hampton especially closely, was Capt. John Esten Cooke, a talented essayist and novelist who was also Stuart's chief ordnance officer. Years later Cooke recalled his initial impression of the South Carolinian, an impression that would deepen, but not materially change, over time:

> The face was browned by sun and wind, and half covered by dark side-whiskers joining a long moustache of the same hue; the chin bold, prominent, and bare. The eyes were brown, inclining to black, and very mild and friendly; the voice low, sonorous, and with a certain accent of dignity and composure. The frame of the soldier—straight, vigorous, and stalwart, but not too broad for grace—was encased in a plain gray sack coat of civilian cut, with the collar turned down; cavalry boots, large and serviceable, with brass spurs; a brown felt hat, without star or feather; the rest of the dress plain gray. . . . What impressed all who saw him was the attractive union of dignity and simplicity in his bearing—a certain grave and simple courtesy which indicated the highest breeding. He was evidently an honest gentleman who disdained all pretense or artifice. It was plain that he thought nothing of personal decorations or military show, and never dreamed of "producing an impression" upon any one. . . . After being in his presence for ten minutes, you saw that he was a man for hard work, and not for display.[40]

This was all to the good, of course, for a great deal of hard work lay ahead, and Stuart's command already had more than its fair share of display.

FIVE

"Theirs was the sleepless watch and the . . . petite guerre."

★ ★ ★

H ampton's introduction to cavalry routine, or what passed for it in
Stuart's command, was a bit disconcerting. One of his worst suspicions
about the cavalry—that it was the province of pampered youth playing at
war—appeared to be confirmed after he reported at Hanover Court House.
On July 29, 1862, Stuart had each of his brigades drill together, in full
panoply, troopers brandishing sabers and pistols with serio-comic ferocity as
they galloped at full tilt across the exercise field. It was the second such exercise the Beau Sabreur had staged in the past two weeks and, like the first, it
resembled a tournament, complete with a crowd of enthralled spectators
including swooning females. Capt. William W. Blackford, Stuart's chief engineer, recalled that he and other staff officers were assigned to squire about "all
the ladies in the country round . . . seeing their carriages well placed and . . .
entertaining them during the intervals of duty." Perhaps with the intention of
inhibiting her husband's flirtatious ways, Flora Cooke Stuart was on hand for
the event, which, as Blackford claimed, she greatly enjoyed. At some point,
presumably, the general introduced his lady to his new second in command.
In her presence, the South Carolinian would not have so much as hinted at
the distaste he felt for such empty pageantry.[1]

As Hampton would learn, a spectacle such as this often preceded a field
campaign. Less than a week after the drill, Hampton found his command
alone in camp, Stuart, Lee, and the Second Brigade having ridden north, at
the behest of army headquarters, to curtail Union depredations against the

87

Virginia Central. That rail line was the major supply link between Lee, who remained around Richmond in company with Longstreet's command, and Jackson, who with twelve thousand men had moved to Gordonsville, sixty miles west of the Confederate capital, to observe the movements of John Pope. Stuart was gone from camp for four days. Hampton used the time to acquaint himself with his acquired subordinates; to inspect their camps, horses, and weapons; and probably also to peruse a tactics manual or two. He would have used every opportunity to assimilate the many and intricate lessons of mounted service.[2]

Within hours of his August 8 return from his punitive expedition, Stuart was off on another extended excursion, this time traveling alone to Orange Court House, seven miles north of Gordonsville. Lee had ordered him to inspect Jackson's cavalry, now led by Tom Munford's successor, the erratic and prickly Brig. Gen. Beverly H. Robertson. In his absence, Hampton was effectively in command of the Cavalry Division, Army of Northern Virginia.[3]

While Stuart was away, word reached Hampton that Lee and Longstreet were preparing to head west in Jackson's footsteps. A sharp, costly encounter between Stonewall's command and nine thousand of Pope's troops had taken place on August 9 at Cedar Mountain, about six miles south of Pope's forward location, Culpeper Court House. The battle ended as a bloody stalemate, thanks to a last-minute counterattack by reinforcements under A. P. Hill, who saved the Rebel line from being outflanked and rolled up like a gray carpet. Lee determined to reinforce his eccentric subordinate before the Federals struck again. Together they would plan a more decisive confrontation, one that would evict Pope from the Rapidan River line.[4]

At the head of Longstreet's column, Lee began to evacuate the Richmond front on August 13. Two days later, Stuart, having completed his study of Robertson's command, returned from Jackson's headquarters. Almost immediately he made plans to retrace his steps in response to Lee's order that the cavalry report to him as soon as possible. Before he again headed west, however, Stuart issued instructions to his subordinates. He would go on ahead by train, while Fitz Lee readied his brigade for an overland march. Fitz and his men were to rejoin Stuart near Raccoon Ford on the Rapidan River, northeast of Orange Court House, by the fifteenth.[5]

Fitz Lee, anticipating an early return to combat, was immediately receptive to the assignment. In all probability, Hampton was less enthused by the mission entrusted to him. He was to remain behind, taking position between

Richmond and McClellan, guarding the former and keeping watch over the latter. Stuart's distribution of responsibilities, although it appeared to relegate Hampton to a secondary role in the unfolding campaign, was grounded in simple logic: the South Carolinian had much to learn before becoming truly proficient in the tactics of his new branch. Being thrown into a field campaign was not the best way to acquire the requisite knowledge. An observation mission, involving only long-range skirmishing, promised a better educational experience. Hampton must have agreed with Stuart's reasoning; at any rate, he does not appear to have protested against it.

While the mission assigned Hampton appeared prosaic enough, it might prove more lively and dangerous than Stuart anticipated. The Army of the Potomac had begun to evacuate Harrison's Landing in mid-July—much of its manpower was earmarked for transfer to Pope—but the operation had truly begun only one day before Stuart returned from Jackson's headquarters. Enough Yankees remained on the James to launch a sudden, heavy strike at Richmond. Thus, when his main body headed for the Rapidan, Robert E. Lee left behind Gustavus Smith, with two and a half divisions of infantry under D. H. Hill and Maj. Gen. Richard H. Anderson, plus artillery under E. P. Alexander. But to observe the enemy properly, infantry and artillery required the eyes and ears that only horsemen could provide. Therefore, Lee intended that Hampton's outfits "keep out scouts and . . . use every means in their power to ascertain General McClellan's movements," while keeping firmly in mind the "necessity of holding Richmond to the last extremity should any attack be made upon it."[6]

Before Fitz Lee left for his rendezvous with Stuart, Hampton moved his command toward the James, where it relieved the pickets of the Second Brigade. He placed a substantial force north of Malvern Hill, which had been the scene of frequent skirmishing until the Federals withdrew from the area on August 7. The remainder of his command he shifted eastward to the Charles City Court House vicinity, filling the space in between with vedettes—mounted pickets. Finally, he sent in skirmishers to fix the enemy and hold them in place by drawing their fire and demonstrating vigorously in their front.[7]

In this arduous and exacting work, Hampton's brigade was assisted by the flying artillery that had reported to it on the tenth. This battery, the Washington Artillery, was the unit that Hampton had organized and armed in 1861 and which, under S. D. Lee, had served the Hampton Legion so ably during its first several months in the field. At its patron's urging, the mounted battery had been reorganized as horse artillery in order that it might continue to support Hampton in his new role as cavalry leader. Now led by Lee's successor, Capt. James Franklin Hart of Charleston, the battery consisted of six howitzers, two 6-pounders and four 12-pounders. Because of the acute shortage of artillery horses in the Confederacy, thus far only about half of Hart's men had been mounted. Even so, Hampton was glad to have the battery, the only artillery support at his disposal. The eight guns of the Stuart Horse Artillery had accompanied Fitz Lee to the Rapidan.[8]

While the pickets, skirmishers, and horse artillerymen plied their trade, a resourceful band of operatives enabled Hampton to gain information from inside the enemy's lines. These so-called "Iron Scouts" included several North and South Carolinians such as Bob Shiver, Bill Mikler, Jack Schoolbred, and Hugh Scott, as well as the daring Texan who commanded them all, Sgt. George Shadburne of the Jeff Davis Legion. On August 16, the scouts sent in word that McClellan's rear echelon was evacuating Harrison's Landing by overland march in the direction of the Chickahominy. Hampton ordered a vigorous but careful pursuit of a force he estimated at more than sixty thousand troops of all arms.[9]

Shadburne and his men tailed the evacuees as far as White House, at the confluence of the York and Pamunkey Rivers. From there they reported that the Federals were being shipped to Aquia Creek, a Potomac River landing northeast of Fredericksburg. Hampton at once turned his command in that direction. By August 25, the scouts had penetrated as far north as Massaponax Church, a few miles below Fredericksburg. After interrogating local citizens, Hampton reported that thirty thousand of McClellan's men had landed at Aquia in recent days. Many had moved on to Pope's new headquarters on the Rappahannock River. The rest were expected to remain in the Fredericksburg vicinity to lend the western general long-range support in his coming confrontation with Lee. As Hampton informed General Smith, via D. H. Hill, the fifty thousand at Fredericksburg were "waiting to hear of Pope's fight, to help him if beaten, to push on to Richmond should he succeed."[10]

By this time, Robert E. Lee, from his headquarters at Jeffersonton on the north fork of the Rappahannock, had learned that McClellan was about to reinforce Pope, if he had not already done so. Hoping to close with the enemy before more additions could arrive, he requested of President Davis that the troops of Smith, Hill, Anderson, and Hampton be sent to him immediately.

Concerned about Pope's cavalry strength, he added, "Hampton's cavalry I particularly require."[11]

Despite the urgency in this request, Davis did not comply until the end of the month, and he released only a portion of the forces his field commander sought. By then it was too late: the confrontation between Lee and Pope had reached its climax, and a major battle had been fought, for the second time in a little over a year, nearly within sight of the U.S. capital.

After adding Longstreet's troops to Jackson's, Lee had attempted to envelop Pope's left along the Rapidan, thus interposing between him and the reinforcements coming in from the east, while also blocking Pope's route of retreat. The plan was rendered inoperable, however, by a number of events, one being Fitz Lee's late arrival near Raccoon Ford. Stuart had come to meet Fitz at nearby Verdiersville, only to barely escape capture by a roving detachment of Union cavalry from the command of Brig. Gen. John Buford. When fleeing from his assailants, the Beau Sabreur left behind papers that detailed Lee's plan to outflank his opponent. Hastened to Pope's attention, the documents prompted him to fall back to the north bank of the more defensible Rappahannock River, thus evading the trap prepared for him.[12]

Disappointed but undaunted, Lee sent Stuart on a looping march into the Union rear, which culminated in the sack of Pope's supply depot at Catlett's Station on the Orange & Alexandria Railroad. When Pope finally turned about, abandoning his secure position to counter what he thought was a major movement against his blind side, Lee responded with a risky maneuver, splitting his army in the face of the enemy. On August 25, 1862, he sent Jackson and the recently returned Stuart, followed less than forty-eight hours later by Longstreet, through the Bull Run Mountains, around Pope's right flank, and into his rear. After trashing Pope's lightly guarded headquarters at Manassas Junction, Jackson on the twenty-eighth tangled with a portion of the now-withdrawing enemy at Groveton, on the Warrenton Turnpike just west of the Bull Run battlefield.

With the main body of his army now on hand, Pope resumed his attack on Jackson, in greater strength, the following day, unaware that Lee and Longstreet had arrived on Stonewall's right and in perfect position to crush the Union left. This Longstreet did beginning in midafternoon on the thirtieth.

The blow was so stunning and so mighty that within an hour the inatten-tive Pope was reeling northward in defeat. Lee followed, and on September 1 he tried again to outflank his adversary, this time at Chantilly (Ox Hill), twenty miles west of the Washington defenses. A poorly coordinated, weather-plagued offensive, coupled with a stubborn defense by the Union rear guard, enabled Pope's survivors to complete their withdrawal to the safety of their capital.[13]

Due to their belated release from the Richmond front, Hampton's troopers were on the road from Fredericksburg to Manassas during the fighting at Bull Run. They finally united with Stuart west of Fairfax Court House on the morning of September 2. With no time to compare notes on their recent oper-ations, Hampton joined Fitz Lee in pursuing Pope's fugitives. At a certain point, Stuart assumed direct command and led both brigades cross-country to the north in the direction of Vienna.

After marching for nearly two miles in search of a flank to attack, the cavalry halted at Flint Hill, a fortified eminence occupied by Pope's rear guard. At Stuart's word, Hampton advanced a line of sharpshooters, backed by a two-gun section of the Stuart Horse Artillery under John Pelham. Hampton reported proudly that after his men dosed them with rifle balls and Pelham laced them with canister, "the enemy retired, and were followed by my brigade." Pushing on, cavalry and artillery soon overtook their quarry once again, when, as Hampton added, "the rifle[d] piece of Captain Pelham opened on them with effect, scat-tering them in every direction. As soon as the cavalry could be brought forward, I pursued them, taking a few prisoners." Only after encountering a much larger body of Federals, who ambushed his men from roadside woods, did Hampton fall back in good order, having suffered a single casualty. So ended the new cavalry-man's first dose of combat other than long-range skirmishing. So ended, too, Lee's campaign to sweep a second Union army off the chessboard of war.[14]

With Pope's survivors bloody and shaken, and many of McClellan's troops still en route to Washington, no Yankees appeared in a position to obstruct Robert E. Lee's next movement. Without hesitation, he began to move north and west toward the Potomac and, beyond, Maryland. He had long consid-ered entering that divided state, which a majority of Americans seemed to regard as Union soil but which was also a hotbed of Confederate sentiment. Once over the river, Lee could range freely through territory capable of sus-taining his army until McClellan or Pope gathered enough nerve to pursue and enough speed to overtake him. In addition to provisions, Maryland might furnish Lee with enough recruits to make good the losses he had suffered in driving McClellan from the gates of Richmond and Pope from the Rapidan-Rappahannock basin. An extended stay in the Old Line State—Lee would have liked to remain there through the coming winter—would also relieve Maryland's several thousand Confederate sympathizers from the yoke of enemy occupation.[15]

On September 3, as Lee's army headed toward the fords of Leesburg, Virginia, the cavalry demonstrated in its rear and on its flanks, keeping the horsemen of McClellan and Pope from interfering with the movement. Two days later, their screening job well done, two-thirds of Stuart's horsemen forded the Potomac in the rear of their infantry comrades. Fitz Lee's Virginians, accompanied by Stuart, were the first to cross, followed by the Deep Southerners under Hampton. Stuart's recently acquired third brigade, once led by Robertson and now under Tom Munford, had relieved Hampton's men at Flint Hill; it would linger in the rear until the main army reached Leesburg. Munford's resumption of command of what would become known as the Laurel Brigade was one result of Stuart's unfavorable report to Lee about Beverly Robertson. On the fifth, the mercurial brigadier had been sent to North Carolina for reassignment.[16]

When Hampton's horses waded the Potomac early in the evening of the fifth, a member of the Jeff Davis Legion beheld "a beautiful sight on that clear moonlight night. The water reached to our saddles, and some small horses had to swim. As Regt. after Regt. reached the Maryland side, the men cheered and the bands played Maryland My Maryland."[17]

As soon as on dry ground, Hampton prepared his command for imminent action. He realized that no matter how timid the Union high command appeared on the offensive, it would not allow an unimpeded invasion of the North. Late that evening, when the First Brigade closed up on the village of Poolesville, Hampton strengthened his rear guard and threw out flankers, while instructing his subordinates to scrutinize the countryside for signs of enemy cavalry. He was right to suppose that the Federals would quickly pick up their trail; just shy of Poolesville, Fitz Lee had to clear blue horsemen from his path, possibly a scouting party from the garrison at Harpers Ferry, twenty miles downriver.[18]

Hampton might be vigilant, but he found his superior more interested in partying than scouting. On the seventh, Stuart moved his headquarters from Poolesville to Urbana, in the heart of a region of Confederate loyalists. There, while his infantry comrades continued northwestward toward Frederick,

Stuart established a semipermanent presence in a most genial location. Jubilant citizens who hailed the newcomers as heroes and deliverers mobbed officers and men and pressed on them all manner of good things—food, drink, even bouquets of flowers.

Stuart, who had a weakness for public acclaim as well as a thirst for genteel entertainment, responded by inviting the better class of locals to a ball, held on the evening of the eighth in a converted female academy on the edge of town. The affair, which featured not only dancing but also choice refreshments and the music of a regimental band, was pronounced a great success by all who attended, including dozens of Stuart's officers. Their superior enjoyed himself immensely, waltzing and flirting the night away among a bevy of female admirers.

Hampton was not one to avoid social responsibilities, but he did not consider the present occasion a suitable time, nor an invaded country the proper place, for merrymaking of this sort. Electing not to caper about a dance-floor in full-dress uniform, he remained with his pickets, clad in the plain but functional attire he favored. It was well that he did, for while the festivities were in full swing bodies of Yankee horsemen advanced from Hyattstown, four miles to the southeast, and attacked his outposts. Several casualties resulted before Hampton could lead reinforcements to the threatened points, forcing the enemy to draw off. The bursts of gunfire brought Stuart's ball to an abrupt halt, especially after wounded pickets were laid on the dance floor for medical treatment. Here was a night few partygoers would ever forget.[19]

Over the next three days, not only Hampton's pickets but also those of Fitz Lee, came under intermittent attack. In every case, the Yankees were repulsed, but the frequency of the assaults and the increasing strength with which they were delivered suggested that the entire enemy army was moving in Stuart's direction. In fact, McClellan, who now commanded not only his old troops but also those of the recently deposed Pope, had led the combined force out of Washington and toward the Potomac crossings on the morning of September 7. By the eleventh, his vanguard was nearing Lee's recent headquarters in Frederick. The Army of Northern Virginia, however, had departed the area three days earlier, heading for the Blue Ridge. Again Lee had split his army in the face of an imminent clash with the enemy. He had accompanied Longstreet's wing toward Hagerstown, while six divisions under Jackson, having passed through the Catoctin Mountains, were advancing south to capture, or at least neutralize, the Yankees at Harpers Ferry.[20]

Stuart's mission was to protect the rear of both columns, but his immediate task was to keep the enemy from interfering with Jackson's operation. Thus he delayed until McClellan was almost within rifle range of his main body, which now included Munford's brigade, before departing Urbana on the twelfth. At his orders, Lee's brigade trotted north from New Market, on the Baltimore & Ohio Railroad, to the village of Liberty. Meanwhile, Munford's brigade moved from Poolesville northwestward, via a pass through Catoctin Mountain, to Jefferson; and Hampton's troops marched from the Urbana area to Frederick. Hampton's designated route placed him between the other columns as well as a few miles in rear of Longstreet's infantry.[21]

As the First Brigade closed up on Frederick, the Iron Scouts informed Hampton that enemy units of all arms were advancing toward him along the historic and commodious National Road. Fearing that two of his squadrons, which he had left in the rear to guard a Monocacy River bridge near Urbana, would be cut off and captured, the brigadier prepared to block the road south of Frederick until the fifty-man party could be recalled. Thanks to the accurate shelling of three of Hart's guns, skillfully supported by a squadron of Butler's Second South Carolina, the advancing Federals failed to gobble up the rear guard.

Upon retiring to the outskirts of Frederick, Hampton found enemy cavalry close on his heels. At the city limits, he halted with the intention of discouraging further pursuit. Hart's guns were soon booming, but the Yankees replied with artillery of their own, some of whose shells landed in the streets of the city, inflicting no casualties but frightening its residents. Appalled by this "unparalleled atrocity," Hampton led a large body of troopers toward the guns and the foot soldiers and dismounted cavalrymen who supported them. Behind him came a mixed force under Butler, including a forty-man provost guard drawn from every unit in the brigade and led by Capt. J. Frederick Waring of the Jeff Davis Legion.

The unexpected attack hit home with intimidating force. Startled Yankees lingered only long enough to fall back, remount, and limber up, whereupon, as Hampton reported, they "scattered . . . in every direction." Even when beyond pursuit, the Federals continued to give way to panic. According to an officer of the Davis Legion, they "ran over each other, upsetting cannon and horses, and firing off their cannon in their own midst, with not a Confederate within fifty yards of them."[22]

The fugitives left behind numerous comrades, including the dead and wounded. Hampton's captures included a colonel of infantry who commanded a brigade, as well as an artillery piece whose team had been killed in their traces. The lack of serviceable horses, however, prevented the Confederates from hauling it off as a prize of war. Even so, as Hampton exulted, "so successful was the charge and so complete the repulse of the enemy that no further attempt to molest me was made, and I withdrew the brigade, at a walk, from the city, bringing off my prisoners."[23]

Leaving Martin's legion, supported by two of Hart's howitzers, to secure the summit of the Catoctin Mountain gap through which the National Road ran, Hampton moved his command toward Hagerstown via Middletown. The next morning, McClellan's advance guard overtook the new rear guard, pelting it with artillery rounds and sharpshooter bullets. Exploiting his own artillery support—shortly after the fight began, Hampton had sent him another section of Hart's battery—Martin returned fire "with good effect," forcing the enemy "to change his position more than once." As more and more Unionists crowded the National Road, Martin himself was forced to shift about until, about 2:00 P.M., his position became untenable. By then Hampton, accompanied by Stuart, had come down to direct the action. Stuart had Martin and Hart withdraw up the pike and through the mountains, rejoining the main body of the First Brigade near Middletown.[24]

As Hampton expected, the Yankees followed. An officer in Colonel Baker's First North Carolina, which covered the retrograde, looked back in wonder as the enemy emerged noisily from the pass and spread out in long lines of advance: "The road from the gap we had just left, clear down to the last line of foot-hills near the village [Middletown], was one dark serried column of all arms of the service pressing on our track. The near clash of hoofs, the clatter of dangling sabres, the accelerated whir and rumbling of artillery wheels, and jangling of chains and the low, shuffling sounds of infantry tramping, told [us] that our energetic foe would soon be upon us again, and it seemed rash presumption, with our insignificant force, to attempt to stand in its way."[25]

But Baker's men, supported by the rest of the brigade, did stand. The position Hampton had selected atop the hills overlooking Middletown was so well chosen, and his men—sharpshooters, skirmishers, and cannoneers—held it so stubbornly, that despite his manpower advantage McClellan could not clear the roadblock until close to sundown. Only when nearly surrounded did Hampton retire, Martin and Hart marching up the pike in the direction of

Boonsboro, the rest of the brigade heading southwestward toward Jefferson, where Stuart wished it to link with Munford's troopers.

The day's fighting left Wade Hampton in an ebullient mood, "both officers and men [having] conducted themselves to my perfect satisfaction. They were exposed to a severe fire of artillery and musketry, which they bore without flinching, nor was there the slightest confusion in the ranks." Stuart, who had closely observed Hampton's disposition and leadership, reported himself just as pleased with the outcome. His newest subordinate was learning the ropes of cavalry combat more quickly than might have been expected of one still in mid-transition from a less mobile style of warfare.[26]

Hampton's heroics were not over. Close to nightfall, as he approached Munford's position near Burkittsville, he discovered, along a parallel road off to his left, two regiments of blue-clad horsemen. Before the Confederates could react, the newcomers spurred across the intervening fields as if to strike the rear of the moving column. Before the blow landed, Hampton ordered the last unit in line, Pierce Young's Cobb Legion, to wheel about and meet charge with countercharge. Within minutes, Young's men were spurring back up the road, swords in hand. A saber charge was not the preferred tactic of Confederate cavalrymen, most of whom, when required to fight at close quarters, resorted to pistols and even shoulder arms. As a recent transferee from the infantry, Hampton had no prejudice against swordfighting—in fact, he favored its use in most tactical situations—and he had communicated his preference to the men he led.

As the opposing forces collided, Hampton led the rest of his command, via a half-circle through the woods that shielded it from enemy view, against the left flank of the bluecoats. One participant later observed that prior to Hampton's arrival, the contest between the Cobb Legion and its assailants— the Eighth Illinois and Third Indiana Cavalry, of the brigade of Brig. Gen. Alfred Pleasonton—had "wavered furiously back and forth over the disputed ground in doubtful struggle." Hampton's attack, however, decided the outcome almost immediately. Seconds later the Federals broke and fled in the direction they had come.[27]

From the wounded that Pleasonton had left behind, Hampton estimated the Yankees had suffered thirty or forty casualties, almost three times as many as his men had absorbed. And yet the Confederates had lost, at least temporarily, some outstanding officers. The highest ranking was Pierce Young, who had taken a gunshot wound in his leg and several saber cuts about the face and head. The lieutenant colonel had also lost several teeth when thrown from his dead horse. One of Young's ablest subordinates, Capt. Gilbert J. Wright, was also rendered hors de combat with a serious wound in the arm.

After caring for the wounded and interrogating his prisoners, Hampton pushed on to Burkittsville and his junction with Munford. The trip proved hazardous, but not because of the proximity of McClellan's infantry. For some reason, Munford, whose brigade was covering the approaches to Crampton's Gap in the South Mountain chain, had not been notified of Hampton's approach on the road from Middletown. Misinformed by his scouts, Munford mistook the newcomers for Yankees and prepared to blast them with Capt. R. Preston Chew's battery of horse artillery. Chew's gunners, lanyards in hand, waited tensely for the horsemen to come into effective range. As Munford later reported, "nothing was required but the word 'fire' to be given." At the last minute Hampton, riding in the vanguard, deduced what was about to happen. Frantically he fashioned a white flag, which he waved so conspicuously that Munford withheld the deadly order.[28]

Thankful that he had not triggered a storm of shell and canister, Hampton compared notes with Munford, coordinated their respective dispositions, then bedded down for the night within supporting range of Crampton's Gap. Stuart joined them there the next morning, September 14. Leaving Munford to hold the pass alone against McClellan's approaching infantry (the colonel would soon be reinforced by one of Jackson's infantry divisions under Maj. Gen. Lafayette McLaws), the Beau Sabreur led the First Brigade to the river at Knoxville. In that area east of Harpers Ferry, Hampton's men spent the rest of the day picketing the width and breadth of Pleasant Valley. Later in the day, after McClellan's advancing legions finally thrust Munford and the infantry away from Crampton's Gap, Hampton's men brought up McLaws's rear as the latter moved to support Jackson at Harpers Ferry. Thanks partially to McLaws's presence on Maryland Heights, above the town, the entrapped garrison surrendered to Jackson before noon on the fifteenth.[29]

After conferring with the victor at Harpers Ferry, Stuart, at Jackson's direction, left Hampton early on the sixteenth and rode north to Sharpsburg, a village west of Antietam Creek and east of the meandering Potomac. There Stuart rejoined Robert E. Lee, who had halted to offer battle to his slow but relentless pursuers. There, too, Stuart reunited with the army leader's nephew, Fitz Lee having returned from an unsuccessful effort to gain McClellan's rear.

Stuart and Fitz were thus available to take part in the limited fighting of the sixteenth and the full-scale battle the following day, which generated 13,700 Confederate and 12,400 Union casualties, making September 17, 1862, the bloodiest single day in American history. One reason for so much carnage was that on this day, as at no other time during the campaign, both armies were close to full strength. Lee's force included the greater part of Jackson's command, which, screened by Hampton's troopers, had made a brisk march to the battlefield from Harpers Ferry. Then, too, the antagonists were prepared to fight to the death: Lee had his back to a nigh impassable river, and McClellan was desperate to end the invasion and reclaim his reputation as the savior of the Union.

Although Hampton started north in company with Jackson, his brigade did not reach Sharpsburg until the afternoon of the seventeenth, by which time the orgy of blood was in full swing. Apparently he did not make direct contact with Stuart, who had taken position on the Confederate left, or upper, flank. Hampton was posted to the other end of the battle line, where Munford's troopers joined him late in the day. In that sector the cavalry saw little action beyond skirmishing on behalf of Jackson's infantry and supporting his artillery. Hampton never went on record as regretting his inability to add to the day's horrific casualty list.[30]

When the fighting finally guttered out, the antagonists appeared equally exhausted but also equally unwilling to quit the field. Late on the eighteenth, Lee was finally persuaded that his position was too precarious to hold any longer. Grudgingly, he began to cross the Potomac into the lower (i.e., the northern reaches of the) Shenandoah Valley.[31]

While Fitz Lee's troopers covered the fording, Stuart selected Hampton for a more dangerous and perhaps more critical mission—a diversionary maneuver in the face of the enemy. His choice of the South Carolinian suggested that he had come to trust, perhaps even to rely on, his coadjutor's leadership. For his part, Hampton vowed to validate that trust. The operation got under way early in the evening. Supplementing the First Brigade with one of Munford's regiments plus an infantry outfit and two howitzers, Stuart led the mixed force on a roundabout route to the north and east. Under cover of darkness, everyone crossed the river at a little-known ford and, once on Virginia soil, looped northward. When opposite enemy-held Williamsport, twelve miles above Sharpsburg, Stuart returned Hampton's men to the Maryland side. At the same time, the regiment detached from Munford's brigade splashed across farther south, and the infantry and artillery fired on the town from the opposite bank.

The dual crossings cut off several pickets and secured Williamsport. Additional prisoners were taken during the next two days as Hampton's men, who had occupied the river bluffs at Williamsport, demonstrated loudly toward the upper flank of McClellan's army. The racket attracted a growing number of the enemy; by early on the twentieth Stuart and Hampton confronted a full division of infantry. Late that day, having been assured that the army had safely crossed, Stuart called everyone to the far side of the river.[32]

By then Hampton, for one, was entirely willing to leave. In common with many of his troopers, he considered the invasion of Maryland a strategic miscalculation, devoid of lasting advantage—devoid of everything, in fact, except hard marching and heavy loss. He would have concurred in Stuart's published assessment of the trials and tribulations experienced by the Cavalry Division, Army of Northern Virginia: "During the Maryland campaign my command did not suffer on any one day as much as their comrades of other arms, but theirs was the sleepless watch and the harassing daily *petite guerre*. . . . There was not a single day, from the time my command crossed the Potomac until it recrossed, that it was not engaged with the enemy." Moreover, the service those troopers had rendered had been "indispensable to every success attained," regardless of how few those successes appeared in retrospect.[33]

Once back in the Old Dominion, Stuart guided his men to a point west of Harpers Ferry, where John Brown had launched his slave uprising, and around Charles Town, where "Old Ossawatamie" had paid for his crime on the gallows. While his troops picketed the Potomac shore, the Beau Sabreur established headquarters at the Bower, the plantation home of the Dandridge family, close friends of his. In that pleasant venue midway between Charles Town and Martinsburg, he and his staff spent the next several weeks enjoying, as William Blackford phrased it, "the most remarkable combination of romance and real life that it had ever been my fortune to encounter." Stuart, "as conspicuous as a leader in a ballroom as he was on a field of battle,"

enjoyed days of partying and parlor games with the Dandridge sons and daughters, and nights of music and dancing.[34]

Such pursuits, however genteel, failed to appeal to Wade Hampton, who spent most of his time with his troopers near Martinsburg, keeping watch over the Yankees beyond the river, wondering if they would ever gain the courage to cross and offer battle. Presumably, he visited the Bower at least once or twice—if not to confer with his superior, then to avail himself of one of the local attractions: the Dandridge estate was surrounded by woods abounding in wild game, including white-tailed deer.[35]

The gaiety of life at the Bower came to a sudden, if temporary, halt on October 9. That morning, in response to Robert E. Lee's request that a body of his cavalry operate against McClellan's rear supply lines, Stuart assembled at nearby Darkesville and Hedgesville a picked force of eighteen hundred. Hampton's complement, which rendezvoused at Hedgesville, consisted of 650 troopers culled from Baker's First North Carolina, Butler's Second South Carolina, Davis's Tenth Virginia, and Lt. Col. W. W. Rich's Phillips (Georgia) Legion, a recent addition to the brigade. Those men drawn from the other brigades in Stuart's command were temporarily under new leaders. With Tom Munford on detached service, Col. William Edmondson "Grumble" Jones had assumed command of the Laurel Brigade, while Rooney Lee had taken the place of his cousin Fitz, who had been disabled by a mule kick. Four cannon, two each under Pelham and Hart, were selected to accompany the raiding force.[36]

When around the rank-and-file, Stuart was closemouthed about his objectives, but Hampton and the other brigade chiefs learned early on that their destination was south-central Pennsylvania. A railroad bridge that crossed a creek north of the Cumberland Valley town of Chambersburg formed a critical link in McClellan's communications network. Were this bridge destroyed, Little Mac would have to get his supplies via the overburdened and vulnerable Baltimore & Ohio. Stuart planned to make that prospect a reality.[37]

The expedition got off to a promising start, suggesting that McClellan was too preoccupied or too lazy to counter it in strength. After daylight on October 10, the vanguard of Hampton's detachment splashed across the Potomac near McCoy's Ferry, seven miles west of Williamsport, and on the other side put to flight a large body of pickets. As soon as the Maryland side was secure, Stuart turned the column toward the Pennsylvania border, only eight miles away. Hampton and his men, who occupied first place in the marching order, proceeded north while casting glances to right and left as well as ahead. They had no idea if enemy troops lurked nearby. They knew only that McClellan's army covered a wide expanse of the Potomac—the laws of probability favored a sudden encounter with some part of it.

But the laws failed to hold. About 8:00 A.M., the column crossed the National Road, where it seized the occupants of a small outpost. The prisoners disclosed that several regiments of infantry, with two cannon, had passed through the area, heading west, about a half hour earlier. In fact, the raiders encountered no roadblock short of their objective, the result of a belated and almost comically inept pursuit by cavalry under Pleasonton and Brig. Gen. William W. Averell. Other would-be pursuers may have been frightened into immobility by exaggerated reports of the size of Stuart's force.[38]

The trail to the Pennsylvania border, which the raiders crossed about ten o'clock, was so clear and the marching pace so unhurried that Hampton had time to take careful note of the mechanics of the operation. Raiding was a new experience for him, but he surmised that its success depended to a great extent on speed and mobility, the salient characteristics of cavalry warfare in general. To maintain both, presumably, a raiding force had to travel light. Ironically, as he would learn, eighteen hundred riders constituted an unusually large, and therefore somewhat unwieldy, column. Overall, however, speed was less important than the ability to gain and maintain the element of surprise, especially during the critical early hours of the march. Stuart had seized the advantage when he dashed across at McCoy's Ferry and captured the guard there. Time would reveal if he could preserve it.

About noon, the column rumbled into the farming village of Mercersburg, ten miles southwest of Stuart's destination. The raiders lingered only long enough to impress from local farmers horses they decreed suitable for cavalry and artillery service. Frightened by Stuart's coming, the townspeople put up little or no resistance. Hampton thereby observed another advantage of a surprise movement. Lacking timely notice of the enemy's approach, civilians could neither spirit away their possessions nor offer effective resistance to their confiscation. Thus unimpeded, the troopers availed themselves fully of the local hospitality. As an example, almost every member of the Second South Carolina supplied himself with boots from a footwear manufactory on the edge of town.[39]

Leaving Mercersburg as abruptly as they had entered it, the raiders pushed on northeastward, their pace slowed by intermittent rain. A couple of hours after dark, the column neared Chambersburg under sodden skies. Hampton, still in the vanguard, approached warily, aware that word of his coming would have raced ahead of him—aware, too, that Chambersburg was large enough to mount a sizable body of home guards. At his order, now-Colonel Butler, with a detail from his regiment, entered the town under a flag of truce. Met by a delegation of local officials, Butler demanded Chambersburg's unconditional surrender, explaining that if his order was complied with, his men would lay a light hand on the place. The town fathers happily assented, whereupon Hampton's main body followed Butler through the dark streets to secure strategic sections of Chambersburg. Hampton established a strong provost guard that prevented—or at least limited—acts of plunder and pillage. By this action he impressed many of the locals, including the editor-politician Alexander K. McClure, who later praised the "respectful and soldierlike manner" the South Carolinian displayed throughout the occupation.[40]

Demonstrating his growing confidence in his second in command, Stuart appointed Hampton "military governor" of Chambersburg. While the raiding leader oversaw the occupation of the surrounding country as well as the effort to wreck the railroad bridge, Hampton spent that night and also the following morning trying to fulfill the secondary and tertiary objectives of the expedition. These encompassed relieving local banks and stores of as much gold and greenbacks as possible and rounding up citizens of prominence to be escorted south and used as hostages against the release of political prisoners in Union hands. Through no fault of Hampton's, neither venture was markedly productive but he accomplished enough to prove that a real effort had been made to comply with Stuart's orders.[41]

Meanwhile, the impressment of farm and dray horses continued. A large quantity of edible livestock—cows, pigs, chickens, geese—also found its way into Stuart's forage wagons. Despite Hampton's best efforts, some unauthorized seizures took place: Several citizens were robbed of their valuables and the few who dared to resist were beaten or pistol-whipped. Hampton was philosophical about these lapses—a certain amount of excess was to be expected of any foraging operation. Then too, while morally indefensible, the pillaging served as partial payment for the more numerous, more diabolical crimes perpetrated by the occupiers of Virginia and her neighbors in rebellion.

After an uncomfortable night in a rain-soaked bivouac, Hampton and his men prepared to accompany Stuart out of town on the morning of the eleventh. Shortly before departing, the raiders ransacked a line of government warehouses on the edge of town, which furnished many ill-clad raiders with

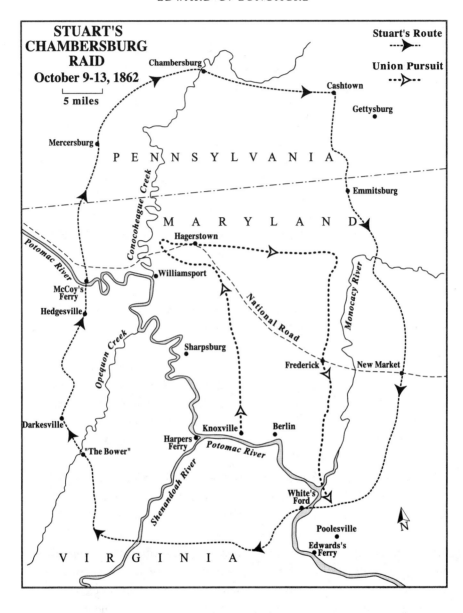

STUART'S
CHAMBERSBURG
RAID
October 9-13, 1862

5 miles

Stuart's Route

Union Pursuit

Chambersburg
Cashtown
Gettysburg

Mercersburg

P E N N S Y L V A N I A

Emmitsburg

Conocoheague Creek

M A R Y L A N D

Hagerstown

Potomac River

Williamsport

National Road

McCoy's
Ferry
Hedgesville

Monocacy River

Opequon Creek

Sharpsburg

Frederick
New Market

Darkesville

Knoxville
Berlin

Harpers
Ferry
Potomac River

"The Bower"

Shenandoah River

White's
Ford

Poolesville

N

Edwards's
Ferry

V I R G I N I A

protection against the wind and chill of October, mainly in the form of spanking-new overcoats of Union blue. As the eastward march resumed, this time
in the direction of a seemingly nondescript little village named Gettysburg,
Hampton's rear guard—Butler's outfit, plus a detachment of Baker's First
North Carolina—torched the warehouses and any supplies that remained.

Stuart's adjutant general estimated the resulting damage at one million dollars. Baker's men also burned the local railroad depot near the point at which details had wrecked a long stretch of track.[42]

These acts constituted the extent of the damage inflicted on local targets of military value. The destruction of the strategic bridge over Conococheague Creek had been entrusted to Grumble Jones, but his Virginians had been duped by local citizens into believing that the span was built of wrought iron and thus was impervious to the axes and crowbars they carried. Aware that the expedition had failed in its primary objective, Hampton vowed that when and if he conducted such an operation, it would be based on better planning and more accurate intelligence.

The return to Virginia, via Cashtown, Pennsylvania, and points south, was almost as leisurely as the journey to Chambersburg. The vigilance of Stuart's scouts and outriders enabled him to bypass Frederick and other places occupied by enemy forces capable of causing him trouble. Assuming that he faced the same lack of opposition as he had encountered on his Chickahominy Raid, the cavalry leader determined to encircle McClellan's spread-out army for the second time in four months, returning to home base by riding across the enemy's rear and around his left flank.[43]

The lack of pursuers, in addition to determining Stuart's return route, drove him to risk-taking. That evening, his column wound through Hyattstown, not far from Urbana, the site of recent merriment. As if he were already home free, in the wee hours of October 12, Stuart, accompanied by some of his aides, rode to the home of a lady friend with whom he had shared several dances during the "Maryland Ball." Hampton did not record his reaction to this unplanned side trip, but it can be assumed that he did not approve of it. In all likelihood, he would have regarded it as a reckless indulgence, an unseemly display of ego and perhaps also libido, and another example of Stuart's disconcerting penchant for mixing pleasure with duty.[44]

Yet the interlude seemed to do no harm. The only resistance the column encountered occurred as it prepared to cross the Potomac into Virginia late the following afternoon. Three forces that had been alerted to the raiders' movements—a fair-sized body of cavalry under Pleasonton in Stuart's rear, a cordon of pickets along the river in his front, and a brigade of infantry near Beallsville, beyond his left flank—attempted to converge on him before he could cross at White's Ford, northwest of Poolesville.

Miscommunication, a lack of coordination, the timidity shown by all involved—especially Pleasonton—and the blue coats worn by many Rebels, which confused their pursuers at a critical juncture, combined to save the raiders just when their capture appeared imminent. At the eleventh hour, almost every Confederate made it across the stream. Hampton claimed that his main body "passed over in perfect safety and without the slightest confu- sion." His rear guard, however, reached the Virginia side only by desperate rid- ing. A detachment of Butler's South Carolinians barely avoided being surrounded as they raced to the river and splashed across under cover of Hart's guns, with Yankee missiles whistling overhead.[45]

To some participants, the hairbreadth escape may have seemed a fitting ending to a bold and daring enterprise. And yet Hampton and many of his men may have wished that their superior had not cut the margin of error so thin. One or two more loping jaunts through enemy territory with little or no regard for the enemy's countermovements and Stuart's command might cease to exist as a viable entity.

SIX

"We have stirred up the Yankees greatly."

Hampton gave the excursion into lower Pennsylvania mixed reviews. On the whole it had been, he believed, "well managed." Stuart's force had outperformed three bodies of pursuers, on whom they had inflicted several casualties, at the cost of a single raider wounded and two others captured. They had seized and brought back dozens of Yankee soldiers; thirty citizens, at least some of whom had value as hostages; and no fewer than twelve hundred horses. These were accomplishments no other expedition of the war had to its credit, not even the celebrated jaunt along the Chickahominy.

Still, certain features of the operation did not please Stuart's senior lieutenant. He did not appreciate the skin-of-one's-teeth return to Virginia, and he suspected that, for all the damage they had done to railroad tracks and warehouses, they could have done more to harm and discomfit McClellan. He did not wholly approve of his superior's decision to ride across the rear of the Army of the Potomac, as if daring the Yankees to stop him. On the other hand, he was impressed by the audacity of the undertaking and the aplomb with which Stuart carried it out.

The many hardships endured without complaint—especially the seemingly endless hours in the saddle—entitled every raider to the thanks of his leader, although Hampton was not certain they would get it. He believed that Stuart was predisposed to "give all the credit to the Virginia Brigades," while overlooking the accomplishments of the participants from the Deep South. It was a complaint Hampton would lodge, loudly and frequently, over the next year and a half.[1]

Upon returning to base and divesting himself of his plunder, Stuart returned to the Bower for another round of balls and parties. The emphasis on extracurricular activities continued to draw his subordinate's disapproval. While Stuart enjoyed himself, Hampton led his troopers back to Martinsburg, where they monitored the movements of the Yankees across the river. The prosaic duty lasted two weeks; it ended in the last days of October, when McClellan's army finally showed signs of stirring. In response to an anticipated advance by its ponderous but powerful enemy, on the twenty-ninth the Army of Northern Virginia began to move from the lower Shenandoah into central Virginia. The next day, McClellan completed the river crossing he had initiated three days earlier, and the stage was prepared for a confrontation somewhere north of the Rappahannock.[2]

Robert E. Lee's primary intent was to get a part of his army below that sluggish stream before the Yankees could strike him. He moved briskly south with Longstreet's command, while Jackson remained in the Valley to observe, and if possible to obstruct, McClellan's movements. Stuart's horsemen were also committed to the blocking mission. Early on October 30, while Jones's Virginians took position in the rear of Jackson's infantry, Stuart moved toward the enemy via the Loudoun Valley, a verdant sanctuary circumscribed by the Blue Ridge on the west and the Bull Run Mountains on the east. He rode at the head of Fitz Lee's brigade (temporarily under Col. Williams C. Wickham, later to give way to Tom Rosser) and the horse artillery of John Pelham. Hampton's men remained near Martinsburg, ready for more active duty once the unfolding campaign assumed definite shape.[3]

Stuart's job, to slow the Federals' progress as much as possible, could only be accomplished by besting the cavalry screening McClellan's vanguard. The barely competent Pleasonton led the largest body of horsemen, but many others followed the highly capable Brig. Gen. George D. Bayard. Of late, both forces had demonstrated aggressiveness, spirit, and staying power, indicating that as a whole Stuart's opponents—their inept performance in pursuit of the Chambersburg raiders notwithstanding—were coming of age. Given the quantitative advantages they enjoyed in manpower, horseflesh, weaponry, ammunition, and equipment, this qualitative increase was a source of continuing unease to Stuart.

Soon after he moved against the enemy, Stuart notified Hampton to stand

ready to join him. The possibility that the advancing Federals would inter-
pose between the two bodies of horsemen, now thirty miles apart, prompted
Hampton to head south, planning to meet his superior near Upperville, in
the heart of the Loudoun Valley, by November 3. In the interim, Stuart
embarked on three days of skirmishing in the northern reaches of the valley,
engaging Pleasonton and Bayard at Mountville, Middleburg, Union,
Piedmont, and Paris.[4]

By late on the third, having gotten the better of his opponents in every
encounter, although not by a wide margin, the Confederate cavalry leader dis-
patched a part of Rosser's command to the foot of the Blue Ridge, to link with
Hampton near Piedmont Station on the Manassas Gap Railroad. Intervening
Federals prevented the junction that Stuart envisioned, but early on the
fourth Hampton reached Linden Station, just west of Piedmont, where he met
D. H. Hill's division of Jackson's command. Stuart rode there to confer with
Hampton, whom he instructed to cross the mountains and meet Rosser at
Barbee's Cross Roads.

Leaving the Phillips Legion to support Hill's infantry, Hampton made for
Barbee's, arriving late that evening. The next morning he took position on
Stuart's left flank outside the crossroads village, while Rosser's brigade held
the right and Pelham placed his guns on high ground overlooking the
probable route of enemy approach. Thus prepared, Stuart engaged the
Federals beginning at 9:00 A.M. Through the rest of the day, fighting swirled
around and beyond the crossroads, punctuated by long-range sharpshooting as
well as saber and pistol attacks and close-quarters combat.[5]

At the height of the action, Stuart heard that the enemy was gathering in
his rear near Warrenton, blocking his path to the Rappahannock. To avoid
entrapment, he ordered a pull-out. Hampton cleared the area via Flint Hill,
Rosser farther east via Orlean. The withdrawal was successful, although
Hampton's rear guard, a detachment of the First North Carolina under Lt.
Col. James B. Gordon, was overtaken and roughly handled by Pleasonton, suffering more than twenty casualties. Some of Stuart's officers blamed Hampton
for Gordon's pummeling. It would appear, however, that Gordon was
responsible for the unfortunate outcome, having turned on his pursuers only
to be lured into an ambush by several times as many Yankees.[6]

If one Tarheel regiment had erred this day, another had distinguished itself.
When, during the retreat from Barbee's Cross Roads, Stuart reached Orlean
in company with Rosser, he learned that the report of Warrenton's occupation

had been false. Union cavalry had attacked the town, but had been repulsed by a recent addition to Hampton's brigade, the Second North Carolina. On November 6, Stuart augmented the North Carolinians with some of Rosser's men, who, although eventually forced out of Warrenton by the reinforced enemy, withdrew in good order to Stuart's newest destination, the upper bank of the Rappahannock.

The withdrawal to the river was facilitated by Hampton's main body, which, after reaching Flint Hill, continued southwest, seeking a good point from which to guard Stuart's left flank. Eventually Hampton laid out a defensive perimeter running south from Gaines's Cross Roads to Sperryville, then east to Amissville. Late in the day, enemy horsemen probed parts of this line. Attacking near Gaines's Cross Roads, they were beaten back by the Cobb Legion, whose men, as Stuart noted in his after-action report, "behaved with great gallantry." Evidently, despite Hampton's fears, the general could be gracious toward Georgians.[7]

By sundown, with a large portion of Stuart's division and Longstreet's entire command dug in below the Rappahannock, the effort to slow McClellan's return to the Old Dominion was nearing an end. What appeared to be the final action of the operation occurred on the seventh, when an accumulation of Union cavalry and infantry forced Hampton to abandon his perimeter and retire to the river.

But the campaign was not quite over. When a large enemy force concentrated near Amissville, Stuart, believing his left flank in danger, determined to dislodge it. He planned to use both of his brigades on hand, but he advanced with only Rosser's. For unknown reasons, Hampton was not alerted to the movement until too late to take part. Apparently the fault was not his for the incident brought him no censure. Without his assistance, however, Stuart's blow was easily parried and he had to neutralize the threat by withdrawing from it.[8]

The success McClellan's army achieved at Amissville proved neither memorable nor satisfying. Later that day Little Mac learned that he had been replaced as commander of the Army of the Potomac by one of his subordinates, Maj. Gen. Ambrose Burnside. To be sure, numerous acts of commission and omission figured in his downfall, but near the top of the list were the two circuits Stuart had made of his army, first on the Peninsula and then in Maryland. Both raids had been personally embarrassing to McClellan as well as damaging to his reputation, but it was the second, in which Wade Hampton had figured so prominently, that caused Abraham Lincoln to lose faith in the man he had chosen to lead the forces of the Republic to victory.[9]

Having studied the technique of the supposed master of the raid, Hampton prepared to try his hand at the business. He eased into it by conducting a couple of medium-range reconnaissance missions. On November 16, following Robert E. Lee's receipt of a report that Warrenton was being evacuated, Stuart directed Hampton to scout west of the town, near Orlean, to determine if the intelligence was accurate. It was. Additional information gathered by Hampton's scouts, coupled with similar findings by the troopers of the now-healthy Fitz Lee, convinced the army leader that McClellan's successor was hustling down the Rappahannock River as if heading for Richmond. By the nineteenth, Lee began to shift Longstreet's newly designated First Corps in the same direction—its destination was Fredericksburg, across the river from the Army of the Potomac's new station at Falmouth. At approximately the same time, Lee recalled Jackson's Second Corps from the Valley to Fredericksburg, a movement not completed until December 2.[10]

Burnside's advance to the lower Rappahannock—which, unbeknownst to Lee, had begun on the fifteenth—marked the start of a fast-moving offensive against the Confederate capital. Burnside might well have reached the city before Lee did but for the fact that upon his arrival at Falmouth he found the now-bridgeless river impassable. Delays in obtaining a pontoon train from Washington proved fatal to Burnside's plan, immobilizing his army until Lee could secure a lodgment on the south bank. What the frustrated commander would do next, now that he had lost the race, was anyone's guess. All that was certain, as Hampton wrote his family, was that Burnside's "quick march to Richmond has been stopped, and he will find trouble before he reaches the city."[11]

Although the bulk of Burnside's massive army confronted Lee across from Fredericksburg, the Union commander maintained a picket line that stretched far to the north and west of Falmouth. The desirability of probing the far end of that line prompted Hampton to launch his second reconnaissance. On the blustery morning of the twenty-seventh, he left his recently established camp at Brandy Station on the Orange & Alexandria Railroad at the head of 174 troopers culled from the ranks of the First North Carolina and the Cobb, Jeff Davis, and Phillips Legions. The column crossed the upper Rappahannock at Kelly's Ford, one of the more accessible points on that stretch of the river, and proceeded east over frost-covered ground toward Morrisville. Late in the day, when nearing their destination, Hampton's scouts learned that a large body of Yankee cavalry was picketing two local roads that led north toward Warrenton. Darkness prevented the Confederates from striking the main picket camp till morning. That night everyone slept—or tried to sleep—without the fires that would have warded off the November chill but also given away their location.

Roused from their cheerless bivouac next morning, the troopers followed Hampton along a woods trail that ran between the roads the enemy was picketing. Upon reaching a strategic location, Hampton had his men strike right and left simultaneously. Charging through the camps of the startled enemy, one detachment bagged a squadron and a half of Yankees almost without resistance. A little farther along the picket line, the second force attacked, surrounded, and captured twenty other sentries. The combined haul amounted to five officers and eighty-seven enlisted men, plus two flags, one hundred horses, and dozens of carbines and pistols—all taken without the loss of a single attacker.[12]

The prisoners were so numerous and Hampton had to detach so many men to guard them that he lacked the manpower to attack other picket posts in the general vicinity. But he had done enough already; after returning to Brandy Station with his prizes, he found himself fairly awash in high-level praise. Stuart lauded the South Carolinian and "his gallant command" for pulling off such a "handsome affair." Robert E. Lee officially expressed his pleasure not once, but twice, on the second occasion declaring of the operation: "The manner in which it was conducted, and the energy and courage displayed by General Hampton and the officers and men under his command . . . are deserving of high commendations." Other tributes flowed from the pens of Hampton's own troopers. More than a few considered the operation the greatest feat of arms thus far in the war. One man, who preferred understatement to hyperbole, observed, "General Hampton has recently troubled the Yankees very much."[13]

The success he had achieved on his reconnaissances persuaded Hampton that he was ready to try long-distance raiding. He delayed only long enough to make a thorough inspection of horses and riders, culling out those he deemed unable to withstand fast travel and hard fighting in severe weather. Among other things, the survey showed that the strength of his command had been severely depleted over the past two months. One reason was that Stuart had restructured the division (which again included Jones's troopers, released from attachment to Jackson's corps) by forming a fourth brigade, which he assigned to the newly promoted Brig. Gen. W. H. F. Lee. Rooney Lee's command consisted not only of two new regiments of Virginians, but also of two outfits transferred from Hampton's brigade, the Tenth Virginia and Second North Carolina.

At present, Hampton also lacked the Jeff Davis Legion, which had been temporarily attached to Longstreet's corps. Although he regained the unit late in November, he soon lost Colonel Martin, whom he replaced with the highly competent J. Frederick Waring. Hampton would be at least partially compensated for these losses: Before year's end, Col. John Logan Black's First South Carolina Cavalry would report for duty at First Brigade headquarters, boosting the command to almost two thousand officers and men.[14]

Despite the recent detaching, Hampton retained enough manpower to make a success of raiding. He was concerned, however, that he lacked sufficient horses. Dozens had broken down from overwork in the weeks following Sharpsburg, many of them during the hard riding to and from Chambersburg. The recent snap of cold weather had played hob with the health of those mounts that had survived the raid. Then, too, the army was so lacking in veterinary facilities and the country in which it served was so bare of provender that, once lost, equine health was almost impossible to restore. "The country is exhausted," Hampton wrote Mary Fisher on November 22, "and I do not see how we are to live." The thought raked to life the lingering resentment he harbored toward his superior: "General Stuart never thinks of that; at least as far as my Brigade is concerned. He has always given us the hardest work to perform and the worst places to camp at. My numbers are already greatly reduced by our hard service, and I fear there will be no chance to restore our horses to condition."[15]

The criticism that Hampton leveled at Stuart from time to time was not always accurate or fair. While it is true that Stuart sometimes displayed favoritism toward his fellow Virginians, there is no evidence that he deliberately neglected the other men and units under his command. The burdens and hardships Hampton described were shared by every officer, enlisted man, and horse in the commands of Fitz and Rooney Lee and Grumble Jones. They were also shouldered by the Yankees across the river.

By all indications, Stuart made a conscientious effort to ameliorate difficulties and make conditions livable for all concerned. In fact, less than a week after Hampton put his latest complaints on paper, the division leader granted his request to establish south of the Rapidan River a camp for recruiting the health of his brigade's mounts, one operated according to "such regulations . . . as will insure the steady return of the convalescent horses to duty." In the long run, this rendezvous would have a beneficial effect on Hampton's command, although it would also ensure that a certain number of troopers—at times, a large number—would linger there, miles from their regiments and the fighting front, waiting for their mounts to recover from ills including spavin, glanders, "grease-heel," and "hoof rot."[16]

For Hampton, the raiding season opened in the second week of December 1862 with a return to familiar territory. His scouts reported that the Dumfries area, which the Yankees had not occupied in force, had nevertheless become an assembly point for the wares of sutlers—civilian merchants licensed to sell to the armies. Dozens, if not hundreds, of wagons filled with all manner of supplies to be delivered to Burnside's troops had been parked on the outskirts of the town as well as farther north at Occoquan. Because the conveyances were privately owned and operated, the army had detailed few soldiers to guard them, making them a tempting target to all but the least enterprising Confederate cavalryman.

Hopeful of supplying his troops from the enemy's larder, Hampton left Brandy Station early on the tenth in company with 520 "thinly clad and scantily fed" troopers—members of the First North Carolina, First and Second South Carolina, and the Davis and Cobb Legions. It took two long, chilly days to reach the Potomac, but by the morning of the twelfth the raiders were within striking distance of a region well known to many of them. A few miles shy of Dumfries, Hampton divided his command between his most trusted subordinates, Butler and Martin, the latter on his next-to-last mission under Hampton. The brigadier directed Butler to attack the outpost from the north, while Martin supported him by deploying his troopers on all sides of the town.[17]

The simple plan worked to perfection, thanks to the energy and efficiency displayed by all involved. Butler's ferocious assault at the head of the First North Carolina, the Cobb Legion, and his own regiment resulted in the quick capture of fifty guards and two dozen sutlers' wagons. Meanwhile, Martin's reserves gobbled up numerous would-be escapees and fended off attacks by bands of neighboring pickets.

Unwilling to linger so near to enemy territory, Hampton gathered up his spoils, burned two wagons found to be too rickety to make a long journey, and headed home. Despite his encumbrances, he moved quickly enough to evade pursuit. By the morning of the fourteenth, the wagons and the people captured along with them, including several luckless merchants, were under guard in Hampton's camp preparatory to conveyance to prison in Richmond. The spoils provided Hampton's command with warm clothing, horse tack, and equipment of all kinds, as well as enough edibles to last more than a week.[18]

Again, Hampton had successfully completed a risky mission without the loss of a single trooper. Again, too, official praise descended upon him and his troops. General Lee believed the operation reflected "great credit" on all involved, while Stuart lauded the raiders' "activity, gallantry, and cheerful endurance." Yet, as if he considered his accomplishments somehow inadequate, no sooner had Lee and Stuart spoken than Hampton was preparing his men for a return to the Occoquan River country.[19]

The new mission, launched on December 17, involved one hundred members of the First South Carolina, eighty from the Phillips Legion, seventy-five each from the First North Carolina and Second South Carolina, and sixty from the Davis Legion. The size of the expeditionary force, only two-thirds of its predecessor's, ensured a faster marching pace. Crossing the river at Rappahannock Bridge upstream from Kelly's Ford, the column rode long and hard through the wintry day. Next morning it approached the town of Occoquan from the southwest, en route seizing every outpost along Neabsco Creek as well as two well-stocked commissary wagons.

Again dividing his force, this time into three detachments commanded by himself, Lieutenant Colonel Martin, and Maj. William G. Deloney of the Cobb Legion, Hampton attacked Occoquan from as many directions. The multipronged offensive not only gave the raiders access to the contents of several local warehouses but also enabled them to capture every picket on the three roads (a total of twenty) and a supply train belonging to Maj. Gen. Franz Sigel's Eleventh Army Corps, overtaken while crossing to the north bank of the Occoquan.

Sigel's train was a real prize, but snaring it was no simple matter. Backed by strategically placed sharpshooters, Hampton had the wagons returned to the lower bank, a difficult operation made even more difficult by a shortage of rafts and ferryboats. Problems mounted when, during the recrossing, a body of Yankee cavalry came down from the general direction of Alexandria—Hampton had been told that twenty-five hundred Alexandria-based Federals were marching his way, intent on halting his depredations. Yet his sharpshooters not only repulsed the interlopers but also propelled them into headlong retreat.[20]

Eventually Hampton, too, was forced to withdraw, without bringing off all the spoils. Credible reports had a larger enemy force endeavoring to cross the river some miles away and gain his rear. To avoid being cut off, Hampton departed the area accompanied by only twenty wagons of supplies, perhaps one-fifth of the captured train. While a rear guard under Colonel Martin held back the Yankees who showed up—they proved to be fewer than Hampton had feared—Colonel Black escorted the wagons homeward. At first, the Federals mounted an aggressive pursuit, but they retired once Martin's men caught up with the rest of the column. Thereafter, the raiders experienced no serious opposition on their journey to the Rappahannock. By the twentieth, they had escorted inside their army's lines the well-stocked wagons, 150 prisoners, thirty stands of rifles, and another regimental flag. Also in tow were a number of civilians—this time not sutlers but Occoquan River Unionists of wide notoriety, including John Underwood, whom Hampton described as "a noted Abolitionist and traitor."[21]

Again the accomplishments of Hampton and his men, magnified by the harsh conditions under which they had ridden and fought, received favorable publicity throughout the army. This time the chain of official commendation extended to Richmond, where the new secretary of war, James A. Seddon, lauded both the mission and the way Hampton had described it in official dispatches: "A very gallant affair and modestly reported. To be remembered in estimating merit for promotion."[22]

This time Hampton vied with his superiors in distributing praise among his troops. His after-action report included mention of more than the usual number of worthies—not only Martin, Black, and other subordinates but also three members of the brigade staff, Captains Barker and Lowndes, and Lt. T. Preston Hampton, aide-de-camp, the newest addition to Hampton's

Lt. Thomas Preston Hampton,
Wade Hampton's second son

military family. All three officers, Hampton declared, "were with me" throughout the operation "and assisted me materially." This marked the first time he had singled out for recognition a subaltern as low ranking as his son. The gesture appeared to indicate nothing more than a large helping of paternal pride.[23]

The reconnaissance of November 27 and the expeditions of December 10–13 and 17–20 had taken a heavy toll of the units involved. "My men are pretty well worn out, by their recent raids," Hampton told his youngest sister. "This sort of work is very hard. . . ." Yet he knew how much the provisions captured on the Occoquan meant to his command, which a member of the First North Carolina, writing in early December, described as "half naked and Barefooted." At least for a time, some of those hardships were relieved by what Hampton called "all sorts of nice things, Christmas presents sent by the Yankees to their friends in the Army."[24]

Those gifts, and the consternation their seizure had caused among the enemy, left Hampton self-satisfied almost to the point of cockiness. "We have stirred up the Yankees greatly of late," he informed Mary Fisher in a Christmas Day letter, "and they swear that my raids shall be stopped. But I shall teach them, that it is hard to catch me, on the ground I know so well. . . ."[25]

Recently the Yankees had been taught another lesson, to their undying regret. During December 11–13, as Hampton headed for Dumfries, Ambrose Burnside had surprised his enemy (and his own army) by crossing the Rappahannock on his long-delayed pontoons and offering battle outside Fredericksburg. Three weeks too late, he had decided to execute his on-to-Richmond strategy. From their now-impregnable positions southeast of the city, the riflemen and cannoneers of Longstreet and Jackson blew apart a suicidal succession of attacks against various sectors of their eight-mile-long line. By sundown, nearly thirteen thousand Federals had fallen dead or wounded; many lay on the frosty earth throughout the night. In stark contrast, the defenders had suffered fewer than fifty-four hundred casualties. Finally persuaded that a golden opportunity had turned to dross, Burnside suspended his offensive and on the evening of the fifteenth withdrew all able-bodied troops to the Falmouth side of the river.[26]

Although Pelham's horse artillery had distinguished itself along the

Confederate right flank, the main body of Stuart's division had seen little action in the great battle. Animated by the thrill of victory, the Beau Sabreur was reluctant to put his men into winter camp without striking the enemy another blow, physical and moral. Studying the results of Hampton's expeditions along the Telegraph Road, he told himself that more spoils could be gathered from that fertile country, which continued to be guarded inadequately. By Christmas Day, Stuart had become convinced that yet another raid in the Dumfries-Occoquan area, one that featured a heavier force than any Hampton had commanded, would cap off perfectly a year's worth of victories by the Army of Northern Virginia.

Robert E. Lee agreed, with the result that on the bracing morning of December 26, almost two thousand troopers and four artillery pieces under Stuart, Hampton, Fitzhugh Lee, and Pelham crossed the river at Kelly's Ford. Once the pickets on the north bank had been captured or dispersed, Stuart led the way northeast to Morrisville, then due north to the crossroads hamlet of Bristersburg, where the expedition spent the night. In line with Stuart's timetable, Hampton roused his slumbering troopers and artillerymen before dawn on the twenty-seventh and put them in motion, for the third time in a month, toward the Occoquan River.

In planning the operation, Stuart had selected an approximately equal number of men from his three brigades on hand (the fourth, Grumble Jones's, had remained in the Shenandoah). Now the Confederate leader sent each of these bodies in a different direction. Hampton moved directly to Occoquan, while Stuart accompanied Rooney Lee on a more southerly route with the intention of striking the warehouses near Dumfries. To guard the lower flank against outlying detachments of Burnside's army, Fitz Lee headed for Chopawamsic Creek, about four miles below Dumfries. If he found no Yankees in that vicinity, he was to sweep northward to assist the other columns as needed.[27]

Stuart hoped for a repeat performance of Hampton's raids, but with a bigger payoff. He intended to ransack wagon trains and supply houses, not in a single locality but in two or three areas at the same time. He figured that the objects of Hampton's attacks would have been restocked by this time and perhaps added to. His secondary mission was to deplete the Union outposts between the Potomac and the Rappahannock by forcing them to detach heavy pursuit forces.

From the outset, however, nothing went according to Stuart's plans. Hampton started out in good style, moving his 870-man column rapidly toward its objective despite poor roads, broken terrain, and plunging temperatures. At Cole's Store, about a mile from Occoquan, his advance encountered a picket post manned by the Seventeenth Pennsylvania Cavalry, a new and inexperienced regiment that guarded the port village and its stores. Hampton attempted to entrap the pickets, preventing them from spreading an alarm to their comrades farther east. But although his brigade should have been intimately familiar with the area, the twenty-five-man party he sent to gain the enemy's rear took a wrong road, alerting the Pennsylvanians to Hampton's coming and permitting them to escape unharmed.[28]

A second trap that Hampton set when he reached the outskirts of Occoquan also failed to close. Entrusting the better part of his command to Calbraith Butler and leaving it west of town with instructions to attack at a certain time, the brigade commander led 260 members of the Jeff Davis and Cobb Legions south of Occoquan to cut off the garrison's escape. When Butler launched his assault, he swept all before him. A North Carolina officer riding with the colonel observed that "after a few sharp cracks [of rifle and carbine fire] they broke and fled, the whole column in full pursuit after them, chasing them through Occoquan, killing, wounding, and capturing twenty-five. . . ." The problem was that Butler had attacked before his superior was in a position to exploit his success. The panic-stricken Pennsylvanians fled so precipitately out the other end of town that Hampton could only watch as they disappeared into the early-evening darkness a few hundred yards south of him.[29]

The enemy's escape was bad enough, but after assembling his troopers in the town, Hampton discovered that it contained few supplies worthy of confiscation. His earlier raids had cleaned out the local quartermaster depot, which, contrary to Stuart's expectations, had not been replenished. This was not the extent of the expedition's failure. When Hampton moved south to rejoin Stuart, he learned that the cousins Lee had fared just as poorly as he had. Not only had they found the recently reinforced garrison at Dumfries too strongly held to take by storm (it had been bolstered, Stuart decided, "in consequence of the numerous descents upon that road by General Hampton"), but the provisions they intended to confiscate had been spirited away a few hours before their arrival. A frustrated Stuart aborted his attack and withdrew, but only after suffering several casualties. His spoils amounted to a handful of prisoners and a small train of sutlers' wagons pulled by some sorry-looking mules.[30]

Foiled in attacking his major objectives, the expeditionary leader considered returning home in defeat. Hampton's thoughts on the matter are not known, but considering his fruitless efforts thus far, the worsening weather, and the fact that in attacking Dumfries from a distance Stuart had expended most of his artillery ammunition, the brigadier probably would have endorsed his superior's thinking. Yet when Stuart decided, instead, to push on in the hope of making something worthwhile of the operation, Hampton dutifully took his place at the head of the northwestward-heading column.

The raiders forged onward into the teeth of an icy wind but also toward the receipt of good news. En route to Brentsville, Stuart met a civilian who had been long seeking him. The man reported that a substantial body of Federals—it proved to be a mixed force of infantry, cavalry, and artillery from the division of Brig. Gen. James White Geary—was moving toward the raiders from the north and east. The intelligence acted like a tonic on Stuart, who surmised correctly that these were pursuers sent down from the lines outside Washington. Just when it appeared that his expedition was bereft of meaning, he had forced the enemy to commit troops to run him to earth. And some of them were foot soldiers—as if they had a prayer of overtaking him![31]

Stuart communicated his restored energy and renewed purpose to his subordinates. Hampton responded by hustling his main body up the road toward the advancing Yankees. At Stuart's direction, he left behind Butler's regiment, which was shunted cross-country to Bacon Race Church. At the old campsite of the Hampton Legion, the Second South Carolina would form a flanking party that would lash the enemy from the west while Hampton and his associates attacked in front.

Again, however, Butler and Hampton failed to coordinate operations, although neither appears to have been at fault. When within a mile of Bacon Race, Butler encountered Geary's mounted pickets, whom he attacked and forced into retreat. Energetically but impetuously, the colonel pursued the fugitives. When rounding a bend in the road, his advance came under a destructive fire from dismounted cavalry and horse artillery that had lain in wait for his regiment. After taking some casualties, Butler fell back, dismounted a squadron or two, and had their men exchange rifle and carbine fire with the enemy. Recalling Hampton's plan, he listened intently but in vain for the sounds of fighting to the east that would indicate the brigadier's involvement with the enemy's main body.

Convinced that something had gone awry, Butler called in his skirmishers and broke contact with Geary's troops. He withdrew by a circuitous route that eventually brought his outfit to the road on which Hampton was supposed to have advanced to the attack. But the only force in the area was the rear of Rooney Lee's brigade. Butler followed Lee, finally catching up with Hampton along the Occoquan.[32]

There Butler learned that Stuart had diverted Hampton from his rendezvous near Bacon Race by moving him farther north in company with the rest of the raiding force. Stuart's action had displeased and concerned his senior subordinate, who naturally felt responsible for the safety of Butler's regiment. In fact, in his official report Hampton implied that by this action Stuart abandoned the Second South Carolina to its fate. He quoted his superior as declaring that after the rest of the raiding column moved on, Butler should return to it "if he could, or retire to camp if he was not able to join us." Neither Stuart not Hampton disclosed whether a courier had been sent to inform Butler of the change in plan. In his own report, Stuart roundly praised the colonel for extricating his outfit from trouble. Even so, it appears that Stuart's decision to abandon the two-pronged attack without notifying Butler created hard feelings that persisted long after the expedition ended.[33]

Hampton seems to have faulted Stuart for acts of commission as well as omission. When the main body left the point where Stuart met his civilian informant, Fitz Lee, leading the column, discovered two regiments of Union cavalry across his path. After Stuart answered a question from his favorite subordinate with a smile and a nod, Lee led his old First Virginia in a charge that routed the enemy. A running fight ensued, as Fitz, with his entire brigade, pursued the fugitives to and across Selectman's Ford on the Occoquan, a distance of five or six miles. When the Yankees tried to re-form on the opposite bank, Stuart chased them away for good. At his order, Rosser's Fifth Virginia forded the shallow, rocky stream under fire, followed by those of Pelham's guns that still had ammunition—a dangerous maneuver, the necessity of which may have been lost on the conservative, pragmatic Hampton.

The Beau Sabreur topped off his suddenly successful expedition with a characteristic flourish, a piece of theatricality that, to Hampton's sensitive nose, may have reeked of excess. Leaving the north side of the Occoquan late that afternoon, the raiding leader directed his column toward Burke's Station on the Orange & Alexandria, only a few miles from the Washington defenses. At that depot he not only saw to the destruction of track and rolling stock but entered the local telegraph hut, appropriated the instrument, and entrusted it to one of his troopers, an experienced telegrapher. Via this man Stuart was able to monitor message traffic to and from the capital, much of it concerned with efforts to overtake his raiders. The general chuckled at reports of pursuers moving hither and yon, in some cases dozen of miles from his route of march. Tiring of this amusement, Stuart had the wires cut, but not before he sent a message of his own, addressed to M. C. Meigs, Quartermaster General of the Union Armies, "in reference to the bad quality of the mules lately furnished, which interfered seriously with our moving the captured wagons."[34]

Then he and his men were off, heading north to challenge the pickets around Fairfax Court House and, when that proved a bad idea ("we were saluted with a heavy volley from the enemy's infantry, posted in their breastworks"), he turned toward the Rappahannock with his plunder. After a frigid night's bivouac, the raiding column reached the Confederate lines via "easy marches." By New Year's Day, Stuart was back in his headquarters outside Fredericksburg, while farther upriver the troops of Hampton and his colleagues were resuming the picket duty they had suspended six days earlier.[35]

Examining the results of the raid, Hampton rendered another mixed review. Again, the cavalry had supplied itself with provisions that would help it remain healthy in winter quarters. The spoils, however, paled in comparison to those Hampton had secured on his earlier forays. The participants had demonstrated tremendous spirit and determination throughout the expedition, even when they seemed unlikely to accomplish anything of lasting value. Yet they, and especially their mounts, had suffered terribly from overexertion and harsh weather. As Hampton reported, "I lost several of my horses, broken down by the long march. . . . many of them are rendered unfit for service."[36]

The raiders had cut many of the communication lines—the roads, railroad tracks, and telegraph wires—that linked Burnside's army to Washington. Yet the damage would be repaired in a few days. They had brought back dozens of prisoners, but had they captured hundreds more they would not have erased the enemy's huge advantage in manpower. Stuart may have added another feather to his raider's cap, but he had acted precipitately in some situations, risking undue harm to his command. The raid had once again pointed up his penchant for grandstanding, behavior that more conservative soldiers like Hampton found boorish and immature.

And yet, on the whole, the expedition had been an exhilarating experience for all involved, primarily because of the risk it entailed, the potential for disaster that lurked at every turn. Hampton could not deny that this mode of warfare—not only raiding, but the myriad other exciting, larger-than-life aspects of cavalry service—made a man feel animated, alert, engaged. In so many ways, it outshone the mundane, predictable life of the foot soldier.

Presumably because he felt this way, Hampton failed to take up Robert E. Lee on an offer the army leader extended to him one week before Stuart's so-called Dumfries Raid got under way—an opportunity to return to the infantry as commander of the South Carolina brigade formerly led by Brig. Gen. Maxcy Gregg, killed at Fredericksburg. "When I proposed your transfer to the cavalry," Lee reminded him, "I understood you, in giving your assent, to say that you did not desire it to be permanent."[37]

But Hampton had changed his mind. He desired the transfer to be permanent. By now he had won his spurs on several fields and, despite some misgivings about the brand of warfare Stuart practiced, he had come to think of himself as a cavalryman. He would serve as one for as long as possible, and if life and luck ran out, he would die a cavalryman.

SEVEN

"A veritable god of war"

Fredericksburg had been so decisive a victory that in after weeks the Army of Northern Virginia looked toward the future with renewed hope and, in many quarters, quiet confidence. A growing number of officers and men believed, or professed to believe, that the new year would see military triumph turned into political victory through a negotiated peace. In the ranks of the cavalry, however, the future did not appear so promising. Stuart's troopers had racked up a succession of victories dating back to the Chickahominy Raid of the previous June. Their opponents, although improving tactically, appeared no match for them; they could not keep up with the Southern horsemen, and rarely overtook them unless Stuart courted a fight. And when it came to combat, the Federals had yet to demonstrate an ability to prevail except when they enjoyed a prohibitive advantage in manpower.

Even so, clouds were hovering above the Army of Northern Virginia's cavalry. Stuart's greatest worry was the growing disparity of physical resources. From the war's outset, his enemy had been better clothed, armed, and equipped, and the mighty Union war machine continued to widen the gap. Of especial concern, the North appeared to draw on an inexhaustible supply of cavalry manpower and horseflesh, while the South could not expand its narrow population base and limited horse breeding capabilities. Perhaps the most critical factor in this unhappy equation was that the two-year period theoretically required to produce an experienced, well-rounded trooper was nearing an end, meaning that the horsemen in blue might soon be overmatched no longer.[1]

As 1863 dawned, Stuart concentrated on how to sustain the health of his finite, and dwindling, supply of horses. So many mounts had broken down during the late-autumn and early-winter campaigning that the rehabilitation camp Hampton had established south of the Rapidan was bursting at its seams. Even those horses still on duty figured to join the sick and disabled ones, the result of an acute shortage of forage throughout middle Virginia. Hundreds of farms had been denuded of their crops and thousands of acres lay untended, their owners having fled and hired hands having gone to war. Like their brethren in the other service arms, cavalrymen could live on rations hauled in from outlying parts of the state, but provender, being bulkier and harder to store, could not be transported from region to region so easily. To survive, cavalry horses had to serve in those areas where forage was available.

Hampton's oft-expressed contention that Stuart was concerned only with the welfare of his Virginians appeared to be borne out by his decision, in early January, to transfer Fitz Lee's brigade from Fredericksburg to King William County, northeast of Richmond, where forage was less scarce. Two weeks later, Stuart removed Rooney Lee's troopers from the war zone and sent them to Virginia's Middle Peninsula; they would spend the middle of winter among the farmlands of Essex County. In their absence, Hampton's command, which had seen more service over the past three months than the other brigades put together, was left to picket the Rappahannock River country, where adequate supplies of hay, oats, corn, and other species of forage were nonexistent.[2]

Predictably, Hampton protested his brigade's treatment, both orally and in writing. Never one to circumvent established procedures, he first complained to Stuart, whom he found sympathetic but unable or unwilling to help. The major general cited three reasons—later repeated by Robert E. Lee in response to an official inquiry into the matter—for leaving Hampton's men on the river: the Rappahannock was the most important theater of operations, Hampton's was the largest brigade in the division, and he was senior brigadier. In other words, as Stuart's ranking lieutenant, he enjoyed the post of honor, with all the hardships and privations it entailed.[3]

An unappeased Hampton, writing from his headquarters near Culpeper Court House, expressed his frustration in a letter to his youngest sister: "All my time and correspondence of late have been taken up in quarreling with Stuart, who keeps me here doing all the hard work, while the Virginia Brigades are quietly doing nothing. His partiality toward these Brigades is as marked, as it is disgusting and it constantly makes me indignant. I do not object to hard work, but I do object to seeing my command broken down by positive starvation. We cannot get forage, and in the course of a few weeks, my Brigade will be totally unfit for service. This is a hard case, but unless Genl. Lee, to whom I have appealed, interferes, Stuart will certainly have my Brigade out of the field before very long."[4]

But the army commander, while echoing the sympathy of his cavalry leader, did little or nothing to rectify the problem. It took a written complaint by Hampton to Jefferson Davis to spur Lee into action—a complaint that may have created some friction between the generals. When Davis contacted him about the perceived bias in Stuart's dispositions, Lee appears to have regarded the inquiry as an implied rebuke. Evidently embarrassed by the imputation of unfair treatment, he replied that the problem was bigger than Hampton made it out to be: "There has been [a] great scarcity of forage in the whole army, & it requires the greatest care of officers & men to keep the horses in condition." He added, however, that "it is my great desire to recuperate the Cavy & if I knew where in Eastern North Carolina Hamptons brigade could be better provided, [I] would gladly send it there."[5]

In the end, Hampton did not have to go so far afield to provide for his horses. Perhaps under Davis's prodding, Lee sent aides to scour Virginia for grazing land not more than a day's ride from the front. The emissaries reportedly favorably on certain quarters of the Shenandoah Valley as well as sections of the Southside, the vast area below the James River. Ultimately, Lee made plans to send Hampton's brigade, or at least a sizable portion of it, to either locale as soon as Fitz or Rooney Lee was available to replace him.

In the interim, Hampton's men continued to shoulder an onerous workload in severe weather. Late in January 1863, when the beaten but still hopeful Burnside suddenly hauled his army out of Falmouth and led it toward his enemy's left and rear, Lee and Stuart responded with alarm, realizing that two-thirds of the cavalry was in no position to halt or even observe the movement. Hampton's troopers had to fill the void. For the four days the advance continued, the officers and men of the First Brigade were almost constantly in the saddle, keeping tabs on Burnside, sending word of his movements to army headquarters, and exchanging rifle and carbine fire with the cavalry in his vanguard. Fortunately, the ill-timed offensive ended when frozen rain, sleet, and snow combined to immobilize the Federals, compel their return to camp, and end Burnside's tenure in army command.[6]

In the wake of what would become known as the "Mud March," Hampton's men returned to picketing the river from United States (or U.S. Mine) Ford, along the army's right flank above Fredericksburg, to a point above the O & A Railroad bridge at Rappahannock Station, eighteen miles to the north. The brigade had its hands full, not only patrolling the riverbank but also reconnoitering across the stream and fending off similar efforts by Union infantry as well as horsemen. On February 5 and 6, the troopers repulsed a vigorous attack in the vicinity of Grove Church, while helping foil an effort to burn the railroad bridge near Rappahannock Station.[7]

Hampton's burdens grew fewer and lighter after February 11, when Fitz Lee's brigade ended its rehabilitation on the Middle Peninsula. A couple of weeks later, Stuart finally removed the First Brigade from its long-held positions while ordering Lee's troopers to sidle downriver to cover the gap thus created. With his superior's permission, Hampton led his men well south of the firing lines, across not only the James but also the Rapidan, North Anna, and South Anna Rivers. In Southside Virginia, which had yet to feel the hard hand of war, enough provisions were available to subsist men and horses for weeks, if not months. With a collective sigh, they settled comfortably into the countryside to enjoy the respite they had feared would be forever denied them.[8]

R. E. Lee believed that Hampton could count on spending at least a month in "a region containing forage, the consumption of which would not interfere with the supplies for the rest of the army" before his presence was again required at the front. The army leader may have spoken too soon. Hampton's absence was widely decried when, in mid-March, a division of Union cavalry attacked Fitz Lee's men, who were caught without ready support. Four weeks earlier, Fitz had crossed the river and surprised General Averell's pickets near Hartwood Church, carrying off dozens of them and embarrassing the division leader and his superiors. Averell, Lee's West Point classmate, took revenge by crossing the river at Kelly's Ford, confronting Fitz near Culpeper, repulsing a charge by each of his four Virginia regiments, mortally wounding the irreplaceable John Pelham, and forcing dozens of proud Confederates into panicky retreat before darkness ended the fight. Here was a shocking illustration of how capable the Yankee horsemen were becoming—hereafter they must be considered a force to be reckoned with in battle.[9]

Quite possibly, Hampton was not saddened by Fitz Lee's plight. Defeat had a way of deflating even the most puffed-up soldier—although Hampton was far from certain it would in Fitz's case. Undoubtedly, Hampton was more upset by his inability to take part in subsequent operations on the Rappahannock, all of which were set in motion by Burnside's successor, Maj. Gen. Joseph Hooker. One of the reasons that "Fighting Joe," as the new army leader was known, had been chosen to lead the Army of the Potomac was that he had a plan for rehabilitating it, physically and psychologically. One of his most visible reforms was to upgrade his cavalry arm, not only by providing it with more and better arms and equipment but also by forming it into a separate corps, thereby increasing its strength, cohesiveness, and morale.[10]

The first major operation of the new command was a raid below the river by eight thousand troopers and horse artillerymen under George Stoneman, who had been McClellan's cavalry chief on the Peninsula. Begun in mid-April, suspended for two weeks by rain, mud, and high water, and resumed on May 3, Stoneman's operation had as its objective the severing of communication lines in Lee's rear. Its larger purpose was to support a simultaneous advance by Hooker and the main army around Lee's left and into his rear near the crossroads known as Chancellorsville, southwest of Fredericksburg. Hooker's reforms may have been of his own devising, but his strategy looked very much like Ambrose Burnside's.[11]

Fortunately for Wade Hampton's peace of mind, neither Stoneman nor Hooker achieved strategic success. Because J. E. B. Stuart considered the cavalry expedition a nuisance raid, he pursued only with Rooney Lee's brigade. He was right to do so. Stoneman inflicted miscellaneous, unpatterned damage to Richmond-area railroads and supply depots before turning back to the Rappahannock after learning that Lee had overwhelmed the irresolute Hooker near Chancellorsville during May 1–3. In no small part, the outcome was attributable to Stuart, who, by remaining with his army instead of going after Stoneman, located a path around Hooker's right flank in the Wilderness. Stuart's find enabled Stonewall Jackson to attack and flatten that flank and force the Yankees back to Falmouth in abject defeat. In the hour of its triumph, however, the Army of Northern Virginia suffered a shattering loss when, late on the second, Jackson went down with a mortal wound.[12]

As soon as Hooker's offensive took shape, Hampton's brigade had been rushed to Culpeper Court House in a belated and fruitless attempt to counter Hooker or Stoneman, or both. Its leader, however, did not accompany his command, for he was hundreds of miles from the front. Late in March, with the permission of Secretary Seddon and General Lee, Hampton had returned to South Carolina, accompanied by 150 unhorsed troopers, to procure remounts for his command.[13]

In Columbia, the brigadier had a joyous reunion with Mary, the children, and the Aunties. Yet he had been at home for only a week when duty called from Charleston, whose harbor defenses had come under attack by the warships of Flag Officer Samuel F. Du Pont. The crisis prompted him to volunteer his services and those of his now-mounted men to his old commander, Beauregard, who had been in charge of the local military department since the previous August. It is not known if Hampton made the trip to the embattled city, but if he did his help was not needed after April 7, when Du Pont's attack on Fort Sumter proved a miserable failure.

By the middle of May, Hampton and his companions had returned to Virginia on a train of boxcars filled with remounts procured in his home state. Upon rejoining the army, he was greeted by his soldier-sons, both of whom pressed him for word of the family, and by brother Frank, whom Hampton found in good health although still mourning the loss of his beautiful wife, who had succumbed to an insidious illness the previous fall.[14]

Upon reaching the front, Hampton reestablished his headquarters at Culpeper Court House. His brigade, its equine health much improved, had preceded him there from the Southside. During its several-month rehabilitation period, the command had devoured acre upon acre of farmland crops. By late April, an officer in the First North Carolina had observed that forage was now so scarce in that region "we can't remain at a place more than three or four days at a time."[15]

The return of spring to central Virginia portended a resumption of active operations. Having been gone from the front for more than three months, Hampton looked forward to the coming campaign, which appeared to offer opportunities for him as well as for his army: "A good deal more cavalry from the South are coming on," he informed Mary Fisher Hampton on May 19, "and Stuart will grab it, if he is allowed to do so. But if a Division of Southern cavalry is made here, I intend to ask for it. This will bring up the question of my promotion and I will see what ground Stuart will take."[16]

Recently, in fact, an opportunity for independent command and perhaps also higher rank had come his way, indicative of the high regard of his superiors. In late February, D. H. Hill, now commanding the Department of North Carolina, petitioned Lee to send Hampton to lead his cavalry and offering to swap Beverly Robertson for him. Months earlier, Jefferson Davis had also suggested Hampton's transfer to North Carolina, but now, as then, Lee refused, explaining that the brigadier was of greater value to the Confederacy in his present position.[17]

Hampton's reaction to Hill's overture and Lee's rejection of it remain unknown, but if the outcome disappointed him he would have contented himself with the truism that the most direct route to advancement was to excel in battle. By late May 1863, battle was imminent, for Lee had decided to launch a second invasion of the North. His intention was not only to spare Virginia from enemy occupation but also to draw Union reinforcements from the West, thereby hampering, if not canceling, Maj. Gen. Ulysses S. Grant's offensive against the Mississippi River stronghold of Vicksburg. Another factor in Lee's decision was the lure of winning a major victory on Northern soil, one that might win foreign recognition of the Confederacy and military intervention on her behalf. By late May his unfolding strategy had gained the approval of Jefferson Davis and his cabinet. On June 2, convinced that Hooker would remain quiescent at Falmouth and that no movement against Richmond from the Peninsula was imminent, Lee put his army in motion northwestward, heading toward the Mason-Dixon Line via the Shenandoah Valley.[18]

In preparation for the invasion, Lee had reorganized his army, retaining Longstreet as senior corps commander, naming Lt. Gen. Richard S. Ewell to succeed the fallen Jackson as head of the Second Army Corps, and creating a third corps under A. P. Hill. He left the cavalry's structure basically unchanged although he augmented Stuart by recalling Jones's brigade from the Valley and (no doubt with D. H. Hill's blessing) a two-regiment brigade under Robertson from North Carolina. He also borrowed two brigades of western Virginia cavalry under Brig. Gens. Albert G. Jenkins and John D. Imboden. Jenkins would meet Ewell in the Valley and screen his movement north, while Imboden would operate on the far left flank of the army for most of the campaign. The additions, minus Imboden, gave Stuart more than nine thousand officers and troopers for the invasion, a greater number than previously assigned him, even temporarily.[19]

To inspect his enlarged force in advance of the campaign and to infuse its people with an appreciation of their own strength and cohesiveness, Stuart on May 22 led his command to an open plain a mile or so northeast of Culpeper Court House, near the O & A depot of Brandy Station. There he staged a review that impressed not only the participants but also the many local folk who turned out to view it. The performance was so well received that Stuart repeated it, on the same ground, on June 5. By then Robertson's demibrigade had arrived from the Carolinas and Jones's troopers had come in from the Valley of Virginia. By then, too, Stuart had gathered at Culpeper an audience of civilian and military officials from Richmond, well-heeled planters and their families, and other distinguished guests. To mark the occasion, the night before the review, the Beau Sabreur held a ball at the courthouse, where he presided over an evening of high-toned revelry.[20]

On the parade ground the next day, the men of Jones and Robertson joined those of Hampton, Fitz Lee (temporarily under Tom Munford while Fitz recovered from a bout with rheumatism), and Rooney Lee, as well as the batteries of the Stuart Horse Artillery, now under Maj. Robert F. Beckham. For the pleasure of the elite audience, troopers and horse artillerymen engaged in mock battle, firing pistols, brandishing sabers, discharging cannon filled with blank rounds, and shouting at the top of their lungs. The spectators were enraptured. It may be, however, that at least one participant grimaced his way through the proceedings: Wade Hampton had lost none of his distaste for such play-acting, and he would have engaged in it only because he had no choice.[21]

Because Robert E. Lee, Stuart's designated guest of honor, had been unable to attend either review, Stuart staged a third performance, strictly for the army leader, early on the eighth. By now Ewell's corps was well on its way to the Shenandoah, with Longstreet's men closing up in its rear and those under A. P. Hill preparing to depart Fredericksburg. The next day, Stuart's troopers were to fall in with the main column, guarding its flanks and rear until the invasion was so far advanced the enemy could not halt it short of Pennsylvania. Foreseeing an early rise and a full day of activity, Hampton was even less enthusiastic than before about his brigade's participation. Still, the event came off smoothly, even if this time the spectators included John Bell Hood's division of Longstreet's corps. Predictably, the foot soldiers greeted the parade ground antics of Stuart's cavaliers with hoots, catcalls, and derisive laughter. If Hampton had been embarrassed by his earlier involvement, he must have been humiliated this time out.[22]

That night cavalrymen and horse artillerists, fatigued by their day-long exertions, slept soundly in bivouac on the south bank of the Rappahannock. In anticipation of an early call to saddle up, the main body of Hampton's command—minus the First South Carolina, which guarded a stretch of the river, and the Phillips Legion, which was on detached duty at Fredericksburg—had bedded down in the farm fields and meadows that surrounded Brandy Station. The brigade's picket line stretched east as far as Kelly's Ford, then south across Mountain Run in the direction of Stevensburg. Stuart's other brigades also contributed men to the picket line, but despite their numbers they failed to safeguard the sleep of their comrades around Brandy.[23]

On the morning of June 9, Stuart's troopers received their wake-up call an hour or so early, but not from their officers. At about four-thirty, they were roused by a dreadful cacophony of gunfire and shouting. Then untold numbers of Yankee horsemen came splashing across the fog-shrouded river at Beverly Ford, four miles northeast of the rail depot. The invaders, members of the corps commanded by Alfred Pleasonton and the division of Brig. Gen. John Buford, drove inland with a wild fury. They threatened not only to collapse the upper flank of Stuart's position but also to capture Beckham's artillery, which was parked beside a woodland chapel, St. James Church. Buford's was one of two mounted columns that Joe Hooker had sent to surprise and thrash Stuart, thereby forestalling what he misinterpreted as an imminent raid into the North. The Yankees had a faulty notion of Stuart's dispositions—they believed he had camped at Culpeper, where they planned to converge on him from three directions. Still, they had succeeded in catching him and his men off-guard, befogged by sleep, and vulnerable to overthrow.[24]

After recovering from the rudest of awakenings, Stuart galloped to the threatened sector, to which he also dispatched the brigades of Hampton, Jones, Munford, and Lee. A half-dressed but fully armed and wholly determined Wade Hampton followed only a few yards back, his brigade trailing out behind him across the open fields north of Brandy Station. En route, in response to Stuart's order to guard the lower flank, Hampton detached the Second South Carolina, Calbraith Butler and Frank Hampton at its head, and directed it to the depot.

Approaching St. James Church, Hampton moved to block the Beverly Ford Road. Jones's men, who had preceded Hampton's, were already furiously engaged, fighting mounted and afoot as the surrounding woods and clearings dictated. Hampton whipped his men into line of battle on Jones's right, with a phalanx of one hundred sharpshooters thrown out in front. This force he doubled when the First South Carolina joined him from Kelly's Ford. Minutes after the First Brigade's arrival, Rooney Lee's men came up to form on Jones's left. Only Munford, who was hampered by garbled orders and a lack of familiarity with the local roads, failed to reach the scene of battle in timely fashion.[25]

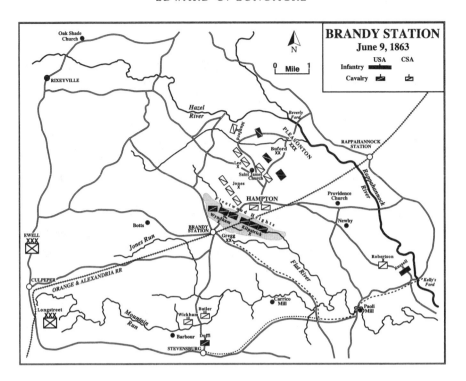

Thanks to the example of commanders such as Hampton, Stuart's rapidly expanding bulwark stood firm. Its men absorbed numerous blows from carbine fire and case shot, as well as a saber charge by a regiment of Pennsylvania volunteers, supported closely by regiments of Regulars. When the charge spent itself and the Pennsylvanians fell back, Hampton advanced part of his line to speed them along, as did Rooney Lee. The latter committed one of Hampton's former outfits, the Second North Carolina. Under the able Solomon Williams, the Tarheels cleared the road from Beverly Ford. Their success was temporary, however, for a seemingly endless stream of Federals continued to push through the trees to the front. Given the numbers engaged on each side, the fighting on Stuart's north flank seemed destined to continue for some time, its outcome long in doubt.[26]

At the height of the combat at St. James Church, the Confederates suddenly faced danger—perhaps disaster—from a new direction. Minutes after the First South Carolina left Kelly's Ford, a second column of bluecoated troopers, under French-born Col. Alfred Duffié, forced its way across at that point, dispersing Robertson's pickets. All but unopposed, the small division proceeded southwestward toward Stevensburg, to which point the Second South Carolina was now heading as well. In Duffié's rear a third column—the much larger division of Brig. Gen. David McMurtrie Gregg—cut through the frigid waters at Kelly's Ford and, upon reaching dry ground, turned north toward Brandy Station. With an air of confident determination, Gregg advanced on the rear of the Confederates opposing Pleasonton and Buford. If he struck his target squarely, Stuart's force would be caught in the jaws of a vise, one capable of squeezing it to death.[27]

Fortunately for the continued survival of the Confederate cavalry, Gregg's column halted at the base of Fleetwood Heights, a long, rugged ridge that jutted north and west of Brandy Station. The delay there, caused by Gregg's mistaken impression that the crest was held in force, enabled Stuart—belatedly apprised of the pincers movement—to turn about and counter it. At his urgent order, much of Jones's brigade, closely followed by Hampton's main body and Hart's battery, remounted and dashed south. Both commands covered the two miles to Fleetwood Heights at an extended gallop, horses and riders bounding over the rough, rocky ground; cannon, limbers, and caissons jouncing along behind; bugles squalling; guidons rippling in the breeze.

Col. Judson "Kilcavalry" Kilpatrick

The first rank of horsemen hit the north slope of Fleetwood Heights without breaking stride. Its people raced to the top, which they found covered with Yankees from the brigade of Col. Percy Wyndham. Jones's men broke into a charge, but because they lacked the time to form properly, they were unprepared for a counterblow. When Wyndham's men attacked, the Virginians went flying off to right and left. The Federals' success, however, lasted only until the head of Hampton's column thundered up the heights to the summit. The Deep South troopers struck Wyndham's flank with a force one Confederate likened to a whirlwind. Their momentum enabled them not only to hurl Wyndham's men from the crest but to slice through recently arrived reinforcements—two New York regiments from Col. H. Judson Kilpatrick's brigade—and force them back just as decisively. At that point, however, Hampton's troopers, their energy spent, were themselves vulnerable to being outflanked.[28]

This occurred as soon as Kilpatrick's First Maine Cavalry reached the crest and attacked. Quickly uprooted, Hampton's troopers streamed down the heights and at its foot raced toward St. James Church, carried along against their will by panicky horses. Several hundred yards from the point of collision, Hampton finally regained control of the column and stanched its retreat. Re-forming his disordered ranks, he turned them about and led them back to the ridge at a rapid gait, then swept up the north slope, the Cobb Legion in advance.

Regaining the summit, the Georgians slammed into the First Maine, whose men had become strung out, and forced them, slowly and grudgingly, to give ground. Under a flurry of sword blows and pistol shots at point-blank range—Hampton using both weapons to dispatch several opponents—the Yankees finally broke contact and raced off. Hampton, Young, and their men spurred after them, ensuring that Kilpatrick's brigade would not rally. They also over-ran the battery Gregg had emplaced at the foot of the ridge, killing or wounding thirty artillerymen and capturing or disabling all six of its guns.[29]

With Gregg thrust off Fleetwood Heights and Buford fought to a standstill around St. James Church, Pleasonton, at about 5:00 P.M., began to withdraw from the battlefield. Although his contemplated trap had failed to close on the enemy, the Union commander was in lofty spirits as he recrossed the river at Beverly Ford and Rappahannock Station; so too were most of his officers and men. For the first time in the war, they had engaged Stuart's cavaliers at full strength and had given them all they could handle. Henceforth, they would confront their once-invincible opponents with a winning combination of power, poise, and self-confidence.

Although Stuart later papered his command with proclamations of a great and glorious victory, few of his men were deceived. They had been taken by surprise and placed on the defensive for much of the fight, and they had held the field by a razor-thin margin. While many were loath to lay the blame at the feet of their commander, Hampton was not, although he was discreet in making his feelings known. As he wrote Stuart's adjutant general after the war, "Stuart managed badly that day, but I would not say so publicly."[30]

Hampton may have blamed a painful personal tragedy on Stuart's faulty leadership. As Gregg's division recrossed the river at day's end, Duffié's command, having been recalled from Stevensburg, closed up in its rear. Hampton was observing Duffié's withdrawal when a courier galloped up from the west with horrible news. Minutes later, an ashen-faced brigadier was accompanying the messenger at top speed out the road to Stevensburg. Learning that the Second South Carolina had established a hospital on the plantation of John S. Barbour, the general arrived there to find his brother barely alive, his face and head bloody from saber slashes, a fatal wound from a pistol ball in his body. An hour or so earlier, Frank Hampton had fallen while trying, at the head of a detachment of thirty men, to block the passage toward Stevensburg of Duffié's entire division. It had been an exercise in futility, but one that illustrated the courage and daring that had defined Frank since boyhood. Wade Hampton remained by his brother's side, clutching his hand, until, at about 8:00 P.M., Frank died of his wounds.[31]

After fighting off his grief and seeing to the disposition of his brother's remains, Hampton spent the rest of the night visiting another severely injured officer. Minutes after Frank's wounding, a battery attached to Duffié's command had unlimbered in the Stevensburg Road. It lobbed a shell at the main body of Frank's regiment, which burst near Calbraith Butler, virtually severing his right foot. While the colonel would recover from the ghastly wound, his recuperation would last almost a year.

Hampton was greatly affected by Butler's disabling, but he would never fully recover from the loss of his brother. He would take his revenge on every Yankee who crossed his path in battle, many of whom he would dispatch with saber or pistol. Nor would he ever forgive Williams Wickham, whose Fourth Virginia had been sent from Munford's sector to reinforce the Second South Carolina. Instead of coming to Frank Hampton's aid, Wickham's men had broken and fled from a charge by one of Duffié's regiments. Hampton always considered the Fourth's behavior a contributing factor in his brother's death and Butler's wounding.[32]

In the chaotic aftermath of June 9, Stuart and his subordinates counted their losses, buried their dead, patched the holes that had been torn in their ranks, and tried to ready their men for the hard work that lay ahead. They would

have the time to do all of this. Although Ewell's corps continued its movement toward the Shenandoah, Robert E. Lee decreed that Stuart should
remain on the Rappahannock until he was certain his command was fit to
join in the invasion.[33]

Thus the cavalry spent the next week on and near the battlefield while
Ewell's advance waded the Potomac River for the second time in nine
months, and Longstreet and Hill poised to start for the Valley. Hampton used
the time to inspect and reorganize his regiments, promoting officers and non-
coms to fill sudden vacancies and redistributing the horses, ammunition, and
supplies of dead and disabled troopers to their able-bodied comrades.

He devoted a part of the period to preparing his brother's body for shipment
home. It was accompanied to Columbia by Lt. Preston Hampton and a small
escort. At Governor Pickens's order, Frank's remains lay in state in the capital,
where Mary Chesnut viewed them: "How I wish I had not looked! I remember
him so well, in all the pride of his magnificent manhood." The diarist described
her fellow mourners as "convulsed with grief. In all my life I had never seen
such bitter weeping." Wade Hampton would have given a great deal to have
witnessed these demonstrations of regret and respect. Only the exigencies of
active service could have kept him so far from his grieving family and the place
where his brother was committed to the soil of South Carolina.[34]

He mourned when and where he could, but the unfolding campaign
claimed most of his attention. By the morning of June 15, Hooker's army
began to withdraw from Falmouth in response to belated reports of Ewell's
invasion of the lower Valley. The enemy gone from his front, Lee sent
Longstreet on Ewell's trail and ordered Hill to fall in behind Longstreet. Early
the next day, after the wagon trains of the army cleared the roads leading
north and west from Brandy Station, Stuart crossed the river with the brigades
of Fitz Lee (Munford still in command), Rooney Lee (led by Col. John R.
Chambliss Jr., Rooney having been seriously wounded near St. James
Church), and Robertson. At Stuart's order, the troopers of Hampton and
Jones would remain on the river until the last of Pleasonton's vedettes left
the opposite shore.[35]

On the seventeenth, Hampton, finding the coast clear, crossed his men at
Beverly Ford and, in company with Jones, trotted north. That night both
commands bivouacked outside Warrenton. The next day, two regiments of
Union cavalry—members not of Hooker's army but of the defense forces of
Washington—came down to reconnoiter the area Hampton had evacuated.

Unwilling to leave so large a force in his rear, he whirled about and sparred with the Yankees for several hours under a drizzling rain. At nightfall, he disengaged and returned to the outskirts of Warrenton, where his men spent a second, soggy evening in bivouac. One of them recalled that between the rain and the enemy who continued to lurk in the vicinity, "we did not get much comfort" at any time during the night.[36]

The next morning, Hampton's brigade—which had been increased by troops just returned from a remount mission in the Carolinas, to a total of perhaps fourteen hundred officers and men—started north to join Stuart. The general led the winding column up the east side of the Bull Run Mountains and through Thoroughfare Gap into the Loudoun Valley. In that fertile region, Virginia's horse-breeding country, Stuart had clashed twice in the past two days with some of the same Federals who had fought him to a draw at Brandy. On the seventeenth at Aldie, at the top of the valley, and farther west at Middleburg two days later, the cavalries had tilted with as much energy and determination as they had on June 9, if on a smaller scale.

At several points during those actions Stuart's troopers had taken hard knocks; they had not, however, been deterred from their primary mission, screening the right flank of the main army beyond the Blue Ridge. Late on the twentieth, when Hampton reached Stuart's headquarters at Rector's Cross Roads, midway between Middleburg and the more westerly village of Upperville, the Yankees continued to lack a firm idea of Longstreet's and Hill's dispositions.[37]

Stuart intended to keep it that way. He realized, however, that the Yankees had not given up hope of demolishing the counter-reconnaissance barrier he had erected. Thus, he warned Hampton as well as the recently arrived Grumble Jones to prepare to join in the continuing effort to hold the enemy east of the mountains. That effort began on the morning of Sunday, June 21, when Union troops—not only horsemen but foot soldiers as well—appeared east of Rector's Cross Roads, spoiling for a fight.

Stuart was not surprised by Pleasonton's addition of infantry. He realized that his counterpart was so desperate to break through to the Shenandoah, he would adopt any expedient that added staying-power to his command. At Brandy Station both Buford and Gregg had enjoyed infantry support, although the foot soldiers had not taken a major part in the fighting. Today, they assuredly would.[38]

Stuart was willing to take on all comers, but at a time and on ground of his choosing. As the foot soldiers advanced on him, their rifles spitting, he moved his main body west along the turnpike to Upperville, while sending couriers to inform other elements of his widely scattered command to move in the same direction. Seeing him fall back, the foot soldiers—members of Col. Strong Vincent's brigade of the Fifth Army Corps—raised a shout of triumph. The sound was echoed by the troopers of David Gregg, who spurred past their infantry friends up the now-empty turnpike. A light battery attached to Gregg's division began to hurl shells at the withdrawing Rebels, as if to hasten their departure.[39]

This day Hampton's brigade moved in the approximate middle of Stuart's column, followed closely by the two regiments under Beverly Robertson. Hampton's duties included safeguarding the divisional supply train, a job that prevented him from making maximum speed in the direction of Upperville. Not surprisingly, the Yankees were soon on his and Robertson's heels. Hampton, who did not appreciate being pushed, halted those units not committed to the train and announced that they were going to make a stand on the east side of town. One bystander, impressed by the determination behind this declaration, described Hampton as "calm and composed as if no battle was in progress."[40]

To strengthen his position, Hampton placed Hart's battery on a commanding ridge and had it duel the cannoneers supporting his pursuers. The men of the Washington Artillery did a valiant job of keeping back Gregg and Vincent until an incoming shell struck one of their limber chests, detonating the ammunition inside. The blast damaged a howitzer so severely that Hampton opined, "Hart has lost a gun this time." He was correct: When the cavalry moved on, the cannon was left behind—the first artillery piece Stuart's division had abandoned to the enemy.[41]

After Hart, at Stuart's order, limbered up and moved off, Hampton resumed his withdrawal. In his rear, Robertson's men attempted various delaying actions, especially along Goose Creek, two miles from Upperville, but the enemy flanked them out of one position after another. Robertson then ordered everyone to hasten to Upperville, whereupon the Federals quickened their pace as well. By hard riding, the head of Gregg's column—Judson Kilpatrick's feisty brigade of New Yorkers and Mainers—overtook Robertson's little command on the edge of the town and chased it through the streets of Upperville, inflicting numerous casualties.

Noting his subordinate's predicament, Stuart, who had reached the far end of the town, about a mile and a half from Ashby's Gap in the Blue Ridge, ordered up reinforcements. First to respond was Hampton, who turned his column about and led what had been its rear guard, Lieutenant Colonel Waring and the Jeff Davis Legion, eastward at a dead gallop. The brigadier presented an imposing sight as he closed the distance to Robertson's assailants. One onlooker described him as "seemingly angered, looking a veritable god of war" as he "drew his saber [and] . . . plunged into the charging column of the enemy."[42]

Following Hampton's example, Waring's troopers shouted a war whoop as they thudded into Kilpatrick's advance. Zeal and momentum permitted the legion to cut a jagged swath through the blue column and bring it to a halt. For several minutes, a shooting, hacking contest swirled along the eastern edge of the village, during which Hampton shot down more than a couple of opponents. Stunned by the savagery of the clash, the antagonists finally broke contact and galloped off in opposite directions.

As if also by mutual consent, both sides halted, regrouped, and added reinforcements. Minutes later, Hampton was leading not only Waring's men but also the First North Carolina and the Cobb Legion through town and into the head of Gregg's enlarged column. As the troopers grappled anew, Hart's gunners returned to the fight, shelling the rear of Kilpatrick's brigade with admirable precision. How long the close-quarters fighting lasted is unknown; but when it ended with simultaneous retreats dozens of horses and riders lay piled in the streets.[43]

For the remainder of the day, Hampton and his comrades carried on the fight at long range, much of the work being performed by Hart's gunners. The lull allowed the fighting that had been going on north of Upperville to take center stage. There, along the upper reaches of Goose Creek, Buford's Yankees had failed to skirt Stuart's left flank, defended by the brigades of Jones and Chambliss. Buford then attempted to support Gregg on the Upperville Pike, but with no more success than he had enjoyed along the creek. Yet the dismounted troopers he sent to Gregg's sector appear to have made Stuart believe he was confronted again by foot soldiers, this time at close range. Fearing the power of the infantry's rifles, the Beau Sabreur pulled Hampton's carbineers west of town and headed for the mountains that shielded Lee's infantry.[44]

By now the day was almost spent; Stuart supposed that the enemy lacked the daylight necessary to top the mountains and locate the Army of Northern Virginia. He was wrong, as Buford's men proved just before sundown. Although Stuart's cavalry and horse artillery blocked access to Ashby's Gap, Yankee scouts climbed a neighboring ridge, gained the summit, and peered into the valley beyond. In the fading light they surveyed the camps of Maj. Gen. Lafayette McLaws's division of Longstreet's corps.

The discovery appeared to be a major coup, and Buford's scouts exulted in their intelligence-gathering prowess. But the sighting had come a few days too late. By now Lee's invasion was so well advanced it could not be slowed, let alone halted—not even if Hooker barged into the Valley with his entire army and attacked with enough intensity to live up to his nickname.[45]

Hampton took quiet pride in his men's performance on the twenty-first, which, while it had cost them heavily, had dealt the enemy a more painful blow, strategically and tactically. It appeared to be a coup de grace of sorts, for on the morning of the twenty-second, Pleasonton, his cavalry, and his infantry supports drew off to the east. Their retreat enabled Stuart to move in that same direction, concentrating his still-scattered forces at Rector's Cross Roads. He spent the next five days in the village, refurbishing and resupplying his command; scouting toward Aldie, where the Yankees had gone into camp; and consulting with General Lee, who from his Valley headquarters was deciding how to use his horsemen to best advantage during the next phase of the invasion.

In quick time, Lee and Stuart developed a promising plan of action. After leaving a substantial force to guide the main army northward, Stuart was to pass east of the Bull Run Mountains and then around or through Hooker's army as it lolled in northern Virginia. If blocked by enemy forces found to be in motion, Stuart was to retrace his steps and rejoin the army. But if he found the road open, he could move on, keeping the Yankees under close observation, reporting their dispositions to Lee and, if possible, cutting their communication lines. If able to pass without hindrance into Maryland and Pennsylvania, he was to link with Ewell's infantry somewhere along the Susquehanna River. Although Stuart's critics would accuse him of being late for this reunion, no date was set for it.[46]

If Hampton had any misgivings about a plan of campaign destined to generate tremendous controversy, he failed to say so at the time. He joined the now able-bodied Fitz Lee and the other brigade commanders in endorsing Stuart's original proposal and the refinements later made to it. Much of the fine-tuning resulted from a conference between Stuart and the partisan leader John Singleton Mosby, who knew the position of Hooker's widely dispersed army and suggested a route through it.[47]

Unsurprisingly, when starting on his expedition, Stuart left behind those brigades whose leaders he relied on the least, Jones and Robertson. He instructed both men to keep in close touch with the army as it moved north, guarding the head, rear, and flanks of Longstreet and Hill. Stuart had no way of knowing that after he left, the brigades would idle well to the rear of their infantry comrades, depriving Robert E. Lee of the powers of perception as he moved through unknown territory.[48]

If James Longstreet, Stuart's immediate superior, had had his way, Stuart would have left behind a more reliable subordinate—Hampton. By now, however, the South Carolinian had become Stuart's strong right arm; the cavalry leader would not consider embarking on such an important and risky mission without Hampton by his side. Accordingly, on the early morning of June 25, Hampton and his men accompanied the cavalry of Fitz Lee and John Chambliss, plus six horse artillery pieces—a total of about forty-five hundred officers and men—toward Glascock's Gap in the Bull Run Mountains.

The first four days of the expedition were without major incident, save that almost at the outset a moving column of Union infantry blocked Stuart's path near Haymarket, precipitating a sharp skirmish. Instead of returning to the army in conformance with his instructions from Lee, Stuart forged onward according to his own plan, although by a more southerly route. The road now clear, the raiders moved on to Gainesville, Buckland Mills, Bristoe Station, and the familiar countryside around Brentsville, before turning north via Fairfax Station and bypassing the outskirts of Washington, D.C. Fording the Potomac near Rushville early on the twenty-eighth, they destroyed boats on the river and a nearby canal, while capturing and paroling the several hundred Federals the vessels had been carrying.[49]

Leaving the river, the troopers plunged into Maryland, nine months after bidding farewell to it after Sharpsburg. Coming up to the Baltimore & Ohio, they demolished track and rolling stock on long stretches of that strategic railroad. Hampton's brigade cheerfully joined in the work, although many of its men were occupied by guarding a supply train that had been bound for Hooker's army. Hard-riding members of the Second South Carolina had captured the 125 mule-driven wagons outside Rockville, Maryland, on the twenty-seventh. Although the wagons would slow him down, Stuart had been unable to resist adding them to his column. They served as proof that he had met one of his objectives, the gathering of provisions for Lee's underfed, ill-clothed army.[50]

Although various elements of the Army of the Potomac, principally detachments of Pleasonton's cavalry, had been sent to locate Stuart, the raiders encountered no opposition until they reached Westminster, Maryland, on the afternoon of the twenty-ninth. At that depot on the Western Maryland Railroad, ninety-five plucky but foolhardy members of the First Delaware Cavalry plowed into Fitz Lee's brigade, inflicting a couple of casualties before being overwhelmed and dispersed. The unexpected clash prompted Stuart to lay over in the town for the remainder of the day. The respite proved fateful, for when his column crossed into Pennsylvania the next day it encountered Kilpatrick's cavalry division on the outskirts of Hanover.[51]

Unable to avoid a confrontation, Stuart attacked the rear of Kilpatrick's column of thirty-five hundred men. The fight began as a series of small-unit actions but expanded into a full-blown battle, one that lasted most of the day. On Stuart's side, most of the fighting was carried on by the troopers of Lee and Chambliss; Hampton continued to guard the long, unwieldy wagon train in the rear. In midafternoon, elements of the First Brigade worked their way to the front to take a more substantial part in the clash, but even then, they were mainly used in a supporting role. Close to sundown, following several hours of fierce fighting, Hampton's men returned to the train and under cover of darkness escorted it around the town. As soon as the brigade cleared Hanover, Stuart, Lee, and Chambliss fell in behind it and made for the Susquehanna River.[52]

Although Kilpatrick failed to pursue, the march from Hanover was a grueling ordeal for everyone involved. Throughout July 1, Stuart pushed northward at a clip that drove horses and riders to the brink of exhaustion. The pace increased after outriders failed to locate Confederate infantry near York, an area that, according to local newspapers, Ewell's corps had recently occupied. Hearing that Ewell might have moved to Carlisle, the Beau Sabreur moved north by northwest, searching desperately for signs of gray infantry—unaware he was moving away from a place where his presence was urgently needed.[53]

Bereft of mounted reconnaissance, Robert E. Lee had stumbled into battle that morning against Hooker's recently appointed replacement, Maj. Gen. George Gordon Meade. The fighting at Gettysburg, fifteen miles west of Hanover, had begun when A. P. Hill's infantry encountered Buford's cavalry west of the town. Before the morning was over, two of Meade's infantry corps had arrived to relieve Buford, while Ewell's foot soldiers had come down from

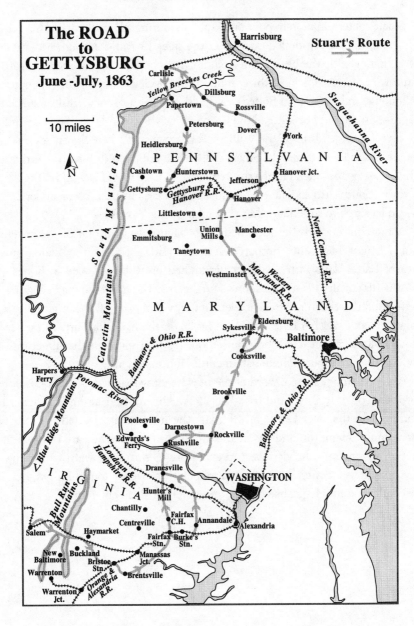

The ROAD to GETTYSBURG
June -July, 1863

Stuart's Route

10 miles

N

PENNSYLVANIA

MARYLAND

VIRGINIA

Harrisburg

Carlisle
Yellow Breeches Creek
Dillsburg
Papertown
Rossville
Petersburg
Dover
Heidlersburg
York
Cashtown
Hunterstown
Hanover Jct.
Gettysburg
Gettysburg & Hanover R.R.
Jefferson
Littlestown
Hanover
Union Mills
Manchester
Emmitsburg
Taneytown
Westminster
Western Maryland R.R.
Sykesville
Eldersburg
Cooksville
Baltimore
Brookville
Poolesville
Darnestown
Edwards's Ferry
Rushville
Rockville
Dranesville
WASHINGTON
Hunter's Mill
Chantilly
Centreville
Fairfax C.H.
Annandale
Alexandria
Salem
Haymarket
Fairfax Stn.
Burke's Stn.
New Baltimore
Buckland
Bristoe Stn.
Manassas Jct.
Warrenton
Brentsville
Warrenton Jct.
Orange & Alexandria R.R.

South Mountain
Catoctin Mountains
Blue Ridge Mountains
Potomac River
Harpers Ferry
Baltimore & Ohio R.R.
Loudoun & Hampshire R.R.
Bull Run Mountains
Susquehanna River
North Central R.R.
Baltimore & Ohio R.R.

Carlisle and York to form on Hill's left. Ewell had reached the field after a brisk march over good roads, including one that Stuart crossed twelve hours later. But by then no foot soldiers lingered in the area to inform the cavalry leader where his colleague was heading.

145

Stuart's determination to push on despite mounting adversity carried his jaded horses and their sleep-dulled riders over the steep foothills of South Mountain. Early that evening the head of the column, Lee's brigade, approached the garrison town of Carlisle, almost thirty miles north of Gettysburg. While Hampton, Chambliss, and the wagons halted near Dillsburg, southeast of Carlisle, for essential rest, Stuart and Lee entered the town, which they found occupied by a militia division under Brig. Gen. William Farrar Smith. When Smith spurned a couple of surrender demands, Stuart shelled the militia with his horse artillery, while some of Lee's men burned the venerable U.S. Cavalry barracks on the edge of town. Smith's troops offered minimal resistance, but their commander continued to refuse to surrender even after taking some casualties.

A merciful end to the one-sided affair occurred when one of the several scouts Stuart had sent through the countryside, seeking the main army, returned after dark with a courier dispatched by Robert E. Lee in hopes of finding his cavalry leader. As soon as he digested the news the messenger carried—a battle still in progress at Gettysburg, victory or defeat hanging in the balance—an upset but relieved Stuart broke off the fight and turned the head of his column about. Lee's brigade led off, trotting south in the direction of Papertown, Petersburg, Heidlersburg, and Hunterstown.[54]

As the march resumed, word of the new heading reached Dillsburg. Before 3:00 A.M. on July 2, Chambliss's brigade was in motion along a westward-leading road that met Lee's path. Finally the movement reached the rear of the column. Hampton and his men, still entrusted with the care of the ponderous wagon train, headed west, preparatory to turning toward Gettysburg, seat of Adams County, Pennsylvania, population twenty-four hundred, home of a college, a theological seminary, and an expansive cemetery.

EIGHT

"Charge them, my brave boys!"

About noon on July 2, 1863, the head of Stuart's column reached Hunterstown, five miles northeast of Gettysburg. There the sounds of combat—the bass tones of artillery, the rolling vibrato of musketry—were perfectly audible to the approaching troopers. As the long line of horsemen wended its way through Hunterstown, Stuart rode on ahead to report to Robert E. Lee. He would explain the reasons behind his belated arrival and learn how he could serve his army in the crisis at hand. In his absence, the brigades of Fitzhugh Lee and Chambliss continued to move southward, followed by Hampton and the wagons.[1]

By 2:00 P.M., the entire column, having passed through Hunterstown, had come to a halt. About a mile south of town, Hampton was sitting his horse, chatting with his subordinates, when he became the target of carbine fire from a roadside woodlot perhaps three hundred yards off. Never one to refuse a challenge, the unhurt brigadier spurred his horse toward the trees, trailed by members of his staff. When he got within two hundred yards of his assailant, Hampton discovered him to be a Federal cavalryman armed with a Spencer repeating carbine. Although the general would not learn the man's name until after the war, he was James C. Parsons, a twenty-five-year-old private of Company I, Sixth Michigan, part of the brigade of Brig. Gen. George Armstrong Custer. Two days earlier Parsons's regiment, a member of Kilpatrick's division, had tilted with Stuart's men in the streets of Hanover. The Sixth was one of several units Kilpatrick had dispersed to scour the countryside around Gettysburg for signs of the Confederate horsemen who had eluded him late on June 30.

Moving to within a hundred yards of his opponent, Hampton engaged him in an improbable duel, answering his carbine blasts with pistol shots. The antagonists fired off several rounds without result, at which point young Parsons raised his hand as if to signal a halt—his weapon had fouled, and he needed a minute to clear the bore. Ever the sportsman, Hampton waited patiently, his pistol cocked but pointed in the air, until the trooper's carbine was again in working order. But no sooner had Parsons raised it into firing position, signaling a resumption of the duel, than Hampton regained his marksman's eye. He put a ball in the trooper's wrist, sending him fleeing through the woods and ending the standoff.

Hampton quickly paid for his chivalry. While he lingered at the tree line, searching for his adversary, an officer from Parsons's regiment, Lt. Charles E. Storrs, galloped out of the woods, saber in hand, and attacked Hampton from the rear. Before the brigadier could turn, Storrs brought the flat of his sword down on the back of the general's head. Hampton's thick head of hair and his old felt hat, in which he may have carried copies of dispatches, partially absorbed the blow, preventing a fatal injury. Bellowing in pain, he turned his horse about and charged Storrs, who raced off along the edge of the woods, seeking an exit. As he followed, Hampton shouted a string of epithets, while snapping his pistol over and over again, but—due to a faulty percussion cap—to no effect. Thus spared, Storrs plunged into the trees and outdistanced his enraged pursuer.[2]

Afire with pain, Hampton rode to the rear, where one of his surgeons treated the four-inch gash on the back of his skull with a court plaster. The patient would spend the rest of the day wracked by a massive headache, but he had to fight a small-scale battle anyway. At about four o'clock, with Hampton's brigade still waiting for word to proceed to Gettysburg, a detachment of the Sixth Michigan, Custer at its head, advanced through the streets of Hunterstown and out its south side.

Supposing that the newcomers intended to attack the rear of the army at Gettysburg, Hampton took steps to hold them in check. He placed his rear unit, the Cobb Legion, across the road from town, blocking Custer's path. On Pierce Young's right he deployed Lieutenant Colonel Rich's Phillips Legion, while positioning Maj. Thomas Lipscomb's Second South Carolina on the left. The rest of the brigade, being much closer to Gettysburg, would take time to countermarch to the endangered point. Yet because the advancing men appeared to be no more than a squadron, Hampton doubted that reinforcements would be needed. He put in a call anyway, along with a request that some horse artillery be sent back from the front of the line.[3]

To his opponent's disbelief, Custer deployed his little force in attack formation. Through his field glasses Hampton could see the enemy force was even smaller than he had supposed—possibly only a single company. Other members of the Sixth Michigan had taken post, as dismounted sharpshooters, on either side of the fence-lined road. Their position was such that if they were not careful, they would do more harm to their mounted comrades than to their enemy. Hampton spied other Yankees on horseback farther north around the town itself. Evidently, Custer had reinforcements at hand but did not intend to use them. The strange situation grew stranger still when the Union leader spurred into a charge and no more than fifty officers and men followed him. With sabers and pistols upraised and shouting a facsimile of the Rebel Yell, the men came at Hampton's line four abreast, all the road could accommodate.

At Hampton's command, dismounted Georgians and South Carolinians unleashed a converging fire at a target even the poorest marksman could not miss. Predictably, men and horses went down in a heap before they reached the Cobb Legion's position, some of them felled, as Hampton had foreseen, by the fire of their badly positioned supports. One of the unhorsed riders was Custer, who escaped death only because one of the few unhurt men took him up on the back of his horse and carried him to safety under a torrent of small-arms fire.[4]

Within minutes, most of the Michiganders who had not been killed or badly wounded had scrambled for the rear. The sobering outcome, and the fact that the road was blocked by downed horses, ought to have rendered a counterattack out of the question. Perhaps because he was suffering the effects of Lieutenant Storrs's attack and thus not thinking clearly, Hampton ordered Pierce Young to charge the fleeing Yankees. It proved to be as costly a mistake as Custer's. No sooner had the Cobb Legion started up the road than its men were felled not only by carbine fire but also by shells from a battery that had been trundled into position in Custer's rear. Before Young could wheel about and dash to safety, he duplicated Custer's experience, flying over the head of his dead horse. His second in command, now-Lieutenant Colonel Deloney, was even more severely injured, being shot and sabered at close quarters. Six other officers and almost sixty men also became casualties.[5]

Repenting his rashness, Hampton recalled Young's survivors and allowed his dismounted skirmishers to carry on the fight. After a time, two cannon came up from Gettysburg to assist him—not horse artillery pieces but two 10-pounder Parrott rifles of a Louisiana mounted artillery unit, on loan from Dick Ewell. The artillery, Hampton reported, "did good service," keeping the enemy back until darkness came down. Soon afterward the fighting sputtered out, but Hampton held his position until morning, when he found the area free of Yankees. Persuaded that the Confederate rear was now secure, he finally followed Fitz Lee and Chambliss toward Gettysburg, where the outcome of the battle—and perhaps the war—remained undecided.[6]

Hampton's head was still pounding when, early on July 3, he led his column across the tracks of the Gettysburg & Hanover Railroad, then onto the turnpike to York. By now he had unburdened himself of the captured supply train; the wagons and their bountiful harvest were safely in the hands of Robert E. Lee's quartermasters. Turning left in response to orders from Stuart, Hampton's men followed Colonel Chambliss's brigade as it moved out the northeastward-leading pike under a cloudless sky. The march continued for almost an hour, the heat of the day slowly rising and the sounds of fighting at Gettysburg growing fainter in the distance.

At some point, Hampton, who was probably in the dark as to the cavalry's mission this day, must have wondered why he and his comrades—which now included Jenkins's brigade of western Virginians, under Col. Milton J. Ferguson—were moving so far afield of their army. The mystery deepened when, at a point about three and a half miles from Gettysburg, the line of march swung south. A nonplused Hampton followed Chambliss across neat parcels of farm land whose ubiquitous fences had to be thrown down, one after another, to permit the passage of horses and riders.

For Hampton, the journey ended at the northern base of a tree-fringed stretch of high ground known as Cress's Ridge. Guided into position by Stuart's staff officers, he halted and dismounted his command, then threw out skirmishers toward the south and east. A few of these he placed in support of the two cannon (later joined by several other pieces) that had unlimbered atop the ridge. Comrades on either side of Hampton's position—Chambliss on his right, the late-arriving Fitz Lee on his left—deployed in similar fashion.[7]

Colonel Ferguson's men held the far right of the line, which rested on land owned by a farmer named Rummel. Some of the Virginians had advanced as far as Little's Run, which ran south from the Rummel farmstead toward belts of timber that evidently shielded enemy cavalry. One regiment was already exchanging fire with mostly unseen Yankees near a dusty crossroads about a half-mile closer to Gettysburg. Hampton learned that the Federals were Custer's, including the same regiment that had charged his line so foolishly, and whom he had countercharged just as foolishly, at Hunterstown. Today, however, Custer's brigade was on the field in something close to full strength. Furthermore, it was supported by a couple of brigades from Gregg's division, most of whose men were ensconced in the woods around that crossroads.

Soon after Hampton's arrival, a Parrott rifle from the battery attached to Ferguson's brigade was hauled into successive positions facing north, south, east, and west. It discharged a round in each direction. No explanation was forthcoming, but some officers, perhaps including Hampton, surmised that it was a signal from Stuart to Robert E. Lee that the cavalry had gotten into its assigned position. Stuart would never explain his reasons for taking up that position. Even so, contemporary observers and latter-day historians would speculate that Lee had ordered him to assault the Union right rear at the same time as an offensive destined to be remembered as Pickett's Charge struck the front of Meade's line below Gettysburg.[8]

Perhaps because Stuart never revealed his intentions, Hampton spent much of the day reacting to enemy movements rather than taking the initiative. Under the circumstances, it is not surprising that affairs on his front—indeed, along the length of Stuart's line—were managed so poorly that, eventually, they got out of hand.

Things began to go awry in midafternoon. Around 2:30 P.M., with the temperature climbing toward ninety degrees, Ferguson's men became heavily engaged with Custer's troopers and their supports. Many of the Virginians, however, had to quit the fight in midcourse, having exhausted their limited supply of Enfield rifle ammunition. To fill the gaps thus created, Chambliss committed a part of his command, mounted and afoot, but Hampton—perceiving no opening for an offensive and with few Yankees in his front clearly visible—kept his brigade sheltered under the trees at the base of Cress's Ridge.[9]

At four-thirty, as Hampton recalled, but probably an hour or so earlier, he was summoned, along with Fitz Lee, to Stuart's field headquarters. Believing it unwise for two brigade leaders to leave the field at the same

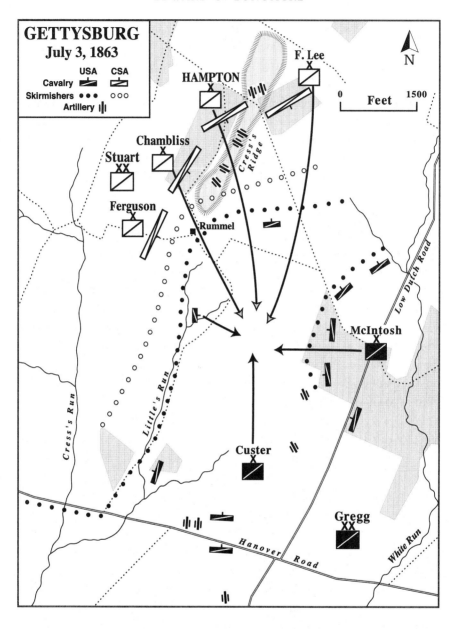

GETTYSBURG
July 3, 1863

USA CSA
Cavalry
Skirmishers ● ● ● ○ ○ ○
Artillery

F. Lee

HAMPTON

Stuart
XX

Chambliss

Cress's Ridge

Ferguson

Rummel

0   Feet   1500

Low Dutch Road

McIntosh

Cress's Run

Little's Run

Custer

Gregg
XX

White Run

Hanover Road

time, Hampton, as senior brigadier, proposed that he be the first to go, Lee
to follow suit upon his return. Fitz assented and Hampton rode off, but he
was back earlier than expected, having failed to locate Stuart. When
almost to the place at which he had left his command, he was shocked to

152

find a large part of it moving from the ridge into a wide clearing in front of the Union position.

From a source he never identified, Hampton learned that Fitz Lee had ordered the brigade to charge in support of Ferguson and Chambliss. Aware that the Yankees had placed at least two batteries near the crossroads, Hampton was concerned that his men would attract a devastating cannonade. He galloped to the head of the column, overtaking Colonel Baker, its leader, before he could order the attack, and countermanded Lee's orders. He did so too late—as he had feared, the movement had already revealed his brigade's position to the enemy, who sent a few shells in its direction. Livid with anger, the brigadier returned the troopers to their former position—"not, however, without loss."[10]

He never disclosed what, if anything, he said to Fitz Lee about his flagrant usurpation of a superior's authority. Not long afterward, however, the same thing happened again, with equally unhappy results. Minutes after countermarching to Cress's Ridge, Hampton was met by a staff officer from Chambliss, whose charging troopers had been taken in flank by an equally mobile and much larger force of Federals, just up from the crossroads. To take the heat off the colonel and permit him to disengage, Hampton sent forward Laurence Baker, with his own regiment and the Jeff Davis Legion. The reinforcements started out in good order, repulsing the nearest Yankees and facilitating Chambliss's withdrawal. To Hampton's chagrin, however, Baker pushed his advance too far. Soon he was in the same trouble as the comrade he had tried to assist—confronted by an enemy force large enough to batter him in front and flank while also cutting into his rear.

Impulsively, Hampton galloped onto the plain with the intention of guiding Baker's men homeward. How he could have accomplished this by himself is problematical, but in the end he did not have to. As he reported, while running his rescue mission, "to my surprise I saw the rest of my brigade (excepting the Cobb Legion) and Fitz Lee's brigade charging." This time the order to advance Hampton's brigade had come from his adjutant, Major Barker, who believed his superior needed reinforcing.[11]

The new advance drew a substantial response. Blue riders advanced on Hampton, Chambliss, and Lee from south and east, some at an extended gallop, sabers and pistols drawn. In the near distance, the Union cannon poured a steady fire into the head of Hampton's column, while Stuart's few guns answered, albeit with less effect. Seeing he could not avoid a collision, Hampton raised his own sword and shouted, "Charge them, my brave boys, charge them!" His brave boys responded with great enthusiasm. Within seconds, horsemen from the Carolinas, Georgia, Alabama, and Mississippi were vying with the Virginians of Chambliss and Lee in galloping toward the oncoming enemy.[12]

As they neared a collision, the adversaries appeared to increase, rather than slacken, their pace. In the middle of the open field, they came together with a resounding crash. A Union participant likened the sound to that of falling timber. The force of the impact was even more impressive: Dozens of horses went down, "turned end over end and crushed their riders beneath them." For several minutes, all was chaos; then men struggled free of the giant tangle and singled out opponents for a frantic session of thrust and parry.[13]

Coolly maintaining his seat, Hampton confronted a succession of Yankees, dispatching each with a deadly swipe of polished steel. For several minutes, as troopers shouted, horses neighed, pistols cracked, and sabers clanged, the brigadier hewed a path through the blue ranks, mingled elements of Custer's and Gregg's commands. Numerous would-be opponents, intimidated by the sweep of his broadsword, gave him a wide berth as he bulled his way forward. Suddenly, however, Union reinforcements—members of Pennsylvania and New Jersey outfits in Gregg's division—slammed into both flanks of Hampton's column. While Hampton was engaged with swordsmen in front, the new arrivals struck from his blind side. Before he could whirl about to parry the blow, a Jerseyman struck him twice about the skull, reopening the previous day's wound and inflicting new, more serious ones.

Dazed by the blows, wracked by pain, almost blinded by the blood pouring from his scalp, Hampton kneed his big bay charger about and headed back to Cress's Ridge. On all sides of him gray troopers, already reeling from the unexpected assaults on their flanks, their momentum spent amid the crush of blue horsemen, turned to follow him. They accompanied him to the rear at a moderate pace, then with increasing speed. In a matter of minutes, most of Hampton's men, as well as the majority of their comrades under Lee and Chambliss were streaming to the rear in full retreat.[14]

Even after disengaging, no rider was home free. Still-arriving antagonists galloped up and sliced through their ranks, cutting off a large portion of Hampton's command from Cress's Ridge. A woozy Hampton had to run a gauntlet of fire from dismounted Federals on his flanks as well as from the batteries to the south that were now showering the retreating troopers with shot and shell. As his horse topped a fence a few hundred yards from the ridge–an obstacle its half-blinded rider could barely make out—a piece of red-hot shrapnel slammed into his right hip. This, his fourth wound in two days, left him almost helpless, barely able to remain in the saddle. Observing his plight, a sergeant in the First North Carolina assisted him to the rear and fended off enemy troopers intent on doing him further harm.[15]

When the general reached the shelter of the trees he had been so reluctant to leave, he slumped into the arms of his staff, who put out a frantic call for the surgeon. When the doctor arrived, he saw at once that if the victim expected to survive, he would require more than a court plaster and a few minutes of rest.

Hampton's wobbly ride to the rear was a harbinger of Confederate defeat. Within minutes of his disengagement, most of Chambliss's, Lee's, and his own men were back at the starting point of their advance, many of them, like him, nursing saber slashes or gunshot wounds. Because their exhausted opponents were content to let them go, the Confederates spent the remainder of the day in the safety of the rear. There they salved not only physical injuries but also less accessible wounds—wounds to the psyche, to pride, to perceptions of invincibility. Although the antagonists had been evenly matched except in artillery strength, Stuart's troopers had been decisively repulsed—they would be in no position to support Robert E. Lee's offensive at Gettysburg.

How much the cavalry could have accomplished, had it broken through the Yankee lines, is a matter of conjecture. It is entirely possible that, even with well-timed help from Stuart, Pickett's Charge would have failed as signally as it did without his support. Forced to cross a mile of open ground exposed to cannon fire and musketry, most of the units involved in the attack were shot to pieces well short of their objective, the center of Meade's line on Cemetery Ridge. Their failure doomed Lee's plan to linger indefinitely in the North. The following day, July 4, 1863, he quit Pennsylvania for Maryland, ending his second and last foray in Union territory.[16]

Wade Hampton left the blood-soaked fields of Gettysburg flat on his back. Accompanied by a hospital steward, he rode south in one of the numerous well-stocked ambulances whose departure marked the start of Lee's retreat. He made the journey in a semiconscious state, the product not only of his injuries but of the opiates given him to dull the searing pain.

He had sent word to his brigade—now in the capable hands of Laurence Baker and attached to Fitz Lee for the rest of the campaign—that he was suffering little and would soon be back in action. One of those who believed this brave declaration rode in another ambulance: Will Deloney of the Cobb Legion, who bore saber wounds much like his superior's, although not as deep or severe. In a letter home, the lieutenant colonel described Hampton's condition as "not dangerous but painful." Those who observed Hampton as he lay bleeding, however, were shocked by the severity of his condition. John Esten Cooke marveled that a man who had been "nearly cut out of the saddle by a sabre stroke," could survive the blows he had received. Cooke lamented that "ten minutes before [his wounding] I had conversed with the noble South Carolinian, and he was full of life, strength, and animation. Now he was slowly being borne to the rear in his ambulance, bleeding from his dangerous wounds." He wondered if he would ever see the brigadier again.[17]

Frequent doses of laudanum prevented Hampton from suffering the full effect of the voyage to the Potomac. Rocking and jouncing over the broken terrain and nearly torn apart by a wind-whipped downpour, the ambulance train inflicted inhuman damage on the already-shattered bodies it conveyed. Dully, Hampton heard other patients cry out in pain and delirium, many begging the drovers to stop and leave them to die by the side of the road, others calling on comrades to end their suffering with a gunshot. But the caravan of misery kept rolling, and the ordeal continued until the column halted along the rain-swollen Potomac at Williamsport, Maryland, on the afternoon of July 5. There it would stay till the water receded or pontoons could be laid across it.[18]

The following day, the cavalry of John Buford, spearheading Meade's pursuit, attacked the ambulances and supply wagons parked at river's edge. Indicative of the severity of Hampton's injuries was his inability to take part in the train's defense, although dozens of ambulatory convalescents including Deloney helped oppose the attackers. The Yankees were put to flight thanks to the fight these men put up in spite of their infirmities and to the large number of cannon that had accompanied the train, including Hart's battery, which was serving alongside Hampton for the first time in three weeks. For another week Hampton and his fellow patients were stranded along the river, although now inside the protective embrace of their entire army. Finally, they crossed to the Virginia side on the floating bridge that Lee's engineers constructed near Falling Waters.[19]

As soon as the wagons crossed, they trundled down to the railhead at

Staunton, where the wounded were placed aboard a train bound for the military hospitals at Charlottesville. Hampton made this leg of the journey in company with his old infantry comrade, John Bell Hood, now a division commander under Longstreet, whose left arm had been shattered on the second day of the battle. By now Hampton was not only conscious but alert and increasingly able to deal with the pain that seemed to wrack his entire body, not merely his cloven skull or perforated thigh.

By the fifteenth, he was occupying a hospital cot in Charlottesville and receiving excellent care. He was able to sit up and read and write. To one correspondent he reported himself as "doing well and hope in a few days to be able to go home." Much of his hair had been shorn to enable the doctors to examine and bandage his most serious wounds. Affecting a jocular mood, he informed Mary Fisher Hampton that "my head is well, *externally*, but seems tender inside; perhaps it is only *weak*. The penitentiary style in which my hair is cut, half the head being shaven, is striking, if not beautiful. It suits all kinds of weather, as one side of my head is sure to be just right, either for cool, or for hot weather. But the flies play the mischief, as they wander over the bald side."[20]

In communicating with his sister, he made no reference to the defeat his army had suffered on enemy soil and ventured no glimpses into the future of their nation. Instead, he commented wryly on his plight ("don't you feel mortified that any Yankee should be able on horse back, to split my head open? It shows how old I am growing, and how worthless"). His one concern was for his eldest son, who was on staff duty in Richmond, recently under threat by Union troops on the Peninsula ("my heart is full of anxiety about Wade. May God in [His] mercy spare him").[21]

He was more expansive in writing Louis Wigfall. To the former Texas senator he expressed confidence that despite its repulse the army remained in good spirits and would rebound speedily from "its terrible and *useless* battle. The Yankees will be defeated if we can get at them on fair ground." His only criticism of the Pennsylvania campaign was a reference to Pickett's Charge: "We could better have stormed the heights of Stafford [at Fredericksburg] than those of Gettysburg." As to the value of, and the wisdom behind, the operation that had taken Stuart's command around Hooker and far afield of Lee, he said nothing. Nor would he ever render a public utterance on the subject. Any opinions he might have expressed in private were never recorded.[22]

If Stuart was not much on Hampton's mind, Hampton was prominent in Stuart's thoughts. Early in August, the cavalry commander wrote Louis

Wigfall that he was "truly glad to hear the favorable accounts you gave of Hampton's, [M. C.] Butler's, and Hood's wounds, and sincerely hope that all three of those glorious fellows will be in the field again for the next fight. Hampton I fear will not soon be with us. His wound[s] must have been very severe. . . ." Stuart surmised correctly; by the time he wrote, Hampton had been invalided home to South Carolina. There an examining surgeon found his wounds serious enough "to incapacitate him for military duty with his Command for at least thirty days, and it may be for a much longer period."[23]

In the bosom of his family, under the care of Mary and the family physician, he healed as rapidly as could be expected. Yet his afflictions were such that almost four months passed before he could even consider rejoining the army. Every twenty days an army surgeon examined him and requested an extension of his leave, a formality always granted, often with a sympathetic endorsement by Stuart or Robert E. Lee. At times, Hampton grew discouraged by the slowness of his recuperation. But then he would think of the longer, more painful recovery faced by Butler, with whom he kept in close touch, and he would feel fortunate that his own condition was no worse.

By late October, the numbing headaches had become tolerable, the shrapnel wound had begun to scar over, and the patient was feeling more and more like his pre-Gettysburg self. Before the month ended, he tore himself away from his family and his bountiful plantation and caught a northbound train. He reached Richmond on November 3, where he stopped at the Adjutant and Inspector General's Office to receive his assignment to active duty. A day or two later he rode a passenger coach on the Virginia Central to the front via Gordonsville and Charlottesville, where he had begun to heal.[24]

On or about November 5, he reported at army headquarters, which had been established in the vicinity of Culpeper Court House. He received a warm greeting from everyone he met, from the commanding general on down. When he repaired to Stuart's encampment on the Rappahannock, the Beau Sabreur expressed his pleasure at again having a second, strong arm on which to lean. As always, he viewed Hampton as a source of mature experience, a counterbalance to the advice he received from the younger, more impetuous Fitz Lee.

Throughout his convalescence, Hampton had kept abreast of events at the front via the newspapers and conversations with officers of his command at home on furlough. Now he was further filled in by his aides, his subordinates, and Stuart.

In his absence, the cavalry had been engaged heavily and often during the many advances and retreats of its army in the wake of its return to Virginia. In mid-July, while Hampton lay abed at Charlottesville, Stuart had driven from the Leetown area a large force of cavalry that had been threatening the army's rear. Days later, by strenuous effort, the cavalry plugged the lower gaps of the Blue Ridge, preventing Meade from pouring through and halting Lee's return to the Rappahannock.[25]

The following month, and again in mid-September, the opposing cavalries had tilted on historic ground, fighting to a bloody draw at Brandy Station and Culpeper while the Southerners fell back to prepared defenses below the Rapidan. Late in September, the increasingly aggressive Yankees of Buford and Kilpatrick returned to the attack, this time nearly surrounding Stuart's command at Jack's Shop (or Liberty Mills), on the Rapidan's north fork. At the eleventh hour, Stuart broke free of encirclement and withdrew in good order, but it had been a near thing.[26]

The September offensive, which produced the combat around Brandy Station, had resulted from Meade's discovery that Lee had reduced his army by a full corps (Longstreet's), which had been sent to assist Confederate forces in the West. The augmentation helped the Army of Tennessee win a resounding victory near Chickamauga Creek, in north Georgia. When Meade countered by sending two of his own corps (the Eleventh and Twelfth) to Chattanooga in late September and early October, Lee advanced on his depleted enemy two weeks later, driving them to the Rappahannock, and beyond. Over the next two weeks Stuart's horsemen saw action time and again. Once more they drove the enemy from the heights around Brandy Station. Near Bristoe Station on the O & A, however, the Beau Sabreur, with a large portion of his command, again avoided being encircled and crushed, this time by infantry and artillery.[27]

Over the next several days, Stuart and his infantry comrades followed Meade across Bull Run to the heights of Centreville before giving up the chase and retiring to the Rappahannock. On the return trip, Kilpatrick's division mounted an injudicious pursuit. With Fitz Lee's assistance, Stuart set a trap near Buckland Mills on the Warrenton Pike, into which the bluecoats obligingly fell. When Stuart turned round and attacked in front and Fitz struck from the flank and rear, more than two hundred Yankees became casualties. So many others fled the scene in panic that the fight became known in both North and South as "the Buckland Races."[28]

Engagements great and small did not exhaust the newsworthy events that had occurred during Hampton's absence. Beginning with preliminary planning in late July and culminating in official orders published two months later, the cavalry of the Army of Northern Virginia had expanded from a division into a full-fledged corps. The reorganization had begun as a way to standardize the size and composition of brigades, each of which henceforth consisted of no more than four regiments or legions. It grew into a means of promoting deserving subordinates who had been denied higher rank due to a shortage of suitable commands.

The redistribution of units resulted in the formation of seven brigades (reduced to six in late August, when Ferguson returned to western Virginia). The remainder was evenly divided among Stuart's senior subordinates. Hampton was assigned a division consisting of the brigades of Butler (Hampton's original brigade, led during Butler's convalescence by Pierce Young), Baker (an expanded version of Robertson's old command, now led by James B. Gordon, Baker having been severely wounded on August 1), and Rosser (successor to Grumble Jones, who while Hampton was away had feuded so bitterly with Stuart that he, like Robertson, had been banished to a far-off theater). The other division went, of course, to Fitzhugh Lee; it encompassed Fitz's old brigade, under Williams Wickham; Rooney Lee's brigade, which continued to be led by John Chambliss (Rooney had been captured while convalescing from his Gettysburg wound, and his return to the field was a matter of doubt); and a newly created brigade assigned to Brig. Gen. Lunsford L. Lomax.[29]

Those elevated to brigade command—even the pro tem leaders, Gordon and Young—had been awarded the wreathed stars of a brigadier general. Hampton was especially pleased by Butler's promotion—he only hoped his long-time subordinate returned to the field to accept it. For his part, Hampton was now a major general, his promotion dating from August 6. This was the proper rank of a division commander; Fitz Lee assumed it as well, although his appointment was of slighter later date, thus preserving Hampton's seniority. Only Stuart failed to gain the extra sleeve lace to which his position appeared to entitle him. Because the cavalry had not been expanded—even Lomax's brigade had been built from existing resources—Robert E. Lee did not consider his mounted chief deserving of a lieutenant general's appointment merely because he now led a corps. Stuart's failure to add rank appears to have been a sore point with him, although he refused to sulk or brood over its withholding, an attitude that would have won points with Hampton.[30]

For three weeks before Hampton reached the front, the armies had been rel-atively quiet, glowering at each other across the Rappahannock. Lee sus-pected, however, that at some point Meade would try to force him back to his former position south of the Rapidan. That attempt occurred on November 7. Meade's objective was a concave line of defense that Lee had erected on the north bank at Rappahannock Bridge. A late-afternoon bayonet assault by ele-ments of the Sixth Corps not only captured the position and a full brigade of defenders but also seized a supporting position downriver near Kelly's Ford. As a result, Lee called an armywide retreat to the lower river.[31]

The cavalry saw no direct involvement in the fighting of the seventh, but stood "to horse" throughout the day in case needed. It was observed that when Hampton rode to the head of his new command, his troopers cheered him long and loudly, "as almost to drown the noise of gunfire." Late in the day—even before he had time to meet with his new subordinates—Hampton led everyone south toward the army's new position. Thereupon, his division joined Fitz Lee's people in guarding the army's flanks and rear as it settled down near Orange Court House, the position it had abandoned at the outset of the Bristoe campaign.[32]

The Federals pursued to the north bank of the river. Hampton spent sev-eral days observing Meade's dispositions and guarding against a movement Stuart believed to be imminent, against the army's right flank and the com-munication lines in its rear. Stuart was so concerned about this prospect that, at his urging, Hampton detached the Laurel Brigade and moved it several miles downriver, stretching to the outskirts of Fredericksburg.

To further guard the right flank, Hampton massed the brigades of Young and Gordon near Orange Springs on the North Anna River, nine miles southeast of army headquarters. Their picket line ran north for twelve miles, as far as Raccoon Ford on the Rapidan. The men were not, however, rooted to these positions. A little over a week after Rappahannock Bridge, Hampton crossed the river with a reconnaissance party that penetrated to within a few miles of Stevensburg, scene of his brother's demise. The trip, seventy miles from start to return, pained his still-tender hip, but the payoff made his discomfort bearable.[33]

Approaching Stevensburg in evening darkness, his outriders discovered an enemy campsite, which, at Hampton's word, the entire party attacked while keening the Rebel Yell. The sleeping occupants, members of a Pennsylvania cavalry regiment with whom Hampton had tangled briefly at Hanover the previous June, awoke with a start, then fled the scene as fast as their horses could carry them. "I never saw such a complete rout as we gave the Yankees," he exulted in a letter to Mary Fisher. "The officers . . . ran off in their drawers and bare-footed, leaving all their clothes behind. The men were scattered all over the woods, and my men were chasing them about like rabbits. It will be a long time before that unfortunate Regt. can get organized again."[34]

Back on the Rapidan and North Anna, Hampton resumed the less exciting chore of guarding the army's right against a possible advance by Meade. On November 26, that prospect became a reality as the Union leader crossed the Rapidan beyond his enemy's right with the intent of maneuvering Lee out of his formidable positions to the west. Meade's superiors had been urging him to take the offensive before cold, wind, and snow suspended operations. In the West, forces under Ulysses S. Grant, the captor of Vicksburg, had recently lifted the siege of Chattanooga, while nearly annihilating the Confederates who had triumphed at Chickamauga. Meade was determined to achieve a victory of similar magnitude before being forced to confine his army to winter quarters.[35]

He hoped to surprise his adversary, thus placing him at a disadvantage from the outset. Thanks to Hampton's troopers, however—specifically, to Rosser's pickets west of the Union cavalry's crossing point at Ely's Ford—word of the advance reached Lee in good season. Suspecting that his enemy was aiming for the army's rear via two parallel routes through the Wilderness, the Orange Turnpike and Orange Plank Road, Lee quickly moved his infantry and artillery eastward. He hoped to wrest the offensive from Meade. Instead, a meeting-engagement took place next day at a forest crossroads east of Mine Run, a little stream on Lee's right flank that would lend its name to the ensuing campaign.

As the main army moved out, there occurred the first in a strange series of mix-ups between Stuart and Hampton that undoubtedly added friction to their relationship. Assigning Fitz Lee to deal with Judson Kilpatrick, whose division was threatening the Confederate left, Stuart pounded off for New Hope Church on the Orange Plank Road. As he rode, he instructed Hampton to meet him near the church that evening. For unspecified reasons, however, the advance element of Hampton's division, Gordon's brigade, did not reach the rendezvous until the next morning, the twenty-seventh. The late arrival rankled Stuart; in his campaign report, he ascribed to it the progress that Meade's First and Fifth Corps made that day toward the Confederate rear.

When Gordon's brigade, minus Hampton, joined Stuart, the corps commander took charge of it, apparently without notifying his senior subordinate. Stuart handled the brigade so effectively that the First and Fifth Corps—the lowermost of Meade's three westward-moving columns—were brought to a halt not far from New Hope Church. When Hampton finally reached the scene at the head of his old brigade, he and Pierce Young attacked afoot with such power that a portion of the Union left came apart; it was repaired with great difficulty.[36]

Presumably, Hampton's performance restored him to Stuart's good graces, if only temporarily. Through their teamwork, a critical element of Meade's offensive was held in check east of Mine Run for some hours. The time they bought Robert E. Lee enabled the vanguard of the main army to reach the threatened point. There it countered not only the First and Fifth Corps but the forces farther to the north, the Second, Third, and Sixth Corps.[37]

Early on the twenty-ninth, following a day of desultory skirmishing east of Mine Run, Stuart and Hampton became involved in another imbroglio, this clearly the result of miscommunication. Responding to an order to reconnoiter the Union left rear, Stuart prepared to join Hampton at the latter's field headquarters on the Catharpin Road, south of and roughly parallel to the Orange Plank Road. Again, the generals failed to rendezvous according to Stuart's timetable. Reaching the appointed place, Stuart found Rosser's brigade, but not Hampton, nor the rest of his division.

After waiting in vain for several minutes, a perturbed Stuart again assumed command of Hampton's forces. He led Rosser's brigade cross-country to Parker's Store on the plank road. There, deep in the woods, he came upon the lightly defended camp of David Gregg's cavalry, most of which was spearheading Meade's advance. Stuart promptly attacked; after a brief struggle, Rosser's men put the guards to flight and captured and ransacked Gregg's supply train.[38]

Word of the assault quickly spread, and soon a large body of Federal cavalry arrived, formed, and launched a counterattack. Suddenly, Stuart and Rosser found themselves hard pressed on all sides. Pressure abated only after Hampton came up with the brigades of Gordon and Young and some guns under his long-time horse artillery subordinate, James Hart. The newcomers counterattacked and soon succeeded in dislodging the enemy. Young's brigade, at the head of Hampton's column, delivered the critical blow.

Writing that night to his sister, Hampton crowed that "my old Brigade . . . did splendidly. No men could have behaved better and the movement made by them, which drove the enemy from the field was executed in the finest style. Stuart, who saw it, said he had seen nothing finer, and I was proud of my brave old soldiers."[39]

Not long after Gregg fell back, Hampton's scouts observed Yankee infantry moving toward Stuart's rear. The Confederates lingered near Parker's Store only long enough to ascertain that the advancing troops were members of Meade's Second Corps, led by Maj. Gen. G. K. Warren. The Federals appeared to be trying to slip around the lower flank of the Army of Northern Virginia and into its rear. Stuart rushed word of the maneuver to army headquarters, then "made a *detour* to the left" that enabled him to avoid contact with Warren.[40]

The intelligence relayed by Stuart prompted Robert E. Lee to dig in behind Mine Run, barring Warren's path. Warren had hoped to strike his unsuspecting enemy at 9:00 A.M. November 30, but after studying the defenses Lee's infantry had constructed the night before, he called off the attack, effectively ending the Union offensive. A frustrated Meade remained in position opposite Lee's extended flank until the morning of December 2, when he returned his army to its camps north of the river.[41]

Thus ended the Mine Run campaign, a well-crafted but ill-starred attempt to win the war in a single stroke before snow began to fall. Its failure would cost Meade unfettered command of the great Union army in the East. Before spring came in, Ulysses S. Grant would be summoned from Tennessee to Washington, to receive promotion to the revived grade of lieutenant general and to assume command of all the armies of the United States. While he would retain Meade in direct command of the Army of the Potomac, Grant would accompany that army in the field, peering over Meade's shoulder every step of the way.[42]

Victory has a way of paving over the rough spots that sometimes mar command relationships. Yet the recent difficulties between Stuart and Hampton were not forgotten so quickly. In his campaign report, which he did not send in until April 1864, Stuart several times faulted Hampton for failing to report to him on time, and he omitted the South Carolinian when citing those worthy of his commendation, a list that included not only Rosser, Young, and Gordon, but also several regimental officers and enlisted men. Hampton's report, which was briefer and less self-congratulatory than Stuart's, gave a straightforward account of the campaign as its author experienced it and remembered it. Unlike Stuart's report, Hampton's was not replete with criticism, although it mildly faulted Stuart for twice assuming direct command of the First Division without notifying its designated leader.[43]

Considering that Hampton had played a key role not only in extricating Stuart from difficulty at Parker's Store but also in detecting Warren's turning-movement, he might have gone to greater lengths to defend himself while more harshly condemning Stuart's abrogation of established lines of authority. But a gentlemen is nothing if not discreet, and Wade Hampton was nothing if not a gentleman.

NINE

"A vast difference between the old and the new"

F ollowing Meade's withdrawal, both armies settled, as comfortably as possible, into winter camp. In his present venue—his headquarters was now near Guiney's Station on the Richmond, Fredericksburg & Potomac Railroad, twenty-some miles southeast of the recent battlefield—Hampton experienced good times and bad. His habitation was a source of comfort and consolation; by the first week in January 1864, he was informing his sister that "we are fixing up our quarters quite snugly, having already put up a fine chimney to our mess tent, and I have one to my tent." When not "at home," he rode for pleasure and hunted in the local woodlands. Long rides continued to hurt his hip and made dismounting and remounting difficult, but he enjoyed the exercise. As for hunting, the area was alive with game but not with Yankees. Of the latter, "none are near me, so we have nothing to do, but to shoot partridges." By New Year's Day 1864 he calculated that almost three hundred game birds had been brought down by him and his staff during the past six weeks.[1]

Another pleasure of life in winter quarters was the occasional opportunity to socialize. Late in January, he took leave in Richmond, during which he dined, along with members of Stuart's staff, as the guest of James and Mary Chesnut. That same month he was gladdened when his nineteen-year-old daughter Sally made an extended visit to the army with a party of South Carolinians. Along with relatives of other high-ranking officers, including Flora Cooke Stuart, Sally took rooms in a local boarding house, which enabled her to see her father almost daily for the duration of her stay. At the same time she could visit her brothers, both of whom now served on their father's staff. Undoubtedly, Sally also spent time in the company of the dashing young Charlestonian she would marry eighteen months hence, Maj. John Cheves Haskell, commander of a mounted artillery battalion attached to Longstreet's corps.[2]

Winter quarters also brought Hampton his share of burdens and problems. At times he was almost overwhelmed by administrative duties, including paperwork on a scale he had not experienced as a brigade commander. "You cannot tell," he wrote Mary Fisher, "how irksome the labors of the 'office' are to me. Some times I have to sign one hundred papers and that is the most tiresome kind of writing."[3]

While his own labors were demanding, he was more distressed by the grueling operational schedule his command shouldered throughout the winter in contrast with the lighter burdens of its comrades. While the First Division remained constantly on picket along the Rapidan and its many tributaries, the rest of the cavalry appeared to idle in the rear, before being entirely detached from the army. In the second week of December 1863, two-thirds of Fitz Lee's division—the brigades of Wickham and Chambliss, plus Beckham's horse artillery—were placed in camp near Charlottesville, more than twenty miles from the front. A few days later, both brigades were removed from Stuart's authority and sent into the new state of West Virginia to counter raids on communication lines by Federal forces too large for the local commander, General Imboden, to counter. Two days after Wickham and Chambliss went west, Rosser's command was ordered to join them. The Laurel Brigade would not return to Hampton for almost five months.[4]

Hampton's subordinate, Brig. Gen James B. Gordon

The departures only increased the already numerous and onerous duties imposed on the units that remained. Now Gordon's and Young's men—with minimal assistance from Lomax's brigade, which Fitz Lee had left on the Rapidan to guard the army's left flank—had to cover almost forty miles of riverbank. The men assigned to this near-constant duty were lacking not only in weapons, ammunition, and equipment, but also in such basic necessities as rations, clothing, and bedding. In one regiment, the First South Carolina, three hundred men lacked the blankets critical to sleeping through the frigid winter nights.[5]

Perhaps worst of all, Hampton's command lacked enough healthy horses to mount an adequate picket force, let alone counter enemy movements. The root of the problem was a historic one: the unavailability of forage in the area of operations. As one of Hampton's regimental commanders observed, throughout the winter Gordon's and Young's brigades were "poorly foraged. . . . Our corn issues for nearly two months did not exceed 3 lbs. to the horse." The officer declared that "it was little better than actual starvation to our poor horses." In common with many of his comrades, he would tie his own mount to an oak sapling, "that the poor creature might eat the bark from it."[6]

The scarcity of provender was a greater problem in Hampton's ranks than in the rest of the cavalry. In mid-January, when Fitz Lee returned from his excursion to West Virginia, he temporarily disbanded most of Wickham's and Chambliss's regiments, permitting their men to subsist themselves and their mounts at home for a part of the winter. When the regiments reassembled six weeks later, Lee furloughed Lomax's brigade in the same fashion. This practice, which also allowed regiments to increase their strength via local recruiting, was not extended to Hampton's division. His Carolinians and Georgians lived too far from the seat of war to make their disbanding a viable expedient.[7]

Believing his troopers unfairly treated, Hampton complained loudly and often, but to no avail. Every suggestion save one that he proposed to Stuart as a means of lessening his division's workload was rejected. The cavalry leader disapproved allowing Gordon's and Young's brigades to remount and reequip in North Carolina, where, as Hampton noted, "forage is abundant & where they will have an opportunity not only of procuring fresh horses but of doing good service." Stuart also turned down Hampton's request that the troopers on the most extended points of his picket line be relieved by infantry. And he tabled Hampton's proposal to move Young's pickets from the lower Rappahannock to the suburbs of Richmond, where proximity to the Quartermaster Department would guarantee regular provisions.[8]

Even the one request of Hampton's that was approved redounded to his detriment, at least in the short run. Late in the winter he persuaded Robert E. Lee to recommend to the War Department that Hampton's most broken-down regiments—the First and Second South Carolina of Young's Brigade—be permitted to return to, and serve in, their home states. In exchange, Hampton would receive a new brigade composed of three large, well-appointed regiments that for the past several months had been defending their state's coastline. These outfits would be assigned to M. C. Butler, who was still a few months away from retaking the field with a cork leg in place of the limb shot away at Brandy Station. This arrangement would permit General Young, who had won his spurs as a brigade commander, to avoid demotion upon Butler's return.[9]

In the end, Jefferson Davis approved the swap and authorized its implementation. The only problem was that the First and Second South Carolina went home in mid-March, while the newcomers—the Fourth, Fifth, and Sixth—were not available for service in Virginia till the end of May. In the interim, Hampton's command had to handle its myriad duties with even fewer resources. The manpower situation worsened even more when, late in the winter, Robert E. Lee did a turnabout and permitted the Fourth and Fifth North Carolina of Gordon's brigade to return to the Tarheel State for recruiting and remounting. The Fifth would rejoin its command in time for the spring campaign, but the Fourth, upon its return to Virginia, would be assigned to duty in the Petersburg defenses instead of with Gordon.[10]

Taking into account every trial that plagued it, Hampton feared that when active campaigning resumed, his command would acquit itself poorly, through no fault of its own. "In this event," he informed his sister in early January, "I shall ask to be transferred to some other army, or I will resign. I am thoroughly disgusted with the way things are managed here, and I have no doubt but that the Yankee cavalry will be better next spring, than ours."[11]

If others had their way, he would leave the Army of Northern Virginia sooner rather than later. Back in November, Hampton's friend and former superior, Joseph E. Johnston, then a few weeks away from assuming command of the Army of Tennessee, had requested Hampton's transfer to Mississippi. Lee had rejected the petition with the simple explanation that "General Hampton cannot be spared." Two months later James Longstreet, who had been given an independent command in Tennessee and would not rejoin Lee's army for some months, wrote the Confederate adjutant and inspector general, Samuel

Cooper, asking that Hampton take command of his cavalry. Longstreet added a generous testimonial: "I have served with General Hampton in the Army of Northern Virginia and know him to be an excellent officer, and I think that he possesses all of the parts so essential in a cavalry officer." Longstreet's effort was of no avail; in rejecting it, Cooper echoed Lee's reply to Johnston: "Major-General Hampton cannot be spared from General Lee's army for this service."[12]

For his part, Hampton hoped that President Davis would transfer him to an area of operations closer to home—if not South Carolina, then some place near his other landholdings. For some months—even when the prospects appeared dim—he clung to the hope that his request to remount at least some of his regiments in the Carolinas would be approved: "If my two brigades are placed in North Carolina," he told Fisher, "I hope the Presdt. will send me to Miss. for the winter." By the early weeks of 1864, however, he came to believe that he hoped in vain. He and his overtaxed troopers would remain in Virginia indefinitely. Moreover, even in their weakened condition, field serv-ice—hard, sometimes punishing service—would be required of them.[13]

In December, Hampton had informed his family that "we are miles away from the enemy, but if he makes a raid, we will be in the right place to catch him." But being in the right place did not necessarily mean within easy marching distance of any Yankees who intended to cause trouble behind the lines. This became evident in early February 1864, when Hampton was ordered to oppose an advance up the Peninsula toward Richmond by four thousand troops under Brig. Gen. Isaac J. Wistar, the commander at occupied Yorktown.

Despite his command's debility, Hampton immediately responded to Robert E. Lee's call to assist in defense of the Confederate capital. First, he assembled a mobile force composed of every horse and rider able to move on such short notice. Then he started south at a pace fast enough, and in weather harsh enough, to be the death of underfed, weakened mounts. En route, how-ever, his fear for the safety of his capital was replaced by other emotions. He was still several miles from the city when he learned that Wistar had been turned back at Bottom's Bridge over the Chickahominy. It turned out that the commander at Richmond, Brig. Gen. Arnold Elzey, had been forewarned of the advance by a Union deserter, enabling him to unplank the bridge, strand-ing the Yankees on the south bank.[14]

A frustrated but relieved Hampton led his men back to the Rapidan, only to be summoned forth, on the same mission, a week later—Elzey had overreacted to rumors of a second attempt on the capital. Fortunately for the health of his division, Hampton refused to leave his camps until assured that an attack was imminent—an action that Robert E. Lee later endorsed. "We saved our horses this time," Hampton informed his sister. "Those panics in Richmond are disgraceful and some of the officers there should be broken"— better them than his men's mounts. He assured Fisher that despite the recent marching and countermarching, "the men are in good spirits, and if we only had horses we could do very well."[15]

But pleas for help from the capital kept coming; one of them responded to a credible threat. Late in the morning of Monday, February 29, Sergeant Shadburne, leader of the Iron Scouts, rushed word to Hampton's new headquarters at Milford Station on the R, F, & P, that a raiding force of considerable size was running loose in the army's rear. Two of Shadburne's people had observed, and later infiltrated, a thirty-five-hundred-man column led by the erratic, reckless, and ambitious Judson Kilpatrick. Having slipped over the Rapidan at Ely's Ford late the previous day, the Yankees were heading for lightly guarded Richmond, where, it was later ascertained, they intended to destroy Confederate industry and government offices, while also freeing the inmates of Libby and Belle Isle Prisons. A detached body of five hundred of Kilpatrick's best troopers, under a dashing young colonel named Ulric Dahlgren, was to cross the James River, reach the city from the southwest, and link with Kilpatrick on March 1 for a cooperative assault on the Richmond defenses.[16]

Those defenses, as Hampton was aware, were held by no more than a few hundred troops—the local garrison, under Elzey, augmented by some militia and a defense battalion made up of government clerks and mechanics. If the crisis were to be met, a contingent from Lee's army would have to retrace Hampton's steps of early January—but in even colder weather, snow having coated central Virginia.

Hampton relayed to Stuart's headquarters the information his scouts had so resourcefully obtained. He received no reply; nor did Stuart respond to either of two later dispatches from him. In fact, the cavalry chief was miles away, having started after yet another raiding column at the head of a detachment of Fitz Lee's division. Members of those regiments had recently returned to the army after disbanding. Stuart, however, was being led astray by diversionary operations far to the west of Kilpatrick's and Dahlgren's columns. George Custer, leading fifteen hundred cavalrymen, was advancing on Charlottesville, where the horse artillery of Lee's army continued to winter. Although the cannoneers would repulse Custer without Stuart's help, the Confederate leader intended to hasten the Yankees on their way home. In Stuart's absence, Hampton alone was in position to counter the much greater threat posed by the horsemen aiming at Richmond.[17]

When he finally learned in which direction Kilpatrick was moving, Hampton cobbled together a pursuit force. He pulled off the picket lines as many men and horses as could be spared—and as many as he believed could endure the hard marching that lay ahead. By early afternoon on that bone-chilling day, he was leading this impossibly small force—305 members of the First and Second North Carolina Cavalry, plus two of Hart's cannon—to Mount Carmel Church, nine miles south of Milford Station. Even as he pushed south, Hampton must have asked himself what he would do with so few soldiers if and when he caught up with his quarry.[18]

As it happened, Kilpatrick had so large a head start and the pursuit was slowed by so many obstacles, including a steadily falling snow, that Hampton failed to overtake Kilpatrick short of the capital. On the morning of March 1, the Confederates reached Hanover Court House, about a dozen miles above Richmond. At that hour, Kilpatrick was tangling with the occupants of the defenses north of the city—regular artillerists, militia, and home guards, many hunkered down behind recently erected breastworks. Cowed by the resistance of which this motley force proved capable, bedeviled by an icy rain that turned to snow and made his horses' footing precarious, and concerned that Dahlgren's party was nowhere to be found, the raiding leader quickly lost his stomach for a fight. After setting in motion a two-column dismounted attack against a key sector of the works, Kilpatrick abruptly changed his mind and ordered everyone to clear out. By early evening, he was leading his cold, tired, lost, and dejected troopers into bivouac at Mechanicsville, northeast of the city, scene of the second of the Seven Days' Battles.[19]

While Kilpatrick advanced and retreated, Hampton and his little band reached Atlee's Station on the Virginia Central Railroad. Peering south through the falling snow, the general saw the light of Kilpatrick's campfires four miles away. He decided on a plan of attack. Although outnumbered ten to one, he realized that a carefully executed assault in the snowy darkness against a sleeping enemy had a chance of succeeding—a slim chance perhaps, but one he felt obliged to take.

Lacking the time to surround the camp and doubting he could sneak up on it, he determined to rush it. Singling out the nearest of three adjacent bivouacs, he trained his artillery on it, then sent one hundred dismounted troopers to strike it, supported closely by the rest of the force on horseback. Kilpatrick's pickets detected the approach of the footmen and fired on them before they could strike home, but then Hart's guns opened, spreading destruction and chaos throughout the bivouac. Under cover of the cannonade, the dismounted men felled the sentinels while their comrades on horseback stampeded through the camp, shooting and shouting, rousting the Federals from their bedrolls.

Many raiders were shot down or captured before they could arm themselves. Those who snatched up weapons found themselves trading pistol balls and saber strokes with horsemen screeching like banshees. After recovering from the initial shock, many Yankees sought to obey officers' orders to mount and move to a better defensive position. But as one raider recalled, "just which way was the query, as it was utterly impossible to distinguish roads, points of compass or anything else" in the dark.[20]

Hampton's assault was not only frightening and deadly but also brief. As the general reported, "the enemy, a brigade strong here, with two other brigades immediately in their rear, made a stout resistance for a short time, but the advance of my men was never checked and they were soon in possession of the entire camp, in which horses, arms, rations, and clothing were scattered about in confusion. Kilpatrick immediately moved his division off at a gallop. . . ." Most of the Yankees raced northeastward toward Old Church. Some of Hampton's men pursued briefly. Realizing the impossibility of coordinating a pursuit in the dark, Hampton quickly recalled them all.[21]

At sunup, after a rest of several hours during which he rounded up and interrogated his captives and tended to the casualties on both sides, Hampton started after Kilpatrick, only to find him gone, having retreated in warm haste down the Peninsula. Hampton followed as far as Old Church, where many of his exhausted horses gave out. After discarding those mounts that could not continue, he led what remained of his force out the Richmond & York River Railroad. For the next three days, he and his remnants lingered about Tunstall's Station "in the hope of being able to strike a blow at the enemy." Kilpatrick, however, would not venture beyond Union-held Yorktown. On March 6, with War Department approval, Hampton led his men back to the place they had departed so hastily a week earlier.[22]

He later learned that by attacking the raiders at Mechanicsville, he had forestalled a second, perhaps more successful, assault on Richmond. Against his better judgment but at the insistence of his subordinates, Kilpatrick had agreed to mount another attempt, this under the command of an officer presumably more courageous and tenacious than he. Hampton also learned what had become of Dahlgren's satellite force. Stymied by the rain-swollen James, the colonel had attempted to reach Richmond from the west instead of the south, but the roundabout route brought him to the city limits after Kilpatrick had retreated. Unable to reestablish contact with his superior, Dahlgren led his detachment northeastward, across the Pamunkey and Mattapony Rivers, trailed by an ever-growing body of civilian warriors and regular troops, including disbanded cavalrymen residing in the areas Dahlgren traversed.

The colonel was finally brought to bay near Stevensville, north of the Mattapony. In a confrontation with his pursuers, Dahlgren was shot dead and his band was decimated and most of its members captured. That should have been the end of the failed mission, but it was not. Papers found on the colonel's body implicated his column, and perhaps Kilpatrick's as well, in a plot not only to seize Richmond but also to burn the city to ashes and to seize and execute President Davis, his cabinet, and as many other high officials as possible. The papers ignited a controversy that burned for weeks and prompted calls for retaliation, including the hanging of all captured raiders.[23]

Hampton followed the cause célèbre from afar but did not weigh in on it. He appears to have believed the Dahlgren Papers to be genuine, as opposed to Kilpatrick's assertion that they were Rebel forgeries. Hampton's only public statement on the subject was a list of recommendations for strengthening Richmond's defenses against future forays such as Kilpatrick's.

In a memorandum to Stuart, Hampton noted that his recent application for a furlough had been approved but that, if he could be of assistance in implementing his proposals, "I will cheerfully forego my visit home." Apparently the high command decided that, for a time at least, the capital was safe and that they could dispense with Hampton's services. By mid-March, the savior of the Confederate capital was en route to Columbia and a joyous reunion with his family.[24]

Hampton's visit to South Carolina was more business than pleasure, meaning that it was not a uniformly pleasant experience. His return to his family, which included his first sight of one-year-old Alfred, his eighth and last child, was joyous in the extreme. But he was troubled by a recent blow-up with his army commander. He was also concerned that he must use all his efforts of persuasion to expand his shrinking command while avoiding a confrontation with an esteemed former superior.

On the eve of his departure from Virginia, he had learned that Rooney Lee, recently returned to Stuart's command following his release from a Yankee prison, was to be promoted to major general and be assigned a division of his own. To man the organization Hampton and Fitz Lee would each have to give up a brigade—Gordon's and Chambliss's, respectively. Given the sad condition of Young's brigade and the fact that the Laurel Brigade would remain in the Shenandoah Valley indefinitely, Hampton was reluctant to part with Gordon, especially because the transfer smacked of nepotism. Hampton may well have viewed the creation of a third division as Stuart's way of currying favor with Rooney Lee's father.[25]

Whether or not he detailed his objections, Hampton complained bitterly of his treatment not only to Stuart but also to Robert E. Lee. Apparently he reminded Lee that he was about to go home on furlough. Mary Chesnut later claimed that Hampton told her Lee's curt and cutting response: "I would not care if you went back to South Carolina with your whole division." The diarist supposed, probably correctly, that Lee had spoken out of frustration, tired of subordinate commanders protesting the orders of their superiors.[26]

Even if Mrs. Chesnut quoted Hampton accurately, Lee's reply could have had an innocuous meaning. Yet the tone in which the army leader spoke was not susceptible of ambiguity: "Wade said his [Lee's] manner made this speech immensely mortifying." She also claimed that months after Hampton first spoke of his "row with General Lee," he repeated the story in greater detail but without altering its substance.[27]

In fact, Hampton went home in the company of only two regiments. The First and Second South Carolina, having been whittled down by hard and almost incessant campaigning to about three hundred effectives, made the trip in passenger and boxcars while Hampton and some of his staff officers shared a more commodious coach on the same train. The undermanned regiments would not return to Virginia—they would be replaced. Hampton carried official authority to remove from General Beauregard's department a substantial number of mounted units, to be added to his command.

After visiting with his family in Columbia, Hampton made the journey to

Charleston, where he presented his old commander with the documents authorizing him to detach not only the Fourth, Fifth, and Sixth South Carolina but also a Georgia regiment serving in Beauregard's domain, and eight unattached companies. Believing his mounted arm already too small, Beauregard objected to Hampton's "taking from this department fifty-two companies of cavalry at a sweep of the pen." His chief of staff, Brig. Gen. Thomas Jordan, sarcastically called the transfer "very much like another advance from Virginia." On another occasion, Jordan unnecessarily reminded his boss of the long-standing enmity between Beauregard and Jefferson Davis: "Can't you guess [the] source of this raid on your cavalry?"[28]

Hampton sympathized with Beauregard's situation, and he treated the matter with as much tact and diplomacy as he was capable of —which was a great deal. In the end, Beauregard, who had no recourse, authorized the transfer. He told Hampton, however, that a certain amount of time must elapse—he could not say how long—before the units could be relieved at their current duty stations, properly replaced, and outfitted for the movement north. His visitor could only smile and nod his head.

In fact, it took more than six weeks for the replacements to be made ready for shipment to Virginia. In one sense, the delay was a boon to Hampton, for it permitted him to extend his stay with his wife and children, including his precious baby. He spent time, also, with M. C. Butler, who was up and about on his artificial foot and planning to rejoin the army in a month, if not sooner. At other times, Hampton visited local recruiters to try to obtain new blood for his old regiments up north. And he inspected the outfits that would accompany him there and acquainted himself with his future subordinates.

On several occasions, he reviewed the South Carolina regiments on parade. As he hoped, the displays of martial might had a good effect on troop morale. A member of the Fifth South Carolina predicted in a letter to his family that "when we all get together in Virginia we will form a glorious phonomial [sic] of strength and will be able to make the yankees quail." Hampton also attended dinners at which he and the regimental commanders were wined and dined by the citizens of Columbia and Charleston.[29]

By April 22, the general realized that the time had come to return to the seat of war. Newspaper reports revealed that the Army of the Potomac—still under the tactical control of Meade, although Grant was traveling with it and plotting grand strategy—was preparing a new offensive. On the twenty-fifth, at Richmond's urging, Hampton boarded a northbound train. His new

177

troops—some of them, at least—made the journey at approximately the same time, but without their horses. Due to inadequate transportation, a problem that affected every Southern railroad by this point in the war, the animals would not reach Virginia until mid-May.[30]

Until they arrived, the troopers who accompanied Hampton would serve as infantry—not on the Rapidan, but at Petersburg. While Meade struck Lee's army with the intention of defeating it outright or forcing it back upon Richmond, a second, smaller Union army in Virginia, the Army of the James, led by Benjamin F. Butler, a notorious but influential political general, would strike at the Confederate capital from below. En route, Butler's command would attack Petersburg, Richmond's principal support center, twenty-two miles to the south, which the new arrivals from South Carolina would help defend. The dismounted troopers would not report for duty with Lee's army until they were joined by another Butler, their new brigade leader. At the time of Hampton's departure for the North, his long-time subordinate was in the final weeks of his convalescence, but he would not reach the front until about the time his brigade's horses did.[31]

On May 2, Hampton reported at his headquarters near Milford Station. He had arrived none too soon; on the morning of the fourth, the Army of the Potomac began to cross the Rapidan in full strength, again aiming to circumvent Lee's right but this time via a route well to the east of Mine Run. That route led through the heart of the Wilderness, where both Hooker and Meade had been stymied and forced into retreat. But Grant was calling the shots now, and he did not intend to quit, as his predecessors had, until he interposed mightily between Lee and Richmond.

Grant was gambling that he could clear the vast expanse of scrub oak and second-growth pine below the Rapidan before Lee could offer battle. As Meade's army crossed the river and entered the forest, its advance was screened by its cavalry, under Alfred Pleasonton's successor, Maj. Gen. Philip H. Sheridan, a pugnacious, bandy-legged Irishman who had served under Grant in the West. Sheridan's troopers did their best to clear a path through the dense foliage, but they could not move stealthily enough to evade detection by Stuart's scouts and Hampton's pickets. The timely warning these observers rushed to Orange Court House enabled Robert E. Lee to hasten east via the Orange Turnpike and Orange Plank Road and bar Meade's path. The result was a two-day slugfest, May 5–6, between opponents not only blinded by tree cover but also slowed by clumps of briar-infested underbrush.[32]

Maj. Gen. Philip H. Sheridan (third from the left) and his subordinates

Twenty-odd miles southeast of the point where the fighting broke out, Wade Hampton awaited the outcome with mixed emotions. As he informed his youngest sister in a hastily written letter, the battle "promises to be the greatest of the war. I hope confidently for success, but at the same time I cannot but feel anxious. . . . If we can gain a decisive victory, I think our cause is safe, and that we shall have fair prospects for peace."[33]

At the time, his primary emotion was frustration. For the first three days of the unfolding campaign, he saw precious little participation, because he was virtually without a command. It was at this time that, with something less than good grace, he prepared to detach Gordon's brigade and entrust it to Rooney Lee's care. He dreaded making the transfer. The Laurel Brigade was still en route from the Valley; its delayed return had driven Hampton to fire off a sharp note to Stuart's headquarters, inquiring of its whereabouts. With Butler's brigade not yet on hand, Hampton was reduced to the command of his original brigade, now Pierce Young's. That organization now numbered no more than two hundred officers and men.

Hampton therefore begged that he be allowed to retain Gordon's brigade. For one thing, if he gave it up, the junior division leader, Rooney Lee, would have a larger force than he, the senior commander. Then, too, he feared that even after Rosser joined him, his command would aggregate less than two full brigades—sending off Gordon would cripple the effectiveness of the units that remained. But he pleaded in vain; the transfer of Gordon's brigade from the First to the Third Division took place, as ordered, on the seventh.[34]

Worse than leading a division unworthy of the name, for days after the campaign began Hampton remained at Milford awaiting orders. Not until the afternoon of the seventh—and only after repeated inquiries to corps headquarters—was he instructed to move to Shady Grove Church, about four miles below the Orange Plank Road.

Hampton reached his assigned position early on the seventh, too late to take part in the fighting amid the Wilderness. Upon arriving, he made contact with Rosser's brigade, which had reached army headquarters at Orange Court House late on May 4 but soon afterward had been appropriated by Stuart to assist Fitz and Rooney Lee in attacking Meade's vanguard. On the fifth, the Laurel Brigade had battered the cavalry in the forefront of the Union advance, the division of Rosser's West Point classmate, Brig. Gen. James Harrison Wilson. The following day, Stuart had hurled the Laurels against the head of another cavalry division, Brig. Gen. Alfred T. A. Torbert's, which had been screening the Union south flank. Again, Rosser's men had given the Yankees some hard knocks, helping ensure that the Army of the Potomac remained bogged down in the Wilderness without hope of circumventing Lee's flank.[35]

Grant, committed as he was to a forward movement in maximum strength, elected to push on through the trees to the open ground beyond. Early on the seventh, he sent Sheridan's cavalry, minus Wilson's division and followed at a distance by the nearest infantry, G. K. Warren's Fifth Corps, southeastward toward Spotsylvania Court House. Troopers and infantry moved by way of Todd's Tavern, an old hostelry at a crossroads along the southern edge of the forest.

The men of Torbert and Gregg started out in good order, until they found the road blocked by dismounted troopers of Fitz Lee's division, who had erected breastworks and other barriers north of Todd's Tavern. Through much of the seventh, Fitz's people, with Stuart as on-scene commander, fought valiantly to hold back the blue tide that surged toward them through the timber and brush. In the end, however, the defenders were overwhelmed, shoved from one line of works to another, until Sheridan had effective possession of the strategic crossroads.[36]

Fitz's people might have been driven off the board entirely were it not for the timely arrival, late in the day, of Hampton's command, which now included Rosser's horsemen. Perturbed to have been denied the Laurel Brigade for so long, but relieved that he at last commanded something larger than a glorified battalion, Hampton galloped to the tavern from the south, determined to succeed where Stuart and Lee had failed. Upon arriving, he sent Rosser's men into action up the road, their flanks protected by Young's little command, fighting dismounted.

Hampton would report that after a short struggle he thrust the Yankees from the vicinity of the tavern. This was something of an overstatement, for by the time he arrived night was coming on and the prudent Sheridan had withdrawn to a point north of Todd's Tavern. Yet by taking the offensive after Lee's men had relinquished it, Hampton did secure the lower reaches of the road running from the tavern to Spotsylvania Court House. This lodgment, which Lee's men helped maintain, ensured that, come morning, Grant and Meade would make slow, fitful progress toward their next objective.[37]

Before sunrise on May 8, Warren's foot soldiers attempted to reach Spotsylvania, there to link with Wilson's cavalry, which had moved to the courthouse by a cross-country route. The Fifth Corps, however, found the road below Todd's Tavern clogged by Sheridan's dismounted troopers, as well as Fitz Lee's men, who were intent on slowing their opponents' progress through fight-and-fall-back tactics. The traffic snarl had two major effects. That morning the infantry advance of the Army of Northern Virginia, the First Corps of Maj. Gen. Richard H. Anderson (successor to Longstreet, severely wounded in the Wilderness) teamed with Fitz Lee to eject Wilson from Spotsylvania. Then the new arrivals dug rifle pits and built breastworks northwest of the village, across the path of Warren's slow-moving corps. Grant's second attempt to outflank his opponent on the road to Richmond had failed.[38]

Cursing his immobility, Warren vented his spleen at the cavalry, which he blamed for his late arrival at Spotsylvania. When Phil Sheridan reached the scene late that morning, he engaged Warren and then Meade in a heated conversation that left all parties with ruffled tempers. Grant heard about the row, which Sheridan had ended by boasting that if Meade would unchain him, he would seek out Stuart, draw him into a fight, and whip him. Grant was so impressed by the cavalry leader's aggressiveness that he granted his request.[39]

For most of that day, the eighth, Hampton remained in position west of Todd's Tavern, helping infantry comrades check the progress of the late-arriving Federals. About midday, he sent Rosser's and Young's men to attack the front and right flank of an enemy force in cooperation with an assault against its left by the infantry division of Maj. Gen. Jubal Early. Hampton reported that "both movements were executed handsomely & vigorously, the enemy falling back rapidly and leaving us in possession of his camp." In the afternoon, Early moved south to join the fighting closer to Spotsylvania, and Hampton accompanied him. Once at the courthouse, he and his horsemen settled down to participate in a siege-like campaign destined to last almost two weeks.[40]

For the first twenty-four hours of that period, while the Yankees launched and the Rebels repulsed a series of desperate attacks, Hampton held a position on the Confederate left. After May 9, he guarded both flanks by himself. That afternoon Stuart abruptly left the siege lines to gallop down the Telegraph Road at the head of Fitz Lee's division and Gordon's brigade. As Hampton learned, Stuart was in pursuit of Phil Sheridan and ten thousand Yankees who appeared to be heading for Richmond. Hampton had no idea that Sheridan's objective was not the Confederate capital, but the Confederate cavalry.

Hampton was kept so busy along the front at Spotsylvania that he had no time to monitor Stuart's pursuit. He probably assumed that, even with his smaller force, the cavalry leader would overtake his foe and thrash them soundly. Thus he was unprepared for the news he received on the twelfth: The previous day, Stuart had run Sheridan to earth near Yellow Tavern, six miles above Richmond. In heavy fighting, Stuart's men had been defeated and dispersed, and Stuart himself had taken a gunshot wound to the body. He would die of the wound that evening.[41]

Despite his distaste for Stuart's gaudy lifestyle and cavalier image, Hampton had long admired his superior's zeal and energy; his dedication to the cause; his tactical skill, especially at intelligence-gathering; and his talent for morale-building—his knack for making officers and men believe themselves invincible, or close to it. Whatever his limitations as a soldier and a man, Stuart had made the horsemen of the Army of the Northern Virginia into the finest light cavalry on the continent, with the possible exception of the Native American horsemen. Stuart had been the heart and soul of the command almost since its inception, and he would be sorely missed.

Hampton put all of these facts into a general order promulgated by his headquarters on May 16. The proclamation, copies of which were read aloud to every unit of the command, noted that "death has at last accepted the offering of a life, which before the admiring eyes of the Army, has been so often, so freely & so nobly tendered on almost every battle field of Virginia. In the death of Maj Genl J. E. B. Stuart the A. N. V. has lost one of its most brilliant, enthusiastic & zealous Military leaders; the Southern cause, one of its earliest, most untiring & devoted supporters & the Cavalry arm of the service a Chieftain who first gave it prominence & value & whose dazzling achievements have attracted the wonder & applause of distant nations. . . ."[42]

Stuart's passing, besides plunging the entire corps into mourning, created a vacancy at the top that produced a minor controversy which would take three months to resolve. As senior major general, Hampton had every right to believe he would succeed to command all three cavalry divisions. This did not happen. For reasons he left unsaid at the time, Robert E. Lee decided not to anoint a formal successor to Stuart. The truth was that despite the solid and sometimes extraordinary performances Hampton had turned in over the past two years, Lee did not know if the South Carolinian—a nonprofessional soldier, a former infantryman, and several years older than the majority of the officers of the corps—could meet the demands of the position. Until he could make an informed decision, "Marse Robert" decreed that whenever Hampton's division served apart from those of Fitz and Rooney Lee, each officer would report directly to army headquarters. Only when the army leader's son and/or nephew served alongside him would Hampton, as senior general officer, exercise overall authority.[43]

In addition to being unusual, the arrangement promised to be awkward, unwieldy, and promotive of friction. By putting it into effect, Robert E. Lee appeared to show favoritism toward Fitz, who, as the quintessential Virginia cavalier, considered himself the rightful heir to Stuart's mantle. Virtually every member of the corps knew that Hampton and Lee did not get along famously; they would watch closely to see how the new arrangement affected an already strained relationship. Many believed it would force one or the other to seek a transfer, or perhaps resign his commission. For a long time, however, Hampton said and wrote nothing to indicate resentment over the decision of his superior; he accepted the situation and recognized Lee's right to impose it. Rather than carp or complain, he would work hard to prove himself a worthy successor to the Beau Sabreur.

For two weeks after Stuart's death, he and Fitz Lee did not serve together.

In accompanying Stuart in pursuit of Sheridan, Fitz had effectively detached himself from the army; by late May he was still serving apart from it. His division, dispersed at Yellow Tavern but subsequently reconstituted, was now guarding Richmond against potential attackers—not only Sheridan, whose raiders had bypassed the city but might return to menace it, but also Ben Butler's army, which by May 16 stood poised to attack the James River defenses on the capital's doorstep. Eventually, both threats evaporated. Sheridan gave Richmond a wide berth on his way back to Meade's army and Butler was soundly defeated at Drewry's Bluff by troops rushed up from the Carolinas under Beauregard. By month's end, the Creole had bottled up his enemy inside Bermuda Hundred, a peninsula formed by the James and Appomattox Rivers.[44]

By May 21 Grant and Meade were planning to depart the stalemate around Spotsylvania. Within forty-eight hours they had taken up a new position above the North Anna, where Lee, by making maximum use of his interior lines of movement, managed to block the road to Richmond yet again. Over the next three days the armies maneuvered on their respective sides of the stream. Meade, adopting an aggressive posture, attacked across the water on two of those days, to no strategic advantage.[45]

During these operations, Hampton's command, which temporarily included Chambliss's brigade of Rooney Lee's division, carried out the same duties it had performed during the sluggish maneuvering around Spotsylvania: guarding its army's flanks, observing Meade's movements, and trying to discern his intentions. At the outset of the departure from Spotsylvania, Hampton's division—specifically, Rosser's portion of it—developed the enemy's movements through a series of aggressive attacks, enabling Lee to track Meade to the North Anna. Later, when the armies clashed along that river, Hampton's men joined in. They saw action mainly against infantry, Sheridan's horsemen having yet to rejoin their army. Although facing the legendary staying-power of foot soldiers, Hampton more than held his own. On one occasion he informed Robert E. Lee that he had been skirmishing with the Ninth Army Corps for two hours or more: "They are pushing on sharply, but I can hold them here for some time."[46]

By late on the twenty-sixth, Grant had withdrawn the Army of the Potomac to the north bank and had begun to move it southeastward yet again, this time toward the Pamunkey. The Union commander hoped to cross in the vicinity of Hanovertown, beyond Lee's right—if his enemy would allow it. Lee would, but only because Meade was feinting in so many directions he was having a hard time deciding where the Army of the Potomac was heading. Lee's cavalry would have to find out. To do a thorough job of scouting, it must be used at full strength for the first time in weeks.

Early on the twenty-seventh, Lee moved his headquarters to Atlee's Station on the Virginia Central, eight miles above Richmond. In that vicinity he reunited with his nephew, whose division had occupied that area for the past two weeks. Bringing up the rear of the army, Hampton linked with the younger Lee late in the day. This enabled cousin Rooney to reclaim Gordon's brigade, which was now under Col. Clinton Andrews, as Gordon had been mortally wounded the day after Stuart fell.

With his horsemen massed, Robert E. Lee gave Hampton orders to head north to scout the Hanovertown area. Earlier that day, Torbert's and Gregg's Union horsemen had crossed the river at the local ferry, as had some of Meade's infantry. This operation, however, might be a feint to mask a crossing by the rest of the army at another point entirely. In command of every horseman in the army, Hampton's initial assignment was to ascertain Meade's intentions and relay them as quickly as possible to headquarters.[47]

When Hampton started for Hanovertown Ferry on the morning of May 28, he took only half of Fitz Lee's command, leaving Lomax's brigade behind. The reason was that Robert E. Lee wished to retain some cavalry in close support of the main army. Although Hampton's preference would have been to take the entire corps, he started east with his own division and Rooney Lee's. He also had the brigade of Williams Wickham, the officer whose Virginia regiment had broken and run at Brandy Station, dooming Frank Hampton, as his brother saw it, to a violent death.

Hampton even managed to compensate for Lomax's absence, for he was also accompanied by half of the brigade that would be assigned to Calbraith Butler—the Fifth South Carolina and a large portion of the Fourth. Newly mounted, wearing natty uniforms that included white linen gloves for the officers, and toting Enfield rifles, the erstwhile coastal defenders were determined to make an effective showing in their first major operation in Virginia. Butler, however, was not with him; late that evening, in company with the Sixth South Carolina, he would reach the front by train from Columbia, two weeks less than a year since losing his foot in battle.[48]

Unknown to Hampton, Sheridan's cavalry was also in motion, on the same mission as he—trying to locate the enemy's infantry. A little before 10:00 A.M.

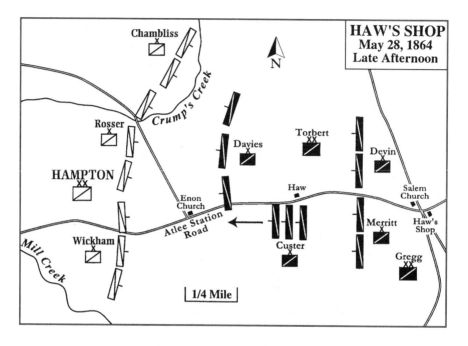

Hampton's column, Wickham's brigade in advance, crossed Totopotomoy Creek, then turned east on the road to Enon Church. Just beyond the church, about two miles west of a crossroads landmark, Haw's Shop, Wickham encountered the pickets of David Gregg's division. Attacking with a will, the Virginians scattered the Yankees in many directions. No sooner had the pickets fled, however, than Gregg's main body pounded up from the east. Several regiments dismounted and dug in between Haw's Shop and Enon Church, training their repeating carbines on Wickham's men. To their rear, Gregg ran horse artillery into position to sweep the road with shell and case shot.

Wickham's troopers also dismounted and began to construct log and fence-rail breastworks on the high ground near the church. As soon as the rest of his column reached the scene, Hampton extended this line on both sides of the road. Dismounted members of Rosser's brigade formed on Wickham's left, while the newcomers from South Carolina went in, afoot, on the right. When Rooney Lee's command, bringing up the rear of the column, arrived, either Hampton or Fitz sent it, along with some guns, out a byroad to the north in hopes of locating and then turning the Union right. "This he was unable to accomplish," Hampton later wrote, "as he feared that his own flank was menaced, but his Artillery, from the position he attained did good service, while he protected Rosser's left."[49]

By the time Hampton's dispositions were complete, an almost equal number of dismounted troopers faced each other across a stretch of country several hundred yards long. So many Yankees fighting on foot as a body was not an unusual occurrence, but it was something of a novelty for Confederate cavalry. Here, visible to every participant, was another characteristic of Hampton's generalship. He had already demonstrated an inclination to take with him into battle as many troopers as available, in contrast to J. E. B. Stuart's predilection for doing the most with the fewest resources—a habit that had cost him dearly at Yellow Tavern. Now Hampton was showing his preference for dismounted fighting, a stark departure from his successor's reliance on mounted warfare with saber and pistol.[50]

Hampton's emphasis on long-range firepower made itself felt. For upwards of seven hours, his troopers exchanged missiles with their opponents, both sides inflicting heavy casualties on each other. Attempts to flank the enemy occurred at intervals throughout the fight, but for the most part it was an old-fashioned, straight-up slugging match. Since both Hampton and Gregg fed in reinforcements from time to time, the tempo of the fighting seemed to grow as the temperature on that late-spring day climbed through the eighties.

The contest finally turned at about 4:00 P.M., when massive additions from the late-arriving division of Torbert, Sheridan at its head, reached the scene and went into line beside and behind Gregg's troopers. At Sheridan's order, one of Hampton's most familiar antagonists, Custer, sent dozens of dismounted sharpshooters of his Michigan Brigade forward along both sides of the road. Despite stubborn resistance, the Wolverines threatened to overrun some sectors in which the defenders had run low on ammunition.

At about the same time, Hampton decided to retract his lines in preparation for quitting the field. By now he had gained the information his superior needed. Among the many prisoners his men had captured were infantrymen; under questioning, they revealed that their comrades had crossed the Pamunkey and were massing just behind the cavalry on the south bank. "It was evidently, therefore, useless to pursue the fight further," wrote Edward Wells, undoubtedly expressing Hampton's view of things. Already his command had suffered severely, and though the toll might be no higher than the enemy's, Sheridan could afford to lose more than his opponent. This was one disadvantage Confederate troops of any arm of the service always confronted.[51]

Because Custer's fresh troops advanced just as Hampton pulled his men to the rear, the Federals would claim they had overwhelmed their enemy. One unfortunate event seemed to confirm this view of things: When it got the word to withdraw, Wickham's brigade did so precipitately, endangering the forces on either side of it. Rosser's men, being veterans, extricated themselves quickly from what otherwise might have been a precarious position. On the right, however, the rookies from South Carolina retained their position in close contact with the Yankees until nearly surrounded and cut off.

Despite their inexperience (until this day, Wells wrote, many of the newer recruits "had never yet heard the 'zip' of a bullet"), they had done much damage with their accurate, long-range Enfields. Wells quoted one Union participant to the effect that this was "the first time we have met those Carolinians of Butler's, and I wish to God it might be the last." Determined that proven fighters such as these would not be sacrificed, Hampton risked life and limb by going forward to help open an escape route. Although he did so at great personal risk, his attitude throughout the ordeal was "calm, cool, and reassuring" to all who saw him. In the end, he managed to haul to safety the great majority of Butler's men.[52]

When, some time after 5:00 P.M., his command finally disengaged and withdrew, Hampton had the satisfaction of knowing that he had accomplished his mission during his maiden outing as Stuart's successor. That he had done so during such a hard-fought contest (he would always consider the fight "the severest the Cavalry had ever been engaged in," an opinion endorsed by many another participant, North and South), made his success loom all the larger.[53]

Then, too, he had given many members of the corps their first look at his brand of leadership, and he believed they liked what they had seen. He was correct: As one officer later put it, "up to this time the Cavalry Corps had not learned the style of their new commander, but now they discovered a vast difference between the old and the new." It was obvious that Hampton's emphasis on maximum resources and fighting as much as possible in infantry fashion, would pay dividends. The advantages, the officer said, were "soon apparent, for while under Stuart stampedes were frequent, with Hampton they were unknown, and the men of his corps soon had the same unwavering confidence in him that the 'Stonewall Brigade' entertained for *their* General."[54]

TEN

"I propose to fight!"

In the bloody aftermath of Haw's Shop, the Union cavalry held the field of battle until relieved by Meade's infantry advance, the Second Corps. At that point Sheridan, with the horsemen of Gregg and Torbert, moved southeast to Old Church and from there to Cold Harbor, a crossroads settlement not far from the old battleground of Gaines's Mill. Foot soldiers were not far behind, for Grant had sized up Cold Harbor as a jumping-off point for one more attempt to envelop Lee's right. With the Chickahominy River ahead, the Federals were fast running out of maneuvering room north of Richmond. Cold Harbor was their last chance to steal that march on the enemy that they had been seeking since crossing the Rapidan.[1]

Lee was committed to countering this latest move, but his ability to do so depended upon the scouting and fighting abilities of his cavalry. From Haw's Shop, Hampton had fallen back to the Virginia Central, Rosser's and Young's troopers going into bivouac near Atlee's Station. Hampton permitted Butler's brigade to camp farther south, near Meadow Bridge, where the railroad crossed the Chickahominy; there the new general could get acquainted with his officers and organize their units as he saw fit. To guard the army's left, or upper, flank, Hampton placed the men of Rooney Lee at Hanover Court House and to protect the right, he advanced Fitz Lee toward Cold Harbor.

Affairs remained quiet until the thirty-first, when both of the Lees came under attack. By then Fitz had dug in north of Cold Harbor; from behind well-constructed breastworks, his troopers repulsed Torbert's strike. Aware that

Meade was moving infantry into the area as well, Robert E. Lee hustled his own foot soldiers to the crossroads village. Not enough arrived in time, however, to fend off a second assault by Torbert, this one augmented by Gregg, with the Fifth Corps not far to the rear. After a three-hour fight, Lee and his supporters were driven out of the village. On June 1, when Yankee infantry began to reach the scene in force, Fitz fell back to Bottom's Bridge to block any further advance by the enemy toward the Chickahominy.[2]

Meanwhile, Rooney Lee's people had been engaging the balance of the Union cavalry along the Virginia Central. On the thirty-first, Wilson's division had driven back Rooney's pickets in front of Hanover Court House. A sharp fight broke out around the town only to die out, then resume the following day. During the engagement of June 1, Wilson's larger force compelled Lee's to fall back, rather precipitately, to Ashland Station.

Perceiving his subordinate's predicament, Hampton led three of Rosser's regiments to Rooney Lee's assistance. Butting into Wilson's column, he chased it as far as Ashland, striking the Union rear again and again. Near Ashland, Lee turned about and attacked afoot against Wilson's front while the relief troops under Hampton struck from the opposite direction, mounted and afoot. Hampton claimed that through a series of "brilliant charges" his men captured "prisoners from eight different Regiments, about two hundred horses & many arms." But the assaults were costly; among Lee's casualties was Pierce Young, seriously wounded at the head of Gordon's old brigade.[3]

When even these blows failed to drive Wilson from the position he had taken along the railroad embankment, Hampton personally led two Virginia regiments and a North Carolina squadron against a weakened sector along the Union right. This effort broke the stalemate, "the enemy giving way at all points. . . . he was pursued until night forced us to halt."[4]

While Hampton had been assisting Rooney Lee against Wilson, the main bodies of both armies had been grappling at Cold Harbor. Thanks to his cavalry's intelligence-gathering expertise, Lee had reached the crossroads first, where he fortified to await Meade's coming. Arriving on the scene and discovering that not all of his opponent's forces were in place, the Union commander attacked and, although failing to turn Lee out of his works, made inroads in a couple of places.

Instead of exploiting his limited success, Meade did not attack on the second, which was also largely a day of rest for his horsemen. By the third, both armies were at Cold Harbor in full strength—Meade's ranks, in fact, included ten thousand men borrowed from the Army of the James. The additions counted for little, for when Meade resumed his assault all along the lines, the well-positioned Confederates hurled it back decisively in less than half an hour. During that interval, almost seven thousand Yankees fell dead or wounded compared to fewer than fifteen hundred Rebels.[5]

While the slaughter was in progress, Hampton moved east of the Virginia Central with the better part of Rooney Lee's command. In response to reports that Wilson's horsemen had occupied the defenses erected there on the twenty-eighth, Hampton returned to Haw's Shop. Confirming the accuracy of the intelligence, he found that Wilson's men were in position to threaten the left flank of the Army of Northern Virginia at Cold Harbor. With Rooney Lee's cooperation, he ordered the North Carolina brigade, now under Col. John Baker, to shove the Yankees east of Haw's Shop. This Baker did in what Hampton called "handsome style . . . driving the enemy to an interior line," where they posed no further problem.[6]

During this second battle at Haw's Shop, the crack of pistols and the rattle of carbines were often drowned out by the sounds of the heavier fighting at Cold Harbor. Edward Wells, whose Fourth South Carolina had supported Baker's attack, found he could follow the progress of the larger battle strictly by ear: "The successive advances and recoils could be numbered by a listener . . . from the awful roar of musketry and artillery, and then the comparative cessation for short intervals." Even before the fighting ended at Haw's Shop, a sudden silence at Cold Harbor bespoke an end to the "fruitless butchery of twenty [Federals] to every one Confederate." Later, Wells came to realize that it also meant that Grant had failed in his final attempt to bypass the Confederates north of the James: "Another move to the left, endeavoring to turn Lee's flank, would put him further from, not nearer to the objective, Richmond." Grant's next move was anyone's guess, although Wells rather doubted it would be a retreat or a surrender.[7]

By June 5, Hampton had begun to wonder if the Union cavalry had slipped away from him. Meade remained at Cold Harbor, where his army continued to unleash sharpshooter and artillery fire without attempting to retake the offensive, but Sheridan's horsemen were nowhere in sight. The mystery deepened until, on the morning of the eighth, the Iron Scouts reported that Little

Phil had crossed the Pamunkey with most, if not all, of his command. For some hours Hampton was able to gain only a sketchy idea of Sheridan's activities north of the river. Even so, he began to suspect that the Irishman was about to raid toward Charlottesville or Gordonsville, with the intention of destroying portions of the Virginia Central, Lee's connection to the "Breadbasket of the Confederacy," the Shenandoah Valley.[8]

Hampton reported his findings to army headquarters and proposed a full-scale pursuit. Even before his plan was approved, he assembled his old division and pointed it westward. Since Fitz Lee was in close contact with Meade, Hampton directed him to follow as soon as he was able to disengage. Given his preference for maximum resources, Hampton intended also to take Rooney Lee with him. Headquarters, however, decreed that he leave the Third Division behind. Although Torbert and Gregg were about to move out under Sheridan, Wilson, with substantial numbers of cavalry and horse artillery, remained with Meade's main body; a corresponding number of Confederate horsemen was required to oppose him. Then too, Robert E. Lee needed mobile reconnaissance units to keep watch over the enemy—the Army of the Potomac would not stay at Cold Harbor indefinitely, and Lee had to know when and where it was moving.

In fact, Grant was planning to decamp for points south. As soon as Sheridan started west, drawing Hampton after him, the lieutenant general would turn his back on Richmond as well as Cold Harbor. He would cross Meade's army and its reinforcements from Butler over the Chickahominy and the James and toward lightly defended Petersburg. By seizing the "Cockade City," Grant would sever the link between Lee and the Deep South, just as Sheridan, by breaking the Virginia Central, would isolate Lee from his source of supply to the west. Petersburg gone, Richmond would fall of its own weight, as would the Army of Northern Virginia.[9]

As soon as he received approval to tail Sheridan westward, Hampton started out in company with Butler's troopers. Because Sheridan maintained a moderate pace on his westward march and kept his column, for the most part, well north of the railroad, Hampton knew he could beat him to his target—whatever it turned out to be. "In two days march," he later recalled, "I accomplished the object I had in view, that of placing myself in front of the enemy." Late on the tenth, his hard-riding division bivouacked at Green Spring Valley, three miles beyond Trevilian Station. Sheridan had encamped about five miles to the northeast, at Ground Squirrel Bridge on the North

Anna River. Meanwhile, Fitz Lee's late-starting column had closed up on Louisa Court House, five miles east of Trevilian.

That night, Hampton's scouts reported that Sheridan had crossed the North Anna at Carpenter's Ford and was descending on the railroad in the vicinity of Trevilian. Hampton quickly backtracked to that point, while sending word that Lee should meet him in the vicinity of Clayton's Store, northeast of the depot. While Lee came on against their flank, Hampton would strike the Yankees head-on with Butler's and Young's brigades, the latter led by Col. Gilbert J. Wright. Rosser's men would take position west of Trevilian, to guard the Confederate left and rear.[10]

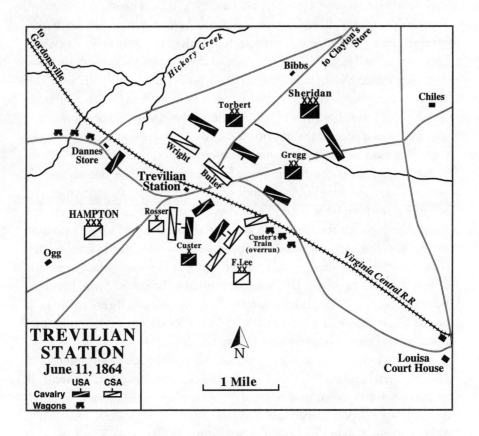

Apparently, Hampton had not communicated his intentions, simple though they were, to his subordinates. Staff officers witnessed a meeting, some time before dawn on the eleventh, between Generals Rosser and Butler. The commander of the Laurel Brigade asked his colleague, "Butler, what is Hampton going to do here today?" Butler's reply was concise: "Damned if I know." Both men rode to the oak-shaded house which Hampton had taken over for his headquarters. They found their superior resting on a table in the front yard, where he had spent the night. After exchanging salutes, Rosser repeated his earlier inquiry: "General, what do you propose to do here today, if I may enquire." Hampton's reply was even pithier than Butler's: "I propose to fight!"[11]

And fight he did. About 5:00 A.M. Hampton, with Butler's and Wright's brigades, moved up the road to Clayton's Store. Two miles or so north of Trevilian Station the Confederates rammed into Sheridan's vanguard, Torbert's division. As befit the philosophy of both cavalries, the encounter became a massive dismounted struggle, hundreds of troopers on each side taking cover behind trees, fences, and some of the thickest underbrush they had ever seen. Edward Wells later observed that this fight, as well as others of later vintage, gave Hampton a reputation in enemy circles "as a 'woods fighter,' as if such tactics were hardly fair play." He called the remark "a compliment . . . [that] gives evidence of the gift he possessed of detecting at a glance advantages of ground and utilizing favorable positions."[12]

For several hours the fighting raged at white heat, each side alternately gaining, losing, and regaining ground, neither willing to retreat, neither able to gain a decisive advantage. Throughout, few reinforcements joined the fight. Although within supporting range of their comrades, Gregg's division and Rosser's brigade remained on the periphery, as if unwilling to corrupt a fair fight by tilting the balance either way. Hampton, of course, wished to expand it with the addition of Fitz Lee, but unaccountably, he saw and heard nothing from the Second Division commander. A series of staff officers galloped to Louisa Court House, but either they could not locate Fitz or they were captured before being able to return to Hampton.

Finally, close to noon, the course of the fighting changed abruptly as Custer's detached brigade, belatedly joining the rest of Torbert's command, trotted down a diagonal road that led to a point below the depot and, providentially for Sheridan, into the Confederate rear. In that sector, the men of Michigan came upon dozens of led horses, those that Butler's and Wright's men had left behind when dismounting to oppose Torbert.

Custer seized as many animals as he could and began to lead them away. Before completing his theft, however, his position was overrun by gray

troopers streaming down from the north. By committing at long last a portion of Gregg's division, Sheridan had dislodged a section of Hampton's line,
sending into retreat a mass of dismounted men who now sought to remount.
On their way to the rear, they detected Custer's presence and deployed to
confront him.[13]

At this point, Hampton pounded up from the rear on his warhorse and
assumed command of the fight. But before he could fashion Butler's and
Wright's fugitives into an assault force, one of Custer's regiments made a dash
for some horse artillery units, including Hart's battery, that had been driven
south by Torbert and Gregg. To prevent their capture, Hampton called up the
nearest body of horsemen—one of the few to have regained their led horses—
and ordered it to charge. This unit, a detachment of the Sixth South Carolina
that included the Cadet Rangers, a company composed of students at the
state's military academy (later known as the Citadel), followed Hampton
through a clearing south of the depot and against the head of the Michigan
regiment. The impact sent the Yankees careening madly about and prevented
them from reaching, let alone seizing, their would-be trophy.[14]

As at Gettysburg and on many other fields, a major charge was quickly followed by a series of individual encounters. In one, Hampton exchanged pistol
shots with a lieutenant of Custer's Seventh Michigan. Due to the bucking and
rearing of his excited charger, the general failed to land a single blow, but neither did his opponent. After the lieutenant had ridden on, Hampton
reloaded, regained his shooting eye, and brought down two other Wolverines
as they tried to flee from him. In later years, when trooper Ulysses R. Brooks
of the Sixth South Carolina gathered material for his book *Butler and His
Cavalry*, he asked Hampton how many Yankees he had personally dispatched.
The figure Hampton came up with seemed low to Brooks, who reminded the
aged general of the two he had shot down at Trevilian Station. Hampton dis-
missed the comment with a wave of his hand: "I did not count them—they
were running."[15]

Thanks at least in part to Hampton's charge, Butler's and Wright's fugitives
not only overran Custer's position but also regained most of their captured animals, and several caissons, limbers, and ambulances that the Wolverines had
begun to carry off. To tighten the squeeze being applied to Custer, Hampton
committed Rosser's brigade to the fight along with several batteries, including
Hart's, under overall command of now-Maj. R. Preston Chew. Custer faced
west against the combined opposition, but he soon found himself also fighting

in the opposite direction. Fitz Lee, finally arriving from Louisa Court House, had slammed into the boy-general's rear and flanks. For perhaps an hour, Custer fought off both encirclement and sunstroke, in the process losing upwards of four hundred men as well as—temporarily, at least—some of his own cannon. Late in the afternoon, however, comrades broke through to rescue his embattled command, effectively ending the frantic action of the day. Each side pulled back to the positions it had occupied at the outset of the fight.[16]

Because Sheridan held his place throughout the night, Hampton suspected he had not yielded his intention of wrecking the railroad and then pressing on to Charlottesville or Gordonsville. Preparing for a second day of hard fighting, that night he ordered Fitz Lee to his side. To make amends for his tardy appearance, Fitz ought to have obeyed as quickly as humanly possible. Instead, it was late in the morning of the twelfth before he completed his detour around Sheridan and joined Hampton west of Trevilian.[17]

As Hampton had suspected, Sheridan began the twelfth by demolishing track on both sides of the depot while his skirmishers prevented the Confederates from interfering. While keeping up a skirmish fire of his own, Hampton waited patiently for the Yankees to drop their crowbars and levers and pick up their pistols and carbines. In the middle of the afternoon, Sheridan finally obliged, sending a mounted column west in search of a bypath to Mallory's Ford, where he intended to recross the North Anna.

Contrary to Hampton's belief, Little Phil considered his mission at an end. He had drawn most of Robert E. Lee's horsemen far afield of Grant's and Meade's movement to Petersburg, an operation now well under way. In fulfillment of a secondary objective, Sheridan's raiders had damaged a several-mile stretch of railroad. A tertiary objective, however, could not be attained. While interrogating some prisoners, the Union leader had learned that continuing on to Charlottesville would accomplish nothing. A small Union army supposed to be operating in that vicinity, which Grant had wished Sheridan to contact and accompany to Petersburg, was wandering far afield of the college town. With a link-up now out of the question, Sheridan was ready to head for home.[18]

He would not get there via Mallory's Ford. To prevent the raiders from continuing west, Hampton had dug in across the road to Charlottesville. The fence-rail works his troopers hastily erected also barred access to Mallory's, forcing Sheridan either to attack him or backtrack to some other crossing site. In the end, he did both. At first unwilling to countermarch, he flung Torbert's men at the barricades, only to see them repulsed in quick order—first, when attacking Lee's men on the southern end of the line and later when trying to smash through Hampton's division along the tracks. Chew's horse batteries offered especially stout resistance. As Lieutenant Colonel Waring of the Jeff Davis Legion noted in his diary, "a terrible fire was poured into the gunners, but they repaid the Yankees with canister, & all [the attackers] ran back except a few sharp-shooters."[19]

According to most accounts, the Confederates repulsed five assaults; Wells insists it was seven. After the war, General Rosser summed up the day's action concisely: "It was a spirited infantry-style attack and a stubborn infantry resistance. Sheridan displayed no skill in maneuvering; it was simply a square stand up fight, man to man, and Hampton whipped him—defeated his purpose and turned him back."[20]

With his casualties mounting—they would eventually top 250 in addition to the 700 or more he had suffered the previous day—and with his command no closer to Mallory's Ford, Sheridan saw he had to withdraw by some other route. Late in the day, when Lomax's brigade moved from the rear of Hampton's line into position to assail his lower flank, the Union raider called retreat. After gathering up his wounded and burying those dead who lay within his lines, he fell back to a less commodious ford east of Trevilian, where his horses waded the river.

Hampton elected not to pursue immediately. After the Yankees had left, his men clambered out of their works to behold a sight that confirmed the wisdom of their commander's preference for "infantry style" fighting, as well as his emphasis on marksmanship over horsemanship. As one of Butler's South Carolinians recalled, "we found the field in our front covered with their dead and wounded."[21]

Hampton was quietly pleased that he and his men had given a strong account of themselves at Trevilian Station, especially on the second day. On the fourteenth, the usually hygienic soldier informed his family that he had been so busy of late, "I have not even changed my clothes for a week. . . . But though I am not very *clean*, I am well, in spite of dirt, and I have again to thank God for his merciful protection of me & mine. I am deeply thankful too that he was pleased to give us success, for I was greatly concerned at the responsibility of my position. The cavalry has never had harder fights or achieved greater success than on this expedition & I am very much gratified that they have done so well under me."[22]

Of course, as he was careful to add, his job was not done. Although compelled to postpone pursuit to rest his tired troopers, succor the wounded, and bury the dead including the dozens of corpses Sheridan had left behind, he intended to bring the Federals to bay as they made their way homeward via White House Landing on the Pamunkey. When Hampton departed Trevilian later that day, he marched in two columns. Fitz Lee took the upper track via Chilesburg, New Market, and Aylett's—the route Sheridan had taken to Trevilian—while Hampton and his division returned the way they had come, along the south side of the railroad.[23]

The divergent routes appeared to symbolize the distant relationship between Hampton and Lee, which had only widened on the eleventh. In his campaign report, Hampton would praise his colleague (Lee "co-operated with me heartily, and rendered valuable assistance"). In later years, however, he would insist that the characterization applied only to the second day of the fight. He would speak harshly of "how greatly he [Lee] had failed me on the first day," while explaining that "my regard for Genl R. E. Lee, induced me to omit all mention of misconduct on the part of Fitz."[24]

His postwar assertion notwithstanding, it is difficult to determine the extent of any animosity or resentment Hampton felt toward Lee at the time. His later criticism may have been prompted by the oft-repeated assertions of subordinates and staff officers that Fitz was to blame for the difficulties the First Division faced on the eleventh, which only Hampton's personal skill and courage had overcome. Hampton's partisans would have been predisposed to blame an outsider for any problems their superior encountered, and the pompous Lee made an appropriate scapegoat.

When Lee rejoined Hampton during the latter stages of the pursuit, Fitz further alienated members of the corps staff. Due to the fact that Sheridan moved east by a more roundabout route, both Confederate columns reached White House on June 20 twenty-four hours before their enemy arrived. By then Hampton had emplaced his horse artillery on high ground west of the Union supply base and had shelled its garrison as well as its wharves, warehouses, and the nine hundred-wagon train that waited there for Sheridan to escort to Meade's army at Petersburg. During the two-hour cannonade, which inflicted heavy but indiscriminate damage to the local facilities, Hampton dismounted hundreds of his men and positioned them for an attack on the garrison. With luck, he would seize all nine hundred vehicles before Sheridan reached the base.[25]

At the eleventh hour, however, Fitz Lee, whose command was included in the storming party, argued against an assault. He stated that his men remained tired from their recent slugging match with Sheridan. Furthermore, they lacked suitable equipment, such as scaling ladders, to gain entrance to the base. Then, too, Hampton's artillery was not in the proper position to support them. After much debate and deliberation, Hampton accepted his colleague's unsolicited advice and called off the assault. When he ordered his subordinates to place their troops in camp south of the landing, Hampton's aides muttered that again Fitz Lee had interfered with the management of the Army of Northern Virginia's Cavalry Corps.[26]

When Sheridan finally reached White House, he rested his horses and riders for forty-eight hours before heading for the Chickahominy and the James. His column had swollen to immense proportions with the addition of Meade's supply vehicles. The elephantine train made a tempting target, and Hampton's men struck at it early and often. They failed to bring it to a halt, however, thanks to the vigilance of its guard. Nor were they able to destroy Jones's Bridge, where Sheridan moved over the Chickahominy. Early on the twenty-third, as the Federals were crossing, Hampton attacked their rear guard, part of Torbert's division, along the Long Bridge Road. Although they inflicted several casualties, the Confederates were driven off, forcing Hampton to devise some other way to overhaul his enemy.[27]

The next day, with Torbert across the Chickahominy and hastening on to the James, Hampton struck again near Samaria Church and Nance's Shop, about seven miles northwest of Charles City Court House. This time, he succeeded in pinning down the rear guard, now composed of David Gregg's men. Hampton was enabled to do so by his superior strength, a rare exception to the normal order of things. Even without adding reinforcements, his command outweighed Gregg's. In addition, now that he was within supporting range of Richmond, he had been joined by Chambliss's brigade of Rooney Lee's division and by a new brigade assigned to duty north of the James, whose ranks contained some familiar faces. Headed by now-Brig. Gen. Martin Gary, former leader of the foot soldiers of the Hampton Legion, the command consisted of the organization Hampton had bankrolled and led to war, since expanded to regimental size and transformed into mounted infantry. Gary's command also comprised two newly organized regiments of cavalry, the Seventh South Carolina and the Twenty-fourth Virginia.[28]

Martin W. Gary, Hampton's wartime subordinate and postwar poltical opponent

Hampton's increased manpower enabled him to hold Gregg's troopers in place with frontal assaults, mounted and afoot, while a large column moved toward the Federals' rear with the intention of blocking their escape to the James. Lieutenant Colonel Waring noted that "the enemy were charged, broke, rallied, and were charged three times more." Hampton failed to cut off his opponent, but he hurt him badly. The defenders suffered almost four hundred casualties (three-quarters of them being prisoners), about seventy more than Hampton. Only the skill with which Gregg shifted units to shore up threatened sectors and repair breaks, and his effective use of his horse artillery, enabled him to break free of the closing trap and withdraw to the river. Waring later claimed that false reports of Union reinforcements caused some attackers to hesitate when within a few hundred yards of seizing the road to Charles City Court House. Through this error, Gregg's men "were allowed time to rally, and blockade the road. They made a stand at dark & we had to stop."[29]

After Gregg escaped to join Torbert at the ferry that would carry their men, horses, artillery, and wagons over the James, Hampton moved in the opposite direction in response to a new assignment. As early as June 22, he had heard that yet another raiding column—Wilson's command, strengthened by Brig. Gen. August V. Kautz's cavalry division of the Army of the James—had been rampaging along the railroads that ran south and west from Petersburg.[30]

The raiders hoped to accomplish a mission that their infantry comrades had botched. A week earlier, Grant and Meade had stolen a march on their adversaries, moving from Cold Harbor to the outskirts of Petersburg almost undetected. For three days they had hammered on the gates of a city defended by a few thousand troops under the peripatetic P. G. T. Beauregard. By any standard of measurement, the attackers should have burst through the outer fortifications and into downtown Petersburg. Providentially for the Confederate cause, a wholesale breakdown in communication, a lack of coop-eration among Meade's subordinates, and a series of egregious tactical blun-ders permitted Beauregard to hold on until the no-longer-deceived Lee arrived on the eighteenth to ensure the city's security. An angry and frustrated Grant now expected a long, enervating siege. Even so, he had struck at Petersburg's railroads in the faint hope of forcing the Confederates to abandon the works that ringed the city on the east, south, and west.[31]

When he learned of Wilson's and Kautz's operation, Robert E. Lee sent his son, with his own division and a Petersburg-based brigade of troopers under Brig. Gen. James Dearing, to shadow the raiders. Rooney Lee lashed their flanks and rear at every opportunity but failed to bring them to bay. Thus, on the twenty-sixth, Hampton was ordered to join the chase. By then all of Sheridan's troopers had passed over the James, leaving him free for service on the Southside.

Leaving Gary's brigade north of the river, Hampton crossed the rest of his command over a pontoon bridge near Chaffin's Bluff, five miles south of Richmond. He then made for Petersburg with as much speed as his jaded mounts could produce. His route lay across the rear of the Howlett Line, the defensive perimeter that had bottled up Ben Butler's army at Bermuda Hundred, then onward to Stony Creek Station on the Petersburg & Weldon Railroad, one of Wilson's targets. At Sappony Church, just west of the depot, Hampton was joined early on the twenty-eighth by two infantry brigades under Maj. Gen. William Mahone. There, too, a few hours later, he encoun-tered the head of Wilson's column returning from wrecking track and rolling stock on the South Side Railroad.[32]

The struggle that broke out upon the raiders' arrival rapidly overflowed the fields and woods on all sides of Sappony Church. Even with Wilson and Kautz caught between two fires—Rooney Lee continued to clout them from the west—the thirty-three hundred-man force was a formidable opponent. The heavy but inconclusive fighting lasted through the day and well into the night.

Before dawn on the twenty-ninth, Hampton's scouts discovered that Wilson had sent Kautz on an end run up the Weldon line to Ream's Station, seven miles south of Petersburg. Hampton pursued, immediately and furiously. Reaching the depot, he took on Kautz before Wilson could disengage from Sappony Church and join him. By the time Wilson moved north, about eight o'clock, hundreds of Mahone's foot soldiers had come up to reinforce Hampton, placing Kautz, and later Wilson as well, in a decidedly tight spot. Hampton and Mahone coordinated operations so expertly that they virtually surrounded the entire raiding force, which they hammered on all sides for hours on end.[33]

Unable to withstand such pressure, in late afternoon the Union line cracked and collapsed. At Wilson's order, the raiders fled for their lives, every man for himself. One described the retreat as "a wild skedaddle through heavy timber, shells from rebel batteries knocking the branches about our ears. . . ."[34]

One body of runaways broke through the line in front of Hampton's field headquarters, which sat atop a small hill. As the general recalled years later, "I was writing an order to [Fitzhugh] Lee, when a company of fugitives nearly ran over me & my staff." He threw his dispatch case aside, mounted, and led the only soldiers near him—aides, couriers, and orderlies—down the hill at the oncoming Yankees.[35]

According to Edward Wells, to whom the general related the incident, Hampton drew his side arms and prepared to use them: "Calling to the Yankees to halt, and then riding up to the leading man, [he] presented his pistol and summoned them to surrender. The man made then as if to draw his weapon, but Hampton told him he would shoot him if he did, when the captain of the band . . . surrendered his men." After the demoralized Federals laid down their arms, some of Mahone's foot soldiers came up to escort them to the rear. They found that Hampton and his little band had captured more than one hundred raiders.[36]

Wilson and Kautz, in their haste to escape, abandoned all their artillery and most of their forage wagons and ambulances, as well as hundreds of runaway slaves who had fallen in with their column in hopes of being delivered from bondage. The forage wagons were found to contain an immense haul of plunder including a communion service stolen from a local church. Although most of the Yankees, including their leaders, eventually reached their army's lines below Petersburg, dozens were overtaken and made prisoner. Their dispersal ended the threat to the railroads outside, and to Lee's army inside, Petersburg. While not all the credit for this outcome belonged to Hampton, he deserved a large slice of it. Once again—as he had when tracking

Kilpatrick and overhauling Sheridan—the pursuer had outmaneuvered, out-fought, and outwitted the pursued.[37]

The near-exhaustion of Hampton's command was a major factor in the ability of so many Yankees to escape capture at Ream's Station. For the past six weeks, the horse soldiers of the Army of Northern Virginia had been marching and fighting on an almost daily basis. Even the stoical Robert E. Lee could see they required an extended rest. When he learned that Sheridan's troopers had gone into fixed camp behind the lines east of Petersburg, Lee ordered Hampton's men to do the same south of the city.

Lee's decree had a therapeutic effect on the entire corps. Officers and men relaxed, resupplied, and refurbished, while taking care to restore the health of their faithful mounts. The duties asked of them were few, mainly scouting and guard duty. "Picketing there was, of course," recalled Edward Wells, "and plenty of it." Another South Carolinian observed that "we are now lying idle . . . awaiting the movements of the Yankee cavalry. As soon as we hear of their moving we will go after them again."[38]

The Yankees did not stir for six weeks, except during a brief period late in July when Meade staged a diversion above the James to pull troops away from the siege lines southeast of Petersburg. In that quarter a regiment of coal miners had dug a 511-foot-long tunnel under a Rebel salient opposite their position, which they filled with four tons of blasting powder. When detonated on July 30, the mine proved a spectacular success, blowing a gaping crater in the enemy line. But a poorly conducted attack in the wake of the blast failed miserably, negating months of careful planning and strenuous labor.[39]

Before the mine blew, Yankee troops on the Northside, including two of Sheridan's divisions, briefly threatened the approaches to Richmond. On the twenty-eighth Robert E. Lee ordered two infantry divisions and elements of Fitz and Rooney Lee's commands to oppose the diversion. Hampton did not take part, perhaps because of a debilitating bout with dysentery. Three days of intermittent skirmishing, which also involved Gary's brigade, proved inconclusive and ended with the Yankees far from their capital. Hours before the fighting at the Crater began, they returned meekly to the south side of the James.[40]

During the mostly inactive period he spent below Petersburg, Hampton appears to have had a run-in with Robert E. Lee that recalled their "row" of the previous spring. The incident may have stemmed from a proposal by the army leader to detach Rosser's brigade and station it, for an indefinite period, on the Northside. A month earlier, Lee had dispatched Jubal Early's infantry to the Shenandoah Valley, initially to oppose the army Sheridan had expected to meet near Charlottesville. Later Lee had Early operate in such a manner as to take pressure off the defenders of Petersburg. On July 5 the feisty division commander crossed the Potomac and advanced on Washington with fourteen thousand troops of all arms. On the twelfth, he attacked Fort Stevens, on the northern outskirts of the capital, where an interested spectator, Abraham Lincoln, came under fire. Early called off the attack after learning of the arrival at Washington of the Sixth Corps, Army of the Potomac, which Grant had reluctantly removed from the siege lines at Petersburg. Early withdrew under pressure and two days later returned to the Valley.[41]

After he left, the Sixth Corps lingered in Washington pending a decision on how to handle the threat that Early continued to pose. The Federals' presence in that quarter bothered Lee. As he informed Hampton, he wished the Laurel Brigade to patrol north of the Virginia Central Railroad "in view of the reported operations of the enemy on the Potomac and the threatening position of Sheridan on the James." He had selected Rosser's brigade "on account of its reliability and the opportunity it would enjoy both of communicating with the Valley, gathering fresh horses, its absentees, &c." In the end, Lee discarded his plan to move Rosser, but only after Hampton strongly objected to it.[42]

Hampton's relations with Lee may also have suffered as a result of the latter's rejection of a request by John Bell Hood that the South Carolinian join him in the West, at a higher grade than he now held. Since recovering from his Gettysburg wound, Hood had gone to Tennessee to accept corps command under another transferee from the Army of Northern Virginia, Joe Johnston. For five months Hood had helped Johnston oppose William T. Sherman's advance toward Atlanta, the most strategically important city in the Deep South. Because Sherman's three armies—a total of ninety-eight thousand officers and men—outnumbered Johnston's command almost two to one, Atlanta's fall may have been inevitable. But when Johnston, who had lost none of his enthusiasm for retreating, refused to pledge he would hold the city to the last, Jefferson Davis on July 17 had replaced him with the more aggressive Hood.[43]

With Sherman now poised to attack the Gate City, Hood wanted Hampton to command the cavalry of his army with the rank of lieutenant general. Although Hampton's feelings on the subject are not known, he may well have favored leaving Virginia for a theater closer to his home state. Almost certainly, he would have appreciated the opportunity for promotion. Thus, he may have resented Lee's refusal to approve his transfer—the latest in a long series of such actions dating to mid-1862.

Even more than promotion, Hampton desired that his duties as de facto commander of the Cavalry Corps, Army of Northern Virginia be formally recognized. By now he had exercised corps command for three months, but without statutory authority. The situation rankled him not only because it implied a lack of confidence on the part of his superior but also because it seemed to encourage Fitz Lee and other subordinates to serve him less than fully and faithfully. Having performed ably, and often exceptionally, on so many hard-fought fields over those three months, he wondered what more he had to do to gain a title that was rightfully his.

Hampton's suspicion that, in Lee's eyes, he remained unworthy of the honors bestowed upon his late, lamented predecessor, appears to have affected his morale. Late in July, he wrote in a sour mood to Mary Chesnut, who had returned with her family to South Carolina. His correspondent noted in her diary that Hampton "says he will be forced to resign because since his tiff with General Lee, that prince and potentate is so prejudiced against him!" Mrs. Chesnut was indignant that Hampton should express anything but cordiality toward the much-beloved army leader, but her husband told her to "let them alone. It will all come [out] right."[44]

James Chesnut was prescient. In fact, Lee had come to appreciate the caliber of Hampton's contributions to the army and was prepared to reward them. As early as July 2, he had written Jefferson Davis, praising the "energy and good conduct" Hampton had displayed during his pursuit of Sheridan to and from Trevilian Station, "and my appreciation of his character and services." On this occasion Lee requested formal authority to place Hampton in charge of his horsemen.[45]

This authority was not conferred until August 11. Significantly, perhaps, it came through only days after Fitz Lee was detached from the Army of Northern Virginia and sent, along with his division, to the Shenandoah. There Fitz would assume command of Early's cavalry, a position roughly equal to Hampton's. Fitz's uncle had decided to beef up Early's command not only with more horsemen but also with an infantry division. The augmentation responded to Grant's August 1 decision to send Sheridan to oppose Early with the Sixth Corps and the cavalry of Torbert and Wilson. In the Valley, Little Phil would assume command of two other infantry corps and a cavalry force under Averell. His job was to rid the Shenandoah of Confederate opposition and then to "peel the land" of crops that would otherwise find their way to Robert E. Lee's army.[46]

If Hampton's advancement had been delayed to save Fitz Lee the embarrassment of serving as his designated subordinate, it brought no complaints from the new corps leader. His attitude toward losing one-third of the strength of his command was another matter. Even so, having gained at last a position to which he had long considered himself entitled, the South Carolinian was content. He made no further mention of his dissatisfaction with his status in the army and no additional accusations that his commander was prejudiced against him.

Upon his elevation, Hampton turned his old division over to M. C. Butler, inspected the field returns of his suddenly reduced command, and overhauled his staff. Most of his aides were holdovers from Stuart's regime, including his inspector general, Maj. A. Reid Venable, and his adjutant general, Maj. Henry B. McClellan. The latter was a first cousin of the deposed commander of the Army of the Potomac, who was about to reenter the public arena as the Democratic Party's presidential candidate in opposition to Lincoln's reelection bid.

Hampton brought a few officers over from the division staff, including his chief surgeon, Dr. Walter Taylor, the faithful Rawlins Lowndes, and Lt. T. Preston Hampton. By now Preston was a veteran not only of staff duty but of hard service in the field, where he had been twice wounded. His father was immensely proud of the reputation his younger son had acquired for courage and coolheadedness under fire. He was no less proud of Preston's brother, who through no fault of his own had enjoyed fewer opportunities to distinguish himself. When Joe Johnston assumed command of the Army of Tennessee, Wade Hampton IV had rejoined his staff. With his long-time superior now deposed, Wade was on the verge of returning to his father's headquarters in the position of acting aide-de-camp.[47]

Within hours of his appointment to corps command, the elder Hampton entered upon a spell of active duty that sent him in several directions to oppose various enemy forces. Late on August 11, army headquarters ordered him, with Butler's division, to far-off Culpeper Court House, there to make a demonstration in favor of the reinforcements heading to the Valley. Dutifully, Hampton marched to the Rappahannock, where he remained for three days. He had come armed with discretion to move against Washington, much as Early had the previous month, "should the enemy move up the Potomac, leaving his capital uncovered." But before he could take advantage of any opportunity, Lee recalled him to the Richmond front, where the Federals had gained a foothold north of the James at Deep Bottom.

On the thirteenth, Grant, believing that Lee had thinned his lines on the Northside to reinforce Early, had sent some of Meade's best troops—the Second Corps, now under Maj. Gen. Winfield Scott Hancock, plus Gregg's cavalry, as well as foot and horse soldiers from Butler's army—to attack out of the Deep Bottom bridgehead. Their objective was to probe the Rebel works near Chaffin's Bluff and, if they proved to be weak, to assault Richmond.[48]

To reach the scene of action, Hampton traversed terrain familiar from his service under Jackson in the Peninsula campaign. Crossing White Oak Bridge over the swamp of the same name, he moved up the Williamsburg Road, then across the fields till he gained the road from Charles City. By 10:00 A.M. on the sixteenth, he and Butler reached White's Tavern, eight miles below the capital. There they made contact with Rooney Lee's division, which they found engaged with Gregg's horsemen. The Yankees had hoped to dash into Richmond while their infantry friends engaged the defenders farther south, including troops that Robert E. Lee had rushed up from Petersburg. Before Hampton arrived, Gregg's larger force had driven in its opponents, in the process killing the hard-fighting John Chambliss. Then Hampton added Butler's men to the fray, dismounting them and leading them in an attack against Gregg's right rear while the younger Lee, with his own division and Mart Gary's brigade, struck frontally.[49]

The combined assault was a dramatic success, the enemy withdrawing in haste and the lost ground being recovered. In this effort, Gary's men distinguished themselves, a fact that, given their somewhat ragtag appearance and lack of experience, may have surprised Hampton. Gary was so proud of his command's performance that when Hampton, in his after-action report, failed to accord it the praise its commander thought due to it, the bald-headed lawyer from Edgefield County took offense. From this incident may be dated the ill feeling that forever after characterized the relationship between Hampton and his one-time protégé.[50]

On the eighteenth, following a day of relative inactivity, Robert E. Lee determined to attack the Second Corps and its supports at Fussell's Mill, almost three miles north of Deep Bottom. This time Hampton's troopers, who went into action alongside Maj. Gen. Charles Field's infantry, attacked breastworks manned by foot soldiers. In this action, as they had on the sixteenth, Rooney Lee and Calbraith Butler joined forces, Hampton and the Virginians striking the enemy's front and the South Carolinians their right flank.

Butler's turning movement—made with the assistance of the Laurel Brigade, which had accompanied Rooney Lee to the Northside but minus its leader (Rosser was recuperating from a wound received at Trevilian Station)—was a thing of beauty. Butler's men drove the Union infantry from their defenses, pursued them for two miles, and captured 167 of them. Largely as a result, the Federals abandoned other sectors of the Fussell's Mill line, although a counterattack by part of the Second Corps restored the balance of power and permitted the Federals to recross the James two nights later. They had learned, to their pain and regret, that the lines below Richmond had not been depleted.[51]

The cavalry's latest triumph drew encomiums from many quarters, including infantry officers who had been impressed—and some doubtless flabbergasted—by Hampton's capture of the works on the Union right. Robert E. Lee wrote to express his appreciation of the "gallant and valuable" services the troopers had rendered, their "skillful execution" of Hampton's orders, and the "signal results" they had produced. Such praise left Hampton excited about his command's prowess as "riding infantry." In a letter to Fisher, he proclaimed, "they charge Infty. and take breast-works, and they are as steady in a fight as our best troops." Of his own conduct he said nothing, although he mentioned the publication of a newspaper report announcing his death in the recent fight. The story had quoted a soldier who had claimed "to '*place me in my coffin.*' I sent a despatch home at once so I hope no uneasiness was felt there. God has spared me through very many dangers and I hope that he will bring us all back in safety to those we love."[52]

Hampton's next experience in infantry-style fighting, while almost as successful as the previous one, proved more costly and left him with doubts about the appropriateness of such tactics. When the Federals crossed back to the Southside on the twentieth, most headed for the railroad south of the city. The attack out of Deep Bottom had represented one-half of a dual offensive by Grant aimed at stretching both of Lee's flanks while also cutting his communications. Since the eighteenth, Warren's Fifth Corps had been wrecking track on the Petersburg & Weldon south of Globe Tavern. At first the vandals were opposed only by Dearing's cavalry and then by A. P. Hill's infantry. The reinforcements drove Warren back to Globe Tavern thus preventing him from making progress toward Lee's rear.[53]

Hancock's corps, still supported by David Gregg's horsemen as well as by a brigade of Kautz's command, arrived from the Northside to reinforce Warren. On the twenty-third, the new arrivals resumed the work of demolishing Weldon Railroad trackage. Over the next two days, while the cavalry watched for the approach of enemy forces, the infantry tore up rails and ties to a point three miles south of Ream's Station. This was as far as Robert E. Lee was willing they should go. On the morning of the twenty-fifth, he sent A. P. Hill, along with Hampton's cavalry (Butler's and Rooney Lee's divisions, the latter temporarily under Brig. Gen. Rufus Barringer), to make them cease and desist.

Attacking at about noon, Hill drove in Gregg's and Kautz's vedettes, then struck the patchwork defenses astride the railroad that Wilson's raiders had thrown up on June 29 and which Hancock's men had slightly improved. One of Butler's troopers described the works as made of "pine logs, sorghum cane and dirt." Despite such inadequate protection, the Second Corps resisted limited attacks that began shortly after 5:00 A.M.[54]

Four hours later, after consulting with Hill, Hampton moved to attack the Union left. Leaving Butler's First Brigade, under Brig. Gen. John Dunovant, to guard the rear, Hampton sent Barringer's men, supported by the rest of Butler's command, up the Halifax and Malone's Crossing Roads, parallel to the railroad. Hampton, riding with the column on the Malone Road, struck Gregg's pickets west of the tracks and drove them, as well as Gregg's main body, toward Hancock's defenses. Yankee infantry rushed up to halt the advance, but Hampton's dismounted troopers, assisted by a two-gun section of Capt. William W. McGregor's horse artillery, held their ground with admirable tenacity. Eventually they withdrew about four hundred yards to the south but only in response to a request from Hill that they try to draw the enemy down the railroad so that he might take them by surprise in rear. The stratagem failed, but not for want of effort on Hampton's part.

Around four o'clock, Hill increased the pressure he was applying to other parts of the enemy position. Throughout the afternoon, wave after wave of attackers, covered by a devastating artillery barrage, struck the center of Hancock's works. For an hour or more, the Federals fended off the onslaught until Hill's men broke through a sector held by new and inexperienced troops. As the gray infantry widened the breach, Hampton attacked the works in his front. In his report he declared that the Yankees "made a stubborn stand, and for a few moments checked our advance, but the spirit of the men was so fine that they charged the breast-works with the utmost gallantry, carried them, and captured the force holding them. This ended the fighting of the day, my men having been engaged for twelve hours."[55]

Due to the lateness of the hour, Hampton did not mount a full pursuit. Instead, he occupied the captured defenses and gathered up the Yankees his men had taken prisoner. Adding these to the far greater number of captives that Hill had taken, nearly 2,100 defenders had fallen into Confederate hands. Six hundred other Yankees had been killed or wounded as against 720 total casualties in Hill's ranks and an unknown number in Hampton's. The victors had also seized nine cannon, twelve colors, and three thousand stands of arms.

Once again, comrades and superiors sang the praises of Hampton's troopers and the dismounted tactics they had employed so effectively. Their leader exulted, "even the Infantry give great praise to our Cavalry. Some one heard an Inft. soldier say the other day, 'That old fellow Hampton is a rusher. He helped us mightily'. . . . I am delighted with the conduct of my men." Later, he took a more sober view of recent events, which had dampened his enthusiasm for storming breastworks: "It is not the work for cavalry. And we have been fighting infty. too much of late. The Yankee Infty. say however that they would rather fight our Infty. than our Cavalry."[56]

Even more than the praise of comrades, Hampton appreciated the plaudits he and his men received from superiors, including Robert E. Lee and A. P. Hill. As he informed Fisher, "Gen. Lee says 'the cavalry *always* fight well now.'" In contrast to the slights Lee had dealt him on more than one occasion, Hampton could now report that his superior "is very civil to me." Such was the healing power of victory.[57]

Following his second fight at Ream's Station in two months, Hampton moved his headquarters into the country ten miles south of Petersburg, "where we get fine water. The Yankees are very quiet in my front and my men drive them off whenever they choose." He had come to this place in response to an order from Lee, received one day after the recent battle: "I wish you now to rest the two divisions as much as practicable, and to take such position as would enable you most speedily to intercept and punish any party which they might send out against our communications."[58]

The threat Lee mentioned did not materialize over the next two weeks, permitting Hampton's men to loll in their camps behind the firing lines, recuperating from their recent hard service. Spared from worrying about defensive operations, Lee began to consider taking the offensive. Recently Hampton's scouts had informed army headquarters that much of Gregg's and Kautz's cavalry had been moved from the Union rear to points closer to Petersburg. The transfer meant, as Lee informed Hampton, "the enemy is very open to attack at City Point [Grant's headquarters on the Appomattox River above Petersburg] and other points where his wagons are parked in his rear. I wish you would have the matter closely inquired into and the roads and distances you would have to travel. A sudden blow in that quarter might be detrimental to him."[59]

Hampton, wishing to sustain his newly improved relations with his superior, at once looked into the matter Lee had brought up. He sent his best operatives, some in civilian dress, some disguised in Union blue, behind the enemy's lines. Two days later, Sergeant Shadburne reported his findings: While the supply wagons at City Point appeared to be well guarded, the cattle herd of the combined Union armies was less so. Almost twenty-five hundred beeves, earmarked for slaughter and consumption by the Federals at Petersburg, had been corralled at Coggin's Point on the James, eight miles east of City Point and twenty-three miles from Hampton's headquarters. The herd had been entrusted to the care of a handful of cavalrymen—a small detachment of Gregg's Thirteenth Pennsylvania—and thirty unarmed civilian drovers. Other troopers, including the First District of Columbia of Kautz's division, picketed the river on either side of Coggin's Point, but no closer than two miles from it.[60]

As his chief scout went on, Hampton began to envision capturing and driving off the herd. Such a mission, if successful, would not only strike a blow at enemy morale but would sustain Lee's habitually underfed army for at least a portion of the coming winter. In addition to its obvious utility, the idea of rustling cattle from under Grant's nose tickled Hampton's fancy and appealed to his sense of the absurd. Apparently it had the same effect on Lee, who promptly approved the project.

It took a week to work out the logistics, select the proper forces, and brief the principal officers on their roles in a most unusual operation. On the morning of September 14, Hampton began to put the carefully developed plan into execution. In predawn darkness, he led some four thousand officers and men—members of the Laurel Brigade (Tom Rosser back in command), Rooney Lee's division, and Dearing's brigade—out of their camps, down the Boydton Plank Road southwest of Petersburg, then through the open country to the east. That night the raiders crossed the sluggish but deep Blackwater River upon a bridge that had been destroyed but which Hampton's engineers and pioneers rebuilt. At dawn on the sixteenth, as planned, Lee's division and Dearing's brigade diverged from the main column to mount diversions on either side of the main objective—mainly west of it, the flank closest to the Union lines at Petersburg. Thereafter, Shadburne and his men guided Hampton and Rosser to Sycamore Church, a mile or so south of the corral at Coggin's Point.[61]

Before sunup, everyone was in position. Moving out, Rosser's brigade surprised the detachment of the First District of Columbia at Sycamore Church, killing, wounding, or capturing 219 of its 250 men and relieving them of the sixteen-shot Henry rifles they carried. Hampton was made a present of one of the prized weapons, which he carried through the rest of the war and into whose stock he proudly carved his name.

Having achieved their initial objective, Hampton and Rosser proceeded to the James. Encountering no opposition en route, they reached Coggin's Point at about 6:00 A.M. They discovered that the civilian drovers (there turned out to be almost seventy of them) had detected their approach and had tried to stampede the cattle to prevent their capture. The tactic failed because the raiders converged on the herd from several directions, boxing it in. Rosser's men chased down the few beasts that escaped, a chore that took more than a mile of hard riding. Once they had rounded up as many as they could catch and had gathered up such other spoils as they could find, the rustlers turned toward home. As Hampton later wrote, "the object of the expedition having been attained by the capture of the whole herd of cattle (2,486), by official return of the officer charged with the care of them, I withdrew everything before 8:00 A. M."[62]

Hearing sketchy but excited reports of the attack, Kautz and Brig. Gen. Henry E. Davies, Gregg's senior subordinate, attempted to overtake the thieves and recover their bovine booty. Given the ponderous pace of the rustlers on their homeward march, this did not seem, at first glance, to be a difficult undertaking. But hours passed before the generals could assemble their scattered forces and pick up Hampton's trail. On the way home, the Confederates again broke up to confuse and slow their pursuers. By the time a coordinated pursuit was in motion, Hampton had an unassailable head start. Then, too, the pursuers were too few to halt the rustlers, had they caught up to them. Davies's brigade consisted of fewer than two thousand men, while Kautz had been able to scrape together no more than seven hundred. When Rooney Lee and Dearing rejoined the main column en route to Petersburg, the Federals were outnumbered almost two-to-one.[63]

Kautz, who pursued Hampton and the herd, made a half-hearted effort to overtake his quarry. His only accomplishment was rounding up eighteen steers that had strayed from the seven-mile-long column. Davies, however, caught up with the Laurel Brigade, which Hampton had sent about two miles north of his own route. Attacking near Ebenezer Church on the Jerusalem Plank Road, Davies drove Rosser's men for about three miles to the south. At Belches's Mill, Rosser made a stand but was so hard pressed that Hampton had to reinforce him with Dearing, then with Rooney Lee's entire division. The enlarged force held Davies at bay until after dark.

While the cavalries sparred, Hampton had the beeves driven across the Blackwater at the reconstructed bridge, then across the Nottoway River at Freeman's Ford and Rowanty Creek via Wilkinson's Bridge. By the morning of September 17, Davies, realizing that he had been delayed too long to over-take Hampton and recapture the herd, broke off the pursuit. Kautz's men had kept pace with the Confederates into the evening of the sixteenth but remained a respectful distance behind them. The next morning, having ensured that his prizes were beyond recapture, Hampton turned about to offer battle, only to find Kautz and his seven hundred troopers gone.[64]

Thus ended the most unusual operation of Hampton's military career, and one of the most satisfying. During the three-day excursion into the enemy's rear, he and his men had marched more than a hundred miles, and had cap-tured, in addition to the cattle, more than three hundred Federals, at the cost of sixty-one casualties. These facts were highly pleasing to all involved in the effort to relieve the chronic hunger pangs of the defenders of Petersburg.

For weeks afterward, Hampton's fling at cattle rustling gave his army ammunition of a different sort to hurl at the enemy. The Confederates rarely missed an opportunity to let fly with what a South Carolina trooper called "one of the best jokes circulating" between the lines: "The Joke is this, that anytime the yankees['] Genls would order a charge & bring their men up toward our lines one of our boys would *bellow tremendously* very much to the annoyances of the yankees no doubt. Much as to say to them we have gotten your beeves."[65]

ELEVEN

"Sherman can be destroyed."

★ ★ ★

O nce again, Hampton and his men basked in praise delivered from on high. Upon returning from the cattle raid, the cavalry leader found a letter waiting from R. E. Lee. It read, in part: "I . . . beg to express my high appreciation of the skill & boldness you have displayed & my gratification at your handsome & valuable success. You will please convey to the officers & men of your command my thanks for the courage & energy with which they executed your orders . . . [and] added another to the list of important services rendered by the Cavalry during the present Campaign." Lee appended instructions for turning over the captured beeves to his commissary officers and assured Hampton that his command would receive as its share "such portion as it requires & as the interests of the service will permit."[1]

Hampton accepted the praise on behalf of his men, especially Shadburne and his scouts, whose daring, resourcefulness, and powers of observation had made the operation possible. Then he filed away the kind words and got back to work. For several days he riveted his attention on improving and extending the breastworks and rifle pits Lee had entrusted to his care. Following Meade's August lodgments on the Weldon Railroad, the Army of Northern Virginia had dug a line of entrenchments, about seven miles long, running southwestward from the original defenses below the city. This line paralleled the Army of the Potomac's defensive perimeter along the railroad and originally extended well below the point at which it ended—at Globe Tavern, three and a half miles from Petersburg. The Confederate line ran as

215

far south as Hatcher's Run, where it was refused at a 90-degree angle toward the west.[2]

The trenches covered the Boydton Plank Road, Lee's last lifeline. That road not only gave access to the South Side, the last intact railroad into Petersburg, but was used frequently by wagons hauling into the city supplies from North Carolina no longer carried by the Petersburg & Weldon. The necessity of keeping the plank road open was always uppermost in Lee's mind—if it were blocked, the city and its defenders were doomed.

For some months, dismounted members of Hampton's command had occupied sections of the main line of entrenchments as well as a second, partial line farther east along the Vaughan and Squirrel Level Roads. Then, two weeks after the cattle raid, Grant launched another series of offensives against both ends of Lee's line. On the Northside, the Army of the James made inroads toward Richmond, capturing fortifications that guarded the southern approaches to the city. Lee was so troubled by this lodgment that when he rushed up troops from below Petersburg, he personally led them in a series of counterattacks that nevertheless failed to recover the forts.[3]

Grant, anticipating that his opponent would denude his trench lines to augment the Northside, ordered Meade to advance below the city. During September 29–30, elements of the Fifth Corps attacked the works on the Vaughan Road, held by the division of the recently promoted Maj. Gen. M. Calbraith Butler. Although most of Butler's men held firm, the Yankees pried some out of their holes and propelled them into retreat. Hampton hustled to the scene of the break, where he assisted his favorite subordinate in driving back the enemy, recovering the lost ground, and taking numerous prisoners.[4]

The success of the counterattack was especially gratifying because Hampton labored at a greater-than-normal manpower disadvantage: His largest brigade was no longer with him. A week earlier Sheridan had defeated Jubal Early's army at Winchester, and three days later he thrashed the Valley Confederates at Fisher's Hill. In hopes of restoring the balance of power in the Shenandoah, the day before Butler was attacked, Robert E. Lee sent the Laurel Brigade to reinforce Early. Its leader would replace Fitz Lee, wounded at Winchester, as commander of Early's horsemen.

Rosser's transfer was bad news for Hampton, but the situation could have been worse: For a time, Rooney Lee's division had been earmarked for transfer north of the James to assist the recently arrived infantry, supported by Gary's cavalry, in opposing the Army of the James. Although the transfer was rescinded before it could occur, Hampton felt as if he were fighting with one hand tied behind him. But there was—as he knew—no help for it.[5]

With remarkable rapidity, matters went from bad to worse. On September 30, Meade's troops assaulted the trenches held by Dearing's brigade, now a part of Butler's division. In Dearing's absence—he was on sick leave—the Yankees captured a long section of his line. Hampton sought to regain the position with the support of Maj. Gen. Henry Heth's division of A. P. Hill's corps. Following a hurried conference, Heth struck the Federals in front, Hampton on their left at the head of two dismounted regiments of Lee's division and McGregor's horse artillery. Hampton reported that his men attacked "in the handsomest style . . . routing the enemy completely, capturing about nine hundred prisoners & ten standards." Staggered by Heth's assault as well as Hampton's, the enemy fell back to their own works.[6]

Hampton expected the Yankees to make another attempt to gain a foothold on the Vaughan Road, and he was not disappointed. On the morning of October 1 they again assailed Butler's position, and again Hampton responded by leading two of Lee's regiments to the rescue, this time via Peebles's Farm, just off the Squirrel Level Road. There he maneuvered toward the rear of the Federals opposing Butler. While he attacked from that direction, Butler launched a frontal assault. The combined effort forced the Federals to give way, but success came at heavy cost, General Dunovant being among the fatalities. Fearing the enemy would rally for yet another go at the Vaughan Road line, Hampton determined to preempt it by taking the would-be attackers in flank and rear. He was arranging infantry support for his maneuver when he heard that the Federals had turned the tables by getting into his rear. By the time he ascertained that the report was erroneous, darkness had descended, halting operations on that part of the field.[7]

By the evening of the first, the Yankee drive on the Southside had been contained, as had Ben Butler's offensive above the James. Meade's lines, however, now stretched three miles west of the Weldon Railroad, while the Army of the James's line enclosed captured positions too close to Richmond for anyone's comfort. His own work well done, Hampton pulled back and returned to camp with those troopers not needed to hold the trenches south of Petersburg.

Quiet abruptly returned to the Petersburg lines; surprisingly, it lingered for almost a month. Hampton's men were involved in no further action until the morning of October 27, when Grant made another, more determined attempt

217

to pass Lee's lower flank. The day was overcast and rainy; before it ended, it would become darker still for Wade Hampton.

This time, Grant was going for broke. He intended to cross the Boydton Plank Road and seize the South Side Railroad, turning Lee out of Petersburg and perhaps Richmond as well. For the movement, Meade made available two of Hancock's divisions, assisted by large portions of Warren's Fifth Corps and the Ninth Corps, now under Maj. Gen. John G. Parke. The movement got underway at 3:30 A.M., and although his supports were unable to make corresponding progress on his right, by noon Hancock had fought his way to the south side of Hatcher's Run, where he ran into Hill's infantry and Hampton's horse soldiers.[8]

Throughout the morning, the defenders put up major resistance, turning back numerous efforts to place bluecoated infantry on the Petersburg side of the run. Regardless of the weather, it was hot work, and it took a toll. Among the many casualties the defenders suffered, Captain Hart went down with a leg wound severe enough to require amputation.[9]

Although Hampton and the infantry who fought on all sides of him—Heth's and Mahone's divisions of Hill's corps—did a good job keeping back the Fifth and Ninth Corps, they failed to detect a turning movement by Hancock's men until almost too late. Early in the day, Hampton had asked that Dearing's brigade be relieved from its entrenchments and be sent to guard the area in his rear, including the Boydton Road. General Hill, however, thought Dearing's transfer too risky and vetoed the request. The upshot was that the Second Corps passed behind Hampton undetected. Shortly before one o'clock, with the rain continuing, now with a cold bite to it, Hampton's scouts informed him that Hancock had not only reached the plank road below Burgess's Tavern but was moving out the White Oak Road, which lay even closer to the railroad. An alarmed Hampton pulled Butler's and Lee's troopers out of line and rushed them west across muddy fields, followed by Hill's foot soldiers.

Galloping ahead of the main body, Hampton outdistanced everyone around him. Unable to keep pace, his staff, including Preston and Wade IV, trailed along in his wake. Reaching Burgess's Mill, he laid out a new line on the White Oak Road, his left resting on the mill itself. As soon as his troopers joined him, he had them dismount and throw up fieldworks. They completed the task just in time to absorb a limited attack by Hancock's vanguard. Then they held their ground stubbornly until the infantry arrived.[10]

At about four o'clock, following inconclusive skirmishing, Hampton learned that Hill was readying a full-scale assault. When the infantry went forward, so did Hampton's troopers. Lee's dismounted men attacked on the plank road, while Butler led his division in a saber charge that helped clear the White Oak Road of the enemy—at least temporarily.

Preston Hampton, unable to resist the temptation to join in the charge, placed himself near the head of Butler's column and put spurs to his mount. His son's impetuosity troubled Hampton, who appears to have been seized by a foreboding. He sent Preston's brother to stop him, then galloped after his older son, followed by his other aides. They reached Butler's column a minute or so too late. As Col. Zimmerman Davis of the Fifth South Carolina Cavalry recounted, "I saw a staff officer, who appeared to be riding to meet me, fall from his horse. I galloped up to see who he was and to render assistance, when General Hampton and his staff rode up. We all dismounted and General Hampton stooped over the prostrate form, gently raised his head and kissed him, saying: 'My son, my son'."[11]

Preston had taken a gunshot wound to the groin. By the time his father reached him, the young man's eyes had rolled up in his head and he was drifting into unconsciousness. While the general and his subordinates bent over Preston, as if to shield him from the rain, a Minié ball thudded into the back of Wade IV, who toppled over almost onto his brother. Davis dragged the older boy from the line of fire, then went looking for Dr. Taylor. By the time he returned with Hampton's surgeon and a wagon in which to convey the brothers to a field hospital, Preston had breathed his last. "Too late, doctor," his father murmured. The general then remounted and rode off to direct Hart's battery as it shelled Hancock's now-wavering ranks. Davis marveled at the accuracy of the battery's fire, which he attributed to Hampton's supervision. Years later, he remembered what "an ennobling and inspiring sight [it was] to see this grand hero, with the kiss from the lips of his dead son still warm upon his own, while the other son was being borne from the field severely wounded, thus subordinating parental affection to duty to his country."[12]

Somehow, he bore up under the unbearable. He had to—he had no choice. Even after Hancock's men withdrew from the Boydton Road, ending the latest—and, to this point, the most severe—threat to Petersburg and Richmond, the war went on and Hampton went with it. It helped that he learned within hours of Wade's wounding that his oldest son's condition was more painful than dangerous. It helped, too, that days after Preston's body had been escorted home by a family friend in Butler's division, Mary McDuffie Hampton traveled to Virginia to comfort her husband and share his grief.[13]

While she was away, unidentified persons—Union deserters, or perhaps disaffected Confederates—vandalized the family's home outside Columbia, ransacking it from top to bottom, stealing everything of value including every piece of Mary's jewelry, and scrawling epithets on the walls. Coming as it did on the heels of his son's killing, the wanton destruction appears to have hardened the general's heart and mind against his enemy. Heretofore, he had fought as a gentleman fights, according to a timeless code of honor that he felt duty bound to uphold. From now on, he would cut down Yankees ruthlessly and without a second thought. Every one he dispatched would be the victim of a personal reprisal, an installment payment in revenge.[14]

His mood grew even darker when November came and Abraham Lincoln won reelection by a respectable margin, the result of a revived war spirit throughout the Union. Grant and Lee might be deadlocked, but Sheridan had won a series of dramatic successes over Early, the most notable being the most recent—in mid-October at Cedar Creek. There Little Phil had turned certain defeat into overwhelming victory as much through the force of his personality as through his advantage in numbers. An even greater factor in reviving a war-weary North was Sherman's early-September capture and occupation of Atlanta, following its abandonment by Joe Johnston's successor, John Bell Hood. No longer would the Deep South be spared the iron fist; no longer would her war industries supply the armies of the Confederacy.[15]

Hampton was astute enough to recognize that Lincoln's victory killed the South's last hope of a negotiated peace, just as Sharpsburg and Gettysburg had killed its chances of foreign aid and intervention. With the armies of the Union everywhere—even at Petersburg—closing in on their starving, ragged, ill-equipped enemy, the war might already be lost. If so, Hampton would see it through, no matter how bitter the finale. Yet, if the end were truly approaching, his preference was to spend it in South Carolina among his people and his possessions. If he had to go down fighting, he wanted to do it while defending hearth, home, and a way of life that had shaped him as a soldier and a man.

The more he went about the business of the war, the more his thoughts turned to protecting his state not only against the people who had violated the sanctity of his home but also against the soldiers he had come to despise. In mid-November, Sherman left burning Atlanta behind and started on a six-week foray through Georgia at the head of sixty thousand men alert to new outlets for their aggression. As 1864 drew to a close, Sherman's armies were in Savannah, where they were poised to turn north and rampage through the Carolinas preparatory to joining Grant for the final bloodletting in Virginia.

Maj. Gen. William T. Sherman

En route, as Hampton foresaw, a blue-clad plague would descend on his state, infamous in the North as the cradle of the rebellion. He had no illusions as to the result. He had heard that his old enemy, Judson Kilpatrick, now Sherman's commander of cavalry, had issued sulfur matches to his troopers with instructions to apply them liberally to the homes and plantations of South Carolinians. Hampton shuddered at the vision of family members, life-long friends, and faithful servants caught in the path of such bestial marauders.[16]

He passed through the final engagements of the year in an abstracted calm, as if his mind were elsewhere. In late November, he worked hard on strengthening and extending his trench lines. Colonel Waring noted in his diary, "Hampton is going to make one continuous line of fortifications" toward the rear of Petersburg. In early December, he opposed enemy infantry and cavalry on familiar ground, Ream's and Stony Creek Stations. These Yankees were vandals, too—destroyers not only of the Weldon Railroad but of private homes along the right-of-way, which they gleefully looted and burned and whose inhabitants—men, women, and children—they assaulted without mercy. Hampton was glad to learn that several of these fiends, stragglers from their regiments, were found dead, their throats cut from ear to ear by outraged pursuers.[17]

For a time, it seemed as if everyone but he was going south to meet the invaders. Late in November, Pierce Young's brigade was permitted to return to Georgia, there to remount, recruit, and assist the small cavalry division of the Army of Tennessee, under Maj. Gen. Joseph Wheeler, the only horsemen actively opposing Sherman's March to the Sea. The following month, Hampton, at Butler's urging, petitioned army headquarters to return the First Division to South Carolina for the same purpose.

Hampton's temporary superior and long-term subordinate, Joseph Wheeler

The prospect that Butler's request would be granted made Hampton all the more hopeful that he, too, might return home in time to parry Sherman's thrust, something he believed was not beyond the realm of the possible. He told his sister early in December, "I am looking with the most profound interest to our state and Geo[rgia]. Surely if active and proper measures are taken, Sherman can be destroyed. He should not be allowed to cross the Savannah [River]. If he gets over we should put an immense force of negroes to block every road. They can do this faster, than he can clear the obstructions, and every hour of delay, benefits us." He added, with an almost audible sigh: "I wish that I could be there, for I should like to strike one blow on the soil of my own State."[18]

As it happened, he would be there. Early in the new year, 1865, if not earlier, he applied to Robert E. Lee for permission to accompany Butler to South Carolina to oversee his command's rehabilitation and then lead it against Sherman. The army leader seemed receptive to the idea, although from the first he regarded any transfer as a temporary expedient. Hampton assured him that if properly managed, South Carolina's defense forces were sufficient to deal Sherman a crippling blow before the winter ended. Lee latched onto this hope, informing Jefferson Davis that he would accede to Hampton's wish, but only "with the understanding that it [Butler's cavalry] is to return to me in the spring in time for the opening of the campaign. May I ask you to impose this condition & let me know."[19]

Nor was Lee willing to let Hampton and Butler go without a basis for believing their recruitment program would succeed: "If the Governor [Andrew G. Magrath] can give no assurance of their procuring mounts, or if Hampton cannot make arrangements for subsistence of the horses, I will not send them." On the other hand, "I think Hampton will be of service in mounting his men & arousing the spirit & strength of the State & otherwise do good. . . ." In the end, Davis gave him the discretion to grant Hampton's petition, and Lee used it. It is not known whether Davis impressed on Hampton Lee's stipulation of an early return to Virginia.[20]

Davis did ensure that Hampton would not go off to a new station at an old rank. On February 4 he directed Adjutant General Cooper to make out a nomination for Hampton as a lieutenant general. Ten days later the nomination cleared the Adjutant and Inspector General's Office, and Davis forwarded it to the Confederate Senate. That body acted with remarkable swiftness—a tribute to the its esteem for Hampton—and by February 15 the president was informed that the nomination had been confirmed. The promotion made Hampton the highest-ranking cavalry commander of the war. The renowned Nathan Bedford Forrest would later attain the same rank but would lack Hampton's seniority.[21]

Hampton would always contend that General Lee had advocated and advanced his promotion. Had Hampton gone to South Carolina as a major general, he would have been subordinate to Wheeler, his senior by several months. Hampton contended that Lee, who had a low opinion of the Georgia-born cavalryman, "refused to let me serve under Wheeler." Here Hampton appears rather more than a little disingenuous. He, not Lee, objected to his serving under Wheeler. Wade Hampton was too old, too proud, and too cognizant of the command experience he had acquired to subject himself to the dictates of an officer eighteen years his junior, regardless of Wheeler's professional education and his own lack of it.[22]

Wheeler was not only a West Point graduate but also a veteran of prewar service in the Regiment of Mounted Rifles. The author of a well-regarded manual of cavalry tactics, he was widely regarded as an authority on the training and employment of his arm. His youth, rank, nickname ("Fightin' Joe"), and long record of service suggested he was an officer of merit, as did the fact that his was the only regular force of any size to oppose Sherman's excursion through Georgia. But his men had acquired a reputation for loose organization and poor discipline, blame for which accrued to their commander.[23]

The army whose cavalry Wheeler had led for more than two years had elected to invade Tennessee rather than pursue Sherman to the coast. John Bell Hood's choice of objectives proved an unwise one. In mid-December, outside Nashville, his army and his career had been shattered by troops under Maj. Gen. George H. Thomas, detached from Sherman's command. Reduced to a shadow of its former size, Hood's once-formidable army had limped out of its namesake state and into northern Mississippi, where it appeared to lie down to die.

Wheeler may have escaped Hood's fate, but his attempt to halt, or at least slow, Sherman failed miserably. During the campaign across Georgia, his command succeeded only in solidifying its reputation as a band of thieves. Many residents swore that Fightin' Joe's troopers did more damage to their homes and possessions than the most avid of Sherman's "bummers" (foragers).[24]

Whatever lay ahead of them, Butler started his men south on January 19. Three days later Hampton, having bade farewell to scores of superiors, colleagues, and subordinates, entrained for Columbia in company with his staff, minus two members who had recently left it—one for the hospital, the other for a grave. Shortly before departing his Virginia camp for the last time, he dashed off a letter to his friend Louis Wigfall: "We are passing through a fiery ordeal but if we 'quit ourselves like men' we must be successful. I do not allow myself to contemplate any other than a successful issue to our struggle."[25]

Hampton, Butler, and their men arrived in Columbia to the huzzahs of an embattled people who viewed them as deliverers. With Sherman's troops already in their state and heading toward them, the local residents were grasping at any sign that their families and homes would be defended. The realists among them, including Governor Magrath, knew better. Even eighteen-year-old Emma LeConte, daughter of one of South Carolina College's leading faculty members, realized that the understrength, horse-poor division could ensure only that "Columbia couldn't be taken by raid."[26]

After parading through the city (astride borrowed mounts) to the cheers and well-wishes of the populace, Butler's command went into camp to begin the nigh-impossible task of regaining its old effectiveness. Meanwhile,

Hampton repaired to Millwood, where Mary and the children were staying, for a joyous if bittersweet reunion with loved ones, family friends, and faithful slaves he had not seen in almost a year. Later he toured his ravaged home, surveying the damage with hooded eyes. Then he returned to the city to assume whatever duties were assigned to him.

At first, he found himself in an anomalous, and somewhat embarrassing, position. Until his promotion was confirmed, he was technically Joe Wheeler's subordinate, although clearly Wheeler did not know what to do with him. While the two men greeted each other cordially enough, from the first there was an awkwardness in their relationship, which they covered up with an elaborate formality.[27]

According to some accounts, Hampton's status was determined on February 7, when he was attached to the corps of Lt. Gen. William J. Hardee. But Hardee was then commanding at Charleston, a post to which Hampton was never assigned. On the same date, Hampton was officially assigned to the command of the troopers he had brought from Virginia, which now included Young's brigade, recently recalled from Georgia. Ten days later, when word of his confirmation as lieutenant general came through, his authority was extended to Wheeler's horsemen as well. Officially, Hampton's command consisted of a corps under Wheeler, plus Butler's division and several unattached regiments and companies. Later it would add the Washington Artillery, which, without Jim Hart, would join Hampton in North Carolina. The total number of troopers at Hampton's disposal was reckoned at seventy-six hundred, but this was an inflated figure—his effective force was probably at least fifteen hundred fewer.[28]

Regardless of how many men he led, Columbia became his primary responsibility. On February 10, the department commander, General Beauregard, arrived in the city en route from Augusta, Georgia. Learning that his old subordinate lacked a command, the hero of Fort Sumter, First Manassas, and Petersburg placed him in charge of all troops in the vicinity of the capital. These included not only the horse soldiers of Wheeler and Butler but the remnant of the infantry division of Maj. Gen. Carter L. Stevenson, a veteran of the Army of Tennessee.[29]

Other troops were, or would soon be, available for the defense of South Carolina, although none would reach Columbia in time to protect it against Sherman. Hardee's command numbered six thousand; but although Hampton hoped it would transfer immediately to Columbia, it did not evacuate

Charleston until mid-February. What remained of Hood's army—perhaps five thousand demoralized troops—was heading for South Carolina, although its fighting ability was questionable. Later a few thousand troops would come down from North Carolina under Gen. Braxton Bragg and Maj. Gen. Robert F. Hoke, but only after failing to prevent the capture of Fort Fisher and the coastal city it had defended, Wilmington, the last operating Southern port of any value.[30]

With so few resources at his disposal, Hampton had no realistic hope of keeping the enemy out of Columbia, which enjoyed neither fortifications nor natural defenses. After February 13, when Beauregard traveled to Charleston, leaving Hampton in command, the latter took such steps as he could with a view to local defense. These included hauling bales of cotton from Columbia's storehouses and piling them in the streets and along outlying roads. Eventually thousands of bales blocked access to key parts of the city. It was a bad idea: The makeshift breastworks would deter no Yankee, only complicate efforts at evacuation. Moreover, as would become horribly clear, the flammable crop posed dangers to inhabitants and their dwellings.[31]

By such an inadequate measure as this, Hampton proposed to hold the city at all costs. On a daily basis he strove to convince the city fathers that he could do so. He may have believed it was possible, or he may have been attempting to buck up morale and prevent panic among the people. In either case, his repeated opinion that Sherman could be kept out of Columbia persuaded many residents to remain when they might have saved themselves and at least some of their possessions by fleeing before the Yankees arrived.

Hampton made other mistakes during his term as local commander—evidence of his inexperience in municipal administration (his stint as "military governor" of Chambersburg, Pennsylvania, notwithstanding). Despite the pleas and protestations of government employees, he failed to institute measures to remove Confederate stores, equipment, ordnance, and treasury holdings before Sherman arrived. He overruled efforts by officials, including Mayor Thomas J. Goodwyn, to destroy the large supply of liquor in Columbia. When the Federals arrived, local merchants, in an attempt to curry their favor, made available a seemingly inexhaustible supply of whiskey and wine, with tragic if predictable consequences. And although he persuaded Beauregard to rescind his order to destroy by fire the cotton stored in and around Columbia, Hampton failed to take the necessary steps to prevent civilians and undisciplined soldiers from torching bale after bale.[32]

The results of Hampton's acts of omission and commission were felt as soon as Sherman's troops drew up on the south bank of the Congaree River and began to shell the city. Around nine o'clock on the morning of February 17, after having engaged the Yankees for some time, the general withdrew his troopers from the south side and led them through the town in retreat. En route, they passed the anguished, upturned faces of residents who knew at last that their city was doomed. Hampton had remained sanguine about his ability to hold the place almost to the last. Hours before the Union guns started in, heralding the approach of four columns of troops, Mayor Goodwyn and the other city fathers had discussed flying a white flag from the steeple of city hall. Learning of their intentions, an angry Hampton sent word that if a surrender banner were run up, he would have it hauled down at once.[33]

On his way out of Columbia, Hampton got a close-up look at some of the material at his command. Butler's division made a stubborn defense, slowing the enemy's advance to and across the river. In contrast, Wheeler's troopers exited the place without any thought of defending it, even briefly. Hampton would claim that "Wheeler's men did not fire a shot in the city." Before departing, they did, however, loot as many stores and homes as time permitted. When Hampton challenged one band of pillagers, several troopers leveled pistols and carbines at him and threatened to shoot if he intervened.[34]

Mary Chesnut's husband, who witnessed this scene, supposed that the thieves "did not know Hampton, or they were drunk, and angry at his being put over Wheeler's head." Before violence occurred, some of Stevenson's foot soldiers happened by and the troopers dispersed. According to Mrs. Chesnut, the confrontation left the general more embarrassed than indignant or fearful: "He did not order any arrests, or want any notice whatever to be taken of this insubordination."[35]

The pillaging by Wheeler's men paled in comparison to what the invaders did when they took full possession of the city. An orgy of drinking, looting, vandalism, and indiscriminate violence—in which not only bummers but also many locals, including just-liberated slaves, indulged—commenced late on the seventeenth. Despite the efforts of Sherman's provost marshals to halt it, the rioting continued through the night. For much of that time, the revelry was bathed in the lurid glow of flames. Around midafternoon, perhaps by accident, some of the cotton that filled the streets caught fire. Later, torches were deliberately applied not only to the improvised barricades but also to stores, offices, factories, and houses throughout the city. Local fire companies and bucket brigades manned by soldiers and civilians proved powerless before the conflagration, which, fed by numberless small fires and fanned by northwest winds, raged out of control for several hours. By the time it burned itself out, about a third of the city had been reduced to charred ruins.[36]

As Hampton retreated via the northeastern suburbs, he saw that the fire had already spread beyond the city limits. Sadly, he saw the direction it was moving in. Within hours, three of his estates east of the city, including his already-ruined home and the majestic expanse that was Millwood, would be totally engulfed in flames. Mary, the children, the Aunties, the family slaves, and the rest of the extended Hampton family had long since fled, so he had no fear that his loved ones would be harmed, at least not physically. Even so,

The ruins of Millwood, a casualty of Sherman's invasion

February 17, 1865, was the most terrible day in the life of a family that had already experienced more than its share of tragedy.[37]

The knife that cut into the heart of the Hampton clan was given a cruel twist by William T. Sherman, who, after the fire died out, publicly accused Hampton of causing it by unwisely burning the cotton piled inside the city: "I declare in the presence of my God that Hampton burned Columbia, and that he alone is responsible for it." When he learned of his enemy's contention, Hampton issued an angry denial and called Sherman a liar. Years later, when penning his memoirs, Sherman not only exonerated Hampton but admitted that he had falsely blamed him—as a representative of that breed of Southern aristocrat that Sherman held responsible for starting the war—in order to lower his standing in the eyes of his fellow South Carolinians.[38]

Even before he learned of Sherman's accusation, Hampton entered into a vitriolic quarrel with the Union commander. During the week following its capture of Columbia, Sherman's army began moving northeastward toward its next objective, Goldsboro, North Carolina. In getting there it encountered much resistance from Hampton's horsemen, mainly Butler's division. The cavalry attacked not only moving columns but also small units operating behind the lines, paying especial attention to bummers. On February 23, Butler, with Young's brigade, overhauled a foraging expedition near Little Lynch's Creek in Kershaw County, capturing and ransacking its wagons. When pursuing infantry later overtook some of the raiders, their commander claimed that two of his men, who fell into Butler's hands, were "brutally murdered in plain view of our skirmishers." The officer relayed the information to Sherman's headquarters, and the following day the Union commander sent a letter, under flag of truce, inside Hampton's lines. To the cavalry leader Sherman complained that "our foraging parties are murdered after capture and labeled 'Death to all foragers'." Although he doubted that Hampton either authorized or condoned such brutality, he declared that "I have ordered a similar number of prisoners in our hands to be disposed of in like manner. I hold about eleven hundred prisoners captured in various ways, and can stand it as long as you." He then attempted to justify his foraging policies by citing historical precedent, and he asserted his right to protect those who executed that policy.[39]

Hampton did not receive Sherman's communication until the twenty-seventh. He replied at once, and with heat. He denied any knowledge of such incidents as Sherman had described and disavowed any intent to murder prisoners unless his opponent began doing so, in which case "for every soldier of mine 'murdered' by you, I shall have executed at once two of yours, giving in all cases preference to any officers who may be in my hands." He further pledged to shoot any bummers caught in the act of burning homes, stressing "the right that every man has to defend his home and to protect those who are dependent on him." Hurling words like darts, he added that "from my heart I wish that every old man and boy in my country who can fire a gun would shoot down, as he would a wild beast, the men who are desolating their land, burning their homes, and insulting their women." This last was a reference to a number of rapes that Sherman's men reportedly committed in Columbia as well as in outlying areas.[40]

No further communication on the subject emanated from the enemy's camp, making Hampton believe he had carried his point. The exchange of correspondence accomplished nothing; atrocities on both sides continued through the remainder of the campaign, although neither Sherman nor Hampton resorted to executing prisoners in retaliation for the offenses of the other. The clash of words and attitudes was further proof that, after almost four years of waging war in honorable fashion, Wade Hampton had removed the gloves. He was willing to pay back in kind any cruelty, any outrage perpetrated by an enemy unbounded by considerations of human decency.

Five days after the occupation and sack of Columbia, Hampton received a new commanding officer. On February 22, Robert E. Lee, the newly installed general in chief of all Confederate forces, reinstated Joe Johnston to overall command in the western theater. Johnston's new domain incorporated Beauregard's department with what remained of the Army of Tennessee. Lee enjoined him to "proceed at once to effect a concentration of all available forces, and make the necessary dispositions to thwart the designs of the enemy operating in these departments."[41]

Those "available forces" were few enough, even after Bragg and Hoke came down from North Carolina, Hardee pulled out of Charleston, and "the complete mob" that was the Army of Tennessee began to assemble near Charlotte. The combined force amounted to no more than twenty-five thousand troops of all arms, many of them poorly clothed and equipped, and others—especially the heavy artillerists of Hardee's old garrison—untutored in field campaigning. In addition to a shortage of combat troops, Johnston was saddled with a plethora of high-ranking subordinates, including two full generals (Bragg and Beauregard), five lieutenant generals (Hardee, D. H. Hill and A. P. Stewart, in addition to Hampton and his former artillery subordinate, Stephen D. Lee), and a gaggle of major generals including Hoke, Stevenson, Lafayette McLaws, and Benjamin F. Cheatham. It seemed possible, perhaps likely, that these subordinates, each of whom jealously guarded the prerogatives of rank and seniority, would get in each other's way, and Johnston's as well, at some point in the campaigning ahead.[42]

Although outnumbered more than two-to-one, Johnston was expected to overtake and halt Sherman's superbly conditioned veterans before they reached Goldsboro. Two additional corps under Maj. Gens. John M. Schofield and Alfred H. Terry were marching to that city from the North Carolina coast to link with the captor of Atlanta and Savannah and raise his manpower to above a hundred thousand. If two-to-one odds were difficult to contend against, Johnston had no chance of prevailing against five times as many Yankees. His only hope of stopping Sherman short of Goldsboro lay in throwing himself into his enemy's path and employing a tactic seemingly alien to his nature—the offensive.[43]

Regardless of the crushing odds the man faced, Hampton was glad of the opportunity to serve under him for the first time in almost three years. Before leaving Virginia, he had asked Louis Wigfall to use his influence to get Johnston reinstated. Upon reaching Columbia, he had confided to Mary Chesnut his opinion that "Joe is equal to even Gen. Lee—if not superior." The diarist attributed Hampton's contention at least in part to his uneven relations with his former commander: "He has not quite forgiven Lee yet that cruel blow to his vanity."[44]

Johnston was in Lincolnton, North Carolina, well to the northwest of Sherman's route of march, when he received word of his assignment. Apprehending an enemy movement into North Carolina, he hastened to Charlotte, where he joined the early arrivals from his old army and where, on February 25, he officially assumed command. There he remained for several days, waiting for his widely dispersed troops to come within range of his authority (as Hampton later wrote of those troops, "it would scarcely have been possible to disperse a force more effectually"). In the meantime, Hampton's troopers scouted the country that lay in the path of the two wings of Sherman's vast army—the Fourteenth and Twentieth Corps, under Maj.

Gen. Henry W. Slocum, on the left flank, and, farther east, Maj. Gen. Oliver Otis Howard, with the Fifteenth and Seventeenth Corps.[45]

As March came in, Hampton tracked the Federals from Lancaster to Cheraw, from which place they unceremoniously evicted Hardee's forces on the second. The invaders then swept across the border into North Carolina with a speed and confidence that overawed many of their opponents. Hampton, however, kept up a series of rearguard actions to prevent Sherman from making even further, faster progress. Every day Butler's troopers, and less frequently Wheeler's, lashed out at the head and flanks of both columns, in places slowing their march to a crawl and sometimes even bringing it to a temporary halt.

Most of Hampton's encounters were with detachments of Kilpatrick's division, which led Sherman's advance. The Yankee troopers rode sleek horses and wielded the most advanced repeating arms. Despite their experience and the formidable appearance they presented, Hampton thought little of their fighting ability and even less of their leader, whom he considered a cowardly braggart in the manner of John Pope. He felt he had a right to be contemptuous of the diminutive Irishman. He had outgeneraled the man on fields including Brandy Station, Hanover, and Hunterstown. A year ago, near Mechanicsville, Virginia, despite being outnumbered ten-to-one, he had whipped the man so soundly that Kilpatrick not only gave up his plan to attack Richmond but soon afterward left the Army of the Potomac in disgrace.

Kilpatrick returned Hampton's scorn, with interest. A poor memory kept him from recalling his past travail at his opponent's hands. He knew only what he saw: a haughty aristocrat in command of dirt farmers neither capable enough nor sizable enough to call themselves cavalrymen. Kilpatrick boasted that his troopers were superior to their enemy in every facet of mounted service—horsemanship, marksmanship, discipline, tactics. He would prove as much to the good people of North Carolina if Hampton would only remain in his path long enough to permit a climactic confrontation.

By the first week in March, it was clear that Sherman was heading for Fayetteville. Thus, Hampton moved in that direction, as did, some miles apart from him, Hardee's corps. On the seventh, Hampton learned that Kilpatrick, with a portion of his command, had interposed between his force and Hardee's, thus presenting an opportunity to stage the showdown his opponent professed to seek. For his part, Kilpatrick saw only that he had gotten between Hampton and Fayetteville. Thus he moved to block the roads the Confederate would have to take to reach the city. In the process, he gambled by dividing his command in the face of the enemy. Only half of it remained with him when, on the ninth, he pitched his headquarters at Monroe's Cross Roads, northwest of Fayetteville.[46]

Taking careful note of Kilpatrick's recklessness—another sign of his arrogance—Hampton called in his outlying detachments and moved into position to launch a second surprise attack on Kilpatrick's camps one year, almost to the day, after the first. From a captured officer, Hampton learned the location of the private dwelling in which Kilpatrick had his quarters. After scouring the vicinity, his scouts reported that Kilpatrick had posted no pickets across the west side of his camp, apparently believing an extensive swamp in that area provided suitable protection. Hampton digested the information and used it to develop a plan aimed at attacking Kilpatrick's camp, routing the several regiments of troopers that surrounded it, and if at all possible, capturing the Yankee leader and carrying him off.

Hampton carefully briefed his subordinates on his proposal, and at sunrise, they and their men moved out to put it to the test. Butler led out, his riders

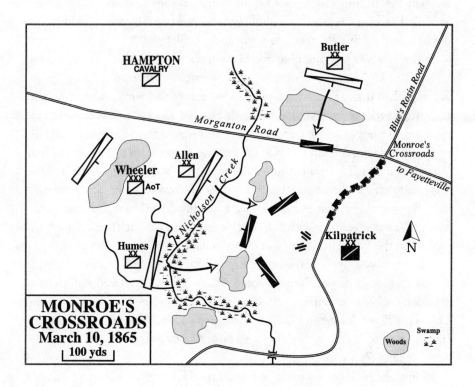

circumventing the swamp and attacking the north side of the camp. They struck with such speed, power, and surprise that within minutes they had captured or put to flight every Yankee within several hundred yards of Kilpatrick's house. Kilpatrick himself later called the attack "the most formidable cavalry charge I have ever witnessed."[47]

The attackers failed, however, to bag the general. Roused from his sleep by the shooting and shouting, Kilpatrick bolted from the house wearing only a shirt over long underwear. Spying him but taking him for a common soldier, one of Butler's officers swooped down, pointed a pistol in his face, and demanded to know General Kilpatrick's whereabouts. Thinking quickly, the Irishman pointed to a passing Yankee and cried, "There he goes on that black horse!" The officer galloped after the rider, whereupon Kilpatrick dashed for the safety of the surrounding woods.[48]

Another resident of the house was soon caught up in the fury and chaos of the assault: Mary Boozer, a comely young woman from a family of South Carolina Unionists, who had willingly accompanied Kilpatrick on his travels through her region. Frightened by the deadly commotion surrounding her, Miss Boozer, clad in a scanty nightgown, escaped harm by taking refuge in a ditch, where she hid through the remainder of the fight.[49]

Beyond its victims' humiliation, Hampton's attack—which later became known in Confederate circles as "Kilpatrick's Shirttail Skedaddle"—accomplished little. The swamp on the west side of the camp and a large contingent of Federals who rallied beside it blocked the path of Wheeler's two columns, neither of which contributed its full weight to the assault. This failure—which Hampton later ascribed not to the enemy's defense but to the halt Wheeler's men made in order to loot a camp they had overrun—enabled the Yankees to rally and counterattack with their Spencer repeaters and later with their horse artillery. Hampton's men were steadily driven back, but many continued to exchange shots with Kilpatrick's men until a detachment of foot soldiers from the Fifteenth Corps came up to chase them away.[50]

Having missed his opportunity to capture Kilpatrick and seriously damage his command—although he had come away with five hundred half-dressed prisoners—Hampton led his brigades on to Fayetteville and beyond, to the Cape Fear River. Johnston's scattered infantry and artillery were also concentrating in that direction, hunting a suitable location from which to make a stand against Sherman.

Riding ahead of his troopers, Hampton reached Fayetteville in advance of the enemy; there he bedded down for the night. Next morning, the general was at breakfast at a local hotel when a large detachment of Kilpatrick's troopers, perhaps seeking revenge for being taken by such surprise the night before, burst into town and began to drive Wheeler's recently arrived troopers through the streets. Hampton left the hotel and tried to persuade Fightin' Joe's troopers to make a stand. Unable to rally more than a handful, he gave up the effort as a lost cause, then turned toward the open country beyond the Cape Fear—only to halt when a stalwart member of the Iron Scouts, eighteen-year-old Hugh Scott, begged him to delay long enough to oppose a fast-approaching body of horsemen.

Hampton responded to the petition by gathering up the only troopers near him, including Edward Wells, and leading them in a hell-for-leather charge through the streets and into the head of a Yankee force that outnumbered his band ten-to-one. When the forces collided, Hampton cut two Federals out of their saddles with his heroic-size sword (according to Union accounts, Hampton killed only one man, who had already been wounded). The rest of the Yankees promptly fled. Hampton, his fighting blood still pumping, chased them down and helped corral a dozen of them. Although dressed in Confederate gray, one of them turned out to be chief of scouts of Sherman's Seventeenth Corps. Hampton entrusted eleven of the prisoners to his provost guard, but he imprisoned the scout with the intention of executing him the following morning. Instead, as befit a member of his branch, the prisoner broke free of his guards during the night and raced to safety aboard a stolen horse.[51]

As he moved northeastward from Fayetteville, Hampton massed the strung-out elements of his command, including as many of Wheeler's troopers as had not deserted or left the army on self-authorized foraging missions. By the sixteenth, he was moving toward Bentonville. Johnston was then at Smithfield, on the railroad between Goldsboro and Raleigh, where a large portion of his main force had collected. His restyled Army of Tennessee consisted of Hardee's corps, Hoke's division (under Bragg), and the contingent of the original Army of Tennessee under A. P. Stewart.

Johnston had made up his mind to fight Sherman before he reached Goldsboro. As a basis for selecting a suitable battlefield, on the seventeenth he asked Hardee—whose corps the previous day had been driven from the crossroads of Averasboro at the crossing of the Cape Fear—for intelligence about

Sherman's latest movements. When he failed to gain what he needed from the infantry leader, Johnston petitioned Hampton, who was then near Bentonville in the path of the Union advance, for the same information. He also solicited suggestions as to the best place to stop and lie in wait for the enemy.[52]

Hampton replied that from what he and his scouts had been able to determine, Sherman's wings were far enough apart that either could be attacked without fear of quick reinforcement by the other. He advised Johnston to strike at the column approaching from Averasboro and recommended Bentonville as a suitable venue for a surprise assault. Johnston accepted his cavalry chief's advice, not realizing that some of it was based on maps that made Sherman's wings look farther apart than they really were. The faulty maps also caused Johnston to underestimate the time necessary to mass his troops, especially Hardee's command, for the coming confrontation. Unaware of these errors, the army leader ordered Hardee, Bragg, and Stewart to converge on Bentonville, where they would attack Slocum's troops as they reached Bentonville via the Goldsboro Road.[53]

On the eighteenth, Johnston conferred at Bentonville with Hampton, who proposed a detailed plan of attack—based on his own careful study of the local terrain—that his superior adopted. Early the next morning, Johnston placed Hoke's troops, screened by Hampton's troopers, astride the Goldsboro Road. Hoke's job was to block the advancing Federals in front, while Hardee and Stewart, from concealed positions in the woods to the northwest, burst forth at a critical juncture to take the enemy in flank and by surprise.

When Slocum's troops arrived, the plan appeared to work perfectly—at first. Despite determined resistance, the Yankee infantry drove in Hampton's troopers. Around 10:00 A.M., the Federals ran into Hoke's men farther east, who from behind prepared defenses opened with musketry as well as with the only brace of artillery in Johnston's command. A testimonial of sorts to the staying-power of Hampton's men was the fact that for over an hour, Slocum believed he was tangling only with cavalry, supported by a few cannon. The wing commander informed Sherman by courier of his situation and opined that he would not require reinforcing.[54]

When Slocum finally understood that he was facing veteran infantry, he pulled back and went over to the defensive. At this moment, the flank drive Hampton had conceived of was supposed to have gone into operation. It was delayed, however, by Hardee's failure to reach his assigned position for another ninety minutes or so, as well as by Bragg's plea that Hoke be reinforced. When Hardee arrived, Johnston weakened his turning movement by detaching troops to assist Hoke.

Hardee's tardiness and the change in plans postponed the envelopment until 3:00 P.M. When Hardee and Stewart finally attacked, they cut off two Fourteenth Corps brigades, pummeled them mercilessly, and forced them into hasty retreat. But the delay in attacking had permitted the Twentieth Corps to come up in rear of the Fourteenth. The newcomers blunted a second advance by Hardee and his supports. Three more times the Confederates attacked; at one point Hoke joined in, before Bragg ordered his troops back to their original position. Worn down by excessive casualties, especially during the fighting of the past six months, Johnston's men could no longer generate the power and tenacity they had once been known for. Desperate fighting continued through the rest of the day and into the evening before Johnston recalled everyone to their preattack positions.[55]

That night, more of Slocum's men reached the field, and the next day Sherman moved with Howard's column to the relief of the Left Wing, ensuring Johnston could accomplish nothing more at Bentonville. On the twenty-first, when Sherman sent a force to cut his line of retreat, Johnston scrambled across Mill Creek, his escape route kept open by the heroic efforts of the troops of Hardee and Hampton.[56]

Although the battle had demonstrated there was fight in the patchwork army Johnston had inherited, his troops had suffered far too many casualties—more than 2,600, to Sherman's 1,650—to offer hope that they could do anything more than occasionally slow the inexorable advance of their enemy. Shrugging off the lumps he had received over the past few days, Sherman resumed his march to Goldsboro, where, on the twenty-third, he joined Schofield and Terry. The Carolinas campaign was over. Nothing barred Sherman from moving to Virginia to help Grant break the Confederate hold on Petersburg and Richmond.

But his presence there was not needed. On April 4, with Johnston's headquarters relocated to Smithfield, his troops received the depressing but perhaps not unexpected news that Petersburg and Richmond had fallen. Both cities had been evacuated two days earlier, and Yankee troops had marched in the following morning. The intelligence made Johnston believe that Sherman would immediately join Grant. To make the link-up as difficult as possible, he ordered Hampton to destroy the railroads outside Goldsboro.[57]

While he moved to comply, Hampton warned his superior that, based on the reports of his scouts, he expected Sherman to leave Goldsboro for Raleigh within a day or so. At 4:00 A.M. on the tenth, Sherman's troops marched out of the city they had occupied three weeks before and started northwestward, just as Hampton had predicted. Over the next three days, as Johnston's little army retreated behind them, Hampton's troopers challenged the oncoming Yankees at several points—along Moccasin Creek, on the Stage Road to Smithfield, and finally on the eastern outskirts of Raleigh.[58]

On the twelfth, as Johnston's sullen troops retreated through the streets of Raleigh, Hampton instructed Wheeler to burn Battle's Bridge over Swift Creek, denying Sherman access to the city. A sharp fight erupted along the stream late that morning when Kilpatrick's cavalry came up to battle Hampton's rear guard, consisting of Colonel Waring and his Jeff Davis Legion, ensconced in rifle pits and behind breastworks above the creek. Finding the bridge unusable, the Federals dismounted and plunged through the stream, cheering raucously as they went. On the far side, they uprooted Waring's men and sent them racing up the tracks of the North Carolina Railroad, while Sherman's main body came up in their rear to take full possession of the city. Captured Confederates, and soon their comrades in Hampton's main body, learned that the cheering had been prompted by the receipt of a news bulletin from Virginia: On April 9, 1865, Robert E. Lee had surrendered the Army of Northern Virginia at Appomattox Court House.[59]

When he heard the report, Hampton refused to credit it, at least when in the company of others. Manly Wellman states that somewhere north of Raleigh, the general formed his troopers into a hollow square and publicly branded the news out of Virginia a falsehood. Wellman also has him hedging his bets by declaring that he would lead everyone willing to go with him on a defiant trek to the Trans-Mississippi Department, where they would fight on no matter what lesser mortals elsewhere chose to do.[60]

Whether Wellman's account is true or not, it suggests that if Hampton denied the report of Lee's capitulation, it was only because he could not bring himself to believe it. Other high-ranking commanders were not so self-delusive. On the day Sherman's troops flooded into Raleigh, Joe Johnston met in Greensboro with Jefferson Davis, who had fled Richmond on the eve of its fall with a party of high-ranking civilians, including most of his cabinet. At the meeting, Johnston presented the officials with a gloomy assessment of his chances of stopping Sherman, and he strongly recommended that Davis authorize a peace parlay with the Union commander.[61]

As a result, Johnston was directed to open communication with Sherman on the subject under discussion. That night, a message went from Johnston's headquarters to Hampton's, near Hillsboro, with a covering request that it be delivered through the lines by a trusted officer of the cavalry corps staff. Hampton was not informed of its contents, but he must have suspected it was a request for an interview to discuss the terms upon which Sherman would receive the surrender of the Army of Tennessee.[62]

The end of the war in the Carolinas was fast approaching, but whether Wade Hampton would accept the fact, or would deny it as strongly as he had denied the "baseless rumor" of Lee's capitulation, remained an open question.

TWELVE

"My reputation is the only thing that I have left."

★ ★ ★

J ohnston's letter produced a meeting with Sherman at the home of a farmer named Bennett, near Durham Station, on April 17. Hampton accompanied his commander, as did five aides including Wade IV, now recovered from his wound and back on Johnston's staff. Although Hampton and Sherman, who had come to detest one another, did not shake hands during the conference, Johnston and his Union counterpart hit it off during this, their first meeting. The interview, however, was marked by an almost palpable tension. Soon after they exchanged pleasantries, Sherman informed Johnston of the news—recently received at his headquarters and not yet announced to his troops—that Abraham Lincoln had been struck by an assassin's bullet three nights before in Washington, D.C.[1]

More mindful than ever of the momentous consequences of their meeting, the commanders came to a relatively quick agreement under which Johnston's troops would lay down their arms. The terms Sherman offered, comparable to those Grant had tendered Lee at Appomattox, struck the Confederate leader as generous. In fact, Sherman went beyond Grant's concessions by attempting to adjudicate political issues, including the disposition of Southern courts and state governments. This intrusion into civil policy would not find favor with Sherman's superiors in Washington, who would reject the surrender "convention" and demand that another, less sweeping agreement be drawn up.[2]

While Sherman and Johnston negotiated inside the Bennett house, Hampton, his son, and the rest of the staff spent the time in the side yard, the

241

general lounging on a carpenter's bench within sight and earshot of Sherman's subordinates. One Union officer found Hampton "bold beyond arrogance," while another noted his "vulgar insolence." When Judson Kilpatrick joined the group, Hampton rose from his seat to tower over his opponent, whom he regarded with a mixture of menace and disdain. One bystander thought Hampton "looked savage enough to eat 'little Kil,' while the latter returned his looks most defiantly." Later Hampton and Kilpatrick, along with members of their respective staffs, engaged in verbal jousting, principally concerning Kilpatrick's near-capture at Monroe's Cross Roads. Their "words grew hot," an eyewitness recounted, until Sherman and Johnston, their negotiations ended, separated the antagonists.[3]

Neither the terms Sherman proposed on April 17 nor the revised agreement that he and Johnston negotiated when they met again at Durham nine days later provided for the surrender of Jefferson Davis and his cabinet. Sherman's objective was the capitulation of a uniformed enemy too few to hurt him but too fast-moving to be overhauled—he did not concern himself with fugitive politicos. Hampton, however, was anxious about the safety of Davis and his entourage, which he hoped to perpetuate. He hoped, in fact, to join the president and escape with him to some place where they could carry on the fight. Union officers who overheard his hard-edged banter with his opponents quoted him as declaring they would "never see me give up. I'll go to Mexico and fight with Maximilian." The reference was to the Austrian prince who headed the puppet government that had been installed in Mexico City the previous year in defiance of the Monroe Doctrine.[4]

Two days after the meeting at the Bennett house, Hampton, having returned to Johnston's headquarters at Hillsboro, wrote a letter to Davis, then thought to be at or near Greensboro. In it he stated his distaste for the surrender agreement reached on the seventeenth. He had recently demonstrated this attitude, having obstructed an attempt by North Carolina governor Zebulon Vance and two of his predecessors to negotiate with Sherman for the surrender of Confederate forces in their state. Now Hampton went further, informing Davis that he would not abide by any terms negotiated by Sherman and Johnston.[5]

Hampton admitted that the military situation looked gloomy, but he refused to consider it hopeless. He assured Davis that "large numbers" of veterans from Lee's and Johnston's armies would willingly form a mounted column that would escort Davis and his party beyond the Mississippi, where

Confederate forces continued to fight on. "When we cross that river," he declared, "we can get large accessions to the cavalry and we can hold Texas. As soon as forces can be organized & equipped, send this heavy cavalry force into the country of the enemy and they will soon show that we are not conquered. My own mind is made up. As to my course I shall fight as long as my government remains in existence, for I shall never take the 'oath of allegiance.' I am sorry that we paused to negotiate, for to my apprehension, no evil can equal that of a return to the Union."[6]

In these words Hampton revealed that his political attitudes had shifted 180 degrees during the past four years. The bitterness he felt at the specter of approaching defeat, the string of tragedies he and his family had endured, and the misery his region had suffered at the hands of a vengeful invader had turned the moderate sectionalist of 1861 into a cast-iron rebel who would not—could not—give up the contest.

Before Johnston's surrender became a fait accompli, Hampton determined to win official acceptance of his escape plan. On the twenty-second he traveled to Greensboro with a few aides for an audience with the fugitive president. Upon his arrival, however, he learned that Davis and his people had forged on toward Charlotte. From Greensboro, Hampton addressed the president a second time, repeating his offer to lead a large escort to the Trans-Mississippi Department: "I can carry with me quite a number and I can get there."[7]

That same day, in reply to Hampton's initial letter, Davis called him to Charlotte for further discussion. Hampton deferred the meeting until the twenty-sixth, by which time he had escorted Johnston back to the Bennett house for his second negotiating session with Sherman. Before the conference concluded, however, Hampton left Durham Station by train, this time accompanied by Joe Wheeler, heading for Charlotte. Later that day, the president and his generals thrashed out the details of the plan Hampton had proposed, which Wheeler supported and which the president viewed as the only way to keep alive the dream of Southern independence. Late in the afternoon, when Hampton and Wheeler left to rejoin their commands, they carried authorization from Davis to form an escort not only by recruiting volunteers but by impressing horses, weapons, and other needed resources.[8]

When the generals reached Greensboro at eleven o'clock that evening, they learned that Johnston had formally surrendered the army. As Hampton later wrote, "this defeated all the arrangements which had been made, for I recognized, of course, that my command had been embraced in the convention entered into between Generals Johnston and Sherman." But the news failed to deter Wheeler, who soon left the army at the head of several dozen members of his command, the nucleus of Davis's escort. Apparently Wheeler believed the order of the president took precedence over the surrender convention. Hampton must have thought so, too, for he made no effort to stop his subordinate or dissuade him from his course.[9]

Although Hampton considered the great majority of his command bound by the terms of the surrender, he was unsure of his own status. When he met with Johnston, he contended that, because he had been absent from the negotiations on a mission from his commander in chief, he was not a party to the proceedings. Johnston sympathized with his cavalry leader but feared he lacked the authority to render a judgment on his situation. He suggested that Hampton seek the advice of Secretary of War John C. Breckinridge, who had assisted Johnston in his talks with Sherman but had since joined the presidential party in Charlotte. Hampton adopted this course, notifying Breckinridge by courier of his claim that he was free to leave North Carolina for more active fields. His declaration was compelling; two days later he received Breckinridge's ruling that, "if not present" at the surrender talks "or consenting" to the terms offered by Sherman and accepted by Johnston, Hampton was "free to come out." But because the officers and men of his command had been on hand for the negotiations, they could avail themselves of no such dispensation.[10]

Even before Hampton received Breckinridge's ruling, most of his men had come to doubt their commander would surrender to Sherman. Many determined to follow his example; late in the day, a large body of Butler's and Young's troopers left the army with the intention of carrying on the fight elsewhere. In a postwar memoir, Hampton implied that as soon as he learned of their action, he recalled them and persuaded them to lay down their arms. In fact, an angry Johnston demanded that he order them to return and, either readily or reluctantly, Hampton complied.[11]

First, he sent couriers to halt the truants before they were beyond his reach; then he rode after them. Shortly after sunrise on April 28, he joined the men in bivouac outside Hillsboro, where he drew them up in column and addressed them as a body for the final time. As he recalled, "I adjured them to prove themselves now, as they had always done, good soldiers, by obeying the command of General Johnston, by whom his army had been surrendered; that I knew they were willing to share my fate, whatever it might be, but they would go as outlaws if they went with me . . . . After a most painful interview, which brought tears, not only from the eyes of many of these brave men, but from my own," he instructed them to return to Greensboro to participate in the surrender ceremonies that were imminent. Giving the command a last salute, Hampton rode off to Charlotte with those few aides who had accompanied him on his earlier journey.[12]

Despite his best intentions and most strenuous efforts, he never rejoined Davis and his party, nor did he reach the Trans-Mississippi. Arriving in Charlotte late on April 28, he found the object of his mission absent, the president and his party having moved on to Yorkville, South Carolina. In that town, Mary McDuffie Hampton and other members of the general's family had taken refuge from Sherman's bummers. Although Hampton had two reasons for proceeding there, his staff had none; with his permission, the aides remained in Charlotte pending the receipt of further orders.[13]

Thus he rode alone to Yorkville, a journey that extended into the small hours of the thirtieth. The long and arduous journey, which culminated in a difficult crossing of the rain-swollen Catawba River, was such an ordeal that by the time Hampton reached Yorkville he was verging on collapse. He was also thoroughly frustrated by his continuing failure to link up with Davis, who had left Yorkville hours earlier for points unknown. Davis's flight would continue for another ten days. On May 10, near Irwinsville, Georgia, the presidential party would be overtaken by Union cavalry and its members returned north under guard. Davis would spend the next two years in close confinement at Fort Monroe, Virginia, before being released to live out his life among the people he had once governed.[14]

An early postwar portrait of Wade Hampton the citizen

Shortly after falling into the

arms of his loving wife, Hampton took to bed in the house where Mary had been staying. It took several days for him to recover from the physical and mental distress he had suffered. In the interim, Mrs. Hampton—ultimately with the assistance of Joe Wheeler, now also in South Carolina and still hopeful of escorting Davis to a safe haven—worked hard to persuade her husband to remain at home until fully recovered. "He finally yielded," Wheeler recalled, "and giving me a letter for Mr. Davis, asked me to tell the President that if, in the future, there should appear any way in which he could serve him, he would do so to the last." By now, however, Hampton must have realized that he had already performed his last service for Jefferson Davis and the dying nation he represented.[15]

One of the arguments by which Hampton's wife and subordinate dissuaded him from further travel was the wretched state of his family's finances, which required his complete and immediate attention. As soon as he could travel, he returned to Columbia in the company of Mary, the children, and hundreds of other veterans of Lee's and Johnston's armies, to survey what remained of his home and property. As he had anticipated, he found Sand Hills, Millwood, and the other plantations in ruins. Once-majestic buildings had been reduced to charred rubble; once-fertile ground lay bare and baking under the sun; and the thousands of slaves who had worked those fields were gone, having run off with Sherman's legions. Hampton would find affairs at Wild Woods and other out-of-state holdings much the same. The Mississippi-grown cotton that had secured his family's fortune had been confiscated by the United States government, while Union troops had stolen jewelry and other valuables there as well as in South Carolina. The vast wealth of the Hampton family had been reduced to millions of dollars in Confederate bonds and currency—worthless symbols of a lost cause. He had no source of income and no prospects for sustenance beyond what he might salvage amid the debris that surrounded him.

A lesser man would have given himself over to despair, wallowing in self-pity, wringing his hands over the utter impossibility of his situation. Had Hampton done so, his enemy would not have been surprised. In a letter to his family, Sherman had opined that, once beset by defeat and poverty, the highest-ranking Rebels—he cited Hampton as an example—would never resign themselves to working for a living.[16]

246

But the Union commander had underestimated at least one of his opponents. Soon after reaching Columbia, Hampton moved his family into "an odd-shaped, quaint looking little cottage" along the Camden Road on the outskirts of the city—formerly an overseer's residence, damaged but not destroyed by enemy soldiers. With the assistance of the few slaves who had resisted the urge to flee, Hampton began to rebuild and expand his cruciform dwelling, which neighbors dubbed "The Southern Cross." Over the next several years, he would divide his time among this modest refuge, his somewhat-less ravaged plantations in Mississippi, and the hunting lodge that remained standing in Cashiers Valley.[17]

After establishing his family in the refurbished cottage, he shaved his wartime beard, doffed his Confederate uniform, donned the less splendid garb of a working man, and set out to make a new life for himself, the children (now including his eldest son, home from the war), his four surviving sisters, and the rest of the extended family that continued to depend on him for financial support. Aware that a quick return to prosperity was out of the question, he planted new crops in old fields. He eschewed cotton and tobacco cultivation and instead grew subsistence crops such as vegetables and fruits. Most of these his family consumed, the rest went to pay the former slaves who remained to assist him.

It was a tremendously difficult life, especially for one unused to living by the sweat of his brow. Yet his personal involvement in planting and harvesting gave him a sense of achievement unlike anything he had experienced through decades of acquisition and accumulation. His growing hope that despite great adversity he and his family would again prosper prevented him from following the lead of other southerners who, unable to cope with the loss of land, wealth, and occupation, left their homes for Mexico or South America. He rejected the overtures of one group who sought to organize an expatriate colony in Brazil, counseling its members to remain at home and devote themselves to "the reestablishment of agriculture and commerce, the promotion of education and the rebuilding of our cities and dwellings which have been laid in ashes."[18]

He added a bit of advice that may have sounded strange coming from a Confederate die-hard: "I recommend that all, who can do so should take the oath of allegiance to the United States Government, so that they may participate in the restoration of Civil Government to our State."[19]

It must have been difficult indeed for Hampton even to consider pledging his fealty to a nation he had warred against so long and with such zeal. But the alternative was to surrender control of South Carolina to the hundreds of federal troops on occupation duty there and to the dozens of Yankee businessmen and politicians descending on the state like locusts with the intention of profiting from her unhappy condition. Steeling himself to the necessity of taking his own advice, on August 2, 1865, Hampton reported to the provost marshal in Columbia and in his presence swore to abide by the Constitution of the United States, including the recently enacted Thirteenth Amendment, which ended slavery throughout the nation.

The following day, he petitioned President Andrew Johnson to pardon him for having taken up arms against the U.S. government. Late in May the president had issued an amnesty proclamation to all who would take the oath of allegiance. The gesture excluded several categories of southerners, including Confederate officers above the rank of colonel and persons owning taxable property valued at more than twenty thousand dollars. Hampton, of course, was disqualified on both counts. Those excluded, however, could apply for individual pardons. In doing so Hampton declared that he acted "from a sense of duty. . . . It is my purpose, if it [his application] is acceded to, to devote myself honestly and zealously to the restoration of law & order in my state & to the interests of my country." Perhaps deliberately, he refrained from his habit of capitalizing the word "State" in contrast to his lower-case rendering of "country."[20]

Hampton's application was warmly supported by Benjamin F. Perry, the South Carolina Unionist whom Johnson had appointed provisional governor of the state. Perry, whom Hampton considered, despite his political leanings, "a distinguished citizen" and "an honest man," acknowledged that the applicant had spent four years waging war against the United States. Even so, Hampton was "no agitator of the Rebellion . . . but he felt it his duty to go with his state when she plunged into the war."[21]

Undoubtedly Perry's endorsement assisted Hampton's effort, although his pardon did not come through until November 13. Even then, Hampton, in common with every other Confederate civil and military leader, was barred from voting and holding public office. His fellow South Carolinians, however, refused to acknowledge these restrictions. By the fall of 1865, Hampton's public and private utterances on various issues of statewide interest, coupled with the prominence accorded him as South Carolina's highest ranking Confederate officer, had brought him unsought opportunities for political service. That summer, for example, he had been named a delegate to the convention Perry had called to rewrite the state's constitution, a step the Republican-dominated U.S. Congress had declared a prerequisite to South Carolina's readmission to the Union and her restoration to self-government.

Although called to serve by the voters of his district, Hampton failed to attend the convention, which met in Columbia in the latter part of September. Wellman and other historians claim that word of his selection reached him at his mountain lodge in Cashiers Valley too late to ensure his participation. Quite possibly, however, he contrived to be inaccessible from a desire to avoid being a party to changing the existing laws of the state. While some additions were an obvious necessity, such as a formal acknowledgment of emancipation, he was unwilling to make the sweeping revisions he feared would be forced upon the delegates.[22]

Three weeks before the forum convened, he had spelled out his views in a letter to the mayor of Columbia, James G. Gibbes. Hampton asked rhetorically: "Are the people of the State willing, by the adoption of a new and totally different constitution, to ignore all the teachings of the past, to subvert the whole order of society, to change, in a moment, its whole organization, and, in a word, to commit political suicide? Yet this is the inevitable tendency of the course recommended by the meeting."[23]

His primary concern was that to reenter the union, the state would have to produce a "constitution representing not the views and interests of the people of South Carolina, but those of Mass[achusetts]." These views included the surrender of political power to the ex-slaves who made up almost 70 percent of South Carolina's population (among all former Confederate states, only Mississippi had a higher percentage of black residents). He agreed wholeheartedly with Benjamin Perry that "this is a white man's government, and intended for white men only," but he doubted the provisional governor wielded enough influence to prevent the adoption of provisions limiting white rule. He suspected, correctly, those most likely to resist substantive changes would be denied representation at the convention. Delegates of less fortitude would acquiesce in the policies of the Republicans in Washington as promulgated by South Carolina's occupation commander, Maj. Gen. Daniel E. Sickles.[24]

Hampton may have had grounds for fearing the outcome of the upcoming convention, but these did not excuse his suggestion to Gibbes that their state wage a form of guerrilla warfare against the federal government. Because nothing achieved at the convention could guarantee the restoration of self-rule, "I recommend . . . taking no action whatever in public affairs. Leave all these matters to the U[nited] S[tates] G[overnment], which will, doubtless in good time provide a government for you. Until that is done, the cartridge-box can take the place of the ballot-box, and the bayonet is a good substitute for the law. It is better to be governed by these than to give your State a constitution which misrepresents . . . humiliates . . . debases . . . [and] degrades."[25]

As it turned out, Hampton might have spared himself much worry and avoided this unfortunate lapse into bellicose rhetoric. The changes the convention adopted were insufficient to overturn the state's age-old reliance on white rule. Emancipation was duly recognized, but a vocal minority of delegates demanded that slave owners be compensated for their loss of property and former chattels be prevented from making a living except as domestics and manual laborers.

While these conditions eventually were dropped, the delegates defiantly refused to repudiate the state's wartime debt or permit African Americans, regardless of their educational or financial attainments, to vote. Numerous historians, especially those writing before the middle of the twentieth century, have maintained that even at this early date Hampton had a more enlightened attitude toward male suffrage, believing it should extended to educated members of both races. Later historians, however, have found no evidence that Hampton either espoused or publicized so enlightened a view at this point in his life.[26]

As Hampton had foreseen, the limited reforms proposed by the delegates at Columbia failed to secure South Carolina's return to the Union fold. She would not be readmitted until June 1868, five months after a second convention—this one dominated by black delegates and their white supporters—made more sweeping revisions to the existing code.[27]

One substantive result of the first constitutional convention was a call for state elections to be held in early October. The leading gubernatorial candidate, the choice of Perry and most of the delegates, was James L. Orr of Craytonville. It is generally acknowledged, however, that Hampton, had he attended the proceedings, would have been the consensus choice. Yet there is no guarantee he would have accepted any call to state office. By the fall of 1865, he appears to have adopted his own advice about "taking no action whatever in public affairs." The prohibitions under which he labored as a

Confederate general would have prevented him from taking office had he been elected to it, and thus in the wake of the convention he made repeated and unambiguous statements of his noncandidacy.[28]

Again however, South Carolinians failed to recognize the laws that restricted the political activities of their favorite son. When they were tallied, Hampton came within 743 votes of defeating Orr. He failed of election only because the voters of his home district, Richland, honored his wishes by giving Orr a ten-to-one majority. Richland did Hampton another favor by refusing to elect him to the legislature. Orr was so chagrined by the narrowness of his victory that he seriously considered refusing to take office; only the urgings of Perry and other influential men persuaded him to serve.[29]

Legal considerations aside, Hampton's refusal to stand for office stemmed from a desire to devote his attention to restoring his family's economic stability. The task was virtually impossible due not only to the war's effect on his finances but also to the steady accumulation of the debts he had assumed upon the death of his father. Interest on his several mortgages had mounted geometrically over the past four years, and now he lacked the resources to make even a dent in the principal. But with Sisyphean determination, he vowed to roll the boulder of debt toward the seemingly inaccessible summit of prosperity.

He sighted a faint glimmer of hope when, in January 1866, he returned to Mississippi to resume cotton production at Wild Woods. The tenants who had managed the Washington County estate in his absence had managed to eke out a living even after the greater portion of their workforce quit the land. Under Hampton's careful guidance, cotton growing increased, although production remained well below prewar dimensions.[30]

Even a marginally improved economic situation served to raise Hampton's spirits, as did the popularity he enjoyed not only in his home state but elsewhere in the South. He had begun to realize the extent of his renown during his first postwar trip to Wild Woods, when, during a stopover in Montgomery, Alabama, he was wined and dined by admiring officials and invited to address the newly seated legislature.

Another factor in Hampton's improved frame of mind was the strengthening of his friendship with Robert E. Lee. Mary Chesnut's observations on their wartime difficulties strike one as somewhat overdrawn. Still, it seems evident that during the first three years of the conflict the two men occasionally rubbed each other the wrong way—mainly due, it would seem, to Hampton's disputes with, and criticism of, J. E. B. Stuart. The situation improved

251

markedly following Hampton's succession to cavalry command. During the last eight months of the conflict Lee had evidenced greater confidence in his subordinate and had treated him with unfailing respect.

The new relationship was cemented by a postwar letter in which Lee called the loss of Hampton and the troopers he had led to South Carolina "the cause of our immediate disaster" at Appomattox. Hampton was touched by the sentiments expressed in Lee's missive, especially by a reference to the battle whose outcome had prompted the evacuation of Petersburg and Richmond and had sent the Army of Northern Virginia on its final retreat: "If you had been there with all of our cavalry, the result at Five Forks would have been different."[31]

The two generals remained close over the next five years. On several occasions, Hampton visited his old commander at his home in Lexington, Virginia, where they reviewed the glories of the past. At Lee's request, Hampton devoted whatever time he could spare to writing a detailed report of his command's operations during the last year of the war. He was still working on it at the time of Lee's death in October 1870, at which point he laid it aside to compose a poignant eulogy to his superior. The work proved so popular that Hampton delivered it as a speech and consented to its publication.[32]

Other seemingly joyful events lifted Hampton's spirits only briefly. Toward the end of the summer of 1866 Mary became pregnant with the couple's fourth and last child. The happy news suggested a reversal of fortune for the beleaguered family, but it proved to be a prelude to tragedy. Born on June 23, 1867, Catherine Fisher Hampton lived less than two weeks, succumbing to illness on Independence Day, a holiday her grief-stricken parents would never again celebrate. Her death was the second such blow in seven months. Wade Hampton's beloved youngest sister, Mary Fisher Hampton, had died the previous December, one month short of her thirty-fourth birthday. Adding to the family's plight was the fact that the health of Mary McDuffie Hampton, which had been poor even before Catherine's birth, declined further in the wake of the child's passing, the result, perhaps, of a difficult pregnancy coupled with an understandable amount of emotional distress.[33]

Even as he mourned and worried, Wade Hampton worked strenuously to gain even a tenth of the prosperity he had known in antebellum years. It was, as he probably suspected, a losing proposition. For three years following his return from the war, he managed to eke out an existence as a South Carolina farmer and a Mississippi cotton grower. Merely to break even, however, he was forced to borrow such money as he could, thus adding to his already crushing financial burdens. Instead of increasing in value, his holdings underwent a steady depreciation throughout the period. The crowning blow came when some of his many creditors filed suit against him.

Unable to pay even a fraction of what he owed to bankers and other lenders, in December 1868 Hampton was forced to declare bankruptcy. In his court petition he listed liabilities in excess of one million dollars and assets that consisted primarily of heavily mortgaged property. To satisfy the debts that had been called, he was forced to liquidate almost all of his land holdings. Most of his Mississippi properties were auctioned off soon afterward, followed less than a year later by his South Carolina lands, including what remained of once-beautiful Millwood. At first he was left with only a portion of Wild Woods but then his creditors permitted him to buy back Southern Cross. In a letter to his former subordinate, James Conner, Hampton explained that he would never renege on his obligation to "pay off my debts. The hope of my life is to do this and I shall devote all my energies to its accomplishment." The effort, however, would remain unfinished upon his death.[34]

The bankruptcy dealt Hampton and his family a stunning blow. Two years earlier, he had informed a family friend that "my reputation is the only thing that I have left and I am jealous of its preservation." His reputation as a businessman, however, suffered as a result of his legal difficulties. Court-appointed trustees discovered a double mortgage on one of his plantations, a lapse that Hampton blamed on lax bookkeeping. One historian who has examined his postwar finances describes Hampton as "a naively optimistic and careless business man." Some of his creditors even accused him of concealing assets. A court hearing was conducted, but no evidence of intentional wrongdoing came to light. Still, the fact that such an inquiry went forward speaks volumes of the depths to which the man once considered South Carolina's wealthiest son had sunk.[35]

Thus it was that Wade Hampton was forced to admit that he could no longer make a life from the soil his family had tended so artfully over the past eight decades. The war had taken from him so much of value: a beloved son and brother, thousands of fertile acres and the hands who tended them, the vision of a free and independent South. Now it had deprived him of a claim to distinction more powerful than the military rank so deservedly conferred upon him—the cherished title of "planter."

Despite an unwillingness to stand for public office, up to the time he filed for bankruptcy Hampton maintained not only an interest, but also an active involvement, in South Carolina politics. Soon after Governor Perry declared, in July 1865, that postwar reconstruction was in effect throughout the state, Hampton began to argue against the constitutionality of certain laws that the Republican-dominated Congress sought to impose on the occupied South. First in private correspondence, then in public statements, he criticized passage of not only the amendment that abolished slavery, but also the Fourteenth and Fifteenth Amendments, which declared, respectively, that every native-born or naturalized American, regardless of race, was a citizen of the United States; and that no male citizen of legal age could be denied the right to vote. He also voiced strong opposition to the Civil Rights Act of 1866, which mandated equal protection under the law, as well as to legislation in support of the newly established Freedmen's Bureau, which provided legal, economic, and educational assistance to ex-slaves.[36]

Hampton did not oppose these acts merely on racial lines. He accepted the demise of the Confederate cause, saw no alternative to emancipation, and had no great aversion to black citizenship or suffrage. He opposed the Thirteenth Amendment only because it was forced on a region that had been deprived of its constitutional rights. He protested selected provisions of other Reconstruction laws, such as those that barred high-ranking Confederates, including himself, from holding office, that forced the South to repudiate its wartime debt, and that levied harsh penalties on states that withheld or limited suffrage.[37]

In time, Hampton's views found a public forum. Beginning in the early autumn of 1865 with a talk to a racially mixed audience at Richland Fork, South Carolina, he delivered a number of cogently argued, clearly worded, and generally well-received political speeches. His early themes were the acceptance of Confederate defeat and emancipation, and the desirability of racial harmony as a prerequisite to rebuilding the region in general and South Carolina in particular. By mid-1867, if not earlier, he had added to his oratory a call for full citizenship for native-born blacks as well as black suffrage "on precisely the same terms as it is to be exercised by the white men," with the addition of "a slight educational and property qualification for *all classes*."[38]

When speaking to all-white audiences, he often coupled his advocacy of interracial cooperation with a ringing condemnation of Reconstruction policies that, in his view, reflected the tendency of the national government to treat the South as a conquered province. A tone of outrage as well as defiance characterized some of his speeches. Addressing a mostly white audience at Walhalla, in the northwestern corner of the state, in the summer of 1867, he argued that "some voice from the South should be raised to declare that, though conquered, she is not humiliated; that though she submits, she is not degraded. . . ."[39]

His own voice had already been raised. The previous August he had addressed a forty-page letter to Andrew Johnson, a native Tennessean and lifelong Democrat whom Hampton viewed as an honest man trying to deal fairly with the South against the frenzied opposition of the Radical Republicans. In the missive, which was published that same month in the columns of New York's *Metropolitan Record*, he nevertheless criticized the president for "not exercising all the power in your hands, to restore to the South as fully and as speedily as might have been done in peace—quiet and the inestimable rights of civil government." He added, however, that Southerners did not doubt Johnson's "earnest disposition to extend to us all these blessings and to bring back the South to the Union with all her rights as well as all her duties intact and unimpaired."[40]

The rest of the letter, which received wide publicity, embraced a list of "grievances and wrongs, inflicted on her [the South] in violation of the terms upon which she had laid down her arms." These included the oppression of occupation forces, especially as practiced by "brutal negro troops," the imposition of provisional state governments ("an anomaly heretofore unknown in a government" of once-sovereign states), and the "mischievous interference of that most vicious institution, the Freedman's Bureau . . . [which] has been used by the basest men, for the purpose of swindling the Negro, plundering the white man and defrauding the government."[41]

He likewise protested the cruel and humiliating treatment of Jefferson Davis, which he called an evil "so deep, so wanton, so stupendous, that in comparison with it all others seem but petty annoyances." He closed with a fervent appeal to Lincoln's successor: "It is for you, Sir, to redress these evils under which we groan. If the South is to resume her long vacant place in the Union, if she is to be restored to it properly, harmoniously, honorably, you, and you alone can accomplish this object."[42]

But Hampton overestimated the president's ability to shape Reconstruction policy. By the time he wrote, the Republican-dominated Congress had become fed up with Johnson's lenient, seemingly apologist attitude toward the South and his apparent affinity for her social and political institutions. They communicated their discontent to the electorate. During that fall's political campaign, the Radicals achieved such an ascendancy that by early 1867 they had taken control of Reconstruction. With the support of moderate elements of both parties who distrusted Johnson's motives, they framed a new series of laws inimical to Southern interests, most of them enacted over Johnson's veto. Johnson's continued attempts to block the Radical Republican agenda would lead to his impeachment in February 1868.[43]

One of the most sweeping pieces of legislation passed despite Johnson's opposition was the First Reconstruction Act (also known as the Military Bill) of February 1867, which divided the former Confederate states, excepting Tennessee, into five military districts. These were to be administered by generals who could be counted on to make the South pay for her experiment in rebellion. Thousands of federal troops would man each district, augmented by state forces in which blacks predominated.[44]

Hampton reacted angrily and vocally not only to the Military Bill but also to a Second Reconstruction Act, enacted the following month, which mandated black voter registration throughout the South. As a long-time slave owner who had learned to control his chattels through a judicious combination of kindness and discipline—preferential to the carrot but willing to apply the stick as needed—he trusted the ability of the old ruling class, absent interference on the federal level, to "direct the Negro vote." In 1866 he had publicized his paternalistic attitudes toward the typical black resident of his state: "As a slave, he was faithful to us; as a free man, let us treat him as a friend. Deal with him frankly, justly, kindly." By early 1867, however, Hampton had detected a swing in political power to freedmen controlled by avaricious carpetbaggers from the North, abetted by local turncoats, or "scalawags." He saw the United States Army as another source of external interference, one that would complicate greatly the effort to harness the black vote.[45]

That vote was prodigious, as the registration rolls revealed. By September 1867, when the voter drive ended, thirty-two thousand more African Americans than Caucasians had been registered in South Carolina, and twenty-one of the state's thirty-one congressional districts were reporting black majorities. Building upon this foundation, the fledgling Republican Party gained power throughout the state, threatening the designs of the old planter aristocracy.[46]

For a year and a half following passage of the Military Bill and the

Reconstruction Act, Hampton worked with other whites to counter the efforts of the Republicans. Their campaign rested on the argument, which Hampton first articulated before a gathering of African Americans in Columbia in March 1867, that black voters should reject the blandishments of politicians who neither understood nor appreciated them and support those local officials who had the best interest of both races at heart. The old guard was the friend of the newly enfranchised black, while the opposition intended to exploit him for political and financial gain.[47]

Too late, Hampton and his associates realized that repeated, emotional-laden appeals to the good sense and patriotic spirit of black voters were ineffective. They failed to influence the composition of, or to control the agenda at, the convention that rewrote South Carolina's constitution early in 1868—the only unobjectionable feature of which, as Hampton saw it, was the return of voting rights to former Confederates. White conservatives suffered an even greater defeat during the army-supervised state elections of that fall, which resulted in Republicans capturing not only the state house but also the legislature. The latter would be composed of eighty-four blacks and seventy-two whites, all but twenty-three of them Republicans.[48]

The old order's defeat mirrored the results of the presidential race. That summer Hampton, as a newly elected member of his party's central state committee, had attended the Democratic National Convention in New York City that nominated New York governor Horatio Seymour to run against the Republican candidate, Ulysses S. Grant. In November, the Union hero easily defeated his opponent, whom the Republicans had painted as a former leader of "Copperhead" (anti-war) Democrats.[49]

Heartsick over his party's defeats, Hampton despaired of seeing his state and region returned as quickly as possible to something approximating their prewar prosperity. Forced by his bankruptcy to concentrate once again on his financial situation, he abruptly retired from active participation in state politics. With the exception of a brief involvement in 1870 in an ill-fated "fusion" campaign of moderate Democrats and Republicans headed by his old subordinate M. Calbraith Butler, his hiatus continued for eight years. During that period he faced for the first time in his life the necessity of securing outside employment as a means of putting food on his family's table.[50]

THIRTEEN

"God bless all my people, black and white."

Wade Hampton took a position in the life insurance industry, a field that attracted many ex-Confederate officials. Early in 1869 he joined with a number of former colleagues, including John Brown Gordon and Alfred H. Colquitt, to direct the affairs of the Atlanta-based Southern Life Insurance Company. In addition to serving on the board of directors of the parent organization, he became vice president of the Baltimore branch of one of its subsidiaries, the Carolina Life Insurance Company. The president of the subsidiary—which, despite its name, had its headquarters in Memphis, Tennessee—was Jefferson Davis, who two years earlier had been released from confinement at Fort Monroe.

To administer the Baltimore branch of Carolina Life, Hampton moved his ailing wife and their unmarried children to the Maryland city. There he found making ends meet a consistent challenge. Although the position granted him an adequate salary, much of it immediately went to his creditors. Then, too, almost from the outset the company experienced financial difficulties of its own, difficulties exacerbated by the financial panic of 1873. Three years later the enterprise folded, an outcome for which Gordon, as its president, received much blame.[1]

Hampton escaped from the collapse with his reputation intact but in tighter financial straits than before. As early as mid-1873 he was desperately attempting to raise capital to fund a business venture of unknown nature in association with former President Davis. He pledged to contribute to the enterprise five thousand dollars of his own money, "all I have in the world." Three years later, when Carolina Life went under, he had even less.[2]

To supplement his income, by late 1872 Hampton had also become president of the Baltimore Fire Extinguisher Works. This position—an offshoot of his involvement in life insurance—proved less remunerative than his position with Carolina Life. During the early 1870s he dabbled in various other ventures, none of which reached fruition. For a time he even considered accepting a cavalry command in the Egyptian army. After both of the Baltimore firms failed, all that kept him and his family afloat was the portion of his Mississippi plantation that the bank's trustees had allowed him to retain. In an ironic twist, the prewar South's most celebrated slaveholder survived by renting "all the land I can" to African American cotton growers.[3]

Perhaps the nadir of Hampton's fortunes occurred late in the winter of 1874. Now approaching his fifty-sixth year, he had begun to suffer, more or less severely, from the effects of his war wounds, especially the one received at Fair Oaks. Then, on March 1, Mary, whose health had deteriorated after the move to Baltimore, died suddenly in a nursing home in Charlottesville, Virginia, not far from the residence of Thomas and Anna Preston, brother and sister-in-law of Hampton's first wife. Mary's passing made her husband a two-time widower and left him "dreadfully restless and oppressed." He returned her body to Columbia, where she was buried beside Margaret Preston Hampton in the cemetery of Trinity Episcopal Church. There would be no third Mrs. Wade Hampton.[4]

In May 1872 Congress had passed an amnesty bill covering all but a select few Confederate officials. Under its terms, Hampton regained the right to hold public office. In that year the Grant administration, although plagued by charges of corruption and mismanagement, won a second term. Grant defeated newspaperman Horace Greeley, a fiery Republican editor during the war who had bolted to the Democrats to run on a reform ticket, one that Hampton and his fellow-Southerners supported with only slight misgivings. At the same time, several former Confederates were elected to the House and Senate, raising the South's hope that the excesses of Radical Republican government might be ameliorated.[5]

In South Carolina, however, political power remained firmly in the hands of the Republican Party as one "carpetbagger administration" succeeded another. In 1874, the Democrats did not even bother to nominate a candidate for governor. Party officials made some overtures to Hampton but found him otherwise occupied. For one thing, he was still trying to make a go of professional life (as he informed Gen. Daniel Harvey Hill, "I must devote all my time & energy to business"). Then, too, he was about to become embroiled in a series of inquiries, orchestrated by the Republicans in Washington, to fix responsibility and award compensation for the February 1865 burning of Columbia. Again Hampton had to refute charges, restated publicly by Sherman, that he was primarily to blame for the conflagration. When evidence to support Sherman's contention failed to surface, the review boards adjourned without rendering a definitive judgment.[6]

Although occupied with outside interests, Hampton kept attuned to the political affairs in his state, and he did not hesitate to protest the fraud, waste, and abuse he saw all about him or to lament its effect on the citizenry. As he wrote a friend in December 1872, "my heart sickens when I contemplate the condition of things in our afflicted State & I fear the spirit of our people is giving way." The public debt had risen dramatically since the Republicans' assumption of power, the result of one boondoggle after another. Few public works had been funded anywhere in the state, and white residents were filing an increasing number of grievances against the high-handed actions of occupation troops and the black-dominated militia.[7]

The state enjoyed a brief respite from its travail when, in the fall of 1874, Massachusetts-born Daniel H. Chamberlain was elected governor. Although he appeared at first glance just another Republican carpetbagger, the former Union officer, a graduate of Yale College and Harvard Law School, proved himself an astute, efficient, and honest administrator. When able to do so without damage to their reputations, Hampton and other fair-minded whites supported his efforts to rid state government of graft and cronyism. By mid-1876, however, it had become apparent that Chamberlain was unable or unwilling to purge his party of its most objectionable officials, some of whom practiced their venality not only behind the governor's back but also under his nose. Leading Democrats desperately sought a means of preventing Chamberlain from winning a second term in the fall of 1876.[8]

Reluctantly at first, then wholeheartedly, Hampton came to the rescue. On June 29, 1876, one day after serving as grand marshal of the parade in Charleston that celebrated the centennial of the Revolutionary War battle of

Fort Moultrie, the general returned to Columbia by train. En route, he conferred with three fellow Confederates, Martin Gary, Johnson Hagood, and Joseph B. Kershaw. All were supporters of M. Calbraith Butler, who in November intended to run for governor on a fusion ticket.[9]

Although Hagood and Kershaw were committed fusionists, Gary, the racist, fiery-tempered "Bald Eagle of Edgefield," was not. Despite the coolness that had existed between the two men since 1864—a coolness that only two years before had allowed the white supremacist to attack publicly Hampton's advocacy of qualified black suffrage—Gary now realized that his old commander was just the man to head a pure Democrat (or, in Gary's words, a "straightout") gubernatorial ticket. With characteristic persistence, he urged such a course on Hampton. The latter attempted to beg off, but at length he repressed his feelings toward Gary and indicated a willingness to run if his party willed it. The added encouragement of Hagood and Kershaw, who shared Gary's conviction that Hampton's immense popularity would carry the election if the Republicans did not steal it, virtually sealed the bargain. All that was missing was Butler's endorsement, which proved to be forthcoming. A few weeks after returning to his modest abode on the outskirts of the capital, Hampton sent Gary a letter of intent to enter the race if nominated at the state Democratic convention.[10]

Wade Hampton in the 1870s

Nomination was a formality, especially once Gary, Butler, and other Hampton supporters packed the convention, held in Charleston in mid-August. By then Gary had helped organize an election committee dedicated to advancing the straightout campaign. To assist the committee at the local level, he had also mobilized an army of Hampton enthusiasts, garbed in red shirts. This simple but effective uniform identified the wearers—whites of

262

every social class, from wealthy professionals to sharecroppers—as soldiers fighting in a holy cause, the redemption of their state from carpetbagger and black rule. Many Red Shirts were Confederate veterans; a significant number were also members of the quasi-military Rifle and Saber Clubs that as early as 1867 had sprung up across the state. Ostensibly private social organizations, the clubs were in fact extralegal constabulary forces designed to counter, and whenever possible overawe, the black militia that supported the Republican regime.[11]

Gary's tactics proved effective from the outset. On August 15, Hampton won his party's nomination by acclamation after two fusion candidates withdrew from the contest in his favor. Over the next three months, Gary and his brightly clothed followers largely shaped the political campaign that saw Hampton pitted against the personable, articulate, but overmatched Chamberlain. While Hampton took to the stump, orating in every county before large, enthusiastic crowds of middle- and lower-class whites, his supporters hounded and badgered his opponent. Wherever Chamberlain spoke, Red Shirts and military club members showered him with boos and catcalls, shouting him down while intimidating his supporters with drawn pistols. On at least one occasion they drove the governor bodily from the speaker's platform.[12]

In later months, Gary loudly contended that he and his little army had been responsible for acts of violence that heavily influenced the outcome of the canvass. His claims were exaggerations, made to enhance his own standing in Democratic circles. Yet many historians have cited his boasts as proof that the campaign of 1876 featured an extraordinary amount of violence by which Democrats intimated Republicans of both races. Such does not appear to have been the case, although a few well-publicized outbreaks of racial warfare marred the campaign and the prelude to it. A small-scale riot had broken out on July 4 in the village of Hamburg, where an angry mob of whites fired on black militiamen, killing nearly two dozen of them. A smaller confrontation at Charleston on September 6 left several members of both races wounded, while in Aiken County, September 15–19, Rifle Club members trapped in and near the town of Ellenton a hundred militiamen, perhaps fifty of whom were shot down before federal troops arrived to avert a greater slaughter. The casualty balance was reversed on October 16 when a black mob precipitated racial violence in Cainhoy, Charleston County; the ensuing confrontation left six white men and one African American dead.[13]

To be sure, the violence provided cause for alarm, and the authorities felt compelled to take action to stop it. Yet most observers agreed that Governor

Chamberlain overreacted when, in the wake of the Hamburg riot, he petitioned Ulysses Grant to augment security throughout the state. The president responded by dispatching several thousand additional troops to Columbia and other cities and towns and ordering the immediate disbanding of the military clubs. These actions exacerbated an already tense and unstable situation throughout the state. By precipitating them, Chamberlain lost the support of fusionists and other white moderates formerly disposed to reelect him.[14]

Although he may have profited indirectly from the bully-boy tactics of Gary and his loyalists, Hampton never condoned them. Whenever incidents of violence and intimidation were brought to his attention, he condemned them in private although not in public, a concession to harsh reality dictated by his inability to rein in the Red Shirts. His own strategy was to appeal to the better nature of the electorate, not to its baser tendencies. In his campaign speeches—which one reporter called "just plain, straight talks" characterized by "strong, clear English" free from "lofty flights of oratory or literature"—he returned to his pre-1868 theme of racial harmony, to his vision of a South Carolina in which whites and blacks worked together for political peace, social stability, and economic prosperity. He continued to criticize carpetbagger and scalawag rule but without the overheated invective to which he had formerly resorted. Instead, aware that the eyes of the nation were turned on his state, he called attention to its political and financial distress and asked fair treatment of its people by the federal government.[15]

He made a special effort to reach and influence the black majority, and he achieved some success. Although Hampton's subsequent claim that seventeen thousand African Americans voted for him in 1876 is probably an exaggeration, he secured the firm support of numerous freedmen disillusioned by the empty promises of Republican leaders. A number of educated, influential blacks campaigned actively for Hampton, including Martin Delaney, the Civil War's highest-ranking African American officer. Gary and his cronies even managed to recruit units of "Black Red Shirts" who, when Hampton campaigned in their communities, paraded through the streets in his honor and cheered loudly and often when he mounted the speaker's stand.[16]

Many latter-day historians and political scientists have argued that the political motives of Hampton and Gary were interchangeable and that any differences between the two were tactical, not ideological, in nature. Yet the only modern, scholarly analysis of Hampton's political rhetoric finds "considerable evidence to establish his active opposition to violence, intimidation, coercion, and fraud as means of dealing with the blacks." Although committed to the overarching principle of white supremacy, he was genuinely desirous of promoting the political rights to which freedmen were entitled under the law, and he consistently strove to protect those rights. At times, however, the opposition of his white constituents to programs advancing African American interests made Hampton despair of a permanent settlement of the race problem. His search for a solution sometimes led him to advocate wholesale black emigration. He advanced this extreme view mainly after leaving the governor's chair, and toward the close of his political career he published a widely circulated and controversial essay on the subject.[17]

In his campaign speeches Hampton attacked the South's imposition of so-called "black codes," which so restricted the freedom of former slaves as virtually to return them to servility. He made consistent and effective appeals to blacks' dreams of a better life, promising them economic, educational, and even political opportunities such as no Democrat had ever offered. A much-repeated pledge was that if elected he would "render to the whole people of this state equal and impartial justice." He won the thanks of African Americans and the grudging respect of many Caucasians when he declared that if any white voter believed "I will stand between him and the law, or grant to him any privileges or immunities that shall not be granted to the colored man, he is mistaken and I tell him if that is his reason for voting for me, let him not vote at all."[18]

So many white South Carolinians did vote for him that the outcome of the campaign remained in doubt to the end—and the end was long in coming. Uncertainty persisted after the ballots were tallied on election day, November 7. The slowly arriving returns eventually gave Hampton a majority of 1,134 ballots, less than 2 percent of the total vote. Yet many counties, especially Edgefield and Laurens, reported what appeared to be inflated counts in his favor, the evident result of repeat voting by numerous Democrats—many smuggled in from Georgia—and the failure to vote by hundreds of blacks intimidated by members of those military clubs that had refused to disband. The total, revised returns also gave the Democrats a slim majority in the joint session of the legislature where the final count would be reviewed and certified.

The situation changed abruptly, however, when the Republican-dominated Board of State Canvassers exercised its recently acquired power to decide contested cases by throwing out the votes of Edgefield and Laurens Counties. This action not only overturned Hampton's apparent victory but, by disqualifying the eight legislators elected from those districts, gave control of the legislature to Chamberlain's party. The state supreme court attempted to restrict the canvassers to tallying votes, but Chamberlain's attorney general issued a ruling in their favor, whereupon the court sought unsuccessfully to jail every member of the board.[19]

The bizarre situation prevailed for the next five months while political opponents exchanged charges, countercharges, threats of force, and, occasionally, appeals to reason and fairness. Only the conspicuous presence of federal forces in and around Columbia prevented an outbreak of violence, and perhaps also bloodshed, on a scale to rival the pre-election riots. During this extended period of high-rising passions, rival legislatures met in session, originally on opposite sides of the same hall, where for days "the confusion of double resolutions and simultaneous speeches reigned." Eventually the bodies vying for control of the lower house separated, sixty-five Democrats adjourning to adjacent Carolina Hall, fifty-nine Republicans, including several blacks, retaining possession of the hall of the House of Representatives. Now free to conduct business on their own terms, the Republican legislators certified Chamberlain as winner of the gubernatorial race, and he was duly inaugurated on December 7.[20]

Chamberlain's grip on power was nevertheless tenuous; it relied on the support of the soldiers who patrolled the capital and kept the warring parties apart. Hampton and his followers—even the quick-tempered Gary—appreciated the importance of refraining from overreacting to Republican provocation. Although he had to stretch his powers of persuasion to the limit, Hampton managed to keep the Red Shirts from any overt act that would play into the hands of their opponents. His repeated calls for patience and restraint won him much favorable publicity not only locally but on the national level as well. Northern politicos and editors began to praise him—in many cases, for the first time—as a badly needed voice of moderation and reason.[21]

One of those favorably impressed by Hampton's conduct was the apparent president-elect, Rutherford B. Hayes, of Ohio. Although a former Union general and a staunch Republican, Hayes was sincerely committed to reuniting the nation by returning the former Confederate states—in spirit as well as in fact—to the Union fold. But in order to bring closure to decades of conflict and contention, the Ohioan had to surmount a contested election that, by all indications, had gone to his Democratic rival, Samuel J. Tilden of New York, the undisputed winner of the popular vote. Many of the same irregularities that plagued South Carolina's gubernatorial contest had left the state's electoral vote in dispute, a situation that also existed in Louisiana and Florida. To be declared the victor, Hayes needed to gain all nineteen of the contested votes held by those Republican-ruled states; to win, Tilden needed only one.

Between November 1876, when the election should have been decided, and the swearing in of the new president the following March, both parties attempted to manipulate the impasse in favor of its candidate, even as they repeatedly charged their opponent with electoral fraud. Eventually, a congressionally appointed national canvassing board was formed to resolve the dilemma. Unsurprisingly, the Republican-dominated board prepared to decide the issue in Hayes's favor but at the risk of igniting sectional warfare in one form or another.

A major constitutional crisis was avoided only when high-ranking Republicans let their counterparts know that if they acquiesced in a Hayes victory, occupation troops would be removed from the southern states. This was a viable course because by 1876, most northerners had come to consider Congressional Reconstruction as a noble experiment gone wrong, a social and political failure to be ended quickly and with a minimum of fanfare. The Republicans' offer was accepted, the South acquiesced in the verdict of the congressional commission, and on March 5, 1877, Rutherford Hayes was sworn in as the nineteenth president of the United States.[22]

Three weeks after his inaugural, Hayes invited Chamberlain and Hampton to Washington for separate, private conferences. Most of what occurred during Hampton's audience at the White House remains unknown, but evidence suggests that the two old soldiers not only reached an accommodation of sorts but also established a close personal relationship. Later they jointly toured parts of the South and stood side-by-side in urging reconciliation between the sections. Shortly after both claimants for the governorship returned to South Carolina, the War Department announced that, excepting the garrisons of the state's coastal fortifications, United States forces would be withdrawn from South Carolina forthwith. The order was carried out on April 10, 1877. Twenty-four hours after the last body of soldiers left Columbia for points north, Chamberlain evacuated the governor's office and Hampton took immediate and peaceful possession. So ended the longest and most hotly disputed gubernatorial contest in American history.[23]

Given his long-delayed assumption of power, Hampton's tenure in office was relatively brief—two months shy of a single two-year term. During that period, he did his utmost to live up to the campaign promises he had made to the black and white people of his state. Even as he reestablished Democratic rule in South Carolina after an absence of almost a dozen years—a feat that won him the honored titles of "redeemer of his state," and the "Moses of his people"— Hampton displayed an admirable tendency toward bipartisanship, appointing some Republicans, including a few African Americans, to state office.[24]

Some of these appointments, especially his naming of a northern-born Republican as chief justice of the state supreme court, drew the ire of white conservatives, notably Martin Gary and one of his most resourceful young lieutenants, Benjamin Ryan Tillman. A one-eyed farmer from Edgefield County and a former saber club leader, Tillman shared his mentor's penchant for physical violence, his gift for invective-laden oratory, and his bitter hatred of blacks, Republicans of either race, and, to a large extent, the aristocratic elite who headed his own party. With increasing frequency, these low-country agitators were regarded with suspicion and unease by the "Bourbon" leader they had helped elect governor. Hampton, secure in his power base, responded to their protests by restating his policy on appointments: He would offer positions to those best qualified to serve, without reference to party or race.[25]

Hampton's political nemesis, Benjamine Ryan "Pitchfork Ben" Tillman

Because of its relative brevity and the need to concentrate on rebuilding state government from top to bottom, Hampton's tenure did not produce a long list of notable achievements. Of those that made that list, however, many had racial overtones. Chief among them was his successful advocacy of a two-mill tax on state property for the education of both races. Here, again, he prevailed against the strident opposition of racists such as Gary, who complained that "nine-tenths of this tax would be paid by white people, and three-fourths of it would be spent in educating piccaninnies."[26]

Hampton also risked his popularity by vetoing one of the first legislative efforts toward the establishment of a chain-gang system, which African American leaders saw as directed at black prisoners. When he reorganized the South Carolina militia in response to white grievances, Hampton ensured that the force at Charleston included a full regiment of black infantry. While the gesture was not specifically race oriented, he also displayed courage in supporting the payment of South Carolina's Reconstruction-era debt. His action was roundly condemned by Gary, Tillman, and others who considered the bills run up by Hampton's Republican predecessors the products of criminal acts and thus not legally binding on the state.[27]

Hampton did not intend that instances of fraud and abuse should go unrecorded and unpublicized. In the winter of 1877–78 he avidly supported an inquiry into the corrupt practices of the carpetbagger regime. The several-month investigation, which placated many of his Democratic critics, produced evidence that "fraud, bribery, and corruption were rife in every department of State government." The sometimes-sensational testimony of those heavily involved incriminated numerous individuals, including a former governor, a sitting United States senator, and an African American state senator. Thirty-one indictments were handed down as a result of the probe, and punishment—including, in a few cases, prison terms—was meted out to several malefactors, white and black. Some of the more flagrant corruptionists, however, had fled the state and thus were beyond the reach of retribution.[28]

For all of Hampton's zeal in uncovering acts of Republican malfeasance, the punishments meted out, as Wellman notes, were "not particularly relentless or severe." In fact, of the thirty-one indicted, only three went to trial, and Hampton pardoned each. While interested in uncovering fraud and abuse, he wished to avoid mass prosecutions that could be construed as political show-trials. "It is very desirable," he informed President Hayes in March 1878, "that all agitation should cease in the state."[29]

In return for his judicious application of leniency, he secured, after months of bargaining, Hayes's pledge of amnesty for all but a few of the eight hundred South Carolina Democrats who had been placed under federal indictment by Chamberlain's attorney general. These persons had been charged with a variety of criminal acts including Ku Klux Klan activities and involvement in the riots at Hamburg, Ellenton, and elsewhere. A certain number were undoubtedly guilty, but the cases against many others had been tainted by judicial excess and by the employment of grand juries composed exclusively of carpetbaggers, scalawags, and uneducated blacks disposed to do the bidding of their white leaders.[30]

Despite the undercurrent of criticism that his conservative critics kept stirring up, Hampton's first term in office was generally judged to be successful. In the fall of 1878 he won renomination without opposition from within his own party or from the Republicans, who knew unassailable popularity when they saw it. Indeed, during the state Republican convention that August, a strong pro-Hampton resolution was introduced, although subsequently voted down. Content that "matters are in a very satisfactory condition now & the opposition has been crushed out," Hampton cruised to reelection: the November 6 vote count was 169,550 to 213 in his favor. Hugging his coattails, Democratic candidates captured all but eight legislative seats.[31]

Riding the peak of his popularity, Hampton undoubtedly expected to influence the South Carolina political scene for many years to come. It is probable that he did not seriously consider the overtures made him by national officials of his party, some of whom advanced him for the vice presidential spot on the 1880 Democratic ticket. Then a sudden intervention by fate altered Hampton's political plans. The night after his reelection, he traveled to Richland County to join some friends on a deer hunt. Arriving late, he mounted a mule, the only available means of transportation, and rode alone to overtake the other hunters, who were already engaged in the sport. Now sixty years old and carrying more than two hundred and forty pounds, Hampton was no longer the agile equestrian he had once been. When a deer suddenly appeared in the brush nearby, he instinctively fired at it. The noise startled his long-eared mount, which began to buck and rear. Hampton alighted from the frightened animal but so awkwardly that he fell, fracturing his right ankle.

Unable to move more than a few feet in any direction, he remained on the ground for hours in great pain until finally discovered and carried to a place where medical attention was available. The long delay in obtaining treatment resulted in the wound's becoming infected. The infection spread to such an extent that in early December, weeks after he had been returned to his home in Columbia, doctors amputated his leg just below the knee.[32]

Although he recovered from the surgery as fully as could be expected, Hampton was reduced by his condition to a less active life. In a sense, the accident also cost him his job, for as he lay abed, awaiting amputation, his friends in the legislature proposed to nominate him for the United States

Senate. Refusing to announce himself as a candidate for the position, he nevertheless declared his willingness to abide by the lawmakers' wishes. The result was preordained; on the day he lost his limb, he was elected to the position by a nearly unanimous vote of both houses.[33]

On February 24, 1879, sporting a well-fitted cork limb such as his new colleague, Sen. M. Calbraith Butler, had received sixteen years earlier following his wounding at Brandy Station, Hampton resigned the office to which he had been twice elected and turned over his duties to the lieutenant governor, W. D. Simpson. Less than six weeks later he was in Washington, where, on April 16, he hobbled for the first time onto the floor of the Senate chamber.[34]

Hampton would spend the next twelve years in the upper house of Congress. Over that span he won appointment to various important committees, his favorite being, logically enough, Military Affairs, although he also actively participated in the affairs of committees devoted to overseeing mining operations and civil service reform. He was a conferee on bills seeking to regulate railroad routes, veterans' homes and pensions, and federal election laws—all issues of interest to him. He offered motions and resolutions on myriad topics and presented reports on issues ranging from naval appropriations to national monuments and cemeteries.[35]

Early in his Senate career he was accused by his Republican colleagues of everything from being a secret Klansman to publicly declaring the Reconstruction legislation of the first postwar Congress null and void. In time, however, he became a well-regarded mainstay of the Senate, his views and his infrequent speeches carefully followed by members on both sides of the aisle. While his limited oratorical abilities and somewhat hobbled presence kept him from standing out from the Senate crowd, he served ably enough—at least in the eyes of the South Carolina legislature—to win a second six-year term in late 1884.[36]

Hampton considered his appointment a high honor, and he strove to uphold the dignity and importance of his position. From the start, however, he enjoyed his work in Washington less than he had the duties of governor, which helps explain why he never distinguished himself as a lawmaker. His political interests lay primarily on the state, not the national, level, and he preferred an executive position to his status as one of seventy-six legislators.

Even so, he never seriously considered resuming his old position, even when state Democrats sought his return to oppose, first, the ambitions of Martin Gary and, later, the inflammatory rhetoric and high-handed tactics of Gary's successors. Yet Hampton must have been at least slightly tempted to reenter the gubernatorial lists after Gary, late in 1879, made a heavy-handed bid to succeed Simpson. As part of his campaign against the Bourbon aristocracy, the Bald Eagle of Edgefield roundly criticized Hampton's record as governor. Many of the charges he hurled about so spitefully and recklessly stung Hampton, but the latter was outraged when Gary claimed that during the election of '76 Hampton had betrayed his party's national leaders, including Tilden, in exchange for a guarantee from the Hayes camp that he would prevail in his race against Chamberlain. Via speeches and newspaper interviews, Hampton hotly denied the charges and strongly implied that his accuser was a liar. His response gave credence to rumors, devoid of substance, that he would return to Columbia to challenge Gary's election bid.[37]

One reason he did not do so was that he did not have to. With Hampton's long-range support and the more immediate assistance of like-minded Democrats in Columbia, Johnson Hagood captured the governor's office in the 1880 election. Gary's defeat, the latest in a long series of blasted hopes, ended his political career. He went rapidly downhill, dying a few months after Hagood's election. He was succeeded by a body of agitators even more strident and more ruthless than he. These included Tillman, whose rise to power began when a severe depression in the late 1880s enabled him to become the leader of an agrarian revolt directed not only at Republicans and African Americans but also at the remnants of South Carolina's tidewater political aristocracy.[38]

Another reason why Hampton refused to return to the rough-and-tumble of state politics was that he lacked the heart for it, especially after his eldest son died in Mississippi in December 1879 of a virulent strain of malaria. "Life seems closed for me," the grieving father wrote his sister-in-law, "and I have nothing but duty to live for. It is very hard, but I try to say, God's will be done." His brave words notwithstanding, he was devastated by Wade's loss. He suffered a second, crushing blow when, toward the close of his Senate career, his daughter Sally—his last surviving child by his first wife—died at the age of forty-three. A year later Sally was followed in death by nine-month-old Wade Hampton V, son of George McDuffie Hampton and his wife, Eloise.[39]

In addition to family tragedies, Senator Hampton was borne down by advancing age and a plethora of physical afflictions. His war wounds flared up with increasing frequency, while the stump of his amputated leg was a source of lingering discomfort that sapped his strength. Then, too, especially toward the end of his second term, he was beset by renewed financial problems. A series of investments, including a mining venture that may have stemmed from his committee work, failed to bring him the added income he believed he needed. By early 1889, beset by "time, sorrow, wounds & trouble," he began to despair that he would leave anything of value to his surviving children. He almost wished he might die in office; in that event, George, Daisy, and Alfred might split his Senate salary, which would be paid for a full year after his passing.[40]

A little over two years later, he had no salary at all. In November 1890, Ben Tillman ("Pitchfork Ben," as he had come to be known) and his supporters in the politically powerful Farmers' Alliance captured the state house in Columbia. One month after ascending to the governor's chair, Tillman purged the state of one of its last Bourbons by blocking Hampton's bid for a third term

U.S. *Senator Wade Hampton*
(D-South Carolina)

in the Senate. Tillman achieved his victory by successfully portraying Hampton as an elitist who scorned his lower-class constituents. The effort was aided by the senator's principled support of a national gold standard, a stance opposed by southern farmers who hoped to pay their debts in a depreciated currency backed by silver. Although Hampton, once Tillman took power, must have anticipated defeat, he appeared stunned by the outcome. When he finally regained equilibrium and composure, he wrote an old army friend that "if my people think that I should no longer serve them I am willing to retire." Yet more than a decade later, with Tillman himself ensconced in the United States

Senate, Hampton continued to express amazement at his rival's meteoric rise: "I never expected to see my friends bolt for Tillman. . . ."[41]

Over that ten-year period, Pitchfork Ben inflicted ever greater pain on Hampton by slowly but surely wiping out his predecessor's political legacy. As soon as he consolidated his grip on statewide power, Tillman inaugurated a systematic campaign to dismantle the political structure that afforded blacks access to patronage jobs. That done, he set out to deprive African Americans of their most basic legal rights. In 1895, he led a successful effort to rewrite the South Carolina constitution in such a way as virtually to disenfranchise every black resident of the state.[42]

Left with no other option, in March 1890 Hampton vacated the Senate seat he had held for a dozen years. He had capped that career with his impassioned opposition to a Republican-sponsored "Force Bill" that mandated, upon the petition of as few as five hundred voters, federal supervision of state elections. Here was legislation too reminiscent of the excesses of Reconstruction rule to please South Carolina's departing solon. Thus, even as he bowed out, he had the satisfaction of knowing that his carefully crafted and clearly expressed arguments had helped send the bill to defeat.[43]

He was not unemployed for long. In November 1892, Grover Cleveland won the second of two discontinuous terms in the White House. The Democratic administration he ushered in proved a boon to Hampton, who the following year was offered the prestigious but largely ceremonial post of United States commissioner of railroads. He quickly accepted the position, which entailed a return from Columbia to Washington.

For the next four years, until Cleveland was ousted by Republican William McKinley, Hampton filled the Interior Department position. Officially, his duties embraced the oversight of federally assisted railroad lines, including the auditing of their annual reports; the inspecting of tracks, rolling stock, and other equipment; and the mapping of existing and proposed rights-of-way. In actuality, the job mainly provided him with a convenient and free means of traveling to such salubrious climes as California and Texas, where he spent most of his time fishing. Following the loss of his leg, that pastime had replaced hunting as Hampton's recreational passion.[44]

By 1897, he was again out of a government job, this time replaced by

McKinley's man, James Longstreet, a Confederate colleague of Hampton's but also an apostate Republican. This time, when he left office he departed Washington for good. Back in Columbia, he lived quietly in his little home on Camden Road within easy reach of his family, which now included three cherished granddaughters. His only surviving daughter, Daisy, kept house for him; she would not marry and move away until five years after his death.[45]

As the old century moved to its close, Hampton lived the life accorded to a stalwart leader in war and peace. Although no longer active in politics, he was consulted by numerous local, state, and national politicians who valued the wisdom and experience he brought to the dispensing of practical advice. On patriotic holidays, admiring townspeople showered him with tributes as he was paraded through the city in an open carriage or was helped onto a speaker's stand to mark the occasion with a few softly spoken but well-received remarks.

His views on national and international events, especially regarding armed conflicts such as America's 1898 war with Spain and Great Britain's Boer War in Africa two years later, were regularly sought by newspapermen and politicians. He was constantly asked to speak or write about his military service. While he rarely complied with such requests, he took pains to keep in touch, through correspondence and attendance at reunions, with many fellow Confederates, especially veterans of the old Hampton Legion.[46]

His memories of certain wartime personalities remained strong. In 1898, when Alfred Hampton sought a volunteer commission on the staff of Fitzhugh Lee, one of a handful of Civil War commanders recalled to service in Cuba and the Philippines, Hampton is reported to have remarked that "under no circumstances would he have a son of his serve under" such an imperious blowhard as Robert E. Lee's nephew continued to be. And when his old subordinate Joe Wheeler, another Rebel who donned a blue uniform to fight the Spanish, published a self-serving and error-ridden volume of reminiscences, it was all Hampton could do to resist tossing it into the fireplace.[47]

In the spring of 1899 Hampton's own home went up in flames, gutted by a fire of unknown origin that destroyed almost every possession of value including years' worth of documents of inestimable historical value. Forced to relocate to an even smaller outbuilding, Hampton tried to keep his spirits up but achieved mixed success. "As I sit in my little shanty," he wrote an old army friend, "I look on the ruins of my house, facing me, & though they may be very picturesque they are sad, for they cover all I possessed, save the ground on which they stand."[48]

He was not homeless indefinitely. Touched by his plight, his neighbors pooled what funds they could spare to erect a new and larger house for him within the city limits. The act of generosity "touched my heart," Hampton admitted, but he could not bring himself to accept so grand and costly a gift. He relented only when his benefactors "flanked" him by presenting the dwelling to Daisy. The gesture, said Hampton, "was more appreciated by me than any gift could be. It is worth something to a man who has tried to do his duty to his state to feel that his fellow citizens regard him with affection. . . ."[49]

It was indeed a fitting, as well as a touching, tribute to a man who for more than forty years had given selflessly of himself to his state and his community, not only when wealthy but also when teetering on the abyss of poverty. He lived out his remaining years in the gift house, dying there of heart disease, "complicated by old age," on the morning of April 11, 1902, two weeks after celebrating his eighty-fourth birthday.[50]

Many of his last words, uttered in a state of delirium, were cries of pain, prompted not by the afflictions from which he suffered but by poignant memories of fields of battle on which his army and his nation had suffered, and where two of his sons had fallen before his eyes. At the last, the anguished murmuring ceased, and the fog that had enveloped him was momentarily lifted. Gazing dreamily at the loved ones who surrounded his bed—his sons and daughter, his three surviving sisters, his beloved grandchildren—he uttered a benediction that bespoke his lifelong struggle to see his state, his region, and his nation grow and prosper:

"God bless all my people, black and white."[51]

NOTES

Abbreviations Used in Notes:

★ ★ ★

B&L	*Battles and Leaders of the Civil War*
CLS	Charleston Library Society
CSR	Compiled Service Record
CV	*Confederate Veteran*
CWTI	*Civil War Times Illustrated*
DU	William R. Perkins Library, Duke University
E-, M-, R-	Entry, Microcopy, Roll
LC	Manuscript Division, Library of Congress
MC	Eleanor S. Brockenbrough Library, Museum of the Confederacy
MFH	Mary Fisher Hampton
MSS	Correspondence or Papers
OR	*The War of the Rebellion: A Compilation of the Official Records of the Union and Confederate Armies*
SHSP	*Southern Historical Society Papers*
UNC	Wilson Library, University of North Carolina-Chapel Hill
USAMHI	U.S. Army Military History Institute
USC	South Caroliniana Library, University of South Carolina
UV	Alderman Library, University of Virginia
VHS	Virginia Historical Society
WH	Wade Hampton III

ONE:

1. John Coxe, "The Battle of First Manassas," CV 23 (1915): 25.

2. John Hennessy, *The First Battle of Manassas: An End to Innocence, July 18–21, 1861* (Lynchburg, Va., 1989), 1–11; Joseph E. Johnston, *Narrative of Military Operations during the Civil War* (New York, 1874), 33–34.

3. Coxe, "First Manassas," 25.

4. OR, IV, 1: 296; Manly Wade Wellman, *Giant in Gray: A Biography of Wade Hampton of South Carolina* (New York, 1949), 50–51.

5. Wellman, *Giant in Gray*, 34–35.

6. Coxe, "First Manassas," 25.

7. *Ibid.*; William C. Davis, *Battle at Bull Run: A History of the First Major Campaign of the Civil War* (Garden City, N.Y., 1977), 142–43.

8. Coxe, "First Manassas," 25; Hennessy, *First Battle of Manassas*, 42, 65–66.

9. OR, I, 2: 566.

10. *Ibid.*, 487–88, 558–59; Hennessy, *First Battle of Manassas*, 39–42; Davis, *Battle at Bull Run*, 110, 162–66.

11. OR, I, 2: 488–89, 566; Ethan S. Rafuse, *A Single Grand Victory: The First Campaign and Battle of Manassas* (Wilmington, Del., 2002), 131–32.

12. Coxe, "First Manassas," 25; Hennessy, *First Battle of Manassas*, 64–65.

13. OR, I, 2: 566; Coxe, "First Manassas," 25.

14. *Charleston Daily Courier*, August 8, 1861.

15. Coxe, "First Manassas," 25–26; OR, I, 2: 566.

16. Kate Va. Cox Logan, *My Confederate Girlhood: The Memoirs of Kate Virginia Cox Logan*, ed. by Lily Logan Morrill (Richmond, Va., 1932), 133.

17. OR, I, 2: 566–67.

18. *Ibid.*, 567; Hennessy, *First Battle of Manassas*, 66–67.

19. Edward L. Wells, *Hampton and Reconstruction* (Columbia, S.C., 1907), 1–2.

20. WH et al., *Family Letters of the Three Wade Hamptons, 1782–1901*, ed. by Charles E. Cauthen (Columbia, S.C., 1953), 165; Wellman, *Giant in Gray*, 9–10.

21. Wellman, *Giant in Gray*, 10–11; Edward L. Wells, *Hampton and His Cavalry in '64* (Richmond, Va., 1899), 10; WH to Edward L. Wells, June 17, 1895, Wells MSS, CLS.

22. Wellman, *Giant in Gray*, 11–12; WH et al., *Family Letters of Three Wade Hamptons*, xi; Francis B. Heitman, comp., *Historical Register and Dictionary of the United States Army* (Washington, D.C., 1903), 1: 496.

23. Wellman, *Giant in Gray*, 12–13; Wells, *Hampton and Reconstruction*, 2–6.

24. "Visit to a Cotton Plantation," *Scientific American* 15 (February 1860): 103.

25. Wellman, *Giant in Gray*, 13–14; "The Wade Hamptons," *Louisville Courier-Journal*, date unknown; WH et al., *Family Letters of Three Wade Hamptons*, xii.

26. Wellman, *Giant in Gray*, 15; Wells, *Hampton and His Cavalry*, 13–22; Wells, *Hampton and Reconstruction*, 5–7; WH to Edward L. Wells, June 11, 1899, Wells MSS, CLS; Heitman, *Historical Register and Dictionary*, 1: 496.

27. Wellman, *Giant in Gray*, 15–16, 37–38; Wells, *Hampton and His Cavalry*, 17–18; "The Late Col. Wade Hampton," *Porter's Spirit of the Times*, date unknown [1858]; WH et al., *Family Letters of Three Wade Hamptons*, xiv–xv, 16n., 20n.

28. WH et al., *Family Letters of Three Wade Hamptons*, xiv, 166; "The Late Col. Wade Hampton."

29. Wellman, *Giant in Gray*, 19; Wells, *Hampton and His Cavalry*, 18–20; Wells, *Hampton and Reconstruction*, 12–13; WH et al., *Family Letters of Three Wade Hamptons*, xiii–xiv.

30. Wellman, *Giant in Gray*, 16; WH et al., *Family Letters of Three Wade Hamptons*, 166.

31. Wells, *Hampton and His Cavalry*, 27; Wells, *Hampton and Reconstruction*, 18; Wellman, *Giant in Gray*, 38–39.

32. Wells, *Hampton and Reconstruction*, 16–17; Wellman, *Giant in Gray*, 4, 17–20, 39; WH to Margaret Preston Hampton, Aug. 12, 1846, Hampton MSS, UNC; Alfred B. Williams, *Hampton and His Red Shirts: South Carolina's Deliverance in 1876* (Charleston, S.C., 1935), 90.

33. U. R. Brooks, *Butler and His Cavalry in the War of Secession, 1861–1865* (Columbia, S.C., 1909), 435–36.

34. Wellman, *Giant in Gray*, 38, 43; WH to William H. B. Richardson, May 18, 1840, March 15, April 21, 1842; all, Hampton MSS, DU; Wells, *Hampton and Reconstruction*, 13–14.

35. Wells, *Hampton and His Cavalry*, 40–41; Wellman, *Giant in Gray*, 43–44; John S. Palmer et al., *A World Turned Upside Down: The Palmers of South Santee, 1818–1881*, ed. by Louis P. Towles (Columbia, S.C., 1996), 212; Wade Hampton II to MFH, Apr. 22, Nov. 17, 1855, Nov. 7, 1857; WH to MFH, May 22, Nov. 8, 1857, Nov. 6, 1859, all: Hampton Family MSS, USC; Henry T. Louthan, "General Wade Hampton, Planter, Soldier, Statesman," CV 40 (1932): 65.

36. Wells, *Hampton and Reconstruction*, 17; Wellman, *Giant in Gray*, 42; WH to Peter D. Torre, Jan. 6, 1836, Hampton Family MSS, USC.

37. James H. Hammond, *Secret and Sacred: The Diaries of James Henry Hammond, a Southern Slaveholder*, ed. by Carol Bleser (New York, 1988), 9, 22–23, 171–75; Drew Gilpin Faust, *James Henry Hammond and the Old South: A Design for Mastery* (Baton Rouge, La., 1982), 241–43; Maury Klein, *Days of Defiance: Sumter, Secession, and the Coming of the Civil War* (New York, 1997), 78–79.

38. Hammond, *Secret and Sacred*, 120, 124, 175, 185; Klein, *Days of Defiance*, 79–80.

39. Hammond, *Secret and Sacred*, 163–66, 169–71, 176–77, 180–81; Faust, *James Henry Hammond*, 244–45, 248, 250, 288–90, 301–02; Klein, *Days of Defiance*, 80–84.

40. Hammond, *Secret and Sacred*, 174, 179–80, 268–69; Faust, *James Henry Hammond*, 314–15, 338–39.

41. Wellman, *Giant in Gray*, 30–32.

42. *Ibid.*, 33–36; *Charleston Mercury*, Dec. 12, 1859; James M. McPherson, *Ordeal by Fire: The Civil War and Reconstruction* (New York, 1982), 109–10.

43. Wellman, *Giant in Gray*, 32–33.

44. *Ibid.*, 19; Wells, *Hampton and Reconstruction*, 15–16.

45. Wellman, *Giant in Gray*, 20; Wells, *Hampton and His Cavalry*, 43–45.

46. WH to James H. Thornwell, Jan. 13, 1853, Hampton Family MSS, USC.

47. WH et al., *Family Letters of Three Wade Hamptons*, xv; Wellman, *Giant in Gray*, 21–22.

48. Wellman, *Giant in Gray*, 22; James DeVeaux to WH, Nov. 1, 1838, Hampton Family MSS, USC.

49. WH et al., *Family Letters of Three Wade Hamptons*, 167.

50. WH to Margaret Preston Hampton, July 27–29, 1846, Hampton MSS, UNC; WH to Harriet Flud Hampton, Aug. 4, 1846, Hampton Family MSS, USC; Wellman, *Giant in Gray*, 23–24.

51. WH to Margaret Preston Hampton, July 29–Aug. 13, 1846, Hampton MSS, UNC; Wellman, *Giant in Gray*, 24–26.

52. Wellman, *Giant in Gray*, 27.

53. *Ibid.*, 16, 21, 23, 27, 37–41; Wells, *Hampton and Reconstruction*, 12–13; WH et al., *Family Letters of Three Wade Hamptons*, xiv-xvii, 38n., 43n.; Louthan, "General Wade Hampton," 65; "Visit to a Cotton Plantation," 103.

54. WH et al., *Family Letters of Three Wade Hamptons*, xv–xvi, 38 and n., 46n., 57n.; Wellman, *Giant in Gray*, 27.

55. WH et al., *Family Letters of Three Wade Hamptons*, xiv–xvi and nn.

56. *Ibid.*, xv and n.; "Visit to a Cotton Plantation," 103.

57. Wellman, *Giant in Gray*, 28–30; WH to Mary Singleton McDuffie, Mar. 1, 1856, Hampton MSS, DU.

58. Wellman, *Giant in Gray*, 46–47; WH et al., *Family Letters of Three Wade Hamptons*, 167.

59. Wellman, *Giant in Gray*, 30; WH et al., *Family Letters of Three Wade Hamptons*, xvi.

60. Arthur M. Schlesinger, Jr., *The Age of Jackson* (Boston, 1953), 34, 95–96; Paul I. Wellman, *The House Divides: The Age of Jackson and Lincoln, from the War of 1812 to the Civil War* (Garden City, N.Y., 1966), 134–42.

61. Ernest M. Lander and Robert K. Ackerman, eds., *Perspectives in South Carolina History: The First 300 Years* (Columbia, S.C., 1973), 135–36; Harold S. Schultz, *Nationalism and Sectionalism in South Carolina, 1852–1860* (Durham, N.C., 1950), 27, 41.

62. Wells, *Hampton and Reconstruction*, 17–18; *Charleston Mercury*, Dec. 12, 1859; Wellman, *Giant in Gray*, 34.

63. *Charleston Mercury*, Dec. 12, 1859.

64. *Ibid.*; Wellman, *Giant in Gray*, 35–36.

Two:

1. McPherson, *Ordeal by Fire*, 117–26.

2. *Ibid.*, 127–29.

3. Wellman, *Giant in Gray*, 47; WH to MFH, Nov. 4, 1860, Hampton Family MSS, USC.

4. E. B. Long and Barbara Long, *The Civil War Day by Day: An Almanac, 1861–1865* (Garden City, N.Y., 1971), 15–16; OR, I, 1: 2–4.

5. McPherson, *Ordeal by Fire*, 127–37.

6. Wellman, *Giant in Gray*, 48.

7. McPherson, *Ordeal by Fire*, 141; OR, I, 1: 134–37, 140; Klein, *Days of Defiance*, 191–99.

8. Long and Long, *Civil War Day by Day*, 43; Davis, *Battle at Bull Run*, 50.

9. Wellman, *Giant in Gray*, 47; WH to MFH, Mar. 27, 1861, Hampton Family MSS, USC.

10. OR, I, 1: 12–25, 29–35; Klein, *Days of Defiance*, 409–16.

11. Wellman, *Giant in Gray*, 50; WH to MFH, Apr. 30, 1861, Hampton Family MSS, USC.

12. One of the more recent publictions of this photograph is in William C. Davis, ed., *Shadows of the Storm: Volume One of The Image of War, 1861–1865* (Garden City, N.Y., 1981), 107.

13. OR, IV, 1: 296; Wellman, *Giant in Gray*, 50–53; Wells, *Hampton and Reconstruction*, 37–38.

14. OR, IV, 1: 305.

15. *Ibid.*, 303–04.

16. Wellman, *Giant in Gray*, 42, 53; WH et al., *Family Letters of Three Wade Hamptons*, 166.

17. OR, IV, 1: 303; Wellman, *Giant in Gray*, 50–51.

18. Coxe, "First Manassas," 24; Davis, *Battle at Bull Run*, 27–28.

19. OR, IV, 1: 296.

20. *Ibid.*; Robert J. Trout, "Galloping Thunder: Horse Artillery of the Army of Northern Virginia," *North & South* 3 (Sept. 2000): 78; Wellman, *Giant in Gray*, 51, 340n.

21. WH to MFH, Sept. 4, 1861, Hampton Family MSS, USC.

22. OR, IV, 1: 303.

23. Wellman, *Giant in Gray*, 50–51, 57; *Echoes from Hampton Day, Charleston, South Carolina, May 14th, 1895* (Charleston, 1895), 31.

24. Coxe, "First Manassas," 26; Samuel J. Martin, *Southern Hero: Matthew Calbraith Butler, Confederate General, Hampton Red Shirt, and U.S. Senator* (Mechanicsburg, Pa., 2001), 1–16; Ezra J. Warner, *Generals in Gray: Lives of the Confederate Commanders* (Baton Rouge, La., 1959), 40–41, 59–60, 102, 183–84, 189–90.

25. Coxe, "First Manassas," 24; Janet Hewett et al., eds., *Supplement to the Official Records of the Union and Confederate Armies* (Wilmington, N.C., 1994–2001), II, 65: 292–314.

26. Coxe, "First Manassas," 24; WH to P. G. T. Beauregard, June 10, 1861, Hampton MSS, DU.

27. Coxe, "First Manassas," 24; Davis, *Battle at Bull Run*, 27–28.

28. Hewett et al., eds., *Supplement to the Official Records*, II, 65: 307; WH to P. G. T. Beauregard, June 10, 1861, Hampton MSS, DU.

29. WH to P. G. T. Beauregard, June 10, 1861, Hampton MSS, DU.

30. Coxe, "First Manassas," 24.

31. *Ibid.*

32. Wellman, *Giant in Gray*, 57–58; WH to MFH, July 13, 1861, Hampton Family MSS, USC.

33. Wellman, *Giant in Gray*, 57; Hennessy, *First Battle of Manassas*, 1–6.

34. WH to MFH, July 13, 1861, Hampton Family MSS, USC.

35. *Ibid.*; Coxe, "First Manassas," 24; WH et al., *Letters of Three Wade Hamptons*, 74n.

36. Davis, *Battle at Bull Run*, 90–92, 132–34.

37. *Ibid.*, 93–130; Coxe, "First Manassas," 24.

38. Coxe, "First Manassas," 24.

39. *Ibid.*; Wellman, *Giant in Gray*, 59; Martin, *Southern Hero*, 19–20.

THREE:

1. Hennessy, *First Battle of Manassas*, 37–77; Davis, *Battle at Bull Run*, 159–201.

2. Hennessy, *First Battle of Manassas*, 68–71; Logan, *My Confederate Girlhood*, 121.

3. Davis, *Battle at Bull Run*, 196–98.

4. OR, I, 2: 567.

5. Hennessy, *First Battle of Manassas*, 68, 104–11.

6. OR, I, 2: 567.

7. *Ibid.*; Hennessy, *First Battle of Manassas*, 104; Wellman, *Giant in Gray*, 64; *Echoes from Hampton Day*, 33; MFH to Mrs. William Martin, Aug. 12, 1861, Hampton Family MSS, USC; *James Conner . . . In Memoriam* (Charleston, S.C., ca. 1883), 12.

8. OR, I, 2: 567; Coxe, "First Manassas," 26.

9. OR, I, 2: 566–67.

10. *Ibid.*, 567.

11. *OR*, I, 2: 474, 500; Logan, My *Confederate Girlhood*, 129.

12. *OR*, I, 2: 567; Logan, My *Confederte Girlhood*, 124.

13. Caroline L. Hampton to WH, n.d. [ca. Aug. 1, 1861]; MFH to Mrs. William Martin, Aug. 12, 1861; both, Hampton Family MSS, USC.

14. Mary Boykin Chesnut, *The Private Mary Chesnut: The Unpublished Civil War Diaries*, ed. by C. Vann Woodward and Elisabeth Muhlenfeld (New York, 1984), 118.

15. MFH to Mrs. William Martin, Aug. 12, 1861; WH to MFH, Sept. 4, 1861; both, Hampton Family MSS, USC.

16. WH to MFH, Sept. 4, 1861, Hampton Family MSS, USC; Long and Long, *Civil War Day by Day*, 101–02.

17. Hewett et al., eds., *Supplement to the Official Records*, III, 1: 369; WH to Thomas Jordan, Sept. 24, 1861; WH to MFH, Oct. 1, 1861; both, Hampton Family MSS, USC.

18. Hewett et al., eds., *Supplement to the Official Records*, III, 1: 369.

19. *Ibid.*, II, 65: 299–319.

20. *Ibid.*, 293, 303–04; Martin, *Southern Hero*, 20.

21. *OR*, I, 5: 913, 1030; Wellman, *Giant in Gray*, 69.

22. WH to Thomas Jordan, Sept. 24, 1861, Hampton Family MSS, USC; Hewett et al., eds., *Supplement to the Official Records*, II, 65: 301, 310, 312; III, 1: 369, 376.

23. WH to MFH, Oct. 1, 1861, Hampton Family MSS, USC.

24. *Ibid.*

25. Mary Boykin Chesnut, *A Diary from Dixie*, ed. by Ben Ames Williams (Boston, 1949), 175.

26. *OR*, I, 5: 986–87; "Hampton's Sabre," n.d., memo in Edward L. Wells MSS, CLS; Wellman, *Giant in Gray*, 69.

27. *OR*, I, 5: 987.

28. *Ibid.*, 987, 1002; WH to MFH, Jan. 3, 1862, Hampton Family MSS, USC; John Coxe, "Bloody Night Affair at Colchester, Virginia," CV 23 (1915): 168–69.

29. *OR*, I, 5: 1002; Hewett et al., eds., *Supplement to the Official Records*, II, 48: 673; WH to P. G. T. Beauregard, Nov. 17, 1861, Sang-Lee Civil War Collection, Seymour Library, Knox College, Galesburg, Ill.; WH to MFH, Dec. 9, 1861, WH Family MSS (1818–1902), LC; WH to MFH, Dec. 25, 1861, Hampton Family MSS, USC; Coxe, "Bloody Night Affair," 168.

30. WH to P. G. T. Beauregard, Nov. 17, 1861, Sang-Lee Civil War Collection; WH to MFH, Nov. 17, 1861; WH to Catherine M. Hampton, Jan. 15, 1862; both, Hampton Family MSS, USC.

31. WH to MFH, Nov. 17, 1861, Hampton Family MSS, USC.

32. WH to MFH, Nov. 17, Dec. 30, 1861, Jan. 3, 1862; all, *ibid.*

33. *OR*, I, 5: 1082; WH to MFH, Mar. 2, 1862, Hampton Family MSS, USC.

34. *OR*, I, 5: 531–32, 1090–92, 1094; 51, pt. 2: 488.

35. *Ibid.*, 5: 530.

36. *Ibid.*, 535; WH to MFH, Mar. 16, 1862, Hampton Family MSS, USC.

37. *OR*, I, 5: 528–31, 533–34.

38. Wellman, *Giant in Gray*, 69.

39. WH to MFH, Mar. 16, 1862, Hampton Family MSS, USC.

40. *OR*, I, 5: 54; Stephen W. Sears, *To the Gates of Richmond: The Peninsula Campaign* (New York,

1992), 14–20.

41. *OR*, I, 11, pt. 1: 5–12.

42. *Ibid.*, pt. 3: 395, 397, 405, 425–26; Sears, *To the Gates of Richmond*, 43–45.

43. Edward G. Longacre, *General William Dorsey Pender: A Military Biography* (Conshohocken, Pa., 2001), 83–84; Bartlett Y. Malone, *Whipt 'em Everytime: The Diary of Bartlett Yancey Malone, Co. H 6th North Carolina Regiment*, ed. by William Whatley Pierson, Jr. (Jackson, Tenn., 1960), 49–50.

44. *OR*, I, 11, pt. 3: 473, 477, 484–85.

45. *Ibid.*, 488–90; Sears, *To the Gates of Richmond*, 47–48, 59–61.

46. *OR*, I, 11, pt. 1: 19–22, 423–26, 444–45, 448–53, 564–79.

47. *Ibid.*, 22, 614–15.

48. *Ibid.*, 615, 627–29.

49. *Ibid.*, 629–33; Sears, *To the Gates of Richmond*, 85.

50. *OR*, I, 11, pt. 1: 629, 632; Sears, *To the Gates of Richmond*, 85–86; Dwight E. Stinson, Jr., "Eltham's Landing—the End Run that Failed," *CWTI* 1 (Feb. 1963): 38–41; Malone, *Whipt 'em Everytime*, 53–54; Wellman, *Giant in Gray*, 71–72.

51. *OR*, I, 11, pt. 1: 569, 629–30.

52. *Ibid.*, 602, 628, 630–31, 633; Wellman, *Giant in Gray*, 72; Gilbert E. Govan and James W. Livingood, *A Different Valor: The Story of General Joseph E. Johnston, C. S. A.* (Indianapolis, 1956), 126.

FOUR:

1. *OR*, I, 11, pt. 1: 25, 276.

2. WH to MFH, June 3, 1862, Hampton Family MSS, USC; Chesnut, *Diary from Dixie*, 259.

3. Wellman, *Giant in Gray*, 72; *OR*, I, 11, pt. 3: 543.

4. *OR*, I, 11, pt. 1: 872–77, 933–34, 943–45.

5. *Ibid.*, 934, 989–90; Gustavus W. Smith, *The Battle of Seven Pines* (New York, 1891), 21–22, 97–98, 133; Gustavus W. Smith, "Two Days of Battle at Seven Pines (Fair Oaks)," *B&L* 2: 244–45; Steven H. Newton, *The Battle of Seven Pines, May 31–June 1, 1862* (Lynchburg, Va., 1993), 76.

6. *OR*, I, 11, pt. 1: 990–91; Smith, *Battle of Seven Pines*, 98–100; Smith, "Seven Pines (Fair Oaks)," 245–47; Clifford Dowdey, *The Seven Days: The Emergence of Lee* (Boston, 1964), 120–21; Walter Clark, ed., *Histories of the Several Regiments and Battalions from North Carolina in the Great War, 1861–'65 . . .* (Goldsboro and Raleigh, N.C., 1901), 2: 772.

7. *OR*, I, 11, pt. 1: 991; Wellman, *Giant in Gray*, 73–74.

8. *OR*, I, 11, pt. 1: 991; Smith, *Battle of Seven Pines*, 100–01; Newton, *Battle of Seven Pines*, 74–82; Longacre, *General William Dorsey Pender*, 94–95.

9. WH to MFH, June 3, 1862, Hampton Family MSS, USC.

10. *Ibid.*; *OR*, I, 11, pt. 1: 991.

11. *Ibid.*, 993; WH to MFH, June 3, 1862, Hampton Family MSS, USC.

12. Wellman, *Giant in Gray*, 74; Chesnut, *Diary from Dixie*, 242, 252, 255.

13. Smith, "Seven Pines (Fair Oaks)," 261; Newton, *Battle of Seven Pines*, 82–83.

14. Chesnut, *Diary from Dixie*, 257; Wellman, *Giant in Gray*, 72–73.

15. Wellman, *Giant in Gray*, 75–76; Chesnut, *Diary from Dixie*, 256; WH et al., *Family Letters of Three Wade Hamptons*, 167.

16. Wellman, *Giant in Gray*, 76; *OR*, I, 11, pt. 2: 483–87.

17. *OR*, I, 11, pt. 1: 991; Longacre, *General William Dorsey Pender*, 106.

18. *OR*, I, 11, pt. 2: 490–92; Fitz John Porter, "Hanover Court House and Gaines's Mill," *B&L* 2: 327–42.

19. *OR*, I, 11, pt. 2: 484, 593–94.

20. *Ibid.*, 556–57; Wellman, *Giant in Gray*, 77.

21. *OR*, I, 11, pt. 2: 557; Edward Porter Alexander, *Military Memoirs of a Confederate: A Critical Narrative* (New York, 1908), 148–49; Edward Porter Alexander, *Fighting for the Confederacy: The Personal Recollections of General Edward Porter Alexander*, ed. by Gary A. Gallagher (Chapel Hill, N.C., 1989), 108.

22. Wellman, *Giant in Gray*, 79; Alexander, *Military Memoirs*, 149–51; Alexander, *Fighting for the Confederacy*, 108–09; Charles Marshall, *An Aide-de-Camp of Lee: Being the Papers of Colonel Charles Marshall . . .*, ed. by Sir Frederick Maurice (Boston, 1927), 109–12; Brian K. Burton, *Extraordinary Circumstances: The Seven Days Battles* (Bloomington, Ind., 2001), 259.

23. Alexander, *Military Memoirs*, 149–51; Alexander, *Fighting for the Confederacy*, 108–09; Marshall, *Aide-de-Camp of Lee*, 109–12; Robert K. Krick, "Sleepless in the Saddle: Stonewall Jackson in the Seven Days," in Gary A. Gallagher, ed., *The Richmond Campaign of 1862: The Peninsula and the Seven Days* (Chapel Hill, N.C., 2000), 80–83, 92n.

24. *OR*, I, 11, pt. 2: 495, 557.

25. Porter, *Fighting for the Confederacy*, 109–10.

26. *OR*, I, 11, pt. 2: 495–97; Fitz John Porter, "The Battle of Malvern Hill," *B&L* 2: 409–23.

27. *OR*, I, 11, pt. 2: 497.

28. John Pope, "The Second Battle of Bull Run," *B&L* 2: 449–55.

29. *OR*, I, 11, pt. 3: 652, 655; 12, pt. 2: 550; pt. 3: 934; Wellman, *Giant in Gray*, 80–81.

30. *OR*, I, 11, pt. 1: 1041; pt. 3: 655.

31. W. T. Robins, "Stuart's Ride around McClellan," *B&L* 2: 271–75; Edward G. Longacre, *Lee's Cavalrymen: A History of the Mounted Forces of the Army of Northern Virginia, 1861–1865* (Mechanicsburg, Pa., 2002), 85–93.

32. *OR*, I, 11, pt. 3: 652 and n.; Martin, *Southern Hero*, 42–43.

33. *OR*, I, 11, pt. 2: 519–20, 530–31; Jennings Cropper Wise, *The Long Arm of Lee; or, The History of the Artillery of the Army of Northern Virginia . . .* (Lynchburg, Va., 1915), 1: 233; Walter H. Taylor, *Four Years with General Lee . . .* (New York, 1877), 41; Henry B. McClellan, *The Life and Campaigns of Maj. Gen. J. E. B. Stuart, Commander of the Cavalry of the Army of Northern Virginia* (Boston, 1885), 83–85; Douglas Southall Freeman, *Lee's Lieutenants: A Study in Command* (New York, 1942–44), 1: 641–43; Alexander, *Fighting for the Confederacy*, 114–15.

34. John Esten Cooke, *Wearing of the Gray: Being Personal Portraits, Scenes and Adventures of the War* (Baton Rouge, La., 1997), 7–9, 14–17; John Esten Cooke, "General Stuart in Camp and Field," in *The Annals of the War, Written by Leading Participants, North and South* (Philadelphia, 1879), 665–76.

35. *OR*, I, 11, pt. 3: 655; 21: 1067; Wellman, *Giant in Gray*, 81–85.

36. Warner, *Generals in Gray*, 178–79; John S. Wise, *The End of an Era* (Boston, 1899), 334–35; Wellman, *Giant in Gray*, 84.

37. Warner, *Generals in Gray*, 184–85, 214–15, 264–65, 348; Trout, "Galloping Thunder," 78–79; Jeffry D. Wert, "His Unhonored Service," *CWTI* 24 (June 1985): 29–34.

38. *OR*, I, 11, pt. 3: 652, 657; McClellan, *Life and Campaigns of Stuart*, 86.

39. *OR*, I, 12, pt. 3: 920; Wellman, *Giant in Gray*, 84.

40. Cooke, *Wearing of the Gray*, 47–52.

FIVE:

1. William W. Blackford, *War Years with Jeb Stuart* (New York, 1945), 87.

2. *Ibid.*, 95; *OR*, I, 12, pt. 2: 118–21, 177; Cooke, *Wearing of the Gray*, 335–36; McClellan, *Life and Campaigns of Stuart*, 87–89.

3. *OR*, I, 12, pt. 2: 184; Blackford, *War Years with Jeb Stuart*, 97; John Hennessy, *Return to Bull Run: The Campaign and Battle of Second Manassas* (New York, 1993), 28–29.

4. *OR*, I, 12, pt. 2: 149–53, 177–86.

5. *Ibid.*, 725; McClellan, *Life and Campaigns of Stuart*, 89; Blackford, *War Years with Jeb Stuart*, 97.

6. *OR*, I, 12, pt. 2: 550n., 725; pt. 3: 930–31; Robert E. Lee, *The Wartime Papers of Robert E. Lee*, ed. by Clifford Dowdey and Louis H. Manarin (Boston, 1961), 255.

7. Wellman, *Giant in Gray*, 87; WH to Lafayette McLaws, Aug. 16, 18, 1862; both, Rives Family MSS, VHS.

8. Trout, "Galloping Thunder," 78.

9. Wellman, *Giant in Gray*, 101; WH to Lafayette McLaws, Aug. 18, 1862, Rives Family MSS.

10. *OR*, I, 51, pt. 2: 611.

11. *Ibid.*, 12, pt. 3: 942.

12. *Ibid.*, pt. 2: 725–28; pt. 3: 934; Cooke, *Wearing of the Gray*, 195–99; McClellan, *Life and Campaigns of Stuart*, 89–91; Blackford, *War Years with Jeb Stuart*, 97; B. J. Haden, *Reminiscences of J. E. B. Stuart's Cavalry* . . . (Charlottesville, Va., ca. 1890), 14–15; Marshall, *Aide-de-Camp of Lee*, 126–27; Walter H. Taylor, *General Lee: His Campaigns in Virginia, 1861–1865* . . . (Norfolk, Va., 1906), 92.

13. Hennessy, *Return to Bull Run*, 74–81, 143–93, 362–406, 449–50; Pope, "Second Battle of Bull Run," 460–94.

14. *OR*, I, 12, pt. 2: 744; 19, pt. 1: 822.

15. *Ibid.*, 144; Longacre, *Lee's Cavalrymen*, 127–28.

16. McClellan, *Life and Campaigns of Stuart*, 109–10; *OR*, I, 19, pt. 1: 814; pt. 2: 595; James Ewell Brown Stuart, *The Letters of Major General James E. B. Stuart*, ed. by Adele H. Mitchell (n.p., 1990), 266.

17. James K. Munnerlyn to his sister, Sept. 8, 1862, Munnerlyn MSS, UNC.

18. *OR*, I, 19, pt. 1: 814–15, 822.

19. *Ibid.*, 815, 822; Blackford, *War Years with Jeb Stuart*, 140–42.

20. *OR*, I, 19, pt. 1: 25–26, 140–42, 815, 822, 839–40, 951–53.

21. *Ibid.*, 815, 822.

22. *Ibid.*, 815, 822–23; Donald A. Hopkins, *The Little Jeff: The Jeff Davis Legion, Cavalry, Army of Northern Virginia* (Shippensburg, Pa., 1999), 92.

23. *OR*, I, 19, pt. 1: 823.

24. *Ibid.*; D. B. Rea, "Cavalry Incidents of the Maryland Campaign," *Maine Bugle* 2 (1895): 117–18.

25. Rea, "Cavalry Incidents," 118–19.

26. *OR*, I, 19, pt. 1: 823–24.

27. Rea, "Cavalry Incidents," 121.

28. *Ibid.*, 121–22; OR, I, 19, pt. 1: 824, 826.

29. OR, I, 19, pt. 1: 818–19, 824, 826–27, 951, 953–55; McClellan, *Life and Campaigns of Stuart*, 115, 120–23.

30. OR, I, 19, pt. 1: 819–20, 824, 874, 971, 1010; Wellman, *Giant in Gray*, 93; McClellan, *Life and Campigns of Stuart*, 127–29; William R. Carter diary, Sept. 17, 1862, Library of Virginia, Richmond; Robert T. Hubard memoirs, 57, DU; R. Channing Price to his mother, Sept. 18, 1862, Price MSS, UNC; John G. Walker, "Sharpsburg," *B&L* 2: 679–80; George W. Beale, *A Lieutenant of Cavalry in Lee's Army* (Boston, 1918), 48–50; Stephen W. Sears, *Landscape Turned Red: The Battle of Antietam* (New Haven, Conn., 1983), 190–91, 258–68, 274–92; James V. Murfin, *The Gleam of Bayonets: The Battle of Antietam and the Maryland Campaign of 1862* (New York, 1965), 213–14, 231, 240; Charles G. Milham, *Gallant Pelham, American Extraordinary* (Washington, D.C., 1959), 160–67.

31. OR, I, 19, pt. 1: 142, 151; Sears, *Landscape Turned Red*, 306–08.

32. OR, I, 19, pt. 1: 820–21, 824; McClellan, *Life and Campaigns of Stuart*, 133; Blackford, *War Years with Jeb Stuart*, 152.

33. OR, I, 19, pt. 1: 821.

34. Blackford, *War Years with Jeb Stuart*, 155.

35. Heros von Borcke, *Memoirs of the Confederate War for Independence* (New York, 1938), 1: 291.

36. OR, I, 19, pt. 2: 55–57; Wells, *Hampton and His Cavalry*, 62–63; Wellman, *Giant in Gray*, 94–95.

37. OR, I, 19, pt. 2: 55; Edward G. Longacre, *Mounted Raids of the Civil War* (South Brunswick, N. J., 1975), 25–26.

38. OR, I, 19, pt. 1; 72; pt. 2: 38–41, 52, 57, 59; 51, pt. 1: 878; Brooks, *Butler and His Cavalry*, 80–81; McClellan, *Life and Campaigns of Stuart*, 138–39; Blackford, *War Years with Jeb Stuart*, 165; Frank Moore, ed., *The Rebellion Record: A Diary of American Events* (New York, 1861–68), 6: 169.

39. OR, I, 19, pt. 2: 52, 57; Brooks, *Butler and His Cavalry*, 81; Blackford, *War Years with Jeb Stuart*, 165–68; William Clark Corson, *My Dear Jennie: A Collection of Love Letters from a Confederate Soldier to His Fiancée During the Period 1861–1865*, ed. by Blake W. Corson, Jr. (Richmond, Va., 1982), 96–97; Chiswell Dabney to his mother, Oct. 21, 1862, Dabney MSS, VHS; Julian T. Edwards to his parents, Oct. 15, 1862, *ibid.*

40. OR, I, 19, pt. 2: 57; Wells, *Hampton and His Cavalry*, 57–59; Wellman, *Giant in Gray*, 96–97; McClellan, *Life and Campaigns of Stuart*, 141; Blackford, *War Years with Jeb Stuart*, 168.

41. OR, I, 19, pt. 2: 52, 57–58; Brooks, *Butler and His Cavalry*, 81; McClellan, *Life and Campaigns of Stuart*, 141.

42. OR, I, 19, pt. 2: 52–53, 58; Brooks, *Butler and His Cavalry*, 81–82; Julian T. Edwards to his parents, Oct. 15, 1862.

43. OR, I, 19, pt. 2: 52–53; McClellan, *Life and Campaigns of Stuart*, 149; Blackford, *War Years with Jeb Stuart*, 149, 172–73; R. Channing Price to his mother, Oct. 15, 1862, Price MSS, UNC.

44. Blackford, *War Years with Jeb Stuart*, 174, 179–80; Clark, *Regiments and Battalions from North Carolina*, 1: 422.

45. OR, I, 19, pt. 1: 73–74; pt. 2: 39–45, 53–54, 58; Wells, *Hampton and His Cavalry*, 67–68; Wellman, *Giant in Gray*, 97–98; Brooks, *Butler and His Cavalry*, 83; McClellan, *Life and Campaigns of Stuart*, 150–60; Blackford, *War Years with Jeb Stuart*, 171–78; Wilbur S. Nye, "How Stuart Recrossed the Potomac," *CWTI* 4 (Jan. 1966): 45–47; R. Channing Price to his mother, Oct. 15, 1862, Price MSS, UNC; Moore, *Rebellion Record*, 6: 17–18.

Six:

1. OR, I, 19, pt. 2: 52–56; WH to MFH, Oct. 24, 1862, Hampton MSS, UNC.

2. OR, I, 19, pt. 1: 87, 152.

3. Ibid., 152; pt. 2: 140–41, 692–94.

4. Ibid., 104–14, 125–26, 136–38, 141–42, 518–19, 524–25; 51, pt. 1: 903–04, 907, 910–12, 916, 921–22; Moore, Rebellion Record, 6: 56–57.

5. OR, I, 19, pt. 2: 143–46; McClellan, Life and Campaigns of Stuart, 180–84; William R. Carter diary, Nov. 4, 1862; Moore, Rebellion Record, 6: 177–79.

6. OR, I, 19, pt. 2: 144; Chris J. Hartley, Stuart's Tarheels: James B. Gordon and His North Carolina Cavalry (Baltimore, 1996), 164–68.

7. OR, I, 19, pt. 1: 88; pt. 2: 144–45; Robert T. Hubard memoirs, 60.

8. OR, I, 19, pt. 2: 145.

9. Ibid., pt. 1: 88; pt. 2: 144–45, 551; Sears, Landscape Turned Red, 338–45.

10. OR, I, 19, pt. 2: 145; 21: 84–87, 550–51, 1014–15, 1019; 51, pt. 2: 646.

11. WH to MFH, Nov. 22, 1862, Hampton Family MSS, USC.

12. OR, I, 21: 15–16; Wellman, Giant in Gray, 102.

13. OR, I, 21: 15–16, 1114; 51, pt. 2: 653; John F. Milhollin to his wife, Dec. 3, 1862, Milhollin MSS, USAMHI.

14. OR, I, 19, pt. 2: 712–13; 21: 544; 51, pt. 2: 648; McClellan, Life and Campaigns of Stuart, 186n.–87n.; Hopkins, The Little Jeff, 112.

15. WH to MFH, Nov. 22, 1862, Hampton Family MSS, USC.

16. OR, I, 51, pt. 2: 652–53.

17. Ibid., 21: 690; Wellman, Giant in Gray, 102.

18. OR, I, 21: 690–91.

19. Ibid., 690, 1114.

20. Ibid., 695–96; Wellman, Giant in Gray, 102–03; Brooks, Butler and His Cavalry, 85–86.

21. OR, I, 21: 696; Brooks, Butler and His Cavalry, 86–87; Edwin R. Sloan to his wife, Dec. 21, 1862, Sloan MSS, DU.

22. OR, I, 21: 697, 1114.

23. Ibid., 696.

24. WH to MFH, Dec. 25, 1862, Hampton Family MSS, USC.

25. Ibid.

26. OR, I, 21: 64–76, 89–95.

27. Ibid., 547, 553, 731–32; R. Channing Price to his mother, Dec. 17, 1862, Price MSS, UNC; McClellan, Life and Campaigns of Stuart, 195–98; Blackford, War Years with Jeb Stuart, 192–93; William H. Mills to "Dear Brother," Dec. 25, 1862, Mills MSS, J. Y. Joyner Library, East Carolina Univ., Greenville; R. L. T. Beale, History of the Ninth Virginia Cavalry, in the War Between the States (Richmond, Va., 1899), 56–57; Wise, Long Arm of Lee, 1: 382–85, 404; Robert T. Hubard memoirs, 63; Edward G. Longacre, "Stuart's Dumfries Raid," CWTI 15 (July 1976): 18–22.

28. OR, I, 21: 732–33, 736.

29. Ibid., 733, 736; Brooks, Butler and His Cavalry, 87; McClellan, Life and Campaigns of Stuart, 199; D. B. Rea, Sketches from Hampton's Cavalry, Embracing the Principal Exploits of the Cavalry in the Campaigns of 1862 and 1863 (Columbia, S.C., 1864), 64; Wellman, Giant in Gray, 104.

30. OR, I, 21: 733–35, 738–42; McClellan, *Life and Campaigns of Stuart*, 198.

31. OR, I, 21: 733; Freeman, *Lee's Lieutenants*, 2: 402–03.

32. OR, I, 21: 733–34, 736–38; Brooks, *Butler and His Cavalry*, 88; Martin, *Southern Hero*, 64–65.

33. OR, I, 21: 734, 736.

34. *Ibid.*, 733–34, 738–42; McClellan, *Life and Campaigns of Stuart*, 199–201; R. Channing Price to his sister, Jan. 20, 1863, Price MSS, UNC; John F. Milhollin to his wife, Jan. 3, 1863, Milhollin MSS; Robert T. Hubard memoirs, 64.

35. OR, I, 21: 734–36, 739; Brooks, *Butler and His Cavalry*, 89; McClellan, *Life and Campaigns of Stuart*, 202; R. Channing Price to his sister, Jan. 20, 1863, Price MSS, UNC.

36. OR, I, 21: 736.

37. *Ibid.*, 1067.

SEVEN:

1. OR, I, 19, pt. 2: 701; Edward G. Longacre, *Lincoln's Cavalrymen: A History of the Mounted Forces of the Army of the Potomac, 1861–1865* (Mechanicsburg, Pa., 2000), 125; Longacre, *Lee's Cavalrymen*, 157.

2. Robert T. Hubard memoirs, 65; Robert B. Jones to his wife, Jan. 3, 1863, Jones MSS, VHS; John Bolling to "My dear Sir," Jan. 21, 1863, Bolling MSS, *ibid.*

3. Robert E. Lee, *Lee's Dispatches: Unpublished Letters of General Robert E. Lee, C. S. A., to Jefferson Davis and the War Department of the Confederate States of America*, ed. by Douglas Southall Freeman and Grady McWhiney (New York, 1957), 71 and n.-73 and n.

4. WH to MFH, Jan. 27, 1863, Hampton Family MSS, USC.

5. Lee, *Lee's Dispatches*, 71–73.

6. OR, I, 21: 752–55, 986, 989, 994, 999–1001, 1101, 1108, 1111.

7. *Ibid.*, 25, pt. 1: 6, 9.

8. *Ibid.*, 795, 1045; McClellan, *Life and Campaigns of Stuart*, 204; R. Channing Price to his sister, Feb. 17, 1863, Price MSS, VHS; WH et al., *Family Letters of Three Wade Hamptons*, 92n.

9. OR, I, 25, pt. 1: 25–26, 47–50, 54–59, 61, 64; pt. 2: 686; J. E. B. Stuart to John Esten Cooke, Feb. 28, 1863, Cooke MSS, VHS; R. Channing Price to his mother, Mar. 2, 21, 1863; both, Price MSS, UNC; R. Channing Price to his sister, Mar. 15, 1863, Price MSS, VHS; McClellan, *Life and Campaigns of Stuart*, 204, 209–17; Blackford, *War Years with Jeb Stuart*, 201–02; Cooke, *Wearing of the Gray*, 116–19; Freeman, *Lee's Lieutenants*, 2: 455–57, 463–66.

10. Longacre, *Lincoln's Cavalrymen*, 124–29.

11. OR, I, 25, pt. 1: 1057–58; pt. 2: 199–200, 204–05.

12. OR, I, 25, pt. 1: 1097–99; Longacre, *Mounted Raids*, 157–74; Stephen W. Sears, *Chancellorsville* (Boston, 1996), 190–91, 231–33, 240–43, 257–72, 290–97.

13. OR, I, 14: 890; 18: 1044.

14. WH to P. G. T. Beauregard, Apr. 6, 1863, CSR of WH, M-331, R-115, NA; C. R. P. Rodgers, "Du Pont's Attack at Charleston," *B&L* 4: 35–41; WH et al., *Family Letters of Three Wade Hamptons*, 166.

15. WH to George Howe, May 19, 1863, Hampton Family MSS, USC; Jesse H. Person to his mother, Apr. 21, 1863, Person MSS, DU.

16. WH to MFH, May 19, 1863, Hampton Family MSS, USC.

17. OR, I, 18: 891.

18. Edwin B. Coddington, *The Gettysburg Campaign: A Study in Command* (New York, 1968), 5–7.

19. *Ibid.*, 11–13; Douglas Southall Freeman, *R. E. Lee: A Biography* (New York, 1934–35), 3: 12–15; OR, I, 25, pt. 2: 789–90, 804–05, 819–21, 825–26, 831, 836–37, 840, 848, 852, 854.

20. OR, I, 27, pt. 3: 5–8, 12–14; McClellan, *Life and Campaigns of Stuart*, 261; Blackford, *War Years with Jeb Stuart*, 211–12.

21. Richard P. Allen to "Dear Captain," June 6, 1863, Allen MSS, MC; Media Evans memoirs, 7, UNC; George M. Neese, *Three Years in the Confederate Horse Artillery* (New York, 1911), 165–69; Daniel B. Coltrane, *The Memoirs of Daniel Branson Coltrane, Co. I, 63rd Reg., North Carolina Cavalry, C. S. A.* (Raleigh, N.C., 1956), 11–12.

22. McClellan, *Life and Campaigns of Stuart*, 261–62; Neese, *Confederate Horse Artillery*, 169–70; John N. Opie, *A Rebel Cavalryman with Lee, Stuart, and Jackson* (Chicago, 1899), 145–46.

23. OR, I, 27, pt. 2: 680; McClellan, *Life and Campaigns of Stuart*, 262; Fairfax Downey, *Clash of Cavalry: The Battle of Brandy Station, June 9, 1863* (New York, 1959), 84–86.

24. OR, I, 27, pt. 1: 170; pt. 2: 748–49, 754–55, 757; pt. 3: 15–17, 27–30, 34–35, 45; 51, pt. 1: 1047; Coddington, *Gettysburg Campaign*, 54–57; Opie, *Rebel Cavalryman*, 147; Neese, *Confederate Horse Artillery*, 170–73; John S. Mosby, *Stuart's Cavalry in the Gettysburg Campaign* (New York, 1908), 9–16, 27–28, 139.

25. OR, I, 27, pt. 2: 721, 726–27, 729, 732; William R. Carter diary, June 9, 1863; Wert, "His Unhonored Service," 32.

26. OR, I, 27, pt. 2: 680, 721, 727, 729, 733; McClellan, *Life and Campaigns of Stuart*, 268–69; Beale, *Lieutenant of Cavalry*, 86; Opie, *Rebel Cavalryman*, 152; Cadwallader J. Iredell to anon., June 13, 1863, Iredell MSS, UNC.

27. OR, I, 27, pt. 1: 950, 961, 1054; pt. 2: 734–36; pt. 3: 42; David McMurtrie Gregg to Henry B. McClellan, Jan. 21, 1878, McClellan MSS, VHS; Blackford, *War Years with Jeb Stuart*, 214–15; Downey, *Clash of Cavalry*, 106–07.

28. OR, I, 27, pt. 1: 950–51, 965–66, 1024, 1053; pt. 2: 681, 684, 755, 769; 51, pt. 2: 722; McClellan, *Life and Campaigns of Stuart*, 269–70; Blackford, *War Years with Jeb Stuart*, 216; Opie, *Rebel Cavalryman*, 153–54; von Borcke, *Memoirs*, 2: 273–74; Daniel A. Grimsley, *Battles in Culpeper County, Virginia, 1861–1865* (Culpeper, Va., 1900), 11.

29. OR, I, 27, pt. 1: 985–86, 996–97, 1024–25, 1027; pt. 2: 722, 732, 755, 763, 769; von Borcke, *Memoirs*, 2: 276; Beale, *Lieutenant of Cavalry*, 94; Lynwood M. Holland, *Pierce M. B. Young, the Warwick of the South* (Athens, Ga., 1964), 72; Franklin M. Myers, *The Comanches: A History of White's Battalion, Virginia Cavalry, Laurel Brig., Hampton['s] Div., A. N. V., C. S. A.* (Baltimore, 1871), 184–85.

30. OR, I, 27, pt. 2: 719–20; WH to Henry B. McClellan, Jan. 14, 1878, McClellan MSS.

31. Wellman, *Giant in Gray*, 108–09; Brooks, *Butler and His Cavalry*, 132, 165–66.

32. Brooks, *Butler and His Cavalry*, 132–33, 166–69; Martin, *Southern Hero*, 73–75.

33. OR, I, 27, pt. 2: 313, 340; Freeman, *Lee's Lieutenants*, 3: 20; Mosby, *Stuart's Cavalry*, 59; Myers, *Comanches*, 103–04, 188.

34. Wellman, *Giant in Gray*, 109; Chesnut, *Diary from Dixie*, 305.

35. OR, I, 27, pt. 2: 306, 315, 357, 366, 613, 652, 673–77, 687–88, 873; pt. 3: 71–72, 80–84, 87–89, 106, 116–17, 887–88; 51, pt. 1: 1054–55; pt. 2: 723; John T. Swann to "Dear Bettie," June 20, 1863, Swann MSS, Georgia Dept. of Archives and History, Atlanta.

36. Brooks, *Butler and His Cavalry*, 172.

37. *Ibid.*, 171–72; OR, I, 27, pt. 2: 688–89.

38. *OR*, I, 27, pt. 1: 911–12; pt. 2: 613–15, 690.

39. *Ibid.*, pt. 1: 954; pt. 2: 614, 690.

40. Brooks, *Butler and His Cavalry*, 174, 176–77.

41. *Ibid.*, 177; *OR*, I, 27, pt. 1: 912; pt. 2: 690.

42. *OR*, I, 27, pt. 1: 614; pt. 2: 690; WH to Henry B. McClellan, Jan. 14, 1878, McClellan MSS; Hopkins, *Little Jeff*, 141–42; George Baylor, *Bull Run to Bull Run; or, Four Years in the Army of Northern Virginia* . . . (Richmond, Va., 1900), 149.

43. *OR*, I, 27, pt. 2: 688, 690–91; WH to Henry B. McClellan, Jan. 14, 1878, McClellan MSS; Edwin R. Sloan to his wife, June 24, 1863, Sloan MSS; Media Evans memoirs, 8–9; McClellan, *Life and Campaigns of Stuart*, 303–04, 311–12; Hopkins, *Little Jeff*, 142–43.

44. *OR*, I, 27, pt. 1: 920–21, 932–33, 946–48, 954; pt. 2: 691, 750–52; Brooks, *Butler and His Cavalry*, 178–79.

45. *OR*, I, 27, pt. 1: 913; pt. 3: 255; Coddington, *Gettysburg Campaign*, 121–22.

46. *OR*, I, 27, pt. 2: 691–92; pt. 3: 914–15; Coddington, *Gettysburg Campaign*, 107–08; Freeman, *Lee's Lieutenants*, 3: 41 and n., 47–48, 550; Randolph H. McKim, "The Confederate Cavalry in the Gettysburg Campaign," *Journal of the Military Service Institution of the United States* 46 (1910): 418; Marshall, *Aide-de-Camp of Lee*, 201–02, 205–06, 208.

47. *OR*, I, 27, pt. 2: 692, 696, 708–09; McClellan, *Life and Campaigns of Stuart*, 315–17; John S. Mosby to L. L. Lomax, Feb. 19, 1896, Mosby MSS, USAMHI.

48. *OR*, I, 26, pt. 2: 692, 751–52, 760; pt. 3: 915; J. E. B. Stuart to Beverly H. Robertson, June 24, 1863, Stuart MSS, Gilder Lehrman Collection, New York, N.Y.

49. *OR*, I, 27, pt. 2: 692–94; pt. 3: 309–10, 318, 376–77, 915, 923; Alexander, *Military Memoirs*, 378; McClellan, *Life and Campaigns of Stuart*, 318–21, 336; Blackford, *War Years with Jeb Stuart*, 223; Cooke, *Wearing of the Gray*, 226–35.

50. *OR*, I, 27, pt. 2: 694–95; WH to Henry B. McClellan, July 29, 1878, McClellan MSS; Beale, *Ninth Virginia Cavalry*, 78–80; Blackford, *War Years with Jeb Stuart*, 224–25; Cooke, *Wearing of the Gray*, 236.

51. *OR*, I, 27, pt. 2: 202, 695–96; McClellan, *Life and Campaigns of Stuart*, 326–27; Blackford, *War Years with Jeb Stuart*, 225–27; Cooke, *Wearing of the Gray*, 239–42.

52. *OR*, I, 27, pt. 2: 695–96; McClellan, *Life and Campaigns of Stuart*, 327–29; Blackford, *War Years with Jeb Stuart*, 225–27.

53. *OR*, I, 27, pt. 2: 696–97; Wellman, *Giant in Gray*, 114.

54. *OR*, I, 27, pt. 2: 220–21, 224, 696–97; Coddington, *Gettysburg Campaign*, 206, 660n.-61n.; Beale, *Lieutenant of Cavalry*, 114; William R. Carter diary, July 1–2, 1863; Cooke, *Wearing of the Gray*, 245.

Eight:

1. *OR*, I, 27, pt. 2: 221, 224, 697, 724; McClellan, *Life and Campaigns of Stuart*, 330–31; Wilbur S. Nye, "The Affair at Hunterstown," *CWTI* 9 (Feb. 1971): 29.

2. T. J. Mackey, "Duel of General Wade Hampton on the Battle-Field at Gettysburg with a Federal Soldier," *SHSP* 22 (1894): 122–26; Wellman, *Giant in Gray*, 115–16.

3. *OR*, I, 27, pt. 2: 724; Mackey, "Duel of General Wade Hampton," 125–26; Nye, "Affair at Hunterstown," 30–33.

4. Edward G. Longacre, *Custer and His Wolverines: The Michigan Cavalry Brigade, 1861–1865* (Conshohocken, Pa., 1997), 141–42.

5. OR, I, 27, pt. 2: 724; William G. Deloney to his wife, July 4, 7, 1863, Deloney MSS, Hargrett Library, Univ. of Georgia, Athens; Holland, *Pierce M. B. Young*, 73; Wiley C. Howard, *History of Cobb Legion Cavalry and Some Incidents and Scenes Remembered* . . . (Atlanta, 1901), 9.

6. OR, I, 27, pt. 2: 724.

7. *Ibid.*, 697, 724; McClellan, *Life and Campaigns of Stuart*, 337–38; Wise, *Long Arm of Lee*, 2: 691.

8. McClellan, *Life and Campaigns of Stuart*, 338–39; Robert J. Trout, *In the Saddle with Stuart* (Gettysburg, Pa., 1998), 83; Longacre, *Custer and His Wolverines*, 144–47.

9. OR, I, 27, pt. 1: 956, 1050; pt. 2: 697–98; McClellan, *Life and Campaigns of Stuart*, 339–40; William E. Miller, "The Cavalry Battle near Gettysburg," *B&L* 3: 400–03.

10. OR, I, 27, pt. 2: 724.

11. *Ibid.*, 724–25.

12. Rea, *Sketches from Hampton's Cavalry*, 116.

13. Miller, "Cavalry Battle near Gettysburg," 404; Wellman, *Giant in Gray*, 118–19; J. W. Biddle to his father, July 16, 1863, Biddle MSS, DU.

14. OR, I, 27, pt. 2: 725; WH to MFH, July 16, 1863, Hampton Family MSS, USC; Miller, "Cavalry Battle near Gettysburg," 404–05; Wellman, *Giant in Gray*, 120; William G. Deloney to his wife, July 4, 1863, Deloney MSS.

15. Louise Wigfall Wright, *A Southern Girl in '61: The War-Time Memories of a Confederate Senator's Daughter* (New York, 1905), 143; Clark, *Regiments and Battalions from North Carolina*, 1: 425.

16. OR, I, 27, pt. 2: 699; Coddington, *Gettysburg Campign*, 538; John D. Imboden, "The Confederate Retreat from Gettysburg," *B&L* 3: 420–22.

17. William G. Deloney to his wife, July 4, 1863, Deloney MSS; Cooke, *Wearing of the Gray*, 247.

18. Imboden, "Confederate Retreat from Gettysburg," 424.

19. *Ibid.*, 425–27; OR, I, 27, pt. 2: 436–38, 488–89, 653, 655; pt. 3; 327; Coddington, *Gettysburg Campaign*, 554; Robert E. Lee to J. E. B. Stuart, July 13, 1863, Stuart MSS, Henry E. Huntington Library, San Marino, Calif.; Robert T. Hubard memoirs, 79; Blackford, *War Years with Jeb Stuart*, 234–35; J. W. Biddle to his father, July 16, 1863, Biddle MSS.

20. WH to MFH, July 16, 1863, Hampton Family MSS, USC.

21. *Ibid.*

22. Wright, *Southern Girl in '61*, 142–43.

23. *Ibid.*, 148; Surgeon's Certificate, Aug. 7, 1863, CSR of WH, M-331, R-115, NA.

24. Endorsements on Surgeon's Certificate, Aug. 14, 1863; Robert E. Lee to Samuel Cooper, Sept. 28, 1863; both, CSR of WH, M-331, R-115, NA; Wellman, *Giant in Gray*, 130; OR, I, 29, pt. 2: 817, 828.

25. OR, I, 27, pt. 2: 706; Andrew A. Humphreys, *Gettysburg to the Rapidan: The Army of the Potomac, July, 1863, to April, 1864* (New York, 1883), 8; Robert T. Hubard memoirs, 79.

26. OR, I, 29, pt. 1: 195–96, 200–02, 207–08, 215, 730–31, 742–43; pt. 2: 743; Hewett et al., eds., *Supplement to the Official Records*, I, 5: 585–89; McClellan, *Life and Campaigns of Stuart*, 372–76; Opie, *Rebel Cavalryman*, 195; Grimsley, *Battles in Culpeper County*, 14–19; Samuel E. Mays, *Genealogical Notes on the Family of Mays and Reminiscences of the War between the States from Notes Written around the Campfires* (Plant City, Fla., 1927), 109–119; Cadwallader J. Iredell to "My dear Mattie," Aug. 2, 1863, Iredell MSS; Charles W. and Henry M. Trueheart, *Rebel Brothers: The Civil War Letters of the Truehearts*, ed. by Edward B. Williams (College Station, Tex., 1995), 172–73, 177; Neese, *Confederate Horse Artillery*, 208–11; Coltrane, *Memoirs*, 20–21; Baylor, *Bull Run to Bull Run*, 156–57.

27. OR, I, 29, pt. 1: 146–95, 410, 439, 442–44, 447–49, 456, 459, 461, 463, 465–66, 474; pt. 2: 167, 169, 172, 220, 227, 706, 720–21; 51, pt. 2: 772–73, 776–77; McClellan, *Life and Campaigns of Stuart*, 378–92; Robert T. Hubard memoirs, 82; Cadwallader J. Iredell to "My Dear Mattie," Oct. 23, 1863, Iredell MSS; Beale, *Lieutenant of Cavalry*, 129–30; Corson, *My Dear Jennie*, 111–12; Coltrane, *Memoirs*, 22–23; Clark, *Regiments and Battalions from North Carolina*, 1: 426–27.

28. OR, I, 29, pt. 1: 411, 449–52, 461, 464, 466; 51, pt. 2: 778; McClellan, *Life and Campaigns of Stuart*, 393–95; Cooke, *Wearing of the Gray*, 265–66; Thomas L. Rosser, *Riding with Rosser*, ed. by S. Roger Keller (Shippensburg, Pa., 1997), 3–5; William R. Carter diary, Oct. 19, 1863; Robert T. Hubard memoirs, 82–84; Cadwallader J. Iredell to "My dear Mattie," Oct. 23, 1863, Iredell MSS; Clark, *Regiments and Battalions from North Carolina*, 1: 427.

29. OR, I, 27, pt. 3: 1068–69; 29, pt. 2: 707–08; Emory M. Thomas, *Bold Dragoon: The Life of J. E. B. Stuart* (New York, 1986), 258–59.

30. Hewett et al., eds., *Supplement to the Official Records*, I, 5: 563; Freeman, *Lee's Lieutenants*, 3: 210–12; Thomas, *Bold Dragoon*, 258–59; J. E. B. Stuart to Flora Cooke Stuart, Sept. 11, 28, Aug. 4, 1863, Stuart MSS, VHS.

31. OR, I, 29, pt. 1: 574–77, 609–16; Grimsley, *Battles in Culpeper County*, 23.

32. Wellman, *Giant in Gray*, 130.

33. OR, I, 51, pt. 2: 783–86; WH to MFH, Nov. 20, 1863, Hampton Family MSS, USC.

34. WH to MFH, Nov. 20, 1863, Hampton Family MSS, USC.

35. OR, I, 29, pt. 1: 11–13; 51, pt. 2: 787; Jay Luvaas and Wilbur S. Nye, "The Campaign That History Forgot," *CWTI* 8 (Nov. 1969): 12–17.

36. OR, I, 29, pt. 1: 898–99; 51, pt. 2: 788.

37. *Ibid.*, 29, pt. 1: 825–30, 898–99, 902–03, 906–07; 51, pt. 2: 788–89.

38. *Ibid.*, 29, pt. 1: 899–906; 51, pt. 2: 790–92; Lee, *Wartime Papers*, 630; Baylor, *Bull Run to Bull Run*, 181; Myers, *Comanches*, 237; William N. McDonald, *A History of the Laurel Brigade, Originally the Ashby Cavalry of the Army of Northern Virginia, and Chew's Battery*, ed. by Bushrod C. Washington (Baltimore, 1907), 206–07.

39. WH to MFH, Nov. 29, 1863, Hampton Family MSS, USC; OR, I, 29, pt. 1: 899–900, 902–03, 906–07.

40. OR, I, 29, pt. 1: 900.

41. *Ibid.*, 12, 17–18, 697–98, 826, 829, 900; 51, pt. 2: 792.

42. *Ibid.*, 33: 663, 669; Ulysses S. Grant, *Personal Memoirs of U.S. Grant* (New York, 1885–86), 2: 116–17.

43. OR, I, 29, pt. 1: 898–902.

NINE:

1. WH to MFH, Jan. 1, 5, 1864, Hampton Family MSS, USC.

2. Chesnut, *Diary from Dixie*, 364; WH to MFH, Jan. 1, 5, 1865, Hampton Family MSS, USC; WH et al., *Family Letters of Three Wade Hamptons*, 167.

3. WH to MFH, Nov. 20, 1863, Hampton Family MSS, USC.

4. OR, I, 29, pt. 1: 924–25, 971; 33: 1119; Hewett et al., eds., *Supplement to the Official Records*, I, 5: 640–43; Neese, *Confederate Horse Artillery*, 244; John J. Shoemaker, *Shoemaker's Battery, Stuart's Horse Artillery, Pelham's Battalion . . .* (Memphis, Tenn., 1908), 65; Jubal A. Early, *War Memoirs: Autobiographical Sketch and Narrative of the War Between the States*, ed. by Frank E. Vandiver (Bloomington, Ind., 1960), 326–28; Thomas L. Rosser to Elizabeth Winston Rosser, Dec. 27, 1863, Rosser MSS, UV; Rosser, *Riding with Rosser*, 14; Haden, *Reminiscences*, 29.

5. WH to MFH, Jan. 14, 1864, Hampton Family MSS, USC; John L. Black, *Crumbling Defenses; or, Memoirs and Reminiscences of John Logan Black, Colonel, C. S. A.*, ed. by Eleanor D. McSwain (Macon, Ga., 1960), 70.

6. Black, *Crumbling Defenses*, 70.

7. OR, I, 29, pt. 1: 924–25; Haden, *Reminiscences*, 29; J. E. B. Stuart to Flora Cooke Stuart, Jan. 27, 1864, Stuart MSS, VHS; Robert J. Driver, Jr., *5th Virginia Cavalry* (Lynchburg, Va., 1997), 71.

8. OR, I, 33: 1153–55, 1162–64; WH to MFH, Jan. 5, 1864, Hampton Family MSS, USC; WH memoirs, 9–15, 38–42, *ibid*.

9. Black, *Crumbling Defenses*, 71; WH memoirs, 19–20, 42; OR, I, 33: 1258–59; 51, pt. 2: 835–36; Martin, *Southern Hero*, 81–83.

10. OR, I, 51, pt. 2: 835–36; Hartley, *Stuart's Tarheels*, 326–27.

11. WH to MFH, Jan. 5, 1865, Hampton Family MSS, USC.

12. OR, I, 31, pt. 1: 588–89; pt. 2: 632, 682; pt. 3: 816–17.

13. WH to MFH, Dec. 22, 1863, Hampton Family MSS, USC.

14. WH to MFH, Dec. 8, 1863, *ibid*.; OR, I, 33: 143–50; J. E. B. Stuart to Flora Cooke Stuart, Feb. 8, 1864, Stuart MSS, VHS.

15. WH memoirs, 21–25; WH to MFH, Feb. 14, 1864, Hampton Family MSS, USC; Lee, *Wartime Papers*, 673–74.

16. OR, I, 33: 201; Wells, *Hampton and His Cavalry*, 108–09; Wellman, *Giant in Gray*, 133–34; Longacre, *Mounted Raids*, 225–41.

17. OR, I, 33: 161–63, 167–68; 51, pt. 2: 823; Hewett et al., eds., *Supplement to the Official Records*, I, 6: 284–85.

18. OR, I, 33: 201.

19. *Ibid*.; Longacre, *Mounted Raids*, 241–44.

20. OR, I, 33: 201; Wells, *Hampton and His Cavalry*, 113–15; Longacre, *Mounted Raids*, 245.

21. OR, I, 33: 201–02; WH memoirs, 31–32; WH to Edward L. Wells, May 10, 1898, Wells MSS, CLS; Noah P. Ford, "Wade Hampton's Strategy: An Attack on Richmond Foiled," *SHSP* 24 (1896): 280–84.

22. OR, I, 33: 202.

23. *Ibid*., 205–10, 219–24; WH memoirs, 36–37; Lee, *Wartime Papers*, 678; J. William Jones, "Kilpatrick-Dahlgren Raid Against Richmond," *SHSP* 13 (1885): 515–60; Longacre, *Mounted Raids*, 244–52.

24. OR, I, 33: 199–200; Wells, *Hampton and His Cavalry*, 121–22.

25. WH memoirs, 6, 11, 44–45; Wellman, *Giant in Gray*, 137.

26. Chesnut, *Diary from Dixie*, 395.

27. *Ibid*., 395, 405.

28. Wells, *Hampton and His Cavalry*, 124–25; OR, I, 35, pt. 2: 362, 364–65.

29. J. Frederick Waring diary, Apr. 12, 1864, UNC; Joseph L. Waring, ed., "The Diary of William G. Hinson during the War of Secession," *South Carolina Historical Magazine* 75 (1974): 14–15; Alfred B. Mulligan, *"My Dear Mother & Sisters": Civil War Letters of Capt. A. B. Mulligan, Co. B, 5th South Carolina Cavalry—Butler's Division—Hampton's Corps, 1861–1865*, ed. by Olin Fulmer Hutchinson, Jr. (Spartanburg, S.C., 1992), 107.

30. J. Frederick Waring diary, Apr. 22, 1864.

31. Zimmerman Davis to Edward L. Wells, Mar. 10, 1895, Wells MSS, CLS; William Farrar Smith, "Butler's Attack on Drewry's Bluff," *B&L* 4: 206–08; Martin, *Southern Hero*, 83, 87–88.

32. J. Frederick Waring diary, May 2, 1864; WH to MFH, May 6, 1864, Hampton Family MSS, USC; OR, I, 36, pt. 1: 1–2, 18–19, 189–90, 1028.

33. WH to MFH, May 6, 1864, Hampton Family MSS, USC.

34. WH memoirs, 6, 11, 44–45; Wellman, *Giant in Gray*, 137–38; Thomas L. Rosser to Elizabeth Winston Rosser, Mar. 1, 1864, Rosser MSS, UV.

35. WH memoirs, 46; Thomas L. Rosser to J. E. B. Stuart, May 5, 1864, CSR of Henry B. McClellan, M-331, R-169, NA; James Harrison Wilson, *Under the Old Flag: Recollections of Military Operations in the War for the Union, the Spanish War, the Boxer Rebellion, etc.* (New York, 1912), 1: 380–83; Wells, *Hampton and His Cavalry*, 136; J. Frederick Waring diary, May 10–11, 1864.

36. Longacre, *Lee's Cavalrymen*, 280–82.

37. Ibid., 281; WH memoirs, 46; OR, I, 51, pt. 1: 248–49; pt. 2: 897–98.

38. OR, I, 36, pt. 1: 540–41; Hewett et al., eds., *Supplement to the Official Records*, I, 6: 804; McClellan, *Life and Campaigns of Stuart*, 408–09; Robert T. Hubard memoirs, 89.

39. Philip H. Sheridan, *Personal Memoirs of P. H. Sheridan* (New York, 1888), 1: 366–67; OR, I, 36, pt. 1: 788–89; pt. 2: 553.

40. Wells, *Hampton and His Cavalry*, 136–37; WH memoirs, 46–47.

41. McClellan, *Life and Campaigns of Stuart*, 409–10; Gordon C. Rhea, *The Battles for Spotsylvania Court House and the Road to Yellow Tavern, May 7–12, 1864* (Baton Rouge, La., 1997), 114–15.

42. WH memoirs, 47–51.

43. Ibid., 51–52; Wells, *Hampton and His Cavalry*, 263–65.

44. Fitzhugh Lee, Report of Lee's Division, Cavalry Corps, Army of Northern Virginia, May-December 1864, [20]-[21], MC; Smith, "Butler's Attack on Drewry's Bluff," 208–12.

45. OR, I, 36, pt. 1: 21, 193, 782, 793, 854, 1030–31; pt. 3: 171, 199; WH memoirs, 54–55.

46. OR, I, 51, pt. 2: 956.

47. Ibid., 962–63; Hewett et al., eds., *Supplement to the Official Records*, I, 6: 810; Hartley, *Stuart's Tarheels*, 361–68.

48. OR, I, 36, pt. 2: 852–54, 1021–22; Hewett et al., eds., *Supplement to the Official Records*, I, 6: 448–49; William Stokes, *Saddle Soldiers: The Civil War Correspondence of General William Stokes of the 4th South Carolina Cavalry*, ed. by Lloyd Halliburton (Orangeburg, S.C., 1993), 135–36; Fitzhugh Lee, Report of Lee's Division, [21], [23]; Martin, *Southern Hero*, 86–88.

49. Robert A. Williams, "Haw's Shop: A 'Storm of Shot and Shell'," *CWTI* 9 (Jan. 1971): 14; John R. Haw, "The Battle of Haw's Shop, Virginia," CV 33 (1925): 373–76; WH memoirs, 55.

50. Myers, *Comanches*, 291.

51. Williams, "Haw's Shop," 15–19; Wells, *Hampton and His Cavalry*, 158.

52. WH memoirs, 56; Wells, *Hampton and His Cavalry*, 159–66.

53. WH memoirs, 57.

54. Myers, *Comanches*, 291.

TEN:

1. OR, I, 36, pt. 1: 782–83, 805, 822; pt. 3: 258–59, 311, 361, 363; Sheridan, *Personal Memoirs*, 1: 402–04.

2. OR, I, 51, pt. 2: 967–68; WH memoirs, 57–58; Fitzhugh Lee, Report of Lee's Division, [26]–[27].

3. WH memoirs, 58–59; Wells, *Hampton and His Cavalry*, 173; Hewett et al., eds., *Supplement to the Official Records*, I, 6: 812.

4. WH memoirs, 59–60; OR, I, 51, pt. 2: 977.

5. Martin T. McMahon, "Cold Harbor," *B&L* 4: 215–19.

6. WH memoirs, 60–61; OR, I, 51, pt. 1: 245–46.

7. Wells, *Hampton and His Cavalry*, 175.

8. WH memoirs, 62–63.

9. *Ibid.*, 63; OR, I, 36, pt. 3: 599, 603, 628–29; Grant, *Personal Memoirs*, 2: 282; Sheridan, *Personal Memoirs*, 1: 413–16.

10. WH memoirs, 64–65; OR, I, 36, pt. 1: 1095; Wells, *Hampton and His Cavalry*, 193–97; J. Frederick Waring diary, June 8–10, 1864; Hewett et al., eds., *Supplement to the Official Records*, I, 6: 815.

11. Brooks, *Butler and His Cavalry*, 239–40.

12. Wells, *Hampton and His Cavalry*, 196–97.

13. OR, I, 36, pt. 1: 1095; WH memoirs, 65–66; Wells, *Hampton and His Cavalry*, 197–200; J. Frederick Waring diary, June 11, 1864; Hewett et al., eds., *Supplement to the Official Records*, I, 6: 815; Brooks, *Butler and His Cavalry*, 241.

14. Brooks, *Butler and His Cavalry*, 245; Gary R. Baker, *Cadets in Gray: The Story of the Cadets of the South Carolina Military Academy and the Cadet Rangers in the Civil War* (Columbia, S.C., 1989), 100–01.

15. Brooks, *Butler and His Cavalry*, 548.

16. Hewett et al., eds., *Supplement to the Official Records*, I, 6: 815–16; Brooks, *Butler and His Cavalry*, 243–47; Jay Monaghan, "Custer's 'Last Stand'—Trevilian Station, 1864," *Civil War History* 8 (1962): 249–55; Longacre, *Custer and His Wolverines*, 229–34.

17. OR, I, 36, pt. 1: 1095; Wells, *Hampton and His Cavalry*, 201–02; Fitzhugh Lee, Report of Lee's Division, [29].

18. Sheridan, *Personal Memoirs*, 1: 422–23; Theophilus F. Rodenbough, "Sheridan's Trevilian Raid," *B&L* 4: 234–35.

19. OR, I, 36, pt. 1: 784–85, 808–09, 824, 845–46, 850–51, 1095–96; WH memoirs, 66–67; Hewett et al., eds., *Supplement to the Official Records*, I, 6: 816; Sheridan, *Personal Memoirs*, 1: 425; Wells, *Hampton and His Cavalry*, 202–05; Brooks, *Butler and His Cavalry*, 247–53; Eric J. Wittenberg, *Glory Enough for All: Sheridan's Second Raid and the Battle of Trevilian Station* (Washington, D.C., 2001), 183–209; Wellman, *Giant in Gray*, 148–49; J. Frederick Waring diary, June 12, 1864.

20. Wells, *Hampton and His Cavalry*, 205; Brooks, *Butler and His Cavalry*, 256.

21. Wittenberg, *Glory Enough for All*, 215–23, 341–42; Brooks, *Butler and His Cavalry*, 253–54.

22. WH to MFH, June 14, 1864, WH Family MSS (1818–1902), LC.

23. OR, I, 36, pt. 1: 1096; Fitzhugh Lee, Report of Lee's Division, [32]; Hewett et al., eds., *Supplement to the Official Records*, I, 7: 337; Wittenberg, *Glory Enough for All*, 220–23.

24. OR, I, 36, pt. 1: 1097; WH to Edward L. Wells, Feb. 22, 1900, Wells MSS, CLS.

25. OR, I, 40, pt. 1: 747; pt. 2: 669–70; 51, pt. 2: 1081; WH memoirs, 68; Wittenberg, *Glory Enough for All*, 239–41.

26. Robert T. Hubard memoirs, 102.

27. *OR*, I, 36, pt. 1: 809–10, 843–44, 855, 1096; pt. 3: 789–91, 795; 40, pt. 3: 14; Sheridan, *Personal Memoirs*, 1: 431.

28. *OR*, I, 40, pt. 1: 209, 645; pt. 2: 687.

29. *Ibid.*, 36, pt. 1: 810, 855–56, 859, 863, 866, 869, 1096–97; pt. 2: 688; pt. 3: 791; 40, pt. 2: 687–88; WH memoirs, 68–70; Fitzhugh Lee, Report of Lee's Division, [33]-[34]; J. Frederick Waring diary, June 24, 1864; Wells, *Hampton and His Cavalry*, 218–27; Brooks, *Butler and His Cavalry*, 268–70; Sheridan, *Personal Memoirs*, 1: 432–35; Wittenberg, *Glory Enough for All*, 265–92.

30. Lee, *Lee's Dispatches*, 258.

31. *OR*, I, 36, pt. 1: 25–26, 884, 889; 40, pt. 1: 12–13, 620, 625, 644–45, 730; pt. 2: 31–32, 35, 70–72, 232, 255–57, 267.

32. WH memoirs, 70–71, 81–83; *OR*, I, 40, pt. 1: 808; Robert T. Hubard memoirs, 103.

33. WH memoirs, 83–91; *OR*, I, 40, pt. 1: 210, 808–10; Fitzhugh Lee, Report of Lee's Division, [34]-[35]; J. Frederick Waring diary, June 29, 1864; Mulligan, "*My Dear Mother & Sisters*," 128–29; Wells, *Hampton and His Cavalry*, 236–44.

34. Edward G. Longacre, *From Union Stars to Top Hat: A Biography of the Extraordinary General James Harrison Wilson* (Harrisburg, Pa., 1972), 140–41.

35. WH to Edward L. Wells, Feb. 22, 1900, Wells MSS, CLS; J. Frederick Waring diary, June 30, 1864.

36. Edward L. Wells memorandum of fighting at Sappony Church and Reams's Station, Wells MSS, CLS.

37. Longacre, *From Union Stars to Top Hat*, 142–44.

38. Wells, *Hampton and His Cavalry*, 250; Mulligan, "*My Dear Mother & Sisters*," 128.

39. *OR*, I, 40, pt. 1: 58–74, 523–30; pt. 3: 636–40, 646, 656–58.

40. *Ibid.*, pt. 1: 612–13, 618–20; pt. 3: 424–25, 435, 437–38, 443, 448–50, 458, 475–78, 482–83, 500, 551, 553, 568–69, 592–93, 596, 600, 602, 613–14, 616, 796, 807–16, 818–19; WH memoirs, 91–92; Grant, *Personal Memoirs*, 2: 310; Sheridan, *Personal Memoirs*, 1: 446–49; Andrew A. Humphreys, *The Virginia Campaign of '64 and '65: The Army of the Potomac and the Army of the James* (New York, 1883), 247–49.

41. Jubal A. Early, "Early's March to Washington in 1864," *B&L* 4: 492–99.

42. *OR*, I, 37, pt. 2: 598.

43. *Ibid.*, 38, pt. 5: 892; Joseph E. Johnston, "Opposing Sherman's Advance to Atlanta," *B&L* 4: 260–77.

44. Chesnut, *Diary from Dixie*, 423.

45. Lee, *Lee's Dispatches*, 268–69; *OR*, I, 42, pt. 2: 1173.

46. *OR*, I, 40, pt. 3: 640–41, 669; 43; pt. 1: 719, 799, 822, 990, 993, 1003–04; Sheridan, *Personal Memoirs*, 1: 461–63.

47. WH memoirs, 94–97; Wellman, *Giant in Gray*, 153.

48. *OR*, I, 42, pt. 2: 1171–72; 43; pt. 1: 996, 999; WH memoirs, 92–93; WH to Robert E. Lee, n.d. [ca. Dec. 1864], Hampton Family MSS, USC; Wells, *Hampton and His Cavalry*, 270–71.

49. WH memoirs, 98–99; Wells, *Hampton and His Cavalry*, 271–74; J. Frederick Waring diary, Aug. 16–17, 1864; John Horn, *The Petersburg Campaign: The Destruction of the Weldon Railroad, Deep Bottom, Globe Tavern, and Reams Station, August 14–25, 1864* (Lynchburg, Va., 1991), 26–47; Charles W. Field, "Campaign of 1864 and 1865: Narrative of Major-General C. W. Field," *SHSP* 14 (1886): 552–54; Waring, "Diary of William G. Hinson," 21–22.

50. Lewis P. Jones, "Two Roads Tried—and One Detour," *South Carolina Historical Magazine* 79 (1978): 212.

51. OR, I, 51, pt. 2: 1035–36; WH memoirs, 99–101; WH to Robert E. Lee, n.d. [ca. Dec. 1864], Hampton Family MSS, USC.

52. Wells, *Hampton and His Cavalry*, 273–74; WH to MFH, Aug. 20, 1864, Hampton Family MSS, USC.

53. Orlando B. Willcox, "Actions on the Weldon Railroad: I. Globe Tavern," *B&L* 4: 570–71.

54. OR, I, 42, pt. 1: 942–43; WH memoirs, 103–05; Wells, *Hampton and His Cavalry*, 277–80; Brooks, *Butler and His Cavalry*, 303–04.

55. WH memoirs, 105–09; Wells, *Hampton and His Cavalry*, 280–86; Brooks, *Butler and His Cavalry*, 304–06; WH to MFH, Aug. 30, 1864, Hampton Family MSS, USC; OR, I, 42, pt. 1: 943–44.

56. OR, I, 42, pt. 1: 940; J. Frederick Waring diary, Aug. 26, 1864; WH to MFH, Aug. 30, Sept. 10, 1864; both, Hampton Family MSS, USC.

57. WH to MFH, Aug. 30, 1864, Hampton Family MSS, USC.

58. *Ibid.*; OR, I, 42, pt. 2: 1204–05.

59. OR, I, 42, pt. 2: 1233–34.

60. *Ibid.*, 40, pt. 3: 1235–36; WH memoirs, 122–25; Brooks, *Butler and His Cavalry*, 111, 312–13.

61. OR, I, 42, pt. 1: 944–45; WH memoirs, 113–15; Wells, *Hampton and His Cavalry*, 288–90; David Cardwell, "A Brilliant Coup: How Wade Hampton Captured Grant's Entire Beef Supply," *SHSP* 22 (1894): 147–51; Richard W. Lykes, "The Great Civil War Beef Raid," *CWTI* 5 (Feb. 1967): 5–8.

62. OR, I, 42, pt. 1: 945–47; WH memoirs, 115–16; Wells, *Hampton and His Cavalry*, 290–93; Wellman, *Giant in Gray*, 157–58; Mulligan, "My Dear Mother & Sisters," 150; Cardwell, "Brilliant Coup," 151–52;

63. Wells, *Hampton and His Cavalry*, 293–96; Lykes, "Great Civil War Beef Raid," 11–12.

64. WH memoirs, 116–18; Wells, *Hampton and His Cavalry*, 296–301; Cardwell, "Brilliant Coup," 152–53; Lykes, "Great Civil War Beef Raid," 47–49.

65. WH memoirs, 118–19; Mulligan, "My Dear Mother & Sisters," 151.

ELEVEN:

1. Robert E. Lee to WH, Sept. 17, 1864, Georgia Callis West MSS, VHS; WH memoirs, 120–21.

2. WH to Samuel Richards Johnston, Sept. 23, 1864, Johnston MSS, VHS.

3. Richard J. Sommers, *Richmond Redeemed: The Siege at Petersburg* (Garden City, N.Y., 1981), 38–149.

4. OR, I, 42, pt. 1: 947; WH memoirs, 126–27; Wells, *Hampton and His Cavalry*, 318–21.

5. Jubal A. Early, "Winchester, Fisher's Hill, and Cedar Creek," *B&L* 4: 522–24; OR, I, 43, pt. 2: 874, 880–81; WH memoirs, 133–34; Rosser, *Riding with Rosser*, 43–44; Wells, *Hampton and His Cavalry*, 312.

6. OR, I, 42, pt. 1: 947–48; Hewett et al., eds., *Supplement to the Official Records*, I, 7: 510–12; WH memoirs, 127–28.

7. OR, I, 42, pt. 1: 948; WH to MFH, Oct. 5, 1864, Hampton Family MSS, USC; WH memoirs, 128–30; Brooks, *Butler and His Cavalry*, 351.

8. OR, I, 42, pt. 1: 949; WH to MFH, Oct. 11, 16, 1864; both, Hampton Family MSS, USC; WH memoirs, 135–37, 140–41; Mulligan, "My Dear Mother & Sisters", 163; Wells, *Hampton and His Cavalry*, 323–29.

9. Wells, *Hampton and His Cavalry*, 329–30, 341; J. Frederick Waring diary, Nov. 27, 1864.

10. OR, I, 42, pt. 1: 949; Hewett et al., eds., *Supplement to the Official Records*, I, 7: 479–82; WH memoirs, 137–39, 141–42; Wells, *Hampton and His Cavalry*, 330–34.

11. OR, I, 42, pt. 1: 949–50; Hewett et al., eds., *Supplement to the Official Records*, I, 7: 482–83; WH memoirs, 143; Wellman, *Giant in Gray*, 160–61; Wells, *Hampton and His Cavalry*, 334–35; Brooks, *Butler and His Cavalry*, 352, 371–72.

12. Brooks, *Butler and His Cavalry*, 532, 534; Wellman, *Giant in Gray*, 161–62; Chesnut, *Diary from Dixie*, 447–48.

13. J. Frederick Waring diary, Oct. 31, 1864; Wellman, *Giant in Gray*, 162–63.

14. Chesnut, *Diary from Dixie*, 455; Marion Brunson Lucas, *Sherman and the Burning of Columbia* (College Station, Tex., 1976), 35; Samuel Carter III, *The Last Cavaliers: Confederate and Union Cavalry in the Civil War* (New York, 1979), 299.

15. Early, "Winchester, Fisher's Hill, and Cedar Creek," 525–30; John B. Hood, "The Defense of Atlanta," *B&L* 4: 341–44.

16. Stephen Z. Starr, *The Union Cavalry in the Civil War* (Baton Rouge, La., 1979–84), 3: 569–78; Charles Colcock Jones et al., *The Children of Pride: A True Story of Georgia and the Civil War*, ed. by Robert Manson Myers (New Haven, Conn., 1972), 1222–33, 1237–40, 1251, 1256, 1284–85.

17. J. Frederick Waring diary, Nov. 24, Dec. 1, 7–8, 1864; WH to Robert E. Lee, Dec. 5, 1864, Hampton MSS, MC; WH memoirs, 152–57; OR, I, 42, pt. 1: 443–46, 950–52; Wells, *Hampton and His Cavalry*, 372–87.

18. OR, I, 46, pt. 2: 1003; WH memoirs, 150–52; Wells, *Hampton and His Cavalry*, 388–89; WH to M. L. Bonham, Dec. 4, 1864, Hampton Family MSS, USC.

19. Lee, *Lee's Dispatches*, 881.

20. Ibid., 881–82; OR, I, 47, pt. 2: 1018; WH memoirs, 159–60.

21. Jefferson Davis to Samuel Cooper, Feb. 4, 1865; Samuel Cooper to "Col Palfrey," Feb. 14, 1865; both, CSR of WH, M-331, R-115, NA; Wellman, *Giant in Gray*, 352n.

22. WH to Edward L. Wells, Apr. 9, 1900, Wells MSS, CLS; John G. Barrett, *Sherman's March through the Carolinas* (Chapel Hill, N.C., 1956), 65–66.

23. Warner, *Generals in Gray*, 332–33; Carter, *Last Cavaliers*, 249–50, 258.

24. Henry Stone, "Repelling Hood's Invasion of Tennessee," *B&L* 4: 444–64; Burke Davis, *Sherman's March* (New York, 1980), 52–53, 144.

25. Wright, *Southern Girl in '61*, 222.

26. Lucas, *Sherman and the Burning of Columbia*, 39; Barrett, *Sherman's March through the Carolinas*, 66.

27. OR, I, 47, pt. 2: 1054.

28. Ibid., 1069–72, 1112, 1207, 1271; WH memoirs, 164–65; Wellman, *Giant in Gray*, 166; John P. Dyer, *"Fightin' Joe" Wheeler* (Baton Rouge, La., 1941), 219; Lucas, *Sherman and the Burning of Columbia*, 66; Burton Harrison to WH, Feb. 15, 1865, CSR of WH, M-331, R-115, NA.

29. Lucas, *Sherman and the Burning of Columbia*, 45 and n.

30. OR, I, 47, pt. 1: 1071; Mark L. Bradley, *This Astounding Close: The Road to Bennett Place* (Chapel Hill, N.C., 2000), 11–14; Nathaniel Cheairs Hughes Jr., *General William J. Hardee, Old Reliable* (Baton Rouge, La., 1965), 277–78; Dyer, *"Fightin' Joe" Wheeler*, 221.

31. OR, I, 47, pt. 1: 1048; Lucas, *Sherman and the Burning of Columbia*, 46.

32. OR, I, 47, pt. 2: 1184; 53: 1052–53; Lucas, *Sherman and the Burning of Columbia*, 58–59, 64–67, 163–64.

33. OR, I, 47, pt. 2: 1211; Brooks, *Butler and His Cavalry*, 466, 571; Charles Royster, *The Destructive War: William Tecumseh Sherman, Stonewall Jackson, and the Americans* (New York, 1991), 8–16; Davis, *Sherman's March*, 158.

34. Lucas, *Sherman and the Burning of Columbia*, 54, 70; J. Frederick Waring diary, Feb. 16–17, 1865; WH to Edward L. Wells, Mar. 25, 1900, Wells MSS, CLS.

35. Chesnut, *Diary from Dixie*, 512.

36. Lucas, *Sherman and the Burning of Columbia*, 163–67; WH to Edward L. Wells, Mar. 25, 1900, Wells MSS, CLS; Emma LeConte, *When the World Ended: The Diary of Emma LeConte*, ed. by Earl Schenck Miers (New York, 1957), 42–50; Brooks, *Butler and His Cavalry*, 571–72; Barrett, *Sherman's March through the Carolinas*, 71–91; Royster, *Destructive War*, 16–33; James G. Gibbes, *Who Burnt Columbia?* (Newberry, S.C., 1902), 4–9; William Gilmore Simms, *Sack and Destruction of the City of Columbia, South Carolina*, ed. by A. S. Salley (Freeport, N.Y., 1971), 32–35; A. R. Chisolm, "Beauregard's and Hampton's Orders on Evacuating Columbia—Letter from Colonel A. R. Chisolm," *SHSP* 7 (1879): 249–50; J. P. Carrol, "The Burning of Columbia, South Carolina—Report of the Committee of Citizens Appointed to Collect Testimony," *SHSP* 8 (1880): 202–14; Albert R. Elmore, "Testimony about Burning of Columbia," *CV* 20 (1912): 117–18; "The Burning of Columbia," *CV* 24 (1916): 61–62; Chapman J. Milling, "Ilium in Flames," *CV* 36 (1928): 212–16.

37. LeConte, *When the World Ended*, 44; Wellman, *Giant in Gray*, 168.

38. OR, I, 47, pt. 1: 21; William T. Sherman, *Memoirs of General William T. Sherman, by Himself* (New York, 1875), 2: 287; WH, "Letter from General Hampton on the Burning of Columbia," *SHSP* 7 (1879): 156–58; James Wood Davidson, "Who Burned Columbia?—A Review of General Sherman's Version of the Affair," *SHSP* 7 (1879): 185–92; "Who Burned Columbia?—General Sherman's Latest Story Examined," *SHSP* 13 (1885): 448–53; Wellman, *Giant in Gray*, 167–68; Alexander, *Fighting for the Confederacy*, 505–06; Thomas Ward Osborn, *The Fiery Trail: A Union Officer's Account of Sherman's Last Campaigns*, ed. by Richard B. Harwell and Philip N. Racine (Knoxville, Tenn., 1986), 131–32; Barrett, *Sherman's March through the Carolinas*, 77–79, 90–92.

39. Brooks, *Butler and His Cavalry*, 422–23; Osborn, *Fiery Trail*, 148–49 and n.; OR, I, 47, pt. 2: 546.

40. OR, I, 47, pt. 2: 596–97.

41. *Ibid.*, 1248; Craig L. Symonds, *Joseph E. Johnston: A Civil War Biography* (New York, 1992), 343–44.

42. OR, I, 47, pt. 1: 1050–51, 1053, 1058–60; Bradley, *This Astounding Close*, 8–10; O. P. Hargis, "We kept fighting and falling back," *CWTI* 7 (Dec. 1968): 42; Symonds, *Joseph E. Johnston*, 344, 346.

43. OR, I, 47, pt. 1: 23, 25–26, 918.

44. Chesnut, *Diary from Dixie*, 475.

45. Davis, *Sherman's March*, 215; Symonds, *Joseph E. Johnston*, 344; WH, "The Battle of Bentonville," *B&L* 4: 701.

46. Brooks, *Butler and His Cavalry*, 472–73; Bradley, *This Astounding Close*, 14; Davis, *Sherman's March*, 211.

47. M. Calbraith Butler to Edward L. Wells, Mar. 27, 1900, Wells MSS, CLS; WH to Edward L. Wells, Apr. 4, 8, 9, 1900, *ibid.*; Wells, *Hampton and His Cavalry*, 397–406; E. L. Wells, "A Morning Call on General Kilpatrick," *SHSP* 12 (1884): 123–27; Brooks, *Butler and His Cavalry*, 424–28, 443–45; Sharyn Kane and Richard Keeton, *Fiery Dawn: The Civil War Battle at Monroe's Crossroads, North Carolina* (Tallahassee, Fla., 1999), 40–64; Barrett, *Sherman's March through the Carolinas*, 126–28; OR, I, 47, pt. 2: 786.

48. Wells, *Hampton and His Cavalry*, 406–07, 412–13; Brooks, *Butler and His Cavalry*, 446–47; Wells, "Morning Call on General Kilpatrick," 127; Kane and Keeton, *Fiery Dawn*, 64–66; Wellman, *Giant in Gray*, 172.

49. Wells, *Hampton and His Cavalry*, 402–03, 408–10; Wells, "Morning Call on General Kilpatrick," 127–28.

50. OR, I, 47, pt. 1: 23, 861–62, 867; pt. 2: 786–87; J. Frederick Waring diary, Mar. 10, 1865; M. Calbraith Butler to Edward L. Wells, Mar. 27, 1900, Wells MSS, CLS; WH to Edward L. Wells, Apr. 4, 8, 9, 1900, *ibid.*; Brooks, *Butler and His Cavalry*, 445–46; Kane and Keeton, *Fiery Dawn*, 68–79; Barrett, *Sherman's March through the Carolinas*, 128–30.

51. WH to Edward L. Wells, Dec. 20, 1899, Wells MSS, CLS; Wells, *Hampton and His Cavalry*, 29–37, 411; Brooks, *Butler and His Cavalry*, 112–13, 428–29, 441–42; WH to James S. Holmes, Feb. 6, 1899, Hampton Family MSS, USC; Osborn, *Fiery Trail*, 175 and n.-176n., 189–90; Sherman, *Memoirs*, 2: 294, 302; Oliver O. Howard, *Autobiography of Oliver Otis Howard, Major General, United States Army* (New York, 1907), 2: 137–38; Wellman, *Giant in Gray*, 173–75; J. Frederick Waring diary, Mar. 11, 1865.

52. WH, "Battle of Bentonville," 701; Hughes, *General William J. Hardee*, 281–86; Barrett, *Sherman's March through the Carolinas*, 148–58.

53. WH, "Battle of Bentonville," 701; Bradley, *This Astounding Close*, 18–20.

54. OR, I, 47, pt. 1: 1055–56; WH, "Bentonville," 701–02; J. Frederick Waring diary, Mar. 19, 1865; Symonds, *Joseph E. Johnston*, 348–50; Barrett, *Sherman's March through the Carolinas*, 162–63.

55. OR, I, 47, pt. 1: 1056, 1131; pt. 2: 1437–39; WH, "Bentonville," 703–04; Howard, *Autobiography*, 2: 145–47; Barrett, *Sherman's March through the Carolinas*, 163–77. The best general accounts of the action on March 19–21, 1865 are: Mark L. Bradley, *Last Stand in the Carolinas: The Battle of Bentonville* (Campbell, Calif., 1996), and Nathaniel Cheairs Hughes, Jr., *Bentonville: The Final Battle of Sherman and Johnston* (Chapel Hill, N.C., 1996).

56. OR, I, 47, pt. 1: 1057, 1113; pt. 2: 1447, 1451–52; WH, "Bentonville," 704–05; J. Frederick Waring diary, Mar. 20–22, 1865; Barrett, *Sherman's March through the Carolinas*, 177–84.

57. OR, I, 47, pt. 1: 76, 1059–60; pt. 2: 1457–59; pt. 3: 762; Bradley, *This Astounding Close*, 68–69; Barrett, *Sherman's March through the Carolinas*, 184–85.

58. OR, I, 47, pt. 3: 771–72, 781–83, 794–95, 797; Bradley, *This Astounding Close*, 80–81.

59. J. Frederick Waring diary, Apr. 12–14, 1865; Bradley, *This Astounding Close*, 100–07.

60. Wellman, *Giant in Gray*, 180.

61. Symonds, *Joseph E. Johnston*, 353–55; Wells, *Hampton and His Cavalry*, 421.

62. Wells, *Hampton and His Cavalry*, 421–22; Sherman, *Memoirs*, 2: 346.

TWELVE:

1. Sherman, *Memoirs*, 2: 346–49.

2. *Ibid.*, 349–50; Bradley, *This Astounding Close*, 160–62; Barrett, *Sherman's March through the Carolinas*, 230–34.

3. Wellman, *Giant in Gray*, 181–82; George Ward Nichols, *The Story of the Great March, from the Diary of a Staff Officer* (New York, 1865), 311; Henry Hitchcock, *Marching with Sherman: Passages from the Letters and Campaign Diaries of Henry Hitchcock . . .*, ed. by M. A. DeWolfe Howe (New Haven, Conn., 1927), 310; Bradley, *This Astounding Close*, 161–62.

4. Nichols, *Story of the Great March*, 311–13.

5. Wellman, *Giant in Gray*, 182–83.

6. *Ibid.*; OR, I, 47, pt. 3: 813–14; Wells, *Hampton and Reconstruction*, 65–66; WH, "An Effort to Rescue Jefferson Davis: Statement of General Wade Hampton . . .," *SHSP* 27 (1899): 132–33.

7. *OR*, I, 47, pt. 3: 829–30; WH, "Effort to Rescue Jefferson Davis," 133–34.

8. WH, "Effort to Rescue Jefferson Davis," 134.

9. *Ibid.*; Wellman, *Giant in Gray*, 187.

10. WH, "Effort to Rescue Jefferson Davis," 134; Michael B. Ballard, *A Long Shadow: Jefferson Davis and the Final Days of the Confederacy* (Jackson, Miss., 1986), 108; OR, I, 47, pt. 3: 841, 845, 851.

11. WH, "Effort to Rescue Jefferson Davis," 134–35; OR, I, 47, pt. 3: 846.

12. WH, "Effort to Rescue Jefferson Davis," 135; Wells, *Hampton and Reconstruction*, 67; J. Frederick Waring diary, Apr. 27, 1865.

13. WH, "Effort to Rescue Jefferson Davis," 135; Wellman, *Giant in Gray*, 188.

14. WH, "Effort to Rescue Jefferson Davis," 135; WH to Edward L. Wells, Mar. 25, 1900, Wells MSS, CLS; OR, I, 49, pt. 2: 555–56; M. M. Buford, "Surrender of Johnston's Army," CV 28 (1920): 171; Longacre, *From Union Stars to Top Hat*, 221–24.

15. Wellman, *Giant in Gray*, 189; Ballard, *Long Shadow*, 126; Dyer, *"Fightin' Joe" Wheeler*, 231.

16. William T. Sherman, *Home Letters of General Sherman*, ed. by M. A. DeWolfe Howe (New York, 1909), 346.

17. Wellman, *Giant in Gray*, 195–96; *Echoes from Hampton Day*, 39; WH to MFH, Jan. 12, 1866, Hampton Family MSS, USC; WH et al., *Family Letters of Three Wade Hamptons*, xvii–xviii, 118n.

18. Wellman, *Giant in Gray*, 195–203; WH to Editor of the *Columbia Daily Phoenix*, July 27, 1865, Hampton Family MSS, USC.

19. WH to Editor of the *Columbia Daily Phoenix*, July 27, 1865, Hampton Family MSS, USC.

20. McPherson, *Ordeal by Fire*, 498; Amnesty Oath of WH, Aug. 2, 1865; WH to Andrew Johnson, Aug. 3, 1865; both, Pardon Files, South Carolina Dept. of Archives and History, Columbia.

21. Benjamin F. Perry to anon., Aug. 9, 1865, Pardon Files, South Carolina Dept. of Archives and History.

22. Endorsement on Amnesty oath of WH; Andrew Johnson to James Speed, Nov. 13, 1865; both, *ibid.*; Wellman, *Giant in Gray*, 198–99; Hampton M. Jarrell, *Wade Hampton and the Negro: The Road Not Taken* (Columbia, S.C., 1949), 6–7.

23. WH to James G. Gibbes, Aug. 20, 1865, Hampton Family MSS, USC.

24. *Ibid.*; WH to D. W. Ray et al., Aug. 29, 1867, *ibid.*; Jarrell, *Wade Hampton and the Negro*, 13–14; McPherson, *Ordeal by Fire*, 501.

25. WH to James G. Gibbes, Aug, 20, 1865, Hampton Family MSS, USC.

26. Wellman, *Giant in Gray*, 199–200; Jarrell, *Wade Hampton and the Negro*, 15–17; Francis Butler Simkins and Robert Hilliard Woody, *South Carolina during Reconstruction* (Chapel Hill, N.C., 1932), 37–43; WH et al., *Family Letters of Three Wade Hamptons*, xviii and n.

27. Wellman, *Giant in Gray*, 219–20; McPherson, *Ordeal by Fire*, 536–37; Jarrell, *Wade Hampton and the Negro*, 22–23; Francis Butler Simpkins, "The Election of 1876 in South Carolina," *South Atlantic Quarterly* 21 (1922): 226.

28. Wellman, *Giant in Gray*, 201.

29. *Charleston Daily Courier*, Oct. 16, 1865; *Columbia Daily Phoenix*, Nov. 24, 1865; Simkins and Woody, *South Carolina during Reconstruction*, 43.

30. WH et al., *Family Letters of Three Wade Hamptons*, xvii–xviii; WH to MFH, Jan. 1, 12, Mar. 1, 19, 28, 1866; all, Hampton Family MSS, USC.

31. Wellman, *Giant in Gray*, 202, 355n.-56n.; Robert E. Lee to WH, Aug. 1, 1865, Edward L. Wells MSS, CLS.

32. Wellman, *Giant in Gray*, 221–22, 230–31; WH to Samuel Richards Johnston, Nov. 21, 1871, Johnston Family MSS; WH to Edward L. Wells, Feb. 4, 1898, Wells MSS, CLS; WH, *Address on the Life and Character of Gen. Robert E. Lee . . .* (Baltimore, 1871).

33. WH et al., *Family Letters of Three Wade Hamptons*, 166–67; WH to "My Dear Sister[-in-Law]," Mar. 28, 1867, Hampton Family MSS, USC.

34. WH et al., *Family Letters of Three Wade Hamptons*, xv-xviii and nn.; Wellman, *Giant in Gray*, 236; Virginia G. Meynard, *The Venturers: The Hampton, Harrison, and Earle Families of Virginia, South Carolina, and Texas* (Easley, S.C., 1981), 255–56; WH to James Conner, Apr. 11, 1869, Hampton Family MSS, USC.

35. WH to Chancellor Carver, May 25, 1866, Hampton Family MSS, USC; WH et al., *Family Letters of Three Wade Hamptons*, xviii and n.

36. Simkins and Woody, *South Carolina during Reconstruction*, 34–35; Wellman, *Giant in Gray*, 209–10; WH to James G. Gibbes, Aug. 20, 1865, Hampton Family MSS, USC.

37. WH to D. W. Ray et al., Aug. 29, 1867, Hampton Family MSS, USC.

38. *Charleston Daily Courier*, Oct. 10, 1866; *Columbia Daily Phoenix*, Aug. 28, 1867; Jarrell, *Wade Hampton and the Negro*, 15–19; Wellman, *Giant in Gray*, 217.

39. Wellman, *Giant in Gray*, 209–10.

40. WH to Andrew Johnson, n. d. [Aug. 1866], Hampton Family MSS, USC. This letter was published verbatim in the *Metropolitan Record & New York Vindicator* (New York, N.Y.) of Aug. 25, 1865.

41. *Ibid.*

42. *Ibid.*

43. McPherson, *Ordeal by Fire*, 520–33.

44. *Ibid.*, 521–22; Wellman, *Giant in Gray*, 215.

45. McPherson, *Ordeal by Fire*, 524; Jarrell, *Wade Hampton and the Negro*, 16–19; WH to John Mullaly, Mar. 31, 1867, Hampton Family MSS, USC.

46. Jarrell, *Wade Hampton and the Negro*, 20; Simkins and Woody, *South Carolina during Reconstruction*, 89.

47. Jarrell, *Wade Hampton and the Negro*, 16–17.

48. *Ibid.*, 22–25; Wellman, *Giant in Gray*, 226–27.

49. *Charleston Daily Courier*, June 10, July 7, 11, 1868; *Columbia Daily Phoenix*, July 26, 1868; Wellman, *Giant in Gray*, 222–23; Jarrell, *Wade Hampton and the Negro*, 28–31.

50. Jarrell, *Wade Hampton and the Negro*, 34–35.

THIRTEEN:

1. Wellman, *Giant in Gray*, 227; WH et al., *Family Letters of Three Wade Hamptons*, 145n.; Allen P. Tankersley, *John B. Gordon: A Study in Gallantry* (Atlanta, 1955), 316–19; Varina Howell Davis, *Jefferson Davis, Ex-President of the Confederate States of America: A Memoir* (New York, 1890), 2: 811–14; William J. Cooper, Jr., *Jefferson Davis, American* (New York, 2000), 585–89, 594–96.

2. WH to Jefferson Davis, July 23, 1873, Sang-Lee Civil War Collection, Knox College.

51. Wellman, *Giant in Gray*, 333; Wells, *Hampton and Reconstruction*, 225–26. For details of Hampton's funeral, which was attended by some 20,000 mourners, see: *Charleston Evening Post*, Apr. 12, 1902, and *Charleston News and Courier*, Apr. 14, 1902. For coverage of memorial services held in South Carolina and elsewhere in the old Confederacy, see the *News and Courier* for Apr. 22, 1902 and the *Evening Post* of the following day.

Wade Hampton survives to this day in marble. In 1906 an equestrian statue, fifteen feet tall, was erected in the South Carolina capitol complex at Columbia, near what is now known as the Wade Hampton Office Building. Twenty-three years later a full-length likeness of Senator Hampton was placed in National Statuary Hall, Washington, D.C.; it stands in a second-floor corridor of the U.S. Capitol Building. Hampton's name has also been affixed to numerous roads, buildings, and sites in South Carolina including Hampton County, near the southern tip of the state, and its seat, the town of Hampton.

3. Wellman, *Giant in Gray*, 230; WH to Joseph E. Johnston, June 23, 1870, Johnston MSS, Earl Gregg Swem Library, College of William and Mary, Williamsburg, Va.; WH to Armistead Burt, Jan. 2, 1871, Dec. 29, 1872; both, Hampton MSS, DU.

4. Wellman, *Giant in Gray*, 237; WH to Joseph E. Johnston, June 23, 1870, Johnston MSS, Earl Gregg Swem Library; WH to Armistead Burt, Sept. 1, Dec. 16, 1871, Nov. 14, 1872, Apr. 12, 1874; all, Hampton MSS, DU; WH to D. H. Townsend, Oct. 2, 1872; WH to Mrs. Thomas L. Preston, Mar. 29, 1873, Apr. 15, 1874; all, Hampton Family MSS, USC.

5. Wellman, *Giant in Gray*, 233–35; McPherson, *Ordeal by Fire*, 568–71.

6. Wellman, *Giant in Gray*, 235–36; WH to Daniel H. Hill, Oct. 11, 1869, Hill MSS, UNC.

7. WH to Armistead Burt, n. d. [Dec. 1872], Hampton MSS, DU; Jarrell, *Wade Hampton and the Negro*, 38–44.

8. Wells, *Hampton and Reconstruction*, 101–05; Jarrell, *Wade Hampton and the Negro*, 41–45; Simkins, "Election of 1876 in South Carolina," 226–31.

9. Wellman, *Giant in Gray*, 240–43; Jarrell, *Wade Hampton and the Negro*, 47–48; Louthan, "General Wade Hampton," 67.

10. Wellman, *Giant in Gray*, 238–44; Simkins, "Election of 1876 in South Carolina," 231–32; Jarrell, *Wade Hampton and the Negro*, 48; William A. Sheppard, *Red Shirts Remembered: Southern Brigadiers of the Reconstruction Period* (Atlanta, 1940), 80–89; Martin, *Southern Hero*, 206–12.

11. Jarrell, *Wade Hampton and the Negro*, 58; Simkins and Woody, *South Carolina during Reconstruction*, 499–501; Simkins, "Election of 1876 in South Carolina," 336–37; Louthan, "General Wade Hampton," 68; Richard Zuczek, "The Last Campaign of the Civil War: South Carolina and the Revolution of 1876," *Civil War History* 42 (1996): 22–23; Peggy Lamson, *The Glorious Failure: Black Congressman Robert Brown Elliott and the Reconstruction in South Carolina* (New York, 1973), 245–46.

12. Wellman, *Giant in Gray*, 245–57; Jarrell, *Wade Hampton and the Negro*, 51–54, 63–75; Wells, *Hampton and Reconstruction*, 107–09; Williams, *Hampton and His Red Shirts*, 78–92.

13. Wellman, *Giant in Gray*, 261–64; Jarrell, *Wade Hampton and the Negro*, 48–51, 63–79, 145–46; Simkins and Woody, *South Carolina during Reconstruction*, 504–06; Simkins, "Election of 1876 in South Carolina," 338–39; Williams, *Hampton and His Red Shirts*, 27–59, 203–14; Zuczek, "Last Campaign of the Civil War," 20–25; Wells, *Hampton and Reconstruction*, 128–31; Walter Allen, *Governor Chamberlain's Administration of South Carolina: A Chapter of Reconstruction in the Southern States* (New York, 1888), 314–17.

14. Jarrell, *Wade Hampton and the Negro*, 79–82; Simkins, "Election of 1876 in South Carolina," 339–41; Wells, *Hampton and Reconstruction*, 125–27, 132.

15. Williams, *Hampton and His Red Shirts*, 89; Jarrell, *Wade Hampton and the Negro*, 61, 68, 73–74; William J. Cooper, Jr., *The Conservative Regime: South Carolina, 1877–1890* (Baltimore, 1968), 18–20, 23–28, 84–97.

16. Jarrell, *Wade Hampton and the Negro*, 61, 66, 99–100; Wellman, *Giant in Gray*, 257–58, 261; Joel Williamson, *After Slavery: The Negro in South Carolina during Reconstruction, 1861–1877* (Chapel Hill, N.C., 1965), 408–11. For details on Hampton's African-American supporters, see: Edmund L. Drago, *Hurrah for Hampton: Black Red Shirts in South Carolina during Reconstruction* (Fayetteville, Ark., 1998).

17. Stephen Kantrowitz, *Ben Tillman & The Reconstruction of White Supremacy* (Chapel Hill, N.C., 2000), 78, 174, 326n.; George C. Rable, "Bourbonism, Reconstruction, and the Persistence of Southern Distinctiveness," *Civil War History* 29 (1983): 152. The study of Hampton's rhetoric on racial issues, with special emphasis on the Campaign of 1876, is: DeWitt Grant Jones, "Wade Hampton and the Rhetoric of Race: A Study of the Speaking of Wade Hampton on the

Race Issue in South Carolina, 1865–1878" (Ph. D. diss., Louisiana State Univ., 1988); see especially pp. 227–48. Hampton's public statements on African-American emancipation are embodied in *Negro Emancipation: Speech of Wade Hampton, a Senator from the State of South Carolina . . .* (Washington, D.C., 1890), and in Wade Hampton and John T. Morgan, "The Race Problem in the South," *The Forum Extra: A Periodical of Short Studies of Living Problems* 1 (Mar. 1890): 1–28. Toward the close of his Senate career he made an uncharacteristically harsh call for black emigration in a letter to a political colleague (WH to "My Dear Sir," Nov. 12, 1889, WH Family MSS [1793–1889], LC).

18. Jarrell, *Wade Hampton and the Negro*, 52, 122. For details on some of the candidate's political promises to African-American voters, see WH, *Free Men! Free Ballots!! Free Schools!!! The Pledges of Gen. Wade Hampton, Democratic Candidate for Governor, to the Colored People of South Carolina, 1865–1876* (n. p., 1876).

19. Wellman, *Giant in Gray*, 267–74; Jarrell, *Wade Hampton and the Negro*, 86–90; WH to Armistead Burt, Nov. 19, 1876, Hampton MSS, DU; Simkins, "Election of 1876 in South Carolina," 342–45.

20. Wellman, *Giant in Gray*, 275–85; Jarrell, *Wade Hampton and the Negro*, 90–112; Wells, *Hampton and Reconstruction*, 154–67; Simkins, "Election of 1876 in South Carolina," 345–47; Zuczek, "Last Campaign of the Civil War," 28–29; Williams, *Hampton and His Red Shirts*, 375–421; WH et al., *Reply of Wade Hampton, Governor of South Carolina, and Others to the Chamberlain Memorial* (Columbia, S.C., 1877), 59–62.

21. Jarrell, *Wade Hampton and the Negro*, 87, 103–08.

22. Ibid., 112–18; McPherson, *Ordeal by Fire*, 599–604; Wells, *Hampton and Reconstruction*, 188–89. For an alternative view of the connection between the national and Southern state elections of that year, see: George C. Rable, "Southern Interests and the Election of 1876: A Reappraisal," *Civil War History* 26 (1980): 347–61.

23. Wellman, *Giant in Gray*, 291–92; Jarrell, *Wade Hampton and the Negro*, 114, 134–39, 170–75; Cooper, *Conservative Regime*, 28–32; *Charleston News and Courier*, Dec. 14, 1876; Simkins, "Election of 1876 in South Carolina," 348–51.

24. Jarrell, *Wade Hampton and the Negro*, 123; Julia Porter Wickham, "Wade Hampton, the Cavalry Leader, and His Times," *CV* 36 (1928): 448.

25. Wellman, *Giant in Gray*, 300; Jarrell, *Wade Hampton and the Negro*, 125; Cooper, *Conservative Regime*, 13–17, 50–64, 89–93; Stephen David Kantrowitz, "The Reconstruction of White Supremacy: Reaction and Reform in Ben Tillman's World, 1847–1918" (Ph. D. diss., Princeton Univ., 1995), 79–81.

26. Jarrell, *Wade Hampton and the Negro*, 125–28; Sheppard, *Red Shirts Remembered*, 215–16; Cooper, *Conservative Regime*, 90, 112.

27. Wellman, *Giant in Gray*, 299; Jarrell, *Wade Hampton and the Negro*, 125–26; Cooper, *Conservative Regime*, 46–50.

28. Wellman, *Giant in Gray*, 298–99; WH and Morgan, "Race Problem in the South," 8–14; Cooper, *Conservative Regime*, 29–32; *James Conner . . . In Memoriam*, 17–18.

29. Wellman, *Giant in Gray*, 299; Jarrell, *Wade Hampton and the Negro*, 135–37.

30. Jarrell, *Wade Hampton and the Negro*, 137–38, 175–85; Cooper, *Conservative Regime*, 31–32.

31. Wellman, *Giant in Gray*, 300–01; Jarrell, *Wade Hampton and the Negro*, 132, 139–41, 148–50; WH to Armistead Burt, Mar. 24, 1878, Hampton MSS, DU.

32. Wellman, *Giant in Gray*, 301–04; Jarrell, *Wade Hampton and the Negro*, 151–52; Wells, *Hampton and Reconstruction*, 210; Palmer et al., *World Turned Upside Down*, 812.

33. Wellman, *Giant in Gray*, 303–04; Cooper, *Conservative Regime*, 58.

34. Wellman, *Giant in Gray*, 304.

35. For WH's committee assignments and some of the more prominent bills sponsored, amendments and resolutions offered, and remarks delivered during his Senate tenure, see: *Congressional Record* (46th Cong., 1st Sess., 1879): 483, 737, 1779–81, 1811; (46th Cong., 3rd Sess., 1881): 14, 954, 1674, 2139–40, 2967–68, 3102, 3737, 4222, 4334; (47th Cong., 2nd Sess., 1882): 710, 905, 944, 1472–73, 2138, 2414, 2769, 3323, 3376; (48th Cong., 1st Sess., 1884): 17, 49, 845, 878, 1043, 1142, 2329–31, 2454, 2748–49, 3689, 3852, 5182, 5332; (48th Cong., 2nd Sess., 1885): 683, 1017, 1730, 2027, 2144, 2451; (49th Cong., 2nd Sess., 1887): 433, 825, 871, 1224, 1281, 1437, 1471, 1572, 2168, 2326, 2519, 2593; (50th Cong., 2nd Sess., 1889): 966, 1919, 2188, 2314, 2434; (51st Cong., 2nd Sess.): 1418, 1965, 2434, 2480, 2536.

36. Ibid., (46th Cong., 1st Sess.): 1358, 1779–81, 1811–12, 2207; Jarrell, *Wade Hampton and the Negro*, 154–55.

37. Wellman, *Giant in Gray*, 261–62, 288, 304–07; Jarrell, *Wade Hampton and the Negro*, 114–20, 133–34, 153; Sheppard, *Red Shirts Remembered*, 279; Cooper, *Conservative Regime*, 62; Jones, "Two Roads Tried—and One Detour," 214.

38. Wellman, *Giant in Gray*, 307, 312–17; Jarrell, *Wade Hampton and the Negro*, 153; Cooper, *Conservative Regime*, 17–20, 60–64, 203–06. The most thoughtful study of Tillman and Tillmanism is Kantrowitz, *Ben Tillman & the Reconstruction of White Supremacy*. Two older but still helpful studies are by Francis Butler Simkins: *The Tillman Movement in South Carolina* (Durham, N.C., 1926), and *Pitchfork Ben Tillman, South Carolinian* (Baton Rouge, La., 1944).

39. Wellman, *Giant in Gray*, 307, 310; WH to Mrs. Thomas L. Preston, Mar. 20, 1880, Hampton Family MSS, USC; WH et al., *Family Letters of Three Wade Hamptons*, 167.

40. WH to Armistead Burt, Aug. 28, 1881, Hampton MSS, DU; WH to Alfred Hampton, Feb. 3 1889, Apr. 6, 1898; both, WH Family MSS (1818–1902), LC.

41. Wellman, *Giant in Gray*, 317–19; Jarrell, *Wade Hampton and the Negro*, 161–62; Simkins *Tillman Movement in South Carolina*, 152–53; Wells, *Hampton and Reconstruction*, 211–12; W to Charles S. Venable, Dec. 6, 1890, Special Collections, UV; WH to Edward L. Wells, S 5, 1900, Wells MSS, CLS.

42. Jarrell, *Wade Hampton and the Negro*, 157–63.

43. Wellman, *Giant in Gray*, 319–21; *Congressional Record* (51st Cong., 2nd Sess., 1891): 141 WH's most notable attack on the bill is reprinted verbatim in *The Force Bill—H. R. 1 Speech of Wade Hampton, a Senator from the State of South Carolina, Delivered in the Senate United States, Friday, February 6* (Washington, D.C., 1891).

44. Wellman, *Giant in Gray*, 321–23; WH to W. G. Curtis, June 12, 1896, Hampton Famil USC.

45. Wellman, *Giant in Gray*, 325; Jeffry Wert, *General James Longstreet, the Confedera Controversial Soldier: A Biography* (New York, 1993), 425; WH to Alfred Hampton, Apr WH Family MSS (1818–1902), LC; WH et al., *Family Letters of Three Wade Hampton*

46. Wellman, *Giant in Gray*, 325–26, 328–29; "Ovation to Wade Hampton," *CV* 173–75; *Echoes from Hampton Day*, 1–48; Wells, *Hampton and Reconstruction*, 216–

47. Wellman, *Giant in Gray*, 326; WH to "My Dear Lowndes," Mar. 27, 1900, Edwa MSS, CLS.

48. Wellman, *Giant in Gray*, 326–27; Wells, *Hampton and Reconstruction*, 216; WH t Johnson, June 3, 1899, Johnson MSS, Earl Gregg Swem Library, College of Willia

49. WH to Bradley T. Johnson, Sept. 17, 1899, Johnson MSS; "South Carolina's T Hampton: A Loving Tribute of a Grateful People," May 22, 1899, Hampton Fami

50. Wellman, *Giant in Gray*, 331–33; *Charleston Evening Post*, Apr. 11, 1902; *Charl Courier*, Apr. 12, 13, 1902.

BIBLIOGRAPHY

★ ★ ★

UNPUBLISHED MATERIALS

Allen, Richard P. Correspondence. Eleanor S. Brockenbrough Library, Museum of the Confederacy, Richmond, Virginia.

Biddle, J. W. Correspondence. William R. Perkins Library, Duke University, Durham, North Carolina.

Blackford, William W. Correspondence. Wilson Library, University of North Carolina, Chapel Hill.

_____. "First and Last, or Battles in Virginia." Library of Virginia, Richmond.

_____. Papers. Alderman Library, University of Virginia, Charlottesville.

Bolling, John. Correspondence. Virginia Historical Society, Richmond.

Butler, M. Calbraith. Correspondence. Historical Society of Pennsylvania, Philadelphia.

_____. Correspondence. South Caroliniana Library, University of South Carolina, Columbia.

_____. Correspondence. William R. Perkins Library, Duke University.

Carter, William R. Correspondence and Diaries, 1862–64. Library of Virginia.

Cooke, John Esten. Correspondence. Library of Congress, Washington, D.C.

_____. Correspondence. Virginia Historical Society.

_____. Correspondence. William R. Perkins Library, Duke University.

_____. Correspondence and Diaries, 1863–65. Alderman Library, University of Virginia.

Cummings, John N. Correspondence. William R. Perkins Library, Duke University.

Curtis, W. A. Memoirs. In private collection.

Davis, Zimmerman. Correspondence. South Carolina Department of Archives and History, Columbia.

Dawson, Francis Warrington. Papers. William R. Perkins Library, Duke University.

Deloney, William G. Correspondence. Hargrett Library, University of Georgia, Athens.

Edwards, Julian T. Letter of October 15, 1862. Virginia Historical Society.

Evans, Media. Memoirs. Wilson Library, University of North Carolina.

Gary, Martin W. Papers. South Caroliniana Library, University of South Carolina.

_____. Correspondence. Virginia Historical Society.

Gordon, James B. Correspondence. North Carolina State Department of Archives and History, Raleigh.

Hampton, Wade, III. Amnesty Papers. Pardon Files, South Carolina Department of Archives and History.

_____. Compiled Service Record, 1861–65. Microcopy 331, Roll 115, National Archives, Washington, D.C.

_____. Correspondence. Bradley T. Johnson Papers. Earl Gregg Swem Library, College of William and Mary, Williamsburg, Virginia.

_____. Correspondence. Colleen Cecilia Yates Collection. Winthrop College Library, Rock Hill, South Carolina.

_____. Correspondence. Conner Family Papers. South Carolina Historical Society, Charleston.

_____. Correspondence. Edward L. Wells Papers. Charleston Library Society, Charleston, South Carolina.

_____. Correspondence. Edward L. Wells Papers. South Carolina Historical Society.

_____. Correspondence. Eleanor S. Brockenbrough Library, Museum of the Confederacy.

_____. Correspondence. Gilder Lehrman Collection, New York, N.Y.

_____. Correspondence. Henry B. McClellan Papers. Virginia Historical Society.

_____. Correspondence. Joseph Walker Barnwell Papers. South Carolina Historical Society, Charleston.

_____. Correspondence. Rives Family Papers. Virginia Historical Society.

_____. Correspondence. Sang-Lee Civil War Collection. Seymour Library, Knox College, Galesburg, Illinois.

_____. Correspondence. South Carolina Historical Society, Charleston.

_____. Correspondence. Wilson Library, University of North Carolina.

_____. Correspondence. Wade Hampton Family Papers (1793–1889). Library of Congress.

_____. Correspondence. Wade Hampton Family Papers (1818–1902). Library of Congress.

_____. Correspondence. William R. Perkins Library, Duke University.

_____. Correspondence and Memoirs. Hampton Family Papers. South Caroliniana Library, University of South Carolina.

_____. Correspondence and Scrapbook. Charleston Library Society.

_____. Governor's Papers. South Carolina Department of Archives and History.

_____. Letter of December 6, 1890. Special Collections. Alderman Library, University of Virginia.

_____. Letter of July 9, 1880. S. Griswold Flagg Papers. Yale University Library, New Haven, Conn.

_____. Letter of June 23, 1870. Joseph E. Johnston Papers. Earl Gregg Swem Library, College of William and Mary.

_____. Letter of May 5, 1889. Civil War Manuscripts Collection. Yale University Library.

_____. Letter of November 21, 1871. Johnston Family Papers. Filson Historical Society, Louisville, Ky.

_____. Letter of October 11, 1869. Daniel Harvey Hill Papers. Wilson Library, University of North Carolina.

_____. Letter of September 23, 1864. Samuel Richards Johnston Papers. Virginia Historical Society.

Hart, James F., L. C. Stephens, Louis Sherfesee, and Charles H. Schwing. "History of Hart's Battery." South Caroliniana Library, University of South Carolina.

Hubard, Robert T. Memoirs. William R. Perkins Library, Duke University.

Iredell, Cadwallader J. Correspondence. Wilson Library, University of North Carolina.

Johnson, Bradley T. Correspondence. Earl Gregg Swem Library, College of William and Mary.

Jones, DeWitt Grant. "Wade Hampton and the Rhetoric of Race: A Study of the Speaking of Wade Hampton on the Race Issue in South Carolina, 1865–1878." Ph.D. dissertation, Louisiana State University, 1988.

Jones, Robert B. Correspondence. Virginia Historical Society.

Kantrowitz, Stephen David. "The Reconstruction of White Supremacy: Reaction and Reform in Ben Tillman's World, 1847–1918." Ph.D. dissertation, Princeton University, 1995.

Lee, Fitzhugh. Correspondence. U.S. Army Military History Institute, Carlisle Barracks, Pa.

_____. Correspondence. Virginia Historical Society.

_____. Report of Lee's Division, Cavalry Corps, Army of Northern Virginia, May–December 1864. Eleanor S. Brockenbrough Library, Museum of the Confederacy.

Lee, Robert E. Correspondence. Georgia Callis West Papers. Virginia Historical Society.

_____. Correspondence. Virginia Historical Society.

Lee, W. H. F. Correspondence. Alderman Library, University of Virginia.

_____. Correspondence. Virginia Historical Society.

Logan, Thomas Muldrup. Papers. South Caroliniana Library, University of South Carolina.

McClellan, Henry B. Correspondence. Virginia Historical Society.

Milhollin, John F. Correspondence. U.S. Army Military History Institute.

Mills, William H. Correspondence. J. Y. Joyner Library, East Carolina University, Greenville, North Carolina.

Mims, Julian L. "Radical Reconstruction in Edgefield County, 1868–77." M. A. thesis, University of South Carolina, 1969.

Mosby, John S. Correspondence. U.S. Army Military History Institute.

Munford, Thomas T. Correspondence. Eleanor S. Brockenbrough Library, Museum of the Confederacy.

_____. Correspondence. Library of Virginia.

_____. Correspondence. William R. Perkins Library, Duke University.

Munnerlyn, James K. Correspondence and Diary, 1864. Wilson Library, University of North Carolina.

Person, Jesse H. Correspondence. William R. Perkins Library, Duke University.

Pickens, Francis W. Governor's Papers. South Carolina Department of Archives and History.

Price, R. Channing. Correspondence. Virginia Historical Society.

_____. Correspondence. Wilson Library, University of North Carolina.

Rosser, Thomas L. Correspondence. Alderman Library, University of Virginia.

_____. Correspondence. Eleanor S. Brockenbrough Library, Museum of the Confederacy.

_____. Correspondence. Library of Congress.

_____. Correspondence. Virginia Historical Society.

Sloan, Edwin R. Correspondence. William R. Perkins Library, Duke University.

Stuart, James Ewell Brown. Correspondence. Alderman Library, University of Virginia.

_____. Correspondence. Gilder Lehrman Collection.

_____. Correspondence. Henry E. Huntington Library, San Marino, Calif.

_____. Correspondence. Virginia Historical Society.

Swann, John T. Correspondence. Georgia Department of Archives and History, Atlanta.

Tyler, John Jr. Papers. Earl Gregg Swem Library, College of William and Mary.

Waring, J. Frederick. Diaries, 1864–65. Wilson Library, University of North Carolina.

Wells, Edward L. Papers. Charleston Library Society.

_____. Papers. South Caroliniana Library, University of South Carolina.

Wickham, Williams C. Correspondence. Eleanor S. Brockenbrough Library, Museum of the Confederacy.

_____. Correspondence. Library of Virginia.

Wright, Gilbert J. Correspondence. Virginia Historical Society.

Young, Pierce M. B. Correspondence. Georgia Department of Archives and History.

NEWSPAPERS

Abbeville Medium

Abbeville Press and Banner

Augusta Chronicle

Charleston Daily Courier

Charleston Evening Post

Charleston Mercury

Charleston News and Courier

Charleston Sun

Columbia Daily Phoenix

Columbia Daily Register

Daily South Carolinian (Columbia, S.C.)

Daily Union-Herald (Columbia, S.C.)

Edgefield Advertiser

Louisville Courier-Journal

Metropolitan Record & New York Vindicator (New York, N.Y.)

Nation (New York, N.Y.)

New York Herald

New York Times

New York Tribune

Porter's Spirit of the Times (New York, N.Y.)

Richmond Daily Examiner

Richmond Dispatch

The State (Columbia, S.C.)

ARTICLES AND ESSAYS

Barney, William L. "Hampton, Wade." In John Garraty and Mark C. Carnes, eds., *American National Biography* (24 vols. New York: Oxford University Press, 1999), 9: 965–67.

Beale, R. L. T. "Part Taken by the Ninth Virginia Cavalry in Repelling the Dahlgren Raid." *Southern Historical Society Papers* 3 (1877): 219–21.

Beauregard, P. G. T. "The First Battle of Bull Run." *Battles and Leaders of the Civil War* 1: 196–227.

Brooks, U. R. "Hampton and Butler: Some Pages of Heretofore Unwritten History." *Southern Historical Society Papers* 23 (1895): 25–37.

Buford, M. M. "Surrender of Johnston's Army." *Confederate Veteran* 28 (1920): 170–71.

"The Burning of Columbia." *Confederate Veteran* 24 (1916): 61–62.

Butler, M. C. "The Cavalry Fight at Trevilian Station." *Battles and Leaders of the Civil War* 4: 237–39.

Cardwell, David. "A Brilliant Cavalry Coup." *Confederate Veteran* 26 (1918): 474–76.

_____. "A Brilliant Coup: How Wade Hampton Captured Grant's Entire Beef Supply." *Southern Historical Society Papers* 22 (1894): 147–56.

Carrol, J. P. "The Burning of Columbia, South Carolina—Report of the Committee of Citizens Appointed to Collect Testimony." *Southern Historical Society Papers* 8 (1880): 202–14.

Chamberlain, Daniel H. "Reconstruction and the Negro." *North American Review* 128 (February 1879): 161–73.

Chisolm, A. R. "Beauregard's and Hampton's Orders on Evacuating Columbia—Letter from Colonel A. R. Chisolm." *Southern Historical Society Papers* 7 (1879): 249–50.

Cooke, John Esten. "General Stuart in Camp and Field." In *The Annals of the War, Written by Leading Participants, North and South* (Philadelphia: Times Publishing Co., 1879): 665–76.

"Correspondence between Colonel S. Bassett French and General Wade Hampton." *Southern Historical Society Papers* 2 (1876): 31–32.

Coxe, John. "The Battle of First Manassas." *Confederate Veteran* 23 (1915): 24–26.

_____. "Bloody Night Affair at Colchester, Virginia" *Confederate Veteran* 23 (1915): 168–69.

Davidson, James Wood. "Who Burned Columbia?—A Review of General Sherman's Version of the Affair." *Southern Historical Society Papers* 7 (1879): 185–92.

Dyer, John P. "The Civil War Career of General Joseph Wheeler." *Georgia Historical Quarterly* 19 (1935): 17–46.

_____. "Some Aspects of Cavalry Operations in the Army of Tennessee." *Journal of Southern History* 8 (1942): 210–25.

Early, Jubal A. "Early's March to Washington in 1864." *Battles and Leaders of the Civil War* 4: 492–99.

_____. "Winchester, Fisher's Hill, and Cedar Creek." *Battles and Leaders of the Civil War* 4: 522–30.

Elmore, Albert R. "Testimony about Burning of Columbia." *Confederate Veteran* 20 (1912): 117–18.

Field, Charles W. "Campaign of 1864 and 1865: Narrative of Major-General C. W. Field." *Southern Historical Society Papers* 14 (1886): 542–63.

Ford, Noah P. "Wade Hampton's Strategy: An Attack on Richmond Foiled." *Southern Historical Society Papers* 24 (1896): 278–84.

"Gen. M. C. Butler as a Confederate." *Confederate Veteran* 8 (1900): 110–11.

"Gens. Fitzhugh Lee and Wade Hampton." *Confederate Veteran* 6 (1898): 156.

Gergel, Richard Mark. "Wade Hampton and the Rise of One Party Racial Orthodoxy in South Carolina." In James O. Farmer, Jr., ed., *The Proceedings of the South Carolina Historical Association, 1977* (Lancaster: South Carolina Historical Association, 1977), 5–16.

Hampton, Wade. "The Battle of Bentonville." *Battles and Leaders of the Civil War* 4: 700–705.

_____. "An Effort to Rescue Jefferson Davis: Statement of General Wade Hampton . . ." *Southern Historical Society Papers* 27 (1899): 132–36.

_____. "Letter from General Hampton on the Burning of Columbia." *Southern Historical Society Papers* 7 (1879): 156–58.

_____. "What Negro Supremacy Means." *Forum* 5 (June 1888): 2–14.

_____, and John T. Morgan. "The Race Problem in the South." *The Forum Extra: A Periodical of Short Studies of Living Problems* 1 (March 1890): 1–28.

Hanson, Joseph Mills. "Wade Hampton, 1818–1902." *Cavalry Journal* 43 (1934): 30–37.

Hargis, O. P. "We kept fighting and falling back." *Civil War Times Illustrated* 7 (December 1968): 37–42.

"Hart's South Carolina Battery—Its War Guidon—Addresses by Major Hart and Governor Hampton." *Southern Historical Society Papers* 6 (1878): 128–32.

Haw, John R. "The Battle of Haw's Shop, Virginia" *Confederate Veteran* 33 (1925): 373–76.

"History of Hart's Battery." *Confederate Veteran* 9 (1901): 500–01.

Holmes, James C. "Tribute to Wade Hampton." *Confederate Veteran* 10 (1902): 313.

Hood, John B. "The Defense of Atlanta." *Battles and Leaders of the Civil War* 4: 336–44.

Imboden, John D. "The Confederate Retreat from Gettysburg." *Battles and Leaders of the Civil War* 3: 420–29.

James, G. Watson. "Dahlgren's Raid." *Southern Historical Society Papers* 39 (1914): 63–72.

Johnston, Joseph E. "Manassas to Seven Pines." *Battles and Leaders of the Civil War* 2: 202–18.

_____. "Opposing Sherman's Advance to Atlanta." *Battles and Leaders of the Civil War* 4: 260–77.

Jones, J. William, comp. "The Kilpatrick–Dahlgren Raid Against Richmond." *Southern Historical Society Papers* 13 (1885): 515–60.

Jones, Lewis P. "Two Roads Tried—and One Detour." *South Carolina Historical Magazine* 79 (1978): 206–18.

"Kilpatrick's and Dahlgren's Raid to Richmond." *Battles and Leaders of the Civil War* 4: 95–96.

Krick, Robert K. "Sleepless in the Saddle: Stonewall Jackson in the Seven Days." In Gary A. Gallagher, ed., *The Richmond Campaign of 1862: The Peninsula and the Seven Days* (Chapel Hill: University of North Carolina Press, 2000): 66–95.

Longacre, Edward G. "Stuart's Dumfries Raid." *Civil War Times Illustrated* 15 (July 1976): 18–26.

Louthan, Henry T. "General Wade Hampton, Planter, Soldier, Statesman." *Confederate Veteran* 40 (1932): 65–69.

Luvaas, Jay, and Wilbur S. Nye. "The Campaign That History Forgot." *Civil War Times Illustrated* 8 (November 1969): 12–42.

Lykes, Richard W. "The Great Civil War Beef Raid." *Civil War Times Illustrated* 5 (February 1967): 5–12, 47–49.

Mackey, T. J. "Duel of General Wade Hampton on the Battle-Field at Gettysburg with a Federal Soldier." *Southern Historical Society Papers* 22 (1894): 122–26.

McAfee, Ward M. "Reconstruction Revisited: The Republican Party Education Crusade of the 1870s." *Civil War History* 42 (1996): 133–53.

McClellan, George B. "The Peninsular Campaign." *Battles and Leaders of the Civil War* 2: 160–87.

McKim, Randolph H. "The Confederate Cavalry in the Gettysburg Campaign." *Journal of the Military Service Institution of the United States* 46 (1910): 414–27.

McMahon, Martin T. "Cold Harbor." *Battles and Leaders of the Civil War* 4: 213–20.

Miller, William E. "The Cavalry Battle Near Gettysburg." *Battles and Leaders of the Civil War* 4: 397–406.

Milling, Chapman J. "Ilium in Flames." *Confederate Veteran* 36 (1928): 212–16.

Monaghan, Jay. "Custer's 'Last Stand'—Trevilian Station, 1864." *Civil War History* 8 (1962): 245–58.

"Monuments of Wade Hampton." *Confederate Veteran* 15 (1907): 134–35.

Mosby, John S. "The Confederate Cavalry in the Gettysburg Campaign." *Battles and Leaders of the Civil War* 3: 251–52.

Nye, Wilbur S. "The Affair at Hunterstown." *Civil War Times Illustrated* 9 (February 1971): 22–34.

———. "How Stuart Recrossed the Potomac." *Civil War Times Illustrated* 4 (January 1966): 45–48.

"Ovation to Wade Hampton." *Confederate Veteran* 3 (1895): 173–75.

Pope, John. "The Second Battle of Bull Run." *Battles and Leaders of the Civil War* 2: 449–94.

Porter, Fitz-John. "The Battle of Malvern Hill." *Battles and Leaders of the Civil War* 2: 406–27.

____. "Hanover Court House and Gaines's Mill." *Battles and Leaders of the Civil War* 2 (1887–88): 319–43.

Rable, George C. "Bourbonism, Reconstruction, and the Persistence of Southern Distinctiveness." *Civil War History* 29 (1983): 135–53.

____. "Southern Interests and the Election of 1876: A Reappraisal." *Civil War History* 26 (1980): 347–61.

Rea, D. B. "Cavalry Incidents of the Maryland Campaign." *Maine Bugle* 2 (1895): 117–23.

Redwood, Allen C. "Following Stuart's Feather." *Journal of the Military Service Institution of the United States* 49 (1911): 111–21.

Rhea, Gordon C. "'The Hottest Place I Ever Was In': The Battle of Haw's Shop, May 28, 1864." *North & South* 4 (April 2001): 42–57.

Robertson, Beverly H. "The Confederate Cavalry in the Gettysburg Campaign." *Battles and Leaders of the Civil War* 3: 253.

Robins, W. T. "Stuart's Ride around McClellan." *Battles and Leaders of the Civil War* 2: 271–75.

Rodenbough, Theophilus F. "Sheridan's Richmond Raid." *Battles and Leaders of the Civil War* 4: 188–93.

____. "Sheridan's Trevilian Raid." *Battles and Leaders of the Civil War* 4: 233–36.

Rodgers, C. R. P. "Du Pont's Attack at Charleston." *Battles and Leaders of the Civil War* 4: 32–47.

Simkins, Francis Butler. "The Election of 1876 in South Carolina." *South Atlantic Quarterly* 21 (1922): 225–40, 335–51.

____. "The Ku Klux Klan in South Carolina, 1868–1871." *Journal of Negro History* 12 (1927): 607–47.

Smith, Gustavus W. "Two Days of Battle at Seven Pines (Fair Oaks)." *Battles and Leaders of the Civil War* 2: 220–63.

Smith, William Farrar. "Butler's Attack on Drewry's Bluff." *Battles and Leaders of the Civil War* 4: 206–12.

Stinson, Dwight E. Jr. "Eltham's Landing—the End Run that Failed." *Civil War Times Illustrated* 1 (February 1963): 38–41.

Stone, Henry. "Repelling Hood's Invasion of Tennessee." *Battles and Leaders of the Civil War* 4: 440–64.

Trescott, William Henry. "Letters on Reconstruction in South Carolina." *American Historical Review* 15 (1910): 574–82.

Trout, Robert J. "Galloping Thunder: Horse Artillery of the Army of Northern Virginia." *North & South* 3 (September 2000): 75–84.

"Visit to a Cotton Plantation." *Scientific American* 15 (February 1860): 103.

"Wade Hampton Monument at Columbia." *Confederate Veteran* 14 (1906): 534.

Walker, John G. "Sharpsburg." *Battles and Leaders of the Civil War* 2: 675–82.

Wallace, D. D. "The Question of the Withdrawal of the Democratic Presidential Electors in South Carolina in 1876." *Journal of Southern History* 8 (1942): 374–85.

_____. "The South Carolina Convention of 1895." *Sewanee Review* 4 (1896): 348–60.

Waring, Joseph I., ed. "The Diary of William G. Hinson during the War of Secession." *South Carolina Historical Magazine* 75 (1974): 14–23, 111–14.

Wells, E. L. "A Morning Call on General Kilpatrick." *Southern Historical Society Papers* 12 (1884): 123–30.

_____. "Who Burnt Columbia?: Testimony of a Confederate Cavalryman." *Southern Historical Society Papers* 10 (1882): 109–19.

Wert, Jeffry D. "His Unhonored Service." *Civil War Times Illustrated* 24 (June 1985): 29–34.

"Who Burned Columbia?—General Sherman's Latest Story Examined." *Southern Historical Society Papers* 13 (1885): 448–55.

Wickham, Julia Porcher. "Wade Hampton, the Cavalry Leader, and His Times." *Confederate Veteran* 36 (1928): 448–50.

Willcox, Orlando B. "Actions on the Weldon Railroad." *Battles and Leaders of the Civil War* 4: 568–73.

Williams, Lou Falkner. "The South Carolina Ku Klux Klan Trials and Enforcement of Federal Rights." *Civil War History* 39 (1993): 47–66.

Williams, Robert A. "Haw's Shop: A 'Storm of Shot and Shell'." *Civil War Times Illustrated* 9 (January 1971): 12–19.

Wittenberg, Eric J. "Confederate Cavalry Command Dilemma." *America's Civil War* 15 (January 2002): 26–32, 56.

Woody, R. H. "The South Carolina Election of 1870." *North Carolina Historical Review* 8 (1931): 168–86.

_____, ed. "Behind the Scenes in the Reconstruction Legislature of South Carolina: Diary of Josephus Woodruff." *Journal of Southern History* 2 (1936): 78–102, 233–59.

Zuczek, Richard. "The Last Campaign of the Civil War: South Carolina and the Revolution of 1876." *Civil War History* 42 (1996): 18–31.

BOOKS AND PAMPHLETS

Abbott, Martin. *The Freedman's Bureau in South Carolina, 1865–1872.* Chapel Hill: University of North Carolina Press, 1967.

Acts and Joint Resolutions of the General Assembly of the State of South Carolina. Columbia, S.C.: The State, 1868.

An Address to the People of the United States, Adopted at a Conference of Colored Citizens, Held at Columbia, South Carolina, July 20 and 21, 1876. Columbia, S.C.: Republican Printing Co., 1876.

Alexander, Edward Porter. *Fighting for the Confederacy: The Personal Recollections of General Edward Porter Alexander*. Edited by Gary A. Gallagher. Chapel Hill: University of North Carolina Press, 1989.

_____. *Military Memoirs of a Confederate: A Critical Narrative*. New York: Charles Scribner's Sons, 1908.

Allen, Walter. *Governor Chamberlain's Administration of South Carolina: A Chapter of Reconstruction in the Southern States*. New York: G. P. Putnam's Sons, 1888.

Baker, Gary R. *Cadets in Gray: The Story of the Cadets of the South Carolina Military Academy and the Cadet Rangers in the Civil War*. Columbia, S.C.: Palmetto Bookworks, 1989.

Ball, William Watts. *A Boy's Recollections of the Red Shirt Campaign of 1876 in South Carolina . . .* Columbia: State Co., 1911.

_____. *The State That Forgot: South Carolina's Surrender to Democracy*. Indianapolis: Bobbs-Merrill Co., 1932.

Ballard, Michael B. *A Long Shadow: Jefferson Davis and the Final Days of the Confederacy*. Jackson: University Press of Mississippi, 1986.

Barrett, John G. *Sherman's March through the Carolinas*. Chapel Hill: University of North Carolina Press, 1956.

Baylor, George. *Bull Run to Bull Run; or, Four Years in the Army of Northern Virginia . . .* Richmond: B. F. Johnson Publishing Co., 1900.

Beale, George W. *A Lieutenant of Cavalry in Lee's Army*. Boston: Gorham Press, 1918.

Beale, R. L. T. *History of the Ninth Virginia Cavalry, in the War Between the States*. Richmond: B. F. Johnson Publishing Co., 1899.

Biographical Directory of the American Congress, 1774–1961. Washington, D.C.: Government Printing Office, 1961.

Biographical Directory of the Senate of the State of South Carolina, 1776–1964. Columbia: South Carolina Archives Department, 1964.

Black, John L. *Crumbling Defenses, or Memoirs and Reminiscences of John Logan Black, Colonel, C. S. A.* Edited by Eleanor D. McSwain. Macon, Ga.: J. W. Burke Co., 1960.

Blackford, William W. *War Years with Jeb Stuart*. New York: Charles Scribner's Sons, 1945.

Bleser, Carol K. Rothrock. *The Promised Land: The History of the South Carolina Land Commission, 1869–1890*. Columbia: University of South Carolina Press, 1969.

_____, ed. *The Hammonds of Redcliffe*. New York: Oxford University Press, 1981.

Boles, John B. *Black Southerners, 1619–1869*. Lexington: University Press of Kentucky, 1983.

_____, ed. *Masters and Slaves in the House of the Lord: Race and Religion in the American South, 1740–1870*. Lexington: University Press of Kentucky, 1988.

Borcke, Heros von. *Memoirs of the Confederate War for Independence*. 2 vols. New York: Peter Smith, 1938.

Boykin, Edward. *Beefsteak Raid*. New York: Funk & Wagnalls Co., 1960.

317

Brackett, Albert G. *History of the United States Cavalry . . . to the 1st of June, 1863.* New York: Harper & Brothers, 1865.

Bradley, Mark L. *Last Stand in the Carolinas: The Battle of Bentonville.* Campbell, Calif.: Savas-Woodbury Publishers, 1996.

_____. *This Astounding Close: The Road to Bennett Place.* Chapel Hill: University of North Carolina Press, 2000.

Brooks, U. R. *Butler and His Cavalry in the War of Secession, 1861–1865.* Columbia, S.C.: State Co., 1909.

Brooksher, William R., and David K. Snider. *Glory at a Gallop: Tales of the Confederate Cavalry.* Washington, D.C.: Brassey's, Inc., 1993.

Burton, Brian K. *Extraordinary Circumstances: The Seven Days Battles.* Bloomington: Indiana University Press, 2001.

Bushong, Millard K., and Dean M. Bushong. *Fightin' Tom Rosser, C. S. A.* Shippensburg, Pa.: Beidel Printing House, Inc., 1983.

Carter, Hodding. *The Angry Scar: The Story of Reconstruction.* Garden City, N.Y.: Doubleday & Co., Inc., 1959.

Carter, Samuel, III. *The Last Cavaliers: Confederate and Union Cavalry in the Civil War.* New York: St. Martin's Press, 1979.

Chesnut, Mary Boykin. *A Diary from Dixie.* Edited by Ben Ames Williams. Boston: Houghton, Mifflin Co., 1949.

_____. *The Private Mary Chesnut: The Unpublished Civil War Diaries.* Edited by C. Vann Woodward and Elisabeth Muhlenfeld. New York: Oxford University Press, 1984.

Clark, Walter, ed. *Histories of the Several Regiments and Battalions from North Carolina in the Great War, 1861–'65 . . .* 5 vols. Goldsboro, N.C.: Nash Brothers; Raleigh: E. M. Uzzell, 1901.

Coddington, Edwin B. *The Gettysburg Campaign: A Study in Command.* New York: Charles Scribner's Sons, 1968.

Coltrane, Daniel B. *The Memoirs of Daniel Branson Coltrane, Co. I, 63rd Reg., North Carolina Cavalry, C. S. A.* Raleigh, N.C.: Edwards & Broughton Co., 1956.

Congressional Record. Washington, D.C.: Government Printing Office, 1879–91.

Connelly, Thomas Lawrence. *Autumn of Glory: The Army of Tennessee, 1862–1865.* Baton Rouge: Louisiana State University Press, 1971.

Conner, James. *Letters of General James Conner, C. S. A.* Edited by Mary Conner Moffett. Columbia, S.C.: R. L. Bryan Co., 1950.

Constitution of the State of South Carolina . . . Adopted by the Constitutional Convention Which was Held at Charleston, and Adjourned on the 17th March, 1868. Charleston, S.C.: The State, 1868.

Conyngham, David P. *Sherman's March through the South, with Sketches and Incidents of the Campaign.* New York: Sheldon & Co., 1865.

Cooke, John Esten. *Wearing of the Gray: Being Personal Portraits, Scenes and Adventures of the War*. Baton Rouge: Louisiana State University Press, 1997.

Cooper, William J. Jr. *The Conservative Regime: South Carolina, 1877–1890*. Baltimore: Johns Hopkins University Press, 1968.

_____. *Jefferson Davis, American*. New York: Alfred A. Knopf, 2000.

Corson, William Clark. *My Dear Jennie: A Collection of Love Letters from a Confederate Soldier to His Fiancée During the Period 1861–1865*. Edited by Blake W. Corson Jr. Richmond, Va.: Dietz Press, Inc., 1982.

Coulter, E. Merton. *The South during Reconstruction, 1865–1877*. Baton Rouge: Louisiana State University Press, 1947.

Cruden, Robert. *The Negro in Reconstruction*. Englewood Cliffs, N.J.: Prentice-Hall, 1969.

Current, Richard N., ed. *Encyclopedia of the Confederacy*. 4 vols. New York: Simon & Schuster, 1993.

Davis, Burke. *Jeb Stuart, the Last Cavalier*. New York: Rinehart & Co., Inc., 1957.

_____. *Sherman's March*. New York: Random House, 1980.

Davis, Varina Howell. *Jefferson Davis, Ex-President of the Confederate States of America: A Memoir*. 2 vols. New York: Belford Co., 1890.

Davis, William C. *Battle at Bull Run: A History of the First Major Campaign of the Civil War*. Garden City, N.Y.: Doubleday & Co., Inc., 1977.

_____, ed. *Shdows of the Storm: Volume One of The Image of War, 1861–1865*. Garden City, N.Y.: Doubleday & Co., Inc., 1981.

Dodson, William C., ed. *Campaigns of Wheeler and His Cavalry, 1862–1865*. Atlanta: Hudgins Publishing Co., 1899.

Donald, David H. *The Politics of Reconstruction, 1863–1867*. Baton Rouge: Louisiana State University Press, 1965.

Douglas, Henry Kyd. *I Rode with Stonewall: Being Chiefly the War Experiences of the Youngest Member of Jackson's Staff . . .* Chapel Hill: University of North Carolina Press, 1940.

Dowdey, Clifford. *The Seven Days: The Emergence of Lee*. Boston: Little, Brown & Co., 1964.

Downey, Fairfax. *Clash of Cavalry: The Battle of Brandy Station, June 9, 1863*. New York: David McKay Co., Inc., 1959.

Drago, Edmund L. *Hurrah for Hampton: Black Red Shirts in South Carolina during Reconstruction*. Fayetteville: University of Arkansas Press, 1998.

Driver, Robert J. Jr. *5th Virginia Cavalry*. Lynchburg, Va.: H. E. Howard, Inc., 1997.

DuBois, W. E. *Black Reconstruction in America, 1860–1880*. Cleveland: World Publishing Co., 1964.

Dubose, John Witherspoon. *General Joseph Wheeler and the Army of Tennessee*. New York: Neale Publishing Co., 1912.

Dunning, William A. *Reconstruction, Political and Economic.* New York: Harper & Brothers, 1907.

Dyer, John P. *"Fightin' Joe" Wheeler.* Baton Rouge: Louisiana State University Press, 1941.

Early, Jubal A. *War Memoirs: Autobiographical Sketch and Narrative of the War Between the States.* Edited by Frank E. Vandiver. Bloomington: Indiana University Press, 1960.

Echoes from Hampton Day, Charleston, South Carolina, May 14th, 1895. Charleston: Camp Moultrie, Sons of Confederate Veterans, 1895.

Edmunds, John B. Jr. *Francis W. Pickens and the Politics of Destruction.* Chapel Hill: University of North Carolina Press, 1986.

Evans, Clement A., ed. *Confederate Military History.* 13 vols. Atlanta: Confederate Publishing Co., 1899.

Faust, Drew Gilpin. *James Henry Hammond and the Old South: A Design for Mastery.* Baton Rouge: Louisiana State University Press, 1982.

Fleming, Walter L. *Documentary History of Reconstruction.* 2 vols. Cleveland: Arthur H. Clark Co., 1906.

Foner, Eric. *Reconstruction: America's Unfinished Revolution, 1862–1877.* New York: Harper & Row, 1989.

Franklin, John Hope. *Reconstruction after the Civil War.* Chicago: University of Chicago Press, 1961.

Freeman, Douglas Southall. *Lee's Lieutenants: A Study in Command.* 3 vols. New York: Charles Scribner's Sons, 1942–44.

_____. *R. E. Lee: A Biography.* 4 vols. New York: Charles Scribner's Sons, 1934–35.

Govan, Gilbert E., and James W. Livingood. *A Different Valor: The Story of General Joseph E. Johnston, C. S. A.* Indianapolis: Bobbs–Merrill Co., Inc., 1956.

Grant, Ulysses S. *Personal Memoirs of U.S. Grant.* 2 vols. New York: Charles L. Webster & Co., 1885–86.

Grimsley, Daniel A. *Battles in Culpeper County, Virginia, 1861–1865.* Culpeper, Va.: Raleigh-Travers-Green Co., 1900.

Haden, B. J. *Reminiscences of J. E. B. Stuart's Cavalry . . .* Charlottesville, Va.: Progress Publishing Co., ca. 1890.

Hammond, James H. *Secret and Sacred: The Diaries of James Henry Hammond, a Southern Slaveholder.* Edited by Carol Bleser. New York: Oxford University Press, 1988.

Hampton, Wade, III. *Address on the Life and Character of Gen. Robert E. Lee . . .* Baltimore: John Murphy & Co., 1871.

_____. *The Force Bill—H. R. 11045: Speech of Wade Hampton, a Senator from the State of South Carolina, Delivered in the Senate of the United States, Friday, February 6.* Washington, D.C.: Government Printing Office, 1891.

_____. *Free Men! Free Ballots!! Free Schools!!! The Pledges of Gen. Wade Hampton, Democratic Candidate for Governor, to the Colored People of South Carolina, 1865–1876.* n. p.: privately issued, 1876.

_____. *Negro Emancipation: Speech of Wade Hampton, a Senator from the State of South Carolina* . . . Washington, D.C.: privately issued, 1890.

_____. *Speech . . . Delivered in the Senate of the U.S., Fri., Jan. 16, 1891.* Washington, D.C.: Government Printing Office, 1891.

_____. *Speech of Hon. Wade Hampton on the Constitutionality of the Slave Trade, Delivered in the Senate of South Carolina, Dec. 10, 1859.* Columbia, S.C.: privately issued, 1860.

_____, et al. *Family Letters of the Three Wade Hamptons, 1782–1901.* Edited by Charles E. Cauthen. Columbia: University of South Carolina Press, 1953.

_____, et al. *In Memory of Hon. Thomas A. Hendricks, Late Vice- President of the United States: Addresses of Senators D. W. Vorhees, of Indiana, Wade Hampton, of South Carolina* . . . Washington, D.C.: Government Printing Office, 1886.

_____, et al. *Reply of Wade Hampton, Governor of South Carolina, and Others to the Chamberlain Memorial.* Columbia, S.C.: Presbyterian Publishing House, 1877.

Hartley, Chris J. *Stuart's Tarheels: James B. Gordon and His North Carolina Cavalry.* Baltimore: Butternut & Blue, 1996.

Haskell, John Cheves. *The Haskell Memoirs.* Edited by Gilbert E. Govan and James W. Livingood. New York: G. P. Putnam's Sons, 1960.

Haworth, Paul Leland. *The Hayes-Tilden Disputed Presidential Election of 1876.* New York: Russell & Russell, 1966.

Heitman, Francis B., comp. *Historical Register and Dictionary of the United States Army* . . . 2 vols. Washington, D.C.: Government Printing Office, 1903.

Hennessy, John. *The First Battle of Manassas: An End to Innocence, July 18–21, 1861.* Lynchburg, Va.: H. E. Howard, Inc., 1989.

_____. *Return to Bull Run: The Campaign and Battle of Second Manassas.* New York: Simon & Schuster, 1993.

Hewett, Janet, et al., eds. *Supplement to the Official Records of the Union and Confederate Armies.* 3 pts., 99 vols. Wilmington, N.C.: Broadfoot Publishing Co., 1994–2001.

Hirshon, Stanley P. *Farewell to the Bloody Shirt: Northern Republicans and the Southern Negro, 1877–1893.* Bloomington: Indiana University Press, 1962.

Hitchcock, Henry. *Marching with Sherman: Passages from the Letters and Campaign Diaries of Henry Hitchcock* . . . Edited by M. A. DeWolfe Howe. New Haven, Conn.: Yale University Press, 1927.

Holland, Lynwood M. *Pierce M. B. Young, the Warwick of the South.* Athens: University of Georgia Press, 1964.

Hollis, John Porter. *The Early Period of Reconstruction in South Carolina.* Baltimore: Johns Hopkins University Press, 1905.

Holt, Thomas. *Black Over White: Negro Political Leadership in South Carolina during Reconstruction.* Urbana: University of Illinois Press, 1979.

Hopkins, Donald A. *The Little Jeff: The Jeff Davis Legion, Cavalry, Army of Northern Virginia.* Shippensburg, Pa.: White Mane Books, 1999.

Horn, John. *The Petersburg Campaign, June 1864–April 1865.* Conshohocken, Pa.: Combined Books, 1993.

_____. *The Petersburg Campaign: The Destruction of the Weldon Railroad, Deep Bottom, Globe Tavern, and Reams Station, August 14–25, 1864.* Lynchburg, Va.: H. E. Howard, Inc., 1991.

Horn, Stanley F. *The Army of Tennessee.* Norman: University of Oklahoma Press, 1953.

Howard, Oliver O. *Autobiography of Oliver Otis Howard, Major General, United States Army.* 2 vols. New York: Baker & Taylor Co., 1907.

Howard, Wiley C. *Sketch of Cobb Legion Cavalry and Some Incidents and Scenes Remembered . . .* Atlanta: privately issued, 1901.

Hughes, Nathaniel Cheairs Jr. *Bentonville: The Final Battle of Sherman and Johnston.* Chapel Hill: University of North Carolina Press, 1996.

_____. *General William J. Hardee, Old Reliable.* Baton Rouge: Louisiana State University Press, 1965.

Humphreys, Andrew A. *Gettysburg to the Rapidan: The Army of the Potomac, July, 1863, to April, 1864.* New York: Charles Scribner's Sons, 1883.

_____. *The Virginia Campaign of '64 and '65: The Army of the Potomac and the Army of the James.* New York: Charles Scribner's Sons, 1883.

Jacobs, Lee, comp. *The Gray Riders: Stories from the Confederate Cavalry.* Shippensburg, Pa.: Burd Street Press, 1999.

James Conner . . . In Memoriam. Charleston, S.C.: Walker, Evans & Cogswell, ca. 1883.

Jarrell, Hampton M. *Wade Hampton and the Negro: The Road Not Taken.* Columbia: University of South Carolina Press, 1949.

Johnston, Joseph E. *Narrative of Military Operations during the Civil War.* New York: D. Appleton & Co., 1874.

Johnston, R. M. *Bull Run: Its Strategy and Tactics.* Boston: Houghton Mifflin Co., 1913.

Jones, Charles Colcock, et al. *The Children of Pride: A True Story of Georgia and the Civil War.* Edited by Robert Manson Myers. New Haven, Conn.: Yale University Press, 1972.

Kane, Sharyn, and Richard Keeton. *Fiery Dawn: The Civil War Battle at Monroe's Crossroads, North Carolina.* Tallahassee, Fla.: Southeast Archeological Center, National Park Service, 1999.

Kantrowitz, Stephen. *Ben Tillman & The Reconstruction of White Supremacy.* Chapel Hill: University of North Carolina Press, 2000.

Kinsley, Ardyce, comp. *The Fitzhugh Lee Sampler*. Lively, Va.: Brandylane Publishers, 1992.

Klein, Maury. *Days of Defiance: Sumter, Secession, and the Coming of the Civil War*. New York: Alfred A. Knopf, 1997.

Knapp, David Jr. *The Confederate Horsemen*. New York: Vantage Press, 1966.

The Ku Klux Klan Conspiracy. (U.S. Congress Joint Select Committee to Inquire into the Condition of Affairs in the Late Insurrectionary States, 42nd Cong., 2nd Sess.). Washington, D.C.: Government Printing Office, 1872.

Lamson, Peggy. *The Glorious Failure: Black Congressman Robert Brown Elliott and the Reconstruction in South Carolina*. New York: W. W. Norton & Co., Inc., 1973.

Lander, Ernest M. *A History of South Carolina, 1865–1960*. Chapel Hill: University of North Carolina Press, 1960.

_____, and Robert K. Ackerman, eds. *Perspectives in South Carolina History: The First 300 Years*. Columbia: University of South Carolina Press, 1973.

LeConte, Emma. *When the World Ended: The Diary of Emma LeConte*. Edited by Earl Schenck Miers. New York: Oxford University Press, 1957.

Lee, Fitzhugh. *General Lee*. New York: D. Appleton & Co., 1894.

Lee, Robert E. *Lee's Dispatches: Unpublished Letters of General Robert E. Lee, C. S. A., to Jefferson Davis and the War Department of the Confederate States of America*. Edited by Douglas Southall Freeman and Grady McWhiney. New York: G. P. Putnam's Sons, 1957.

_____. *The Wartime Papers of Robert E. Lee*. Edited by Clifford Dowdey and Louis H. Manarin. Boston: Little, Brown & Co., 1961.

Leland, John A. *A Voice from South Carolina*. Charleston, S.C.: Walker, Evans & Cogswell, 1879.

Logan, Kate Virginia Cox. *My Confederate Girlhood: The Memoirs of Kate Virginia Cox Logan*. Edited by Lily Logan Morrill. Richmond, Va.: Garrett & Massie, Inc., 1932.

Long, A. L. *Memoirs of Robert E. Lee: His Military and Personal History* . . . New York: J. M. Stoddart & Co., 1886.

Longacre, Edward G. *The Cavalry at Gettysburg: A Tactical Study of Mounted Operations during the Civil War's Pivotal Campaign, 9 June–14 July 1863*. Rutherford, N. J.: Fairleigh Dickinson University Press, 1986.

_____. *Custer and His Wolverines: The Michigan Cavalry Brigade, 1861–1865*. Conshohocken, Pa.: Combined Publishing, 1997.

_____. *From Union Stars to Top Hat: A Biography of the Extraordinary General James Harrison Wilson*. Harrisburg, Pa.: Stackpole Books, 1972.

_____. *General William Dorsey Pender: A Military Biography*. Conshohocken, Pa.: Combined Publishing, 2001.

_____. *Lee's Cavalrymen: A History of the Mounted Forces of the Army of Northern Virginia, 1861–1865*. Mechanicsburg, Pa.: Stackpole Books, 2002.

_____. *Lincoln's Cavalrymen: A History of the Mounted Forces of the Army of the Potomac, 1861–1865*. Mechanicsburg, Pa.: Stackpole Books, 2000.

_____. *Mounted Raids of the Civil War*. South Brunswick, N. J.: A. S. Barnes & Co., Inc., 1975.

Longstreet, James. *From Manassas to Appomattox: Memoirs of the Civil War in America*. Philadelphia: J. B. Lippincott Co., 1896.

Lucas, Marion Brunson. *Sherman and the Burning of Columbia*. College Station: Texas A&M University Press, 1976.

Malone, Bartlett Y. *Whipt 'em Everytime: The Diary of Bartlett Yancey Malone, Co. H 6th North Carolina Regiment*. Edited by William Whatley Pierson Jr. Jackson, Tenn.: McCowat-Mercer Press, Inc., 1960.

Marshall, Charles. *An Aide-de-Camp of Lee: Being the Papers of Colonel Charles Marshall . . .* Edited by Sir Frederick Maurice. Boston: Little, Brown, & Co., 1927.

Martin, Samuel J. *"Kill Cavalry": The Life of Union General Hugh Judson Kilpatrick*. Rutherford, N. J.: Fairleigh Dickinson University Press, 1996.

_____. *Southern Hero: Matthew Calbraith Butler, Confederate General, Hampton Red Shirt, and U.S. Senator*. Mechanicsburg, Pa.: Stackpole Books, 2001.

Mays, Samuel E. *Genealogical Notes on the Family of Mays and Reminiscences of the War between the States from Notes Written around the Campfires*. Plant City, Fla.: Plant City Enterprise, 1927.

McClellan, Henry B. *The Life and Campaigns of Maj. Gen. J. E. B. Stuart, Commander of the Cavalry of the Army of Northern Virginia*. Boston: Houghton, Mifflin & Co., 1885.

McCrady, Edward, Jr., and Samuel A. Ashe, eds. *Cyclopedia of Eminent and Representative Men of the Carolinas of the Nineteenth Century*. 2 vols. Madison, Wis.: Brant & Fuller, 1892.

McDonald, William N. *A History of the Laurel Brigade, Originally The Ashby Cavalry of the Army of Northern Virginia, and Chew's Battery*. Edited by Bushrod C. Washington. Baltimore: Sun Job Printing Office, 1907.

McPherson, James M. *Ordeal by Fire: The Civil War and Reconstruction*. New York: Alfred A. Knopf, 1982.

Meynard, Virginia G. *The Venturers: The Hampton, Harrison, and Earle Families of Virginia, South Carolina, and Texas*. Easley, S.C.: Southern Historical Press, 1981.

Moore, Frank, ed. *The Rebellion Record: A Diary of American Events*. 12 vols. New York: various publishers, 1861–68.

Mosby, John S. *The Letters of John S. Mosby*. Edited by Adele H. Mitchell. n. p.: Stuart-Mosby Historical Society, 1986.

_____. *Stuart's Cavalry in the Gettysburg Campaign*. New York: Moffat, Yard & Co., 1908.

Mulligan, Alfred B. *"My Dear Mother & Sisters": Civil War Letters of Capt. A. B. Mulligan, Co. B, 5th South Carolina Cavalry—Butler's Division—Hampton's Corps, 1861–1865.* Edited by Olin Fulmer Hutchinson, Jr. Spartanburg, S.C.: Reprint Co., 1992.

Murfin, James V. *The Gleam of Bayonets: The Battle of Antietam and the Maryland Campaign of 1862.* New York: A. S. Barnes & Co., Inc., 1965.

Myers, Franklin M. *The Comanches: A History of White's Battalion, Virginia Cavalry, Laurel Brig., Hampton['s] Div., A. N. V., C. S. A.* Baltimore: Kelly, Piet & Co., 1871.

Neese, George M. *Three Years in the Confederate Horse Artillery.* New York: Neale Publishing Co., 1911.

Newton, Steven H. *The Battle of Seven Pines, May 31–June 1, 1862.* Lynchburg, Va.: H. E. Howard, Inc., 1993.

Nichols, George Ward. *The Story of the Great March, from the Diary of a Staff Officer.* New York: Harper & Brothers, 1865.

Nichols, James L. *General Fitzhugh Lee: A Biography.* Lynchburg, Va.: H. E. Howard, Inc., 1989.

Opie, John N. *A Rebel Cavalryman with Lee, Stuart, and Jackson.* Chicago: W. B. Conkey Co., 1899.

Osborn, Thomas Ward. *The Fiery Trail: A Union Officer's Account of Sherman's Last Campaigns.* Edited by Richard B. Harwell and Philip N. Racine. Knoxville: University of Tennessee Press, 1986.

Palmer, John S., et al. *A World Turned Upside Down: The Palmers of South Santee, 1818–1881.* Edited by Louis P. Towles. Columbia: University of South Carolina Press, 1996.

Pike, James Sheppard. *The Prostrate State: South Carolina under Negro Government.* New York: D. Appleton & Co., 1874.

Proceedings of the Constitutional Convention of South Carolina, Held at Charleston, South Carolina, Beginning January 14th and Ending March 17th, 1868. Charleston, S.C.: John W. Denny & Co., 1868.

Proceedings of the Taxpayers Convention of South Carolina, Held at Columbia, Beginning May 9th and Ending May 12, 1871. Charleston, S.C.: privately issued, 1871.

Rafuse, Ethan S. *A Single Grand Victory: The First Campaign and Battle of Manassas.* Wilmington, Del.: Scholarly Resources, Inc., 2002.

Rea, D. B. *Sketches from Hampton's Cavalry, Embracing the Principal Exploits of the Cavalry in the Campaigns of 1862 and 1863.* Columbia, S.C.: South Carolina Press, 1864.

Report of the Joint Legislative Committee on Frauds. Columbia, S.C.: The State, 1877.

Reynolds, John S. *Reconstruction in South Carolina, 1865–1877.* Columbia, S.C.: State Co., 1905.

Rhea, Gordon C. *The Battles for Spotsylvania Court House and the Road to Yellow Tavern, May 7–12, 1864.* Baton Rouge: Louisiana State University Press, 1997.

Rosser, Thomas L. *Addresses of Gen'l T. L. Rosser, at the Seventh Annual Reunion of the Association of the Maryland Line* . . . New York: L. A. Williams Printing Co., 1889.

_____. *Riding with Rosser.* Edited by S. Roger Keller. Shippensburg, Pa.: White Mane Publishing Co., Inc., 1997.

Royall, William L. *Some Reminiscences.* New York: Neale Publishing Co., 1909.

Royster, Charles. *The Destructive War: William Tecumseh Sherman, Stonewall Jackson, and the Americans.* New York: Alfred A. Knopf, 1991.

Schlesinger, Arthur M., Jr. *The Age of Jackson.* Boston: Little, Brown & Co., 1953.

Schultz, Harold S. *Nationalism and Sectionalism in South Carolina, 1852–1860.* Durham, N.C.: Duke University Press, 1950.

Sears, Stephen W. *Chancellorsville.* Boston: Houghton Mifflin Co., 1996.

_____. *Landscape Turned Red: The Battle of Antietam.* New Haven, Conn.: Ticknor & Fields, 1983.

_____. *To the Gates of Richmond: The Peninsula Campaign.* New York: Ticknor & Fields, 1992.

Sheppard, William A. *Red Shirts Remembered: Southern Brigadiers of the Reconstruction Period.* Atlanta: Ruralist Press, 1940.

Sheridan, Philip H. *Personal Memoirs of P. H. Sheridan.* 2 vols. New York: Charles L. Webster & Co., 1888.

Sherman, William T. *Home Letters of General Sherman.* Edited by M. A. DeWolfe Howe. New York: Charles Scribner's Sons, 1909.

_____. *Memoirs of General William T. Sherman, by Himself.* 2 vols. New York: D. Appleton & Co., 1875.

Shoemaker, John J. *Shoemaker's Battery, Stuart's Horse Artillery, Pelham's Battalion* . . . Memphis, Tenn.: S. C. Toof & Co., 1908.

Simkins, Francis Butler. *Pitchfork Ben Tillman, South Carolinian.* Baton Rouge: Louisiana State University Press, 1944.

_____. *The Tillman Movement in South Carolina.* Durham, N.C.: Duke University Press, 1926.

_____, and Robert Hilliard Woody. *South Carolina during Reconstruction.* Chapel Hill: University of North Carolina Press, 1932.

Simms, William Gilmore. *Sack and Destruction of the City of Columbia, South Carolina.* Edited by A. S. Salley. Freeport, N.Y.: Books for Libraries Press, 1971.

Smith, Gustavus W. *The Battle of Seven Pines.* New York: C. G. Crawford, 1891.

Snowden, Yates, ed., *History of South Carolina.* 5 vols. New York: Lewis Publishing Co., 1920.

Sommers, Richard J. *Richmond Redeemed: The Siege at Petersburg.* Garden City, N.Y.: Doubleday & Co., Inc., 1981.

South Carolina in 1876: Testimony as to the Denial of Elective Franchise in South Carolina at the Elections of 1875 and 1876 (U.S. Senate, 44th Cong., 2nd Sess.). Washington, D.C.: Government Printing Office, 1877.

Stampp, Kenneth M. *The Era of Reconstruction, 1865–1877.* New York: Alfred A. Knopf, 1966.

Starr, Stephen Z. *The Union Cavalry in the Civil War.* 3 vols. Baton Rouge: Louisiana State University Press, 1979–85.

Stokes, William. *Saddle Soldiers: The Civil War Correspondence of General William Stokes of the 4th South Carolina Cavalry.* Edited by Lloyd Halliburton. Orangeburg, S.C.: Sandlapper Publishing Co., Inc., 1993.

Stuart, James Ewell Brown. *Letters of General J. E. B. Stuart to His Wife, 1861.* Edited by Bingham Duncan. Atlanta: Emory University Publications, 1943.

———. *The Letters of Major General James E. B. Stuart.* Edited by Adele H. Mitchell. n. p.: Stuart-Mosby Historical Society, 1990.

Symonds, Craig L. *Joseph E. Johnston: A Civil War Biography.* New York: W. W. Norton & Co., 1992.

Tankersley, Allen P. *John B. Gordon: A Study in Gallantry.* Atlanta: Whitehall Press, 1955.

Taylor, Alrutheus A. *The Negro in South Carolina during the Reconstruction.* Washington, D.C.: Association for the Study of Negro Life and History, 1924.

Taylor, Walter H. *Four Years with General Lee . . .* New York: D. Appleton & Co., 1877.

———. *General Lee: His Campaigns in Virginia, 1861–1865 . . .* Norfolk, Va.: Nusbaum Book & News Co., 1906.

———. *Lee's Adjutant: The Wartime Letters of Colonel Walter Herron Taylor.* Edited by R. Lockwood Tower. Columbia: University of South Carolina Press, 1995.

Testimony on the Recent Election in South Carolina (U.S. House of Representatives, 44th Cong., 2nd Sess.). Washington, D.C.: Government Printing Office, 1877.

Thomas, Emory M. *Bold Dragoon: The Life of J. E. B. Stuart.* New York: Harper & Row, 1986.

Thomason, John W. Jr. *Jeb Stuart.* New York: Charles Scribner's Sons, 1930.

Thompson, Henry T. *Ousting the Carpetbagger from South Carolina.* Columbia, S.C.: R. L. Bryan, 1926.

Tillman, Benjamin R. *The Struggle of 1876: Being the Story of the Red Shirt Movement.* Anderson, S.C.: privately issued, 1909.

Tindall, George Brown. *South Carolina Negroes, 1877–1900.* Columbia: University of South Carolina Press, 1952.

Trout, Robert J. *In the Saddle with Stuart.* Gettysburg, Pa.: Thomas Publications, 1998.

Trueheart, Charles W., and Henry M. Trueheart. *Rebel Brothers: The Civil War Letters of the Truehearts.* Edited by Edward B. Williams. College Station: Texas A&M University Press, 1995.

Wallace, David Duncan. *The History of South Carolina*. 4 vols. New York: American Historical Society, 1934.

_____. *South Carolina: A Short History, 1520–1948*. Chapel Hill: University of North Carolina Press, 1951.

Warner, Ezra J. *Generals in Blue: Lives of the Union Commanders*. Baton Rouge: Louisiana State University Press, 1964.

_____. *Generals in Gray: Lives of the Confederate Commanders*. Baton Rouge: Louisiana State University Press, 1959.

The War of the Rebellion: A Compilation of the Official Records of the Union and Confederate Armies. 4 series, 70 vols. in 128. Washington, D.C.: Government Printing Office, 1880–1901.

Webb, Alexander S. *The Peninsula: McClellan's Campaign of 1862*. New York: Charles Scribner's Sons, 1881.

Welch, Stephen W. *Stephen Elliott Welch of the Hampton Legion*. Edited by John Michael Priest. Shippensburg, Pa.: Burd Street Press, 1994.

Wellman, Manly Wade. *Giant in Gray: A Biography of Wade Hampton of South Carolina*. New York: Charles Scribner's Sons, 1949.

Wellman, Paul I. *The House Divides: The Age of Jackson and Lincoln, from the War of 1812 to the Civil War*. Garden City, N.Y.: Doubleday & Co., Inc., 1966.

Wells, Edward L. *Hampton and His Cavalry in '64*. Richmond, Va.: B. F. Johnson Publishing Co., 1899.

_____. *Hampton and Reconstruction*. Columbia, S.C.: State Co., 1907.

Wert, Jeffry. *General James Longstreet, the Confederacy's Most Controversial Soldier: A Biography*. New York: Simon & Schuster, 1993.

Williams, Alfred B. *Hampton and His Red Shirts: South Carolina's Deliverance in 1876*. Charleston, S.C.: Walker, Evans & Cogswell Co., 1935.

Williams, G. Croft. *A Social Interpretation of South Carolina*. Columbia: University of South Carolina Press, 1946.

Williamson, Joel. *After Slavery: The Negro in South Carolina during Reconstruction, 1861–1877*. Chapel Hill: University of North Carolina Press, 1965.

Wilson, James Harrison. *Under the old Flag: Recollections of Military Operatrions in the War for the Union, the Spanish War, the Boxer Rebellion, etc.* 2 vols. New York: D. Appleton & Co., 1912.

Wise, Jennings Cropper. *The Long Arm of Lee; or, The History of the Artillery of the Army of Northern Virginia . . .* 2 vols. Lynchburg, Va.: J. P. Bell, 1915.

Wise, John S. *The End of an Era*. Boston: Houghton, Mifflin Co., 1899.

Wittenberg, Eric J. *Glory Enough for All: Sheridan's Second Raid and the Battle of Trevilian Station*. Washington, D.C.: Brassey's, Inc., 2001.

Woodward, C. Vann. *Origins of the New South, 1877–1913*. Baton Rouge: Louisiana State University Press, 1951.

Wright, Louise Wigfall. *A Southern Girl in '61: The War-Time Memories of a Confederate Senator's Daughter*. New York: Doubleday, Page & Co., 1905.

Zuczek, Richard. *State of Rebellion: Reconstruction in South Carolina*. Columbia: University of South Carolina Press, 1996.

INDEX

Bold-faced numbers indicate illustration